Problem Representation
in Foreign Policy Decision Making

Previous studies of foreign policy decision making have largely focused on the choice among specified options rather than the prior question of how the options were specified in the first place. Such "problem representation" is the focus of this volume. How do the game theorists' options and utilities come about? Concretely, for example, how and why in the Cuban missile crisis were blockade, air strike, and invasion chosen as options? To answer such questions, the editors contend that the representation of the problem to which the options are a response, the determinants of that representation, and its ramifications must all be analyzed. The contributors to the volume consider these issues both conceptually and empirically, employing the methods of both political science and political psychology.

Professor Donald A. Sylvan has been on the faculty of the Department of Political Science at Ohio State University since 1974. He is also a Faculty Associate at Ohio State's Mershon Center and a member of the Executive Committee of the university's Cognitive Science Center. Sylvan has authored or edited three books about foreign policy and international relations and has written many articles in professional journals. He has done extensive research on foreign policy decision making, political cognition of international leaders, and reasoning in foreign policy. He has been active in the International Studies Association, a major professional organization of international relations scholars, which he has recently served as President of its Midwest Region and has also served as President of its Foreign Policy Analysis Section.

James F. Voss is Professor of Psychology and of Political Science at the University of Pittsburgh and has served as Associate Director of the Learning Research and Development Center at that institution for a number of years. His research interests are primarily in how people learn, especially from text, and how reasoning and problem solving take place in political science and history.

Problem Representation in Foreign Policy Decision Making

Edited by

DONALD A. SYLVAN

and

JAMES F. VOSS

CAMBRIDGE
UNIVERSITY PRESS

PUBLISHED BY THE PRESS SYNDICATE OF THE UNIVERSITY OF CAMBRIDGE
The Pitt Building, Trumpington Street, Cambridge, CB2 1RP, United Kingdom

CAMBRIDGE UNIVERSITY PRESS
The Edinburgh Building, Cambridge CB2 2RU, UK   http://www.cup.cam.ac.uk
40 West 20th Street, New York, NY 10011-4211, USA   http://www.cup.org
10 Stamford Road, Oakleigh, Melbourne 3166, Australia

© Donald A. Sylvan and James F. Voss 1998

First published 1998

Printed in the United States of America

Typeset in Times Roman 10/12 pt, in Penta [RF]

A catalog record for this book is available from the British Library.

Library of Congress Cataloging-in-Publication Data

Problem representation in foreign policy decision making / edited by
Donald A. Sylvan, James F. Voss.
p.   cm.
Includes index.
ISBN 0-521-62293-X (hb)
1. International relations – Decision-making.   2. International
relations – Psychological aspects.   I. Sylvan, Donald A.   II. Voss,
James F., 1930–
JZ1253.P76   1998
327.1 – dc21   97-41729

ISBN 0-521-62293-X hardback

Contents

v

Part III: Empirical Analysis

Part IV: Conclusion

Contributors

Ryan Beasley, Department of Political Science, University of Kansas

Robert S. Billings, Department of Psychology, Ohio State University

Marijke Breuning, Department of Political Science, Truman State University

Martha Cottam, Department of Political Science, Washington State University

Katherine M. Gannon, Department of Psychology, Texas Tech University

Deborah M. Haddad, Department of Political Science, Ohio State University

Charles F. Hermann, George Bush School of International Relations, Texas A&M University

Joel Kennet, Department of Psychology, Pennsylvania State University

Dorcas E. McCoy, Department of Political Science, University of Central Florida

Helen E. Purkitt, Department of Political Science, U.S. Naval Academy

Silvana Rubino-Hallman, Department of Political Science, Syracuse University

Tonya E. Schooler, Department of Psychology, University of Pittsburgh

Laurie Ney Silfies, Department of Psychology, University of Pittsburgh

Donald A. Sylvan, Department of Political Science, Ohio State University

Charles S. Taber, Department of Political Science, State University of New York at Stony Brook

James F. Voss, Department of Psychology, University of Pittsburgh

Jennifer Wiley, Department of Psychology, University of Massachusetts at Amherst

Michael D. Young, Department of Political Science, Ohio State University

PART I

INTRODUCING PROBLEM REPRESENTATION

CHAPTER 1

Introduction

Donald A. Sylvan

> To agree on the problems we have with one another is the most important step in negotiations. We haven't yet agreed on problem definition with Syria. We have agreed on problem definition with Jordan. – Aviv Sharon, Director of Public Affairs, Ministry of Foreign Affairs, State of Israel, July 10, 1994

Aviv Sharon has expressed the importance of a critical variable in the understanding and explanation of foreign policy decision making. The manner in which a problem is defined and represented is crucial to the possible solution of that problem.

A great deal of scholarship in the area of foreign policy decision making concentrates on what Sylvan and Thorson (1992) term the *option selection* stage. Much rational-choice/game-theoretic work carefully illuminates the tradeoffs between alternative courses of action. The subject to be explained is usually the choice between specified options. That is also the subject to be explained by many more traditional, less mathematical studies of foreign policy decision making. In his classic work, Graham Allison (1971) tries to help the reader understand alternative ways of viewing the way in which ExCom (President Kennedy's Executive Committee during the Cuban missile crisis) decided between such specified options as blockade, air strike, and invasion.

"Problem Representation"

What these works do not do is ask the prior question, *How did the options get specified in the first place?* That is the subject of this volume, and we term it *problem representation*. How do the game theorist's options and utilities come about? Why were blockade, air strike, and invasion initially chosen as potential options? To answer these questions, we contend that one should

3

understand how the problem to which the options are a response has been represented. One should focus on both the determinants of that representation and its ramifications. This volume explores each of those issues.

In the academic community, Pennington and Hastie (1987), Voss, Wolfe, Lawrence, and Engle (1991), and Sylvan and Thorson (1992), have all discussed the importance of problem representation. Pennington and Hastie study jury deliberations and decision making and determine that a "story model" best accounts for the way in which jurors represent the problems they face. Voss defines problem representation in terms of understanding goals and constraints in a particular situation. Sylvan and Thorson argue that a person's ontology constrains the manner in which that person can represent a problem, and that option selection, in turn, follows from problem representation. Sylvan and Thorson illustrate their points with reference to decision making in the Cuban missile crisis.

Our research is based on one of the observations of Sylvan and Thorson. It is that the way in which foreign policy decision makers choose options can best be understood by first studying the way in which they represent the problem they see themselves as facing. The research we have undertaken and communicate in this volume explicates these themes in more detail, and we examine them in a variety of different foreign policy decision-making contexts.

The Context: Political Psychology and International Relations

The scholarship put forth in this volume lies at the intersection of political psychology and international relations. It is, therefore, appropriate to point out where the work here fits within the broader schools of thought in each of those two academic communities.

Political psychologists tend to study either elite or mass political behavior. In other words, either they tend to focus on those individuals who are influential in politics or to concentrate on understanding general attitudes and dispositions of a political populace. This volume clearly deals mostly with the first category, elite behavior. Within the study of elite political psychology, some scholars concentrate on roles while others concentrate on processes. In the former category, bureaucratic politics (e.g., Allison 1971) and political leadership (e.g., Hermann 1977) are good examples. Each concentrates on roles, with the former focusing on what bureaucrats have in common while the latter often differentiates between the styles of various leaders. Those whose works focus on political psychological processes, as opposed to roles, often study beliefs and the manner in which they are constructed. Studies as varied as Holsti (1976), Schank and Abelson (1977) and Simon (1985) fall in this category. Some in this grouping of scholarly works employ such cognitively oriented constructs as scripts and schema. Others change the emphasis to socially influenced processes such as discourse (e.g., Sylvan, Majeski, and Milliken 1991). This volume is an attempt to contribute to the understanding of political psychology by studying elites and psychological processes. Most of the authors in this volume employ cognitively oriented constructs, with Rubino-Hallman diverging to employ the less cognitive, more socially constructivist discourse analytic approach.

Within the study of international relations, a predominant concentration is on systemic approaches. Many adopt a realist (e.g., Morgenthau 1956; Schweller 1996) or neo-realist (e.g., Waltz 1979) approach, with clear assumptions of rationality at the level of the nation-state. Even liberal and neo-liberal institutionalists (e.g., Keohane 1986), who disagree with realism on most issues, also tend to focus on the international system and often to assume rationality at the nation-state level. The authors in this volume tend to diverge from the assumptions of both of these approaches and to follow more in the footsteps of Snyder, Bruck, and Sapin (1954). The emphasis is on decision making, with rationality of both individuals and nation-states an open question. Understanding problem representations employed in foreign policy decision making is one important way of getting at the empirical issue of when and under what circumstances individuals and nation-states act rationally.

Organization of the Volume

This volume is divided into four parts. Part I introduces the general topic of problem representation in foreign policy. Donald Sylvan's introductory chapter is followed by James Voss's explication of an information-processing approach to problem representation. An information-processing approach highlights the goal-oriented nature of much foreign policy decision making and helps us focus systematically on the role of problem representation in that process. Voss's chapter serves as a reference point for terminology that is employed in many of the following chapters.

Part II addresses overarching conceptual issues involved with studying problem representation. In Chapter 3, Charles Taber addresses the issue of how decision makers construct initial representations of problems facing them. Following on that concentration of initial representations, Robert Billings and Charles Hermann confront the issue of re-representation of problems in Chapter 4. The process of problem representation in groups is the backdrop for Chapter 5, as Ryan Beasley sets forth aggregation principles by which groups deal with initial problem representations of group members. In Chapter 6, Martha Cottam and Dorcas McCoy examine the relationship between images and problem representation.

Part III presents empirical analyses that involve problem representation. In Chapter 7, Helen Purkitt employs "think aloud" protocols to study South African politics. In Chapter 8, Donald Sylvan and Deborah Haddad employ laboratory experiments to test alternative models of problem representation of foreign policy situations, and they relate them to styles of reasoning. Michael Young uses a computational approach in Chapter 9 to analyze the foreign policy content of President Jimmy Carter's speeches. Katherine Gannon's Chapter 10 is the only chapter in which the content is domestic politics rather than foreign policy, as she garners insights on problem representation from Senate Judiciary Committee hearings. Silvana Rubino-Hallman uses computational tools and a discourse analytic perspective in Chapter 11, as she examines the workings of the Presidential Commission on Women in Combat. Gulf War speeches in the United States Senate are the focus of James Voss and his colleagues in Chapter 12. Marijke Breuning's Chapter 13 closes Part III as she employs both Parliamentary debates and analysis of government expenditures to study foreign assistance problem representations of three European nation-states.

Chapter 14 is the final chapter and the brief fourth part of the volume, wherein Donald Sylvan reflects on the study of problem representation by comparing the impact of alternative means of studying the concept.

Origins of this Volume

Having set forth some of the basic ideas that served as catalysts for this volume, as well as the outline of chapters to come, a brief explication of the genesis of this collaborative effort is in order. All of the contributors to this volume have been involved in a Research and Training Grant from the National Science Foundation.[1] That grant has focused on the role of cognition in collective political decision making and was funded for a five-year period that has now ended. The authors involved in this volume have presented their ideas and research to each other on numerous occasions throughout the life of the N.S.F. Research and Training Grant. This volume represents the revisions of those efforts after feedback from the group and the editors to each chapter author. Taken together, we hope our efforts help point the way toward a fruitful path of inquiry that will help us better understand both foreign policy decision making and political psychological processes.

Note

1 This research was supported by a grant from the National Science Foundation (DIR-9113599) to the Mershon Center Research Training Group on the Role of Cognition in Collective Decision Making at the Ohio State University. We thank David Bearce for constructing the index for this volume.

References

Allison, Graham (1971). *Essence of Decision*. Boston: Little, Brown.

Hermann, Margaret (1977). *A Psychological Examination of Political Leaders*. New York: Free Press.

Holsti, Ole R. (1976). ''Foreign policy decision-makers viewed psychologically: 'Cognitive Processes' approaches.'' In J. N. Rosenau (ed.), *In Search of Global Patterns*. New York: Free Press.

Keohane, Robert O. (ed.) (1986). *Neorealism and Its Critics*. New York: Columbia University Press.

Morgenthau, Hans (1956). *Politics among Nations*. New York: Knopf.

Pennington, Nancy, and Reid Hastie (1987). ''Explanation Based Decision Making.'' *Proceedings of the Ninth Annual Meeting of the Cognitive Science Society*, pp. 682–690.

Schank, Roger C., and Robert P. Abelson (1977). *Scripts, Plans, Goals, and Understanding*. New York: John Wiley and Sons.

Schweller, Randall (1996). ''Neo-realisms: Status-quo bias: What security dilemma?'' *Security Studies*, Vol. 5, No. 3, Spring, pp. 90–121.

Simon, Herbert A. (1985). ''Human nature in politics: The dialogue of psychology with political science.'' *American Political Science Review*, Vol. 79, pp. 293–305.

Snyder, Richard, H. Bruck, and B. Sapin (1954). *Foreign Policy Decision Making*. Glencoe, IL: Free Press.

Sylvan, David J., Stephen J. Majeski, and Jennifer L. Milliken (1991) ''Theoretical categories and data construction in computational models of foreign policy.'' In Valerie Hudson (ed.), *Artificial Intelligence and International Politics*. Boulder: Westview Press.

Sylvan, Donald A., and Stuart J. Thorson (1992). ''Ontologies, problem representation, and the Cuban missile crisis.'' *Journal of Conflict Resolution*, Vol. 36, No. 4, December, pp. 709–732.

Voss, J. F., C. R. Wolfe, J. A. Lawrence, and R. A. Engle (1991). ''From representation to decision: An analysis of problem solving in international relations.'' In R. J. Sternberg and P. Frensch (eds.), *Complex Problem Solving: Principles and Mechanisms* (pp. 119–158). Hillsdale, NJ: Lawrence Erlbaum.

Waltz, Kenneth N. (1979). *Theories of International Politics*. New York: McGraw-Hill.

CHAPTER 2

On the Representation of Problems: An Information-Processing Approach to Foreign Policy Decision Making

James F. Voss

Interactions such as conflict and cooperation that occur between states do not just happen. As noted even by Thucydides (1950), such interactions are regarded as a product of the interests and goals of one state and how such factors impact upon the interests and goals of another state. But a state's interests and goals are not simply given; instead, they are arrived at by the decision makers of that state. Thus, thought processes of the decision makers are critical to the interaction of states, such processes being a function of the person's beliefs and knowledge as well as the person's perceptions of the other states and their interests, goals, and motives. Hence, when a problem situation arises, individuals define the problem by developing a definition of the situation (Snyder, Bruck, and Sapin 1954, 1962) in which their own knowledge and beliefs play a major role. In other words, they develop a problem representation (Newell and Simon 1972). In a general sense, this position is constructivist in nature, that is, individuals are assumed to build models of their environment and act upon the contents of these models, solving problems and making decisions. The models, moreover, can be modified in relation to each person's experience.

In an epistemological sense, the extent to which such models "really" reflect a person's environment is virtually unknown because the representations are products of the individual's own knowledge, beliefs, and experiences and other genetically based or acquired characteristics. Indeed, an important means of evaluating a model is pragmatic – that is, whether it is consistent and helps the individual function in his or her environment. This neo-Kantian view is generally held in psychology, explicitly or implicitly, especially because humans are regarded not simply as passive recipients of environmental input but as active processors of incoming information, interpreting the input in relation to their knowledge, beliefs, attitudes, and motivation – indeed, even seeking and selecting the information in relation to these factors.

8

An important function of representation development is that with the help of a person's memorial capacity, that person is able to develop a sense of stability of the world that helps that person meet his or her needs and goals. Moreover, individuals acquire strategies and tactics that facilitate subsequent goal attainment. When we apply these notions to the domain of foreign policy decision making, individuals are assumed to build models of the world, with such representations being assumed to play a major role in mediating their actions and policy preferences and choices.

The Information-Processing Model of Problem Solving

The idea of problem representation employed in this chapter is based upon Newell and Simon's (1972) information-processing model of problem solving. Other theoretical views in which representational concepts play an important role are those involving mental models (Johnson-Laird 1983), discourse analysis (Shapiro, Bonham, and Heradstveit 1988), the operational code (Leites 1953; George 1969), cognitive mapping (Axelrod 1976), and a variety of conceptual developments in artificial intelligence (e.g., Nilsson 1980). Such efforts suggest that what is considered a representation can be difficult to define, a point discussed by Beasley (this volume), Rubino (this volume), and Young (this volume). Using the information-processing model, this chapter has the following goals: to describe this particular framework of problem representation, especially showing how the concept is of importance to foreign policy decision making; and to consider difficulties of this view of representation, difficulties that need to be overcome if the concept is to be used in studies of foreign policy designed to advance theory or improve practice.

Description of the Model

Although the issue of problem finding has received relatively little study (e.g., Mintzberg, Raisinghani, and Theoret 1976) and is beyond the scope of the present chapter, problems generally may be said to arise when an individual, group, or organization has a goal and that goal is not being obtained. Indeed, this idea, that a goal cannot be obtained because of some type of barrier, is the type of definition of a problem often found in the psychological literature (e.g., Bourne, Dominowski, Loftus, and Healy 1986).

When problems are identified, they are found to occur under particular environmental conditions, and the statement of the problem and the context or set of conditions in which the problem occurs is, in the information processing model, termed the *task environment* (Newell and Simon 1972). In proving a theorem of geometry, for example, there are "Givens" and a "To prove'' statement that define the problem. A problem of this type, moreover, is usually interpreted by geometry teachers and students in a similar way because they have acquired particular conventions about problem structures and solution processes in geometry.

The processing of the problem is assumed to take place in what is termed a *problem space*, which is in the individual's mental structure. The problem space consists of (1) all the possible *states* of the problem, including the initial state and the goal(s), (2) the *operators* that allow a person to move from one state to another, and (3) the constraints of the problem (Newell and Simon 1972).

With respect to problem states, the initial state consists of the ''givens'' of the problem, as stated and as elaborated upon by the solver, and the problem's goal state. Included also are all possible states that could intervene between the initial state and the goal state, including those that may not be appropriate with respect to the solving of the problem.

Operators constitute the means by which an individual moves from one problem state to the next. In a mathematical problem, operators, for example, may include adding and carrying numbers. In a geometry proof, an operator may be ''to find a theorem that is needed in this given situation.'' The type of operator used is thus a formation of the problem that is being considered.

Problem constraints are limitations imposed upon the solving of the particular problem. In proving a geometry theorem, for example, the solver may only be able to use theorems that have been proved. The problem goal itself is a constraint because it exerts a substantial constraining influence on the solution process. Moreover, as will be shown, constraints are often generated during the solving of the problem, especially in the case of ''ill-structured'' problems. Thus, problem solving, according to the information-processing model, consists of moving from state to state via use of operators; or within a spatial metaphor, the solver ''walks'' through the problem space (Newell and Simon 1972).

An additional question is what strategy an individual may use in walking through the problem space. One of the earliest computer programs of problem solving, the General Problem Solver (Reitman 1965), used means–ends analysis. This is a relatively common strategy in which an individual, in a given state, considers the goal and tries to determine how to take a step that places the solver closer to the goal. This strategy thus requires an evaluation component in order to determine whether via that particular step the solver is indeed progressing toward the solution. On the other hand, if the solver knows how to solve the problem, there is no need to use such a means–ends strategy, because the solver is able to ''work forward,'' going step-by-step to the solution (cf. Larkin, McDermott, Simon, and Simon 1980).

As to what constitutes a good problem solution for problems that are relatively well structured, such as proving a geometry theorem, a correct solution is usually already known, having been established in previous work. Sometimes one path to a given solution may be more direct than another, and solutions thus may differ in parsimony or in "elegance." For a novice, the "good" solution will typically be to obtain the correct answer, and possibly to do so via an appropriate procedure – that is, for example, not by guessing.

Assumptions of the Model

Two assumptions of the information-processing model are noted. One is that the human is assumed to be a serial processor, meaning that individuals process information one step at a time, moving from one state to the next, perhaps stopping to evaluate. There has in psychology been a long history of the question of whether the human is a serial or parallel processor, the latter referring to processing a number of bits of information at one time. To some extent the question is a level of analysis issue, because at the level of consciousness, humans, with few exceptions, seem to be serial processors. On the other hand, parallel processing seems to occur at lower levels of cognitive functioning, with some models, for example, assuming parallel distributed processing (e.g., Rumelhart and McClelland 1986). Nevertheless, at the conscious level, we tend to think of one thing at a time.

The second assumption, related to the first, is that humans have a working memory system that has a finite capacity. In general, this assumption not only indicates that an individual can think of only one or at most a few things at any given time, but also that search is a critical component of the problem-solving process because the solver needs to search for and retrieve information from memory or from elsewhere that is germane to the problem.

Ill-Structured Problems

But all problems are not as structured as proving a geometry theorem. Instead, many problems are ill structured. Reitman (1965) first discussed ill-structured problems, noting that many problems do not have well-defined initial states, goals, constraints, and/or means to reach the goal. Reitman used the act of composing a fugue as an example. In such composing, the goal is indefinite; there is no single outcome that is correct, although the quality of the completed fugue may be critically evaluated. Also, a number of constraints are generated during the solving process that are not in the problem statement; instead, they are generated in the solution process. Thus, while the need to stay within the structure of a fugue provides an initial constraint, the composer's selection of a key in which to write the fugue and the composer's writing of the earlier sections of the fugue establish constraints regarding what can be legitimately written. Yet there is a latitude for the composer, and no two composers are at all likely to compose the same fugue. Another and related characteristic is that in many ill-structured problems, the constraints generated often serve as criteria to evaluate a particular aspect of the solution or the solution as a whole. Because of this, one way to view problem solving within the context of the information-processing model is as constraint satisfaction (Simon 1973).

Another important point about constraints is that individuals may differ with respect to what constraints are regarded as relevant to a given problem and/or how different constraints should be weighted. Moreover, solvers often need to attack constraints during the solving process in order to produce an acceptable solution. Furthermore, as Reitman (1965) has pointed out, the differences in constraint recognition and evaluation among individuals is a major reason why the evaluation of solutions to ill-structured problems typically does not produce unanimity or sometimes even consensus. In other words, the solutions to ill-structured problems are often evaluated via constraints as they relate to a person's beliefs, attitude, knowledge, and personality. This point is extremely important with respect to foreign policy decision making.

In addition, in many ill-structured problems, there is usually an implicit set of stop-rules that determine when an individual stops the solving process. In composing a fugue, stop-rules operate to the extent that the composer continues to revise different parts of the composition. There is a point at which the composer will likely stop, although of course many composers have revised a given work over a period of years.

With respect to operators, ill-structured problems involve the use of a number of operators, the operators being germane to the problem and discourse structure (see Voss, Greene, Post, and Penner 1983a). Thus, in analyzing a political editorial, operators may include state premise, state conclusion, state counterargument, refute counterargument, and state example.

Solving Ill-structured Problems

Studying the solving of ill-structured problems in a political context, Voss, Tyler, and Yengo (1983b) and Voss et al. (1983a) collected protocols from subjects who were experts or novices with respect to the Soviet Union. Each subject was asked to assume that he or she was Head of the Ministry of Agriculture in the Soviet Union, and to answer what he or she would do to improve it, given the low productivity in Soviet agriculture. The individual then developed a solution that had the form of a verbal protocol, which was recorded and subsequently analyzed by the experimenters. An outline of the solution stated by one expert is presented in Figure 2.1. As shown in the

Representation Phase
Statement of constraints: land, water, and poor weather
Prior history of problem
  Czar period
  Revolutionary period (since 1917)
  Exhortation
  NEP (New Economic Plan) plans
  Modernization (inadequate at this time)

Solution Phase
Solution – invest in mechanization
  (Constraint)   need to fight with decision-making bodies; approach (Gosplan, the economic planning agency) for investment; can do so by arguing for agricultural self-sufficiency, not dependent upon West.
  (Constraint) – peasants lack education. Develop educational programs using agricultural stations run by knowledgeable people, not party members as is currently done.
  (Constraint) – wages too low; need to raise wages with modernization efficiency.
  (Constraint) – wages too low; develop the private plot to sell products. Against system (constraint).
  Outcome – tractor repair parts increase.
  Outcome – infrastructure in plastics develops.
  (Constraint) – amount of arable land; consider irrigation.

Figure 2.1. Diagram of problem solution of one expert. (See Penner and Voss 1983 for a more detailed description of analyses of experts, novices, and post-novices in Voss, Greene, Post, and Penner 1983a.)

figure, the solving of ill-structured problems usually consists of two phases, a problem-representation phase and a problem-solution phase.

The representation phase of the expert solver described in Figure 2.1 began with the statement of two constraints, the small amount of water and arable land in the Soviet Union, the assertion supported by a percentage statement, and the poor weather. From this point, he developed his representation by looking into the history of the problem. This step apparently had three functions: (1) Given that the solver had not recently thought about the problem, the history provided a review; (2) the historical review helped the solver isolate the causes of the problem; and (3) the review enabled the solver to look at previous solutions and why they did not work. The solver examined the problem's history by pointing out that the problem goes back to the time of the czars when there was a strong aristocracy–peasant distinction and a middle class did not develop, as it did in England. The solver then pointed out that since the 1917 revolution, there had been three solutions, which he described, none of which had worked. The third solution, however – agricultural modernization – had not been pushed as much as it should have been. The problem was thus represented as one of insufficient modernization. Moreover, given this problem representation, the solution generated was that the government needed to invest more money in agriculture.

An important point about the solution process, as described to this point, is that the solver did not generate a number of alternatives. Instead, the representation quite readily led to the solution. In a sense, then, there was not a decision.

Another point is that the solution statement per se was relatively abstract. It did not tell how to obtain or how to invest the money. However, quite importantly, the solver did not stop at this point. Rather, he continued with a critical part of the solving process; namely, he built a case for his solution by showing why his solution would work and considering potential objections to it. The objections, moreover, usually took the form of constraints. The solver, however, reacted to them in order to show why they would not negate his solution.

In building his case, the solver pointed out how greater investment would allow for the development of a plastics infrastructure, something needed because, as he stated, 50 percent of the fertilizer is lost due to the weather when it is in paper bags. He pointed out how more investment could develop a needed transportation infrastructure, and how badly needed tractor repair parts could be produced. On the other hand, he noted that the undereducated peasants who would not be able to deal with modern methods and machinery constituted a constraint. He addressed this by noting the need for agricultural training stations that would require instruction by agricultural experts who knew how to run the stations, as opposed to the agriculturally ignorant party people who currently ran them (another constraint). He also addressed the issue of the need to modify the government's allocation of financial resources, indicating that the argument could be made to Gosplan (the economic planning agency) that greater investment in agriculture is needed to reduce dependency on the West for grain. The solution phase of the solving process thus consisted of the solver arguing why the solution would work, what in essence was a justification.

Examination of the Solution

Goals, Operators, and Constraints: The Soviet agriculture problem was quite ill structured. The goal, "improve agricultural productivity," was indefinite: The task environment included only the statement of low productivity and the role of the solver. In examining the solution of a number of individuals, Voss et al. (1983b) delineated two structures as components of the solving process: a problem-solving structure, which was employed at a relatively high level in the process, and a reasoning structure, which comprised elements at a lower level and implemented the operators of the problem-solving structure. Two classes of operators were thus delineated. Problem-solving operators included state constraint, state subproblem, state solution, interpret problem statement, provide support, evaluate, and summarize. Reasoning-structure operators included state argument, state assertion, state fact, present specific case, state reason, state outcome, compare and/or contrast, elaborate and/or clarify, state conclusion, and state qualifier (Penner and Voss 1983).

The foregoing account provides an example of how constraints were identified and how the solver attacked particular constraints during the solving process in order to reduce or eliminate their restrictive power. Not all constraints were attacked, however; for example, in one part of the protocol, the solver suggested an increase in privatization, with individuals being allowed to sell more products grown in their own family's private plot, but this solution was rejected because it would violate the existing Soviet system and government policy.

Use of Weak Methods: Another of the important aspects of solving ill-structured problems is the typical use of weak problem-solving methods (Newell 1980). Strong methods of problem solving typically involve mathematics or computer algorithms, methods that are powerful in that they often lead to a single solution but that are limited with respect to when they may be applied. Weak methods, on the other hand, are not as powerful, but they may be applied in a variety of situations. Weak methods include decomposition (dividing a problem into subproblems), conversion (transforming a problem into another problem that can be better analyzed), means-ends analysis, analogy, and generate-and-test. These methods are not taught in schools; nevertheless, people usually acquire them. Moreover, these methods are usually used in a more or less automatic way, in the sense that one does not usually say "I am going to convert the problem." Instead, the person proceeds with solving the problem, hardly aware that such methods are being used, as when a person says, "Well, let's consider the worst-case scenario." This is a generate-and-test procedure. Weak methods are of course used in the solving of ill-structured problems because strong methods usually cannot be employed. In the example solution of Figure 2.1, the solver used problem conversion as he transformed the problem as stated into another problem, that of inadequate modernization. In a sense, the weak methods are heuristics that aid the search process, also serving as higher-level operators.

Solution Evaluation: An important issue is that of how solutions to ill-structured problems are evaluated. At the planning stage, which, as noted, is essentially the stage of the Figure 2.1 solution, what the solver is doing is providing an argument. Indeed, the structure of the argument is that of an enthymeme, or a claim supported by a reason (Aristotle 1960). The claim is that agricultural productivity in the Soviet Union will be increased, the supporting reason being that modernization of the agricultural industry will produce the increase. (The argument could also be stated in conditional form.) The entire solution thus is essentially a backing to this argument.

How may the solution to such arguments be evaluated? In the same way other informal arguments are evaluated (cf. Voss, Perkins, and Segal 1991), namely, by examining the acceptability or plausibility of the supporting reasons (acceptable, that is, to the person evaluating the argument) and the extent to which each reason is judged to support the related claim. In addition, one may determine whether counterarguments have been considered, that is, are there reasons supporting the claim that agricultural productivity will not improve (cf. Angell 1964)? Thus, the solution of Figure 2.1 may be evaluated via the evaluation of the overall argument as well as the component arguments.

It is important, however, to note the subjective nature of the evaluation. Because different evaluators may have different views about reason acceptability, relevance of the reason to the claim, and counterargument strength, what constitutes a ''good'' solution, is, as previously noted, a function of who is doing the evaluation. This may not be an entirely satisfactory outcome, but because of the probabilistic nature of such arguments, because there is no ''correct'' answer, and because the contents of the argument must be considered in argument evaluation, such an outcome cannot be avoided. But even more importantly, the evaluation of the argument of necessity is a function of the beliefs and knowledge of the individual evaluating the argument.

Use of Stop-Rules: The solution of Figure 2.1 was essentially a plan, with the solution components generally not unpacked beyond a particular point. For example, the question of how to implement the training of peasants was assumed to be handled once there were appropriate instructions. Thus, the solver apparently used stop-rules to terminate the solving process at various points, quite likely when he thought the particular issue he was addressing was satisfactorily handled.

Reduction of Ill-Structured to Well-Structured Problems: Presumably because well-structured problems are usually easier to solve than ill-structured problems, one finds in political decision making as well as in general the tendency to convert ill-structured into well-structured problems, a process that often leads to oversimplification. A good example of this is the action proposed by Congress with respect to violence in the United States. An ill-structured problem occurring in the United States is how to reduce violence. The general goal is clearly to reduce violence, with some index of violence being needed to demonstrate a reduction, if it would occur. If in developing a representation of the problem, however, individuals attempted to isolate causes, there would not likely be agreement about their relative importance. Drugs would be considered a causal factor, as may the availability of guns, economic conditions as found especially in inner cities, a general breakdown of morality and concern for others, and other factors, with some individuals accepting or maximizing some of these factors while rejecting or minimizing others. Clearly, arguments would need to be made that provide support for each possible factor. However, the American Congress and the executive branch may develop a bill to increase prison capacity, put more policemen on the job, and develop stiffer prison sentences, with one political party typically trying to outdo the other with who is "tougher on crime." How, then, are the party leaders representing the problem?

The implicit representation of the "tough-on-crime" solution is that crime is occurring because not enough is being done to catch and put away criminals, especially for a long time, a representation that likely is quite incorrect, although it sounds good. But why persist in this position? In part, persistence occurs because the representation consists of converting a difficult, ill-structured problem into a relatively easier-to-deal-with, well-structured problem. It involves, in other words, a process of simplification. Crime will be reduced because catching and punishing criminals serves to reduce the number of criminals and (supposedly) to deter crime. The idea that the violence involves economic and other conditions for which there are perhaps no simple answers is apparently ignored. Or perhaps answers that violate some relatively "sacred cow" constraint such as gun control are ignored for political reasons. So, with the simplified representation, political posturing continues, and the people apparently are appeased by it, even though violence continues. Indeed, perhaps appeasing the people is the primary goal because it produces votes, thereby yielding the achievement of this all-important goal.

Solving Ill-Structured Problems and Decision Making

Decision theory typically involves the selection of one alternative from a number of alternatives. Decision theory, however, has been criticized for its reluctance to indicate how the alternatives are generated (e.g., Simon 1985). The model discussed in this chapter notes two points about alternative generation. First, it suggests that making decisions is often avoided because a given representation may lead to a particular solution without a need to generate alternatives. But this is not always the case. How, then, does the problem-solving model deal with alternative generation and selection?

The need to generate alternatives is assumed to occur because the representation that is developed does not lead to a solution, and this requires that the solver should try to further develop the representation. In order to do this, alternatives are generated. This is a generate-and-test procedure in which a solver, by examining the possible positive and negative consequences of alternatives, is able to enhance the representation. The evaluation of consequences in turn is usually related to the constraints involved and their weighting.

Voss, Wolfe, Lawrence, and Engle (1991) addressed the question of the relation between representation and solution by collecting two sets of protocols, one on German reunification and the other on the issue of nuclear war potential as viewed by American and Australian activists. In addition, writings concerned with the Cuban missile crisis and the U.S. intervention in Korea were examined. In the Cuban missile crisis, the decision to "quarantine" or blockade the Soviets from Cuba rather than bomb the missile sites can be interpreted in terms of representational differences involving the weighting of constraints. Those in favor of bombing tended to weight the risk of a third world war as less constraining than those who favored a blockade. But those who favored bombing also thought it would provide a greater benefit in terms of U.S.–Soviet relations because it was a more forceful response. To these people, the perceived benefits were apparently worth the risk. President Kennedy, however, was dissatisfied with answers he received when he asked what the Soviets would do in response to the bombing (Allison 1971). The decision was thus made via the evaluation of the possible consequences of the two actions and how the consequences related to the individual's representation of goals and constraints.

Another finding noted here is that in the work on the views of activists about how to deal with the possibility of nuclear war, individuals who developed a more vague and general representation concerning how to prevent nuclear war also provided a more general and vague solution, a solution often of questionable merit and implementation. On the other hand, more specific representations led to more specific solutions. Indeed, in general, the quality of the solution was a function of the quality of representation.

Origins and Changes of Problem Representations

So far in this chapter, the importance of goals, constraints, and operators has been considered, but little has been discussed about the origins of a person's problem representation, especially as related to ill-structured problems. In such problems, factors such as a person's goals, knowledge, beliefs, and attitudes play an important role as do cultural factors. Indeed, how these components play a role in representations is one of the most frequently addressed topics by the authors of this volume. One factor held to play a role in problem representation is the image that the leaders of one state have of another state, a point developed in another chapter in this volume (Voss, Wiley, Kennet, Schooler, and Silfies). However, the issue of what feeds into a problem representation is also one of the most difficult aspects of the problem representation model.

Returning briefly to the Cuban missile crisis, one may ask about the origins of President Kennedy's representation of the problem. It seems clear that a number of goals were involved. There was, of course, the need to try to avoid a potentially disastrous war. But at the same time there was an urgent need to confront the Soviet action because of domestic reasons. There was a strong anti-Soviet sentiment in the country, and Kennedy felt he might possibly be impeached if he did not address the issue. He therefore rejected Stevenson's suggestion that he take the issue to the U.N., because that would not be a sufficiently strong response (Allison 1971). Similarly, a "weak" response would have opened him to Republican criticism. Also, just as Bruening (this volume) argues that the historical origins of each respective country influenced Belgium's and Holland's policy about foreign aid, so likewise could it be argued that the traditional role of the United States as the dominant force in the Americas, as portrayed, for example, by the Monroe Doctrine, was an influential cultural belief. Thus, when there was a distinction made between a Soviet missile in a submarine a few miles off the Atlantic coast and a Soviet missile in Cuba, the latter was in a sense viewed as a territorial infringement in the Americas, even though the Cuban government was communistic. The relative importance of these various goals and constraints was thus complicated, and it is difficult to ascertain the role each played in Kennedy's decision. But it is likely that President Kennedy would have had difficulty in isolating the weightings.

An important question about representation is whether perhaps the issue of trying to define a representation in terms of a person's beliefs, goals, and constraints is assuming that such decision making is more complex than it really is. There are a number of avenues of research which suggest that perhaps we do not need to know the complexities of mental functioning in order to provide a reasonable idea of President Kennedy's representation of the Cuban missile crisis. First, as previously noted, there is the tendency to simplify, to modify ill-structured problems so they become well-structured problems. President Kennedy explored the two primary alternatives but did not come to a solution such as "The Soviets are aggressors here. Send the bombers." He did not simplify to this point. Nevertheless, his behavior apparently focused upon the analysis of consequences, questioning which solution was more agreeable within the context of the constraints. Second, research in argumentation indicates that individuals, when justifying a given position, typically state only a few reasons to support an argument, even though they may know many more (Hoch 1984; Voss and Means 1991). It is as if they rest their case on a few arguments they regard as highly cogent and only generate more, although not many more, if they are induced to do so under particular circumstances. Thus, it could be that we use less information than we think we do in making a decision. While considering a number of alternatives and consequences, we may generally eliminate some and "zero in" on only a few, thereby simplifying the decision.

In addition to origin, one must also consider the question of how a problem representation changes. This question is currently a major area of inquiry in psychology, where the general issue is termed that of conceptual change or of cognitive restructuring. Individuals often have concepts of physical phenomena that are erroneous according to the domain of physics, and these frequently persist despite such interventions as taking physics courses (e.g., McCloskey 1983). In general, the data on conceptual change, reviewed by Chinn and Brewer (1993), indicate what some contributors of this volume assert (e.g., Beasley, Bruening, Cottam, and McCoy), namely, that change is relatively difficult to effect.

But let us consider cognitive restructuring in the foreign policy decision-making context. A representation is developed and a solution is determined, either with or without consideration of alternatives. When is this representation likely to change? First, one result (Newell and Simon 1972) is that when an individual follows a solution path and comes to a dead end, the solver typically goes back only to the previous choice point and then considers an alternative; the solver does not go back to "Square 1." Further backtracking may occur, but only under quite demanding circumstances does the solver return to the representation. In other words, when the solution does not work, the first reason the policy maker may state is that some unpredictable thing happened, a foreign leader made a completely unanticipated "irrational" action, or perhaps there was some event of nature that interfered. Second, one may claim that the decision was not implemented appropriately, and this led to a negative outcome. Third, immediate subordinates did not carry out the order appropriately, thereby not instructing the implementers appropriately. Finally, at some point, there may be an admission, often private, that "we need to rethink the problem." When Americans were killed by a car bomb in the barracks in Lebanon, it was not the policy that was questioned; it was terrorist activity that produced the outcome. Subsequently, when troops were moved to ships, they were placed "in a more strategic position." Rationalizations are not uncommon when policies do not work.

The research on cognitive restructuring indicates that one of the most important factors in producing representational change is the availability of another representation that is acceptable (Chinn and Brewer 1993); that is, individuals are more likely to remain fixated on their own representation if they do not perceive a viable alternative representation. Some of the other factors noted by Chinn and Brewer (1993) that play a role in cognitive re-structuring were consistent with factors noted by Billings and Herrmann (this volume), factors such as commitment to one's position, and one's epistemo-logical commitments, as in, for example, reference to consistency. Dunbar (1995), however, studied four biological research centers, paying special at-tention to conceptual change that occurred in the investigators. Dunbar noted that the biologists usually did in fact change their views when contradictory data were obtained, as opposed to the notion that people often disregard conflicting data. However, perhaps of greater importance was the finding that the biologists often tended to change their beliefs as a result of meetings of their own lab staff, during which time the scientist's hypotheses and interpre-tation of results were questioned. The social context, in other words, is ap-parently quite important in effecting conceptual change (cf. Voss, Wiley, and Carretero 1995 for further development of this point). The result is reminis-cent of George's (1980) work, which pointed out the importance of having a policy maker hear positions other than one's own.

Problem Representation: Some Additional Issues

A longstanding issue in the study of international relations is the level-of-analysis problem (Singer 1969). The levels referred to are the individual, with possibly the bureaucratic level included, the state level, and the system level. Waltz (1979) has argued essentially that the distribution of capability across states is the most powerful determiner of what states do. Morganthau and Thompson (1985) have argued that the state is the unit of analysis to use for the study of international relations, with power being the most important motivating factor. Although the question of the validity of these positions goes beyond the scope of this chapter (see, however, Hollis and Smith 1990 for a discussion of the level-of-analysis issue), the present model falls within the general context of the approach termed *foreign policy decision making* (cf. Chan and Sylvan 1984).

Within the foreign policy decision-making context, the international sys-tem may be regarded as a constraint; indeed, it may be a powerful constraint. It simply cannot explain behavior, however. As shown in cases such as the Cuban missile crisis, the decisions made are not solely determined by sys-temic constraints. Judgments of decision makers are critical. Similarly, Mor-ganthau's position of realism oversimplifies the international scene; individ-uals do make a difference. Unfortunately perhaps, life has no control groups, so one sometimes needs to argue counterfactually to demonstrate this point, which of course is problematic.

It is of further importance to note that a given situation may be reported quite differently by two individuals. Khrushchev, for example, believing that the United States was going to invade Cuba, regarded his withdrawal of missiles in Cuba as a victory because he felt that, with President Kennedy's assurance not to invade, he had insured that communism would gain a foothold in the Western hemisphere. In addition, Sergeev, Akimov, Lukov, and Parshin (1990), in analyzing the speeches of President Kennedy, found that a counterfactual-oriented computer program suggested that the Cuban crisis was moderated by a sense of "sincerity" and "restraint" between Kennedy and Khrushchev.

Problems with the Problem-Solving Model

The Need for a Metric

One of the most serious problems in the use of the concept of a problem representation is the need for a metric. How does one determine whether two people have approximately equivalent representations or whether one person's representation changes over time? How can we provide some measures for comparison? How can we determine what goals and constraints a person considers to be important? The issue here is not strictly quantification in the sense of giving a representation a number; it is the issue of how to define the parameters of a representation and how to employ some measure of parameter occurrence that permits us to determine occurrence and weightings.

Groups and Organizations

The information-processing model has not been extensively developed for application to groups and organizations; whether this is due to neglect or lack of applicability is not clear. But briefly considering applicability, the following points would need to be noted. Boynton (1991) has presented representation-based arguments in the working of the Senate foreign relations committee. Thus, given an ill-structured problem, individuals in a group may have different goals, if only on a personal basis, and, if they represent different departments in a bureaucracy, the differences would likely be stronger (Halperin 1974). This would mean that, depending upon the problem, the goals and constraints could vary considerably across individuals. (Consider analogously a faculty meeting in which an academic department debates about the area of interest in which a new faculty member should be hired.) Second, a debate could ensue that would focus upon which constraints, including policies, to violate and which to maintain.

Goals and Databases

One of the difficulties of the present model in the foreign policy context is that the data needed to feed into the model are often incomplete. As previously discussed, in the case of the Cuban missile crisis, what were the goals of President Kennedy? How important was satisfying the domestic goal regarding the importance of "standing up" to communism, the goals related to allies, and the goal related to the avoidance of war? Each goal, in a sense, served to constrain possible actions in relation to other goals. We have no good way of knowing how individuals weight the goals, especially which goal comparisons are made. The difficulty then is defining and relating the goals and constraints in a way that can specify those most important.

A second matter is that of the database. There is much information that an individual may use in solving a complex problem, and how this information is selected and generated is a critical issue. Why is some information retrieved rather than other information? Rephrased, the question involves how the solver goes from one state to another in solving an ill-structured problem. The states represent the taking of steps in the solving process, and as previously noted, operators that were found in a problem-solving structure and an argumentation structure were employed. But how are the operators selected? How are connectivity and coherence produced in solving an ill-structured problem? Such questions are at the heart of the difficulties of analysis. Indeed, the same subject does not repeat the same account when given a second opportunity, suggesting that the step-by-step solving process may be varied and truncated (Voss et al. 1983a).

A third matter related to goal and database issues is that of prediction. To what extent can knowledge of a person's problem representation be used to predict the actions and/or choices of the individual? There are at least two answers to this question. The first is that having some idea of how a person represents a problem may give us a better idea of what an individual is likely to do, as suggested by some work reported in this chapter. A second answer, however, is that the goal of prediction is a rather lofty positivistic ideal. Prediction and control have been the watchwords of being "scientific," at least from a positivistic perspective, but prediction is quite difficult in any subject matter domain and usually only possible under highly controlled circumstances. Moreover, because control of conditions is so difficult in the social sciences, and because there often is a "moving target," prediction is quite probably for the most part an unrealistic goal. This point is driven home when, for example, the "experts" differed as to whether Saddam Hussein would withdraw his troops from Kuwait when President Bush gave the ultimatum. Policy analysts and personality analysts were not especially in agreement, and their rationales were basically weak. Indeed, psychology, in which laboratory control is possible, at least for some phenomena, has difficulty in predicting behavior. In a field like foreign policy decision making, then, how can one be expected to predict what a given leader is going to do in a given situation? Tendencies may be observed, but specific, accurate predictions are extremely difficult to produce successfully. Perhaps greater emphasis should be placed on "understanding," in the sense of being able to build a case for the nature of the way in which individuals represent the particular problem and how they act (cf. Hollis and Smith 1990).

Summary

This chapter is an endeavor to develop the idea that the way in which a problem is mentally represented is a critical factor in determining how political choices are made. Moreover, it is held that problem representations are a function of a person's beliefs, attitudes, and knowledge, as well as other personal characteristics, which makes it difficult to provide a complete understanding of the nature of a given representation. Nevertheless, the notion of problem representation constitutes a particular concept that adds specificity to the arguments made by Snyder et al. (1954, 1962) and Jervis (1976) two decades ago regarding the importance of perception in decision making in international relations.

Author's Note: The preparation of this chapter was supported by the Mellon Foundation via an award to the Learning Research and Development Center of the University of Pittsburgh. The contents of the chapter do not necessarily reflect the positions of these organizations.

References

Allison, G. T. (1971). *Essence of Decision: Explaining the Cuban Missile Crisis.* Boston: Little, Brown.
Angell, R. B. (1964). *Reasoning and Logic.* New York: Appleton-Century-Crofts.
Aristotle (1960). *Rhetoric* (L. Cooper, trans.). New York: Appleton-Century-Crofts.
Axelrod, R. (ed.). (1976). *Structure of Decision. The Cognitive Maps of Political Elites.* Princeton, NJ: Princeton University Press.
Bourne, L. E., Dominowski, R. L., Loftus, E. F., and Healy, A. F. (1986). *Cognitive Processes* (2nd ed.). Englewood Cliffs, NJ: Prentice-Hall.
Boynton, G. R. (1991). "The expertise of the senate foreign relations committee." In V. M. Hudson (ed.), *Artificial Intelligence and International Politics* (pp. 291–309). Boulder, CO: Westview Press.
Chan, S., and Sylvan, D. A. (1984). "Foreign policy decision making: An overview."

In D. A. Sylvan and S. Chan (eds.), *Foreign Policy Decision Making* (pp. 1–19). New York: Praeger.

Chinn, C. A., and Brewer, W. F. (1993). "The role of anomalous data in knowledge acquisition: A theoretical framework and implications for science instruction." *Review of Educational Research, 63*(1): 1–49.

Dunbar, K. (1995). "How scientists really reason: Scientific reasoning in real-world laboratories." In R. J. Sternberg and J. Davidson (eds.), *The Nature of Insight* (pp. 365–395). Cambridge, MA: MIT Press.

George, A. L. (1969). "The 'operational code': A neglected approach to the study of political leaders and decision-making." *International Studies Quarterly, 13:* 190–222.

——— (1980). *Presidential Decision Making in Foreign Policy: The Effective Use of Information and Advice.* Boulder, CO: Westview Press.

Halperin, M. H. (1974). *Bureaucratic Politics and Foreign Policy.* Washington, DC: The Brookings Institution.

Hoch, S. J. (1984). "Availability and interference in predictive judgment." *Journal of Experimental Psychology: Learning, Memory, and Cognition, 10*(4): 649–662.

Hollis, M., and Smith, S. (1990). *Explaining and Understanding International Relations.* New York: Clarendon Press.

Jervis, R. (1976). *Perception and Misperception in International Politics.* Princeton, NJ: Princeton University Press.

Johnson-Laird, P. N. (1983). *Mental Models.* Cambridge, MA: Harvard University Press.

Larkin, J., McDermott, J., Simon, D. P., and Simon, H. (1980). "Expert and novice performance in solving physics problems." *Science, 208:* 1335–1342.

Leites, N. (1953). *A Study of Bolshevism.* Glencoe, IL: Free Press.

McCloskey, M. (1983). "Naive theories of motion." In D. Gentner and A. L. Stevens (eds.), *Mental Models* (pp. 299–324). Hillsdale, NJ: Lawrence Erlbaum.

Mintzberg, H., Raisinghani, D., and Theoret, A. (1976). "The structure of 'unstructured' decision processes." *Administrative Science Quarterly, 21*(2): 246–275.

Morganthau, H. J. and Thompson, K. W. (1985). *Politics among Nations: The Struggle for Power and Peace* (6th ed.). New York: Alfred A. Knopf.

Newell, A. (1980). "One final word." In D. T. Tuma and F. Reif (eds.), *Problem Solving and Education: Issues in Teaching and Research* (pp. 175–189). Hillsdale, NJ: Lawrence Erlbaum.

Newell, A., and Simon, H. A. (1972). *Human Problem Solving.* Englewood Cliffs, NJ: Prentice Hall.

Nilsson, N. J. (1980). *Principles of Artificial Intelligence.* Palo Alto, CA: Tioga.

Penner, B. C., and Voss, J. F. (1983). *Problem solving skills in the social sciences: Methodological considerations* (LRDC No. 1983/15). Learning Research and Development Center, University of Pittsburgh.

Reitman, W. (1965). *Cognition and Thought.* New York: Wiley.

Rumelhart, D. E., and McClelland, J. L. (eds.). (1986). *Parallel Distributed Processing* (Vol. 2). Cambridge, MA: MIT Press.

Sergeev, V. M., Akimov, V. P., Lukov, V. B., and Parshin, P. B. (1990). "Interdependence in a crisis situation." *Journal of Conflict Resolution, 34:* 179–207.

Shapiro, M. J., Bonham, G. M., and Heradstveit, D. (1988). "A discursive practices approach to collective decision-making." *International Studies Quarterly, 32*(4): 397–419.

Simon, H. A. (1973). "The structure of ill-structured problems." *Artificial Intelligence, 4:* 181–201.

(1985). "Human nature in politics: The dialogue of psychology with political science." *The American Political Science Review, 79:* 293–304.

Singer, J. D. (1969). "The global system and its subsystems: A developmental view." In J. N. Rosenau (ed.), *Linkage Politics: Essays on the Convergence of National and International Systems.* New York: Free Press.

Snyder, R. C., Bruck, H. W., and Sapin, B. (1954). *Decision-making as an Approach to the Study of International Politics.* Princeton, NJ: Princeton University Press.

(1962). "Decision making as an approach to the study of international politics." In R. C. Snyder, H. W. Bruck, and B. Sapin (eds.), *Foreign Policy Decision Making* (pp. 14–185). New York: Free Press.

Thucydides. (1950). *The History of the Peloponnesian War* (R. Crawley, trans.). New York: Dutton.

Voss, J. F., Greene, T. R., Post, T. A., and Penner, B. C. (1983a). "Problem solving skill in the social sciences." In G. H. Bower (ed.), *The Psychology of Learning and Motivation: Advances in Research Theory* (Vol. 17, pp. 165–213). New York: Academic Press.

Voss, J. F., and Means, M. L. (1991). "Learning to reason via instruction in argumentation." *Learning and Instruction, 1*(4): 337–350.

Voss, J. F., Perkins, D. N., and Segal, J. (eds.). (1991). *Informal Reasoning and Education.* Hillsdale, NJ: Lawrence Erlbaum.

Voss, J. F., Tyler, S. W., and Yengo, L. A. (1983b). "Individual differences in the solving of social science problems." In R. F. Dillon and R. R. Schmeck (eds.), *Individual Differences in Cognition* (pp. 205–232). New York: Academic Press.

Voss, J. F., Wiley, J., and Carretero, M. (1995). "Acquiring intellectual skills." *Annual Review of Psychology, 46:* 155–181.

Voss, J. F., Wolfe, C. R., Lawrence, J. A., and Engle, R. A. (1991). "From representation to decision: An analysis of problem solving in international relations." In R. J. Sternberg and P. A. Frensch (eds.), *Complex Problem Solving: Principles and Mechanisms* (pp. 119–158). Hillsdale, NJ: Lawrence Erlbaum.

Waltz, K. N. (1979). *Theory of International Politics.* New York: Random House.

PART II

OVERARCHING CONCEPTUAL ISSUES

CHAPTER 3

The Interpretation of Foreign Policy Events: A Cognitive Process Theory

Charles S. Taber

Foreign policy scholars have long recognized the importance of the initial stages of decision making – the perception and interpretation of information (e.g., Boulding 1956; Holsti 1962, 1967; Snyder, Bruck, and Sapin 1962; Kelman 1965; Jervis 1970, 1976; Anderson 1981; Lebow 1981; Bennett 1981, 1982; Tetlock 1983; Rosati 1984, 1995; Cottam 1986; Powell, Dyson, and Purkitt 1987; Vertzberger 1990; Banerjee 1991; Ensign and Phillips 1991; Khong 1992; Shimko 1995). Much of this work focuses on distortions and errors in the process, arguing that the imperfect images decision makers rely on to interpret the world are a frequent source of misperceptions and poor decisions. Yaacov Vertzberger, for example, develops this theme in his recent book on the information-processing approach to foreign policy analysis, arguing that "accumulated misjudgments, misevaluations, wrong inferences, and simple unawareness of relevant data are likely to carry over to the next stages [of decision making], with negative ramifications for the quality of the overall coping process" (1990: 8). In short, the initial problem representation strongly constrains subsequent behavior.

One may view the information interpretation process at either the organizational or the individual level, although more work in the area of foreign policy decision making has focused on the impact of images or belief systems on the problem representations of individual elites. This work, in my view, remains somewhat dissatisfying, in part because it does not usually consider organizational patterns in the flow of information or institutional memory and rules (but see Beasley, this volume; Vertzberger 1990; Haney 1995). A second problem for scholars in this area has been the insufficiency of the modeling languages available for expressing theories of foreign policy decision making. Computational modeling offers one important set of methods for representing and exploring the descriptively rich theoretical ideas that have developed in this area (Taber 1992; Taber and Timpone 1994, 1996a, 1996b; Duffy and Tucker 1995; Schrodt, in press), just as experimental methods allow us to test these ideas empirically (Geva, DeRouen, and Mintz 1993; Sylvan, Ostrom, and Gannon 1994).

This chapter focuses on one component of a distributed information-processing theory of event interpretation. After briefly sketching the broad outlines of an organizational process theory, I turn to a more detailed discussion of the cognitive level – how individual decision makers within the larger organizational structure interpret the information they receive as inputs. In other words, I am interested in how they construct an initial representation of the problem facing them. Not surprisingly, this process viewed more generally has been a focus of research in cognitive science (for overviews, see Collins and Smith 1988; Eysenck and Keane 1990; Feigenbaum and Feldman 1995). Several theoretical frameworks have been advanced to explain interpretation and perception processes, with significant effort put into testing these frameworks in the laboratory. I review this literature, with a focus on the work of Schank and Abelson (1977, 1995), and attempt to build a cognitively plausible theory of the perception and interpretation of foreign policy events. The measure of my success in pulling together a coherent theory will be taken as I build a computational model – the Event Interpreter (EVIN) – that represents the cognitive theory using a sample of U.S. foreign policy beliefs as the knowledge base. But a detailed description of EVIN (Taber and Rona 1995) is beyond the scope of this chapter, which develops the underlying theory.

An Organizational Framework for Foreign Policy Event Interpretation

The foreign policy–making system is distributed among a variety of organizational, small group, and individual actors. Organizational actors – such as intelligence services, foreign policy bureaucracies, and military bureaucracies – are themselves composed of a variety of subactors, including suborganizations, small groups, and individuals (March and Simon 1958). This complex arrangement of actors, their relative power and influence, and the patterns and rules that constrain behavior within the system define a particular foreign policy–making system at a particular point in time. For example, the U.S. foreign policy–making system is composed of several "central" organizational actors – the president; the National Security Council; the Congress; the departments of State, Defense, Treasury, Commerce, Agriculture, and Labor; and the intelligence community – and an ill-defined set of peripheral groups and institutions – members or critics of the "foreign policy establishment"; interest groups and lobbies, both foreign and domestic; and the media.

The flow of *information* through this system of distributed actors is, for my purposes, the central issue (Deutsch 1964). Channels that transmit information, bottlenecks in this transmission, institutional rules or norms that regulate communication, and the many "filters" that distort information are key ingredients in a general organizational theory. Although it is certainly true that individual people make decisions, those decisions are heavily constrained by organizational pressures (which are, in part, a product of the individual actions of others within the system, past and present). In particular, an individual's cognitive processing depends partly on the informational inputs from within the system, in addition to informational inputs from outside the system and the individual's own prior knowledge (see Doran 1985; Masuch and Warglien 1992; Ripley 1993, 1995).

Despite the importance of an organizational framework for understanding information flows in foreign policy event interpretation, I will for now set aside the macro theory and focus on its cognitive component. Treating the informational inputs to an individual as exogenous, how does the individual process that information to interpret it?

Cognitive Theories of Perception and Interpretation

Before external stimuli can affect cognitive states or behavior, they must be perceived and, at least for conscious processing, interpreted. Although terminology differs across theorists, interpretation is basically the process of constructing an understanding – a mental model – of the external world (Lippmann 1922; Sowa 1984; Eysenck and Keane 1990). In the words of Riesbeck and Schank (1989: 3), "An understander of the world is an explainer of the world. In order to understand a story, a sentence, a question, or a scene you have witnessed, you have to explain to yourself exactly why the people you are hearing about or viewing are doing what they are doing." Foreign policy decision makers, like other information processors, must interpret the events that concern them; that is, they must build subjective understandings of world events. This section will review the theories of cognitive structure and interpretation processes on which the foreign policy theory is based.

Cognitive Structure

Most models of human information processing assume two structural components, although cognitive scientists differ on many of the specifics (Lodge 1993). One of the oldest tenets of psychology is that human thought depends on a large permanent memory store, or long-term memory (LTM), which is organized associatively so that meaningful packets of information can be remembered together. The dominant architectural model of LTM represents associative memory as a network of linked nodes, where each node contains conceptual information and each link represents conceptual associations (e.g.,

Anderson 1983). For example, if one constructs an understanding of the Bosnia conflict as a variant of the Vietnam Quagmire metaphor, this association might be stored in LTM as a link between the nodes signifying Bosnia and Vietnam Quagmire.

The second functional component is a working memory (WM), corresponding to those things we actively pay attention to at a given moment (Belmore 1986; Fiske 1980). Because of its limited capacity (Miller 1956), serial processing, and slow transfer of learned associations to LTM, working memory is the bottleneck of cognition and the primary reason for the boundedness of human rationality (Baddeley and Hitch 1974; Baddeley 1986). WM is the seat of conscious processing; it is where interpretations are constructed.

Top-Down versus Bottom-Up Processing

Generally speaking, two information sources may be used to understand the external world: informational inputs from the environment and relevant past knowledge and experience stored in LTM. When perceptions of the world are dominated by characteristics of the informational inputs, we call it bottom-up or data-driven processing. Top-down or conceptually driven processing emphasizes the role of stored knowledge from LTM in perceptions. Obviously, perception depends on both types of processing, so the theoretically interesting questions concern how each affects perceptions, the conditions under which each type dominates, and the consequences of reliance on each type of processing.

Most cognitive scientists now emphasize top-down processing in interpretation (for an opposing view, see Gibson 1979). These constructive theories assume that (1) perception is an active process of constructing a mental model, (2) perception is the result of "the interactive influences of the presented stimulus and internal hypotheses, expectations, and knowledge" (Eysenck and Keane 1990: 85), (3) perception is an inferential process, and (4) perception is prone to error introduced by reliance on prior knowledge and expectations, which may be faulty or may not fit the current situation (Bruner 1957; Neisser 1967; Gregory 1972, 1980). These theorists argue forcefully for the necessity of inferential interpretation in building perceptual models. Until they are mapped onto some already stored system of meaning, these inputs have no intrinsic meaning to the perceiver. Moreover, informational inputs are nearly always sketchy and incomplete, but people must form some interpretation of the world in order to act with any coherence. The bottom line is that people must actively use their existing knowledge to make sense of input information. The input information has no meaning without the application (or sometimes misapplication) of prior knowledge. And different individuals will interpret the same input information differently because they have different prior knowledge (different in both content and organization). This does not mean that features of input information have no impact on interpretation – clearly they do. Rather, input information affects how prior knowledge is used but does not control the interpretation process.

An interesting recent development has been the work on explanation-based understanding, which emphasizes the constructivist position even more than most cognitive scientists. According to this approach, people actively construct multiple candidate explanations for important events, eventually selecting one as the believed explanation. But people are not disinterested understanders. They have rather strong predispositions for and against certain possible explanations. Leake (1991; Ram and Leake 1995) argues that these predispositions are essentially derived from one's goals toward the situation requiring explanation. For example, assume that a Middle East peace negotiator constructs an interpretation of Israel's crackdown on militant settlers following the Hebron massacre, taking Israeli explanations at face value, guided by their goal of keeping negotiations alive. A Palestinian, having different goals in the situation, would surely construct a completely different explanation for that Israeli action. Leake's argument ties in nicely with the need for reintegrating motivation in information processing, which is discussed later in this section.

The Structure of Knowledge

If knowledge stored in LTM is central to perception and interpretation processes (and also to subsequent reasoning), how that knowledge is structured is an important question. Do people have a large collection of associated but relatively atomistic concepts in LTM, or do they rely more on larger structures or packets of knowledge? How tightly organized is knowledge?

Most cognitive scientists favor what might be called a "molecular" format for knowledge, in which larger structures are composed of more "atomic" entities (Eysenck and Keane 1990; Minsky 1968; Sowa 1984). The atomic building blocks of knowledge are concepts and conceptual relations. Following the chemistry metaphor, knowledge is information that has been composed into molecular units out of conceptual atoms according to rules of conceptual relations. These knowledge molecules are related to each other in the associative network of LTM, so that knowledge may be composed of quite complex memory objects.

Some scholars take the molecular metaphor to its extreme, arguing that a finite (perhaps quite small) number of basic primitive concepts exist, the various combinations of which can represent all conceptual knowledge. Roger Schank (1975; see also Schank and Abelson, 1977), for example, developed the theory of conceptual dependency (CD), in which all information is conceptualized as either active – in the form Actor Action Object Direction – or stative – in the form Object (is in) State (with Value). CD is particularly useful (and controversial) in its treatment of verbs, which may be represented by sequences of primitive ACTs. Virtually all action may thus be based on a finite (in Schank's theory, quite small) set of primitive action concepts, including MOVE, GRASP, SPEAK, and so forth.

Several types of knowledge molecules have been described by cognitive scientists, and although this proliferation of terms for similar constructs sometimes confuses more than clarifies, I will distinguish three: schemas, scripts, and cases. They differ functionally but are identical in terms of cognitive architecture and processes. Schemas are general semantic knowledge bundles that people may use to attach meaning to and draw inferences about a stimulus (for a general discussion of schemas in foreign policy decision theory, see Larson 1994). They are organized around general semantic categories. George Bush undoubtedly constructed a schema representation to understand Saddam Hussein, drawing on more general schemas (perhaps a political dictator schema, Middle East schemas, a Hitler/Munich schema, and an international aggression schema). Each of these contain hierarchically linked concepts, allowing Bush to draw a variety of inferences without a great deal of cognitive effort (if Hussein is interpreted on the basis of the Hitler schema, for example, then one might infer he is a madman not to be negotiated with).

The Hitler/Munich schema might be distinguished from purely semantic schemas in that it represents a particular historical case. Cases seem especially important in the domain of foreign policy interpretation, because people so frequently invoke past historical examples in explaining their understandings of new cases (Mefford 1987). Such cases may have particular "vividness" for decision makers, suggesting that they may actively seek past examples that may provide policy precedents (Kolodner 1988; Riesbeck and Schank 1989). On the other hand, some recent experimental work questions how much we use case information in reasoning about foreign policy (Sylvan et al. 1994).

We can also distinguish the international aggression schema, which represents a generalized sequence of events called a *script*, from more general semantic schemas. This type of knowledge bundle takes on special importance in a theory of understanding developed by Schank and Abelson (1977), who maintain that scripts, and the experiential memory they represent, can account for the majority of human understanding (for experimental evidence supporting this view see Bower, Black, and Turner 1979; Galambos, Abelson, and Black 1986). People find themselves in similar situations more than once: going to the bank, ordering food at a restaurant, watching a political debate, reading about international aggression, and for U.S. foreign policy decision makers, negotiating an arms control agreement, sending troops abroad, and putting together a coalition of allies for some purpose. In each of these situations, it appears that people rely heavily on expectations to understand what happens and how they should respond. They behave as if their actions were scripted. Of course, different individuals will internalize the scripts for different types of event sequences, or even somewhat different scripts for the same event sequence.

The major advantage of complex bundles of knowledge – scripts, schemas, cases, etc. – is that they require very little cognitive effort of understanders:

> This view says, in essence, that you need do very little thinking at all, that everything is pre-packaged and thus subject to very little spontaneous thought. In other words, under this view of the world, thinking means finding the right script to use, rather than generating new ideas and questions to think about during the course of participating in an event. (Riesbeck and Schank 1989: 4)

On the other hand, these convenient packets of knowledge may lead to misperception in the interpretation process, as scholars in the field of foreign policy decision making have emphasized.

Pattern Matching

Clearly knowledge from LTM, whether scripts, conceptual schemas, or experiential cases, must be brought to bear on new information in WM to interpret it. This process relies on feature recognition and pattern matching to identify the appropriate knowledge structures from LTM (Eysenck and Keane 1990; Leake 1991; Mefford 1987; Schrodt 1991). A great deal of work has been done seeking the features of patterns that are most important in pattern matching, but theorists are divided on whether people reduce stimulus patterns to arrangements of features and compare those features to schemas (the feature approach) or whether they evaluate and compare patterns as a whole (the Gestalt approach). The strongest evidence appears to support the feature position (Eysenck and Keane 1990).

In deciding, for example, whether the U.S. invasion of Panama is an instance of international aggression, one might evaluate the degree of match between the overall pattern of relationships and sequence of events for the Panama case and that for the aggression script, or one might key the pattern match on particular important relationships. Consider a simplified hypothetical script for international aggression containing three actors – an innocent small victim, an unjustified powerful bully, and an appalled international community – and a sequence of likely events: (1) rising threats aimed at victim by bully; (2) increasingly desperate attempts at conciliation of bully by victim; (3) military attacks on victim by bully citing justifications related to earlier threats; (4) indignant condemnation of bully by international community, perhaps including economic and diplomatic sanctions; (5a) victim quickly succumbs while community denounces but does no more or (5b) victim manages to hold on while world pressure on bully grows, possibly leading to intervention. According to the Gestalt approach, the Panama invasion would be considered international aggression by the individual holding this script in WM only if the *overall match* exceeds some threshold of similarity. That is, the pattern matcher would not focus attention on particularly diagnostic features of the pattern but would assess how much of the overall pattern in the event resembles the aggression script. By contrast, the feature approach requires only that *the key features* of the script match, and these key elements will vary by script. In this example, the key features in the aggression script might be the existence of a victim and a bully and the first three stages of the aggression sequence. Of course, either approach may result in a match in this case, depending on the individual's beliefs about the invasion.

The Content of Knowledge

Obviously, the specific knowledge content stored by an individual will powerfully constrain that individual's interpretation of external events. Up to this point, we have talked purely about the form that knowledge takes. Here again, several issues divide the cognitive literature.

One of the classic goals (some would say fantasies) of artificial intelligence was that human problem solving could be reduced to a manageable set of general problem-solving rules (Newell and Simon 1972). These rules would form the core of most problem-solving behavior so that relatively little specialized knowledge would be needed – indeed, specific knowledge was simply the result of the application of more general principles. Cognitive science has moved far from this original goal of AI. Expert systems researchers, for example, generally assume that expert knowledge is almost entirely domain-specific. Current research suggests that interpretation and reasoning processes rely on both general problem-solving knowledge (e.g., one general heuristic proposes that difficult problems should be broken into subtasks) and domain-specific knowledge (e.g., knowledge about the nature and effectiveness of specific weapons systems or the geography of the Middle East).

A second issue concerns the distinction between declarative and procedural knowledge, between "knowing that" and "knowing how." We know that Paris is the capital of France (declarative). We know how to ride a bike, although we may not be aware of how we do it (procedural). This distinction is really somewhat arbitrary, although it can be conceptually useful. In the

Policy Arguer (POLI) project, for example, I used this distinction functionally (Taber 1992). Declarative knowledge was used to interpret events, and procedural knowledge was used to infer courses of action in response to those events. Despite its conceptual convenience, however, the distinction between declarative and procedural knowledge has become very controversial (Duffy and Tucker 1995; Reichgelt 1991). Complex interpretations – more than a simple mapping of stored declarative concepts – require more complex combinations of declarative and procedural knowledge. Part of the power of scripts and schemas is that they can represent both kinds of knowledge together in a single package; a lot of experimental evidence suggests that people integrate their knowledge about things and what to do about those things.

Third, although most cognitive scientists leave the content of knowledge idiosyncratic, a few argue that we can usefully study knowledge structures at slightly higher levels of aggregation (Abelson 1973; Carbonell 1978). To the extent that individuals share knowledge structures, we may be able to ignore analytically the content of individual minds in instantiating our theories of cognitive process; we may be able to use shared knowledge content (e.g., liberals, conservatives, hawks, and doves share many important political beliefs with others of like mind). The POLI project took this approach, finding three important shared-belief systems (paradigms) in the cold war U.S. foreign policy system: militant anti-communism, pragmatic anti-communism, and isolationism (Taber 1992; Taber and Timpone 1994). Particular individuals could be viewed as agents of the paradigm they shared with others.

Finally, there is the practical issue of determining the relevant knowledge content for a model. Expert system research, for example, depends heavily on properly representing expert knowledge. Experts must be identified and interviewed, and the relevant knowledge must be represented in the model. In international relations, data sources may be very difficult to find, especially since decision makers are strategic actors; their public statements may have little to do with their actual ''operational codes.'' In fact, one reason for representing paradigms instead of individual beliefs is the greater validity and ease in collecting shared belief systems (for a fuller argument, see Taber and Timpone 1994, 1996a).

The Role of Motivation

A classic criticism of cognitive science is that it pays insufficient attention to motivational or affective factors (Eysenck 1984; Zajonc 1984). Traditionally, affect has been left out of an already complex picture of human cognition. But this means that a variety of phenomena cannot be explained in these

theories. A number of researchers have recently become interested in inte-
. grating motivational factors (Kunda 1990; Taber, Lodge, and Glathar in
press). There are basically three approaches to this issue: Affect could be
largely independent of cognition; it could be reinterpreted in purely cognitive
terms; or it could have important interactions with cognition.

Zajonc (1984) has made the most consistent claims that affect is independent of cognition. He argues that stimuli may be evaluated on purely affective
terms, so that "affect could be generated without a prior cognitive process"
(1984: 117). For example, we might remember no details of a stimulus
though we do have a strong evaluative response. We might remember nothing
about a melody, but know that we liked it. This position has been sharply
attacked by Lazarus (1982), among others, who claims that we must at least
interpret/perceive a stimulus before it can stir an affective response in us. The
fact that we may not remember the details does not prove that they were not
cognitively processed and then forgotten.

At the other extreme are theorists who would reinterpret all motivation in
purely cognitive terms (Miller and Ross 1975; Nisbett and Ross 1980). In
this view, people "may draw self-serving conclusions not because they
wanted to but because these conclusions seemed more plausible, given their
prior beliefs and experiences" (Kunda 1990: 480). Did Ronald Reagan call
the Soviet Union an "evil empire" because he hated communism (affect) or
because he believed that to be the conclusion that best fit the facts, as filtered
through his perceptions (cognitive reinterpretation)?

In the third approach, which I will adopt, both these interpretations of
Reagan's statement are valid. Affect and cognition have an interactive effect,
with people generally striving for two sets of goals in their interpretations
(Kunda 1990): accuracy goals and directional goals. In this view, motivation
affects reasoning by biasing the cognitive processing of information (what
gets retrieved from LTM, how it is constructed into an interpretation, and
how the interpreted stimulus is then evaluated). People are often motivated to
be accurate in their interpretations, since inaccuracy may bring adverse consequences. So they may expend more effort and attention in building interpretations when they are motivated to be accurate. But people are also subject to
directional biases; they often find in their interpretations what they want to
find, or what they expect to find. This process is not as unconstrained as we
sometimes suppose, however. Most people feel pressure to justify their reasoning, at least to themselves; they must maintain an "illusion of objectiv-
ity," which can counter their directional biases under some conditions (Pyszczynski and Greenberg 1987; Petty and Cacioppo 1986). Accuracy goals can,
but often will not, counter the effects of directional goals. As you might
expect, there is evidence that very deep biases can be quite resistant to accu-
racy-based correctives (Kunda 1990).

A Cognitive Theory of Event Interpretation

A "complete" theory of event interpretation by a foreign policy decision maker might explain several levels of information processing that I will ignore in the current treatment. For example, I am uninterested in some of the basic issues of language comprehension – my model will not be able to parse and represent English text (note the RELATUS model of Alker, Duffy, Hurwitz, and Mallery 1991; Mallery 1991). I am more interested in how decision makers interpret international events, which may (for now) be represented in stylized form as ACTOR VERB TARGET (CONTEXT). This research choice forecloses some of the flexibility of English input but seems reasonable given the complexity of the model as it stands. The theory is presented as a series of propositions, building directly off of the preceding discussion and beginning with basic structures.

Proposition 1: Foreign policy decision makers are information processing systems, whose responses to stimuli are conditioned by (1) internally stored information (knowledge and beliefs) and (2) externally presented or collected information. Thinking and reasoning are the result of combinations and sequences of "elementary information processes."

Proposition 2: The interpretations of foreign policy events are constructed "on the fly" rather than simply recalled from memory. Perception is an inferential process. Moreover, sometimes the process is "highly constructive," so that multiple possible interpretations are assembled among which the decision maker can choose.

Propositions 3 through 6 lay out the basic structures and processes of memory and knowledge.

Proposition 3: Foreign policy decision makers have a long-term, associatively organized memory (LTM). More activated portions of LTM have a greater probability of affecting conscious information processing than less activated portions. Activation spreads through memory in response to informational stimuli according to the nature and strengths of the associations in memory. Associations in LTM decay through time. LTM contains both semantic and affective knowledge.

Proposition 4: Foreign policy decision makers have a limited-capacity working memory (WM), in which all conscious information processing occurs. WM is transitory and can only accommodate serial processing.

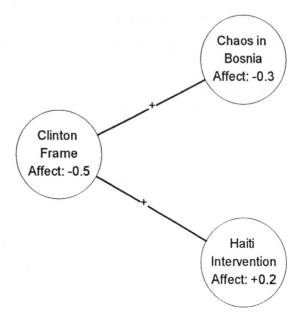

Figure 3.1. Semantic network fragment.

In this theory, WM is the site of conscious processing. Information must be retrieved from LTM or from the environment to affect processing. But as we have seen, WM is transitory and of limited capacity and can only accommodate serial processing. Foreign policy decision makers are only boundedly rational because of the bottleneck of working memory. LTM, on the other hand, is relatively permanent and unlimited and may be capable of parallel processing.

Following what has become the standard form, LTM is expressed as a network of linked nodes, where each node represents a bit – or possibly a larger bundle – of conceptual knowledge or experiential memory. Moreover, in addition to its semantic content, each node carries an *affective tag* to represent the direction and strength of positive or negative feelings about the node concept or experience (Taber et al. in press). For example, Figure 3.1 shows a simple network fragment representing some hypothetical person's beliefs about Bill Clinton and two linked nodes. This person dislikes Clinton, has negative affect about the chaos in Bosnia, and supports intervention in Haiti. Moreover, Clinton is (at least partly) blamed for the Bosnian problem and gets some credit for the Haiti intervention. I now discuss how each of these nodes may represent a detailed schema, case, or script.

This LTM structure can be modeled rather simply by allowing each node to be a data object with four attributes: (1) strength of current activation; (2) semantic content (declarative or procedural, and as complex as can be constructed within the limits of WM); (3) affective content; and (4) a list of links that define the associations of this data object with others in the network, including strength, type, and direction of link.

Node activation represents the degree of "energy" a node currently possesses as the result of hearing, seeing, or thinking about the node concept. Activation is distributed across the network according to four basic rules. First, the *working memory rule* says that LTM nodes that are currently in WM receive some small continual activation. Second, according to the *processing activity rule*, LTM nodes in WM receive a "sharp jolt" of activation when they become part of current conscious processing. Third, the *fan rule* asserts that activated nodes in LTM spread activation to directly linked nodes, according to the strengths of nodes and links. And finally, activation in LTM *decays* rapidly.

Proposition 5: Memory objects, represented as nodes in LTM, may be singular concepts, as described earlier, or bundles of tightly associated knowledge, or schemas. A schema occupies that same "space" in WM as a single node.

I mentioned earlier that the nodes displayed in Figure 3.1 may each contain larger data structures. Bill Clinton, for example, may be known to this person as "Slick Willie" – an untrustworthy, insincere politician, who is pro-choice and pro-death penalty (Figure 3.2). Of these features, which make up the Clinton schema, the only one with positive affect for our hypothetical citizen is his support of capital punishment. If asked about Bill Clinton, this citizen is likely to look first to the beliefs contained within the schema before traveling across the network to linked nodes (e.g., to Clinton's Haiti policy, which the person liked). Similarly, for foreign policy sophisticates, the chaos in Bosnia and the Haiti intervention may contain crystallized beliefs in the form of cases. If, however, we assume that our hypothetical citizen is relatively uninformed, these may be very unspecified cases and a more generalized script for police action may be needed to provide interpretations.

Note, finally, that a new more detailed case for Haiti may be assembled in WM and encoded as a packet to LTM, if motivation is strong. The information in this new case will be the retained features of the input information (probably news stories) as interpreted by appropriate memory structures and perhaps heavily influenced by a general police action script. Priming effects, well known in the experimental literature, are explained in this theory by the power of primed memory structures to frame the mental understanding of the stimulus. How different might the understanding of the Haiti case be if news stories or Republican opponents invoked an "international aggression" or

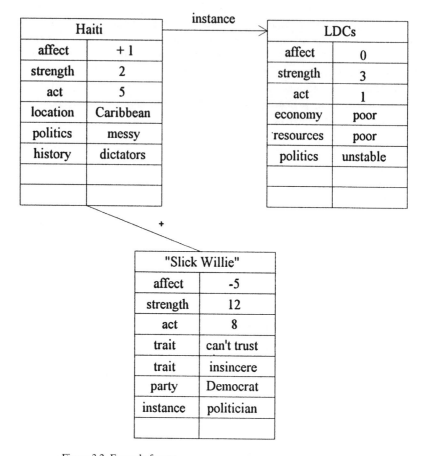

Figure 3.2. Example frames.

"domestic primacy" structure to frame the information about Haiti rather than the police action script.

More generally, schema-, script-, or case-based processing of information is the basis for metaphorical and analogical reasoning (Khong 1992; Shimko 1995). For example, foreign policy decision makers appear to rely heavily on several powerful images of international relations – e.g., Vietnam Quagmire, Munich Metaphor, and Domino Theory – which they may store as schemas or cases in LTM.

Proposition 6: Processing is subject to motivational biases introduced by accuracy or directional goals.

Motivational biases have their greatest impact by biasing memory search (Kunda 1990). Perhaps the simplest mechanism to account for this processing bias is a system of motivational filters on memory search, triggered by one's goals. Accuracy goals, which will arise when the decision task has been made salient (perhaps through experimental manipulation or, in the real world, because people think the decision can have an impact on their lives), will produce much more thorough and deeper processing, and they may compensate to some degree for directional biases. People motivated by directional goals, on the other hand, are less likely to seek all relevant information, being satisfied with interpretations that conform with preconception. If new information does not fit preconception, moreover, strong directional goals may lead people to discount the new information or actively counterargue. I have suggested that these processes can work through a system of memory retrieval filters that would either prevent counterattitudinal information from getting into WM or tag it as dubious (Taber et al. in press).

Directional goals arise when LTM nodes are retrieved into WM, bringing their affective and their semantic content. Early in the process of constructing an interpretation in WM for the event, directional goals will be established if the beliefs and knowledge retrieved from LTM carry strong positive or negative affect. For example, an ''international aggressor'' schema may carry strong negative affect. If it is drawn into WM early in the process of interpreting the Iraqi invasion of Kuwait, it may establish a directional goal to construct a negative understanding of the event. Of course, other considerations that enter WM early in the process also will affect the directional goals that arise.

Proposition 7: In addition to the activation rules already mentioned, LTM nodes that ''partially match'' items in WM receive a jolt of activation.

Schemas in LTM that are not identical to but share features with structures in WM may also become activated. This is an important part of the inferential process, allowing reasoning from metaphor or analogy. For example, someone (as many people did) might understand Saddam Hussein by reference to a Hitler schema (Spellman and Holyoak 1992). This requires that the pattern of features of the emerging representation of Hussein match to some degree the pattern of features in the Hitler schema.

In this theory, pattern matching is a function of four factors. First, the degree of similarity between the semantic content in WM and schemas in LTM (e.g., similarity of actors, targets, or verbs). Second, the matcher looks first to strong potential matches – it is guided by node strength. Third, the matcher favors schemas with affective implications consistent with existing directional goals. And fourth, strong accuracy goals deepen the search for matches by allowing even weaker pattern matches to qualify. It may seem paradoxical that a concern for accuracy leads the decision maker to accept weaker matches in building understandings, but remember that the accuracy motive leads one to process more deeply, considering a wider range of possible interpretations.

Proposition 8: When motivation (either directional or accuracy) is strong and WM holds "new" information, old memory structures may be modified or new memory structures may be assembled in WM and transferred to LTM. This learning responds to information from the environment.

Four types of learning take place in this theory. First, the strength of nodes and links changes with the history of activation; activation passing through nodes and links increases their strength. Second, existing associations among nodes in LTM may be actively altered because of information in WM (e.g., if one hears that Clinton now opposes further intervention in Haiti, that link would be changed). Third, new associations might be learned. And fourth, new schemas might be constructed and linked into LTM. For example, if input information (perhaps a news story) associates Haiti with the earlier Somalia case, a respondent may construct an understanding of the Haiti case by reference to the stored knowledge of the Somalia case. This understanding might then be encoded as a new structure in LTM.

These eight propositions form the core of a theory of event interpretation. Note that this theory is intended to provide a general explanation for both elite interpretation and the perceptions of citizens. They will undoubtedly differ in the amount of knowledge they have and in how tightly structured it is. Note also that the theory is separate from the actual knowledge content used to interpret events. To initiate the theory as a model, I will have to endow it with knowledge about the world that is at least similar to the knowledge people make use of. A computational model (the Event Interpreter, or EVIN) is currently being developed to explore formally the implications of the theory.

A Formal Model of Event Interpretation

EVIN is the cognitive level of a distributed organizational politics model of foreign policy event interpretation (hinted at earlier). Ultimately, EVIN will be embedded in a social structure defined by rules and procedures for information flow among individuals, but I consider only the cognitive component in this chapter. Because the emphasis in this chapter has been on developing

Stim Obj						
actor						
target	1	2	3	4	5	6
verb						
goals						

Figure 3.3. Working memory.

the theory that stands behind EVIN, the overview in this section is intended to illustrate rather than fully describe the model.

As described in the last section, EVIN's structure divides into two basic components: LTM, which represents an individual's knowledge and beliefs relevant to foreign policy, and WM, which provides a limited "scratch pad" for current information processing. LTM is modeled as a network of linked frames, each of which contains semantic content (e.g., a Haiti frame may contain an individual's knowledge that Haiti is a poor island country in the Caribbean Sea), affective content (in the form of a single numerical summary tag), a current activation level (which is a function of the activation rules already described), and a current node strength (which is a function of the node's history of activation and its "usefulness" in processing). WM is limited to seven slots, six of which can each contain one frame from LTM. The seventh slot is always occupied by the "stimulus object," which represents the person's current understanding of the stimulus event (Figure 3.3). Initially, the stimulus object contains only markers for the elements of the stimulus event (ACTOR, VERB, TARGET, and CONTEXT), but it becomes more elaborate as interpretation proceeds.

Processing in EVIN occurs in discrete steps, successively iterating the same processes until the interpretation is deemed satisfactory. As we can see in Figure 3.4, processing cycles between a series of LTM processing steps and a series of WM steps. In general, processing in LTM involves the spread of activation across links, while processing in WM uses a pattern matcher to assess the relevance of recalled memory objects for the task at hand. To illustrate the flow diagram, consider the interpretation processes that might ensue for the event "Iraq/Saddam Hussein attacks Kuwait," assuming the limited knowledge of a typical American citizen. First, markers for the three elements of the event are placed in the stimulus object slot in WM (for simplicity, we will assume that WM is otherwise empty). Activation is applied to a simple corresponding LTM frame for "Iraq" and to several frames corresponding to "attack" (e.g., a "cavalry charge" frame, a "mugging"

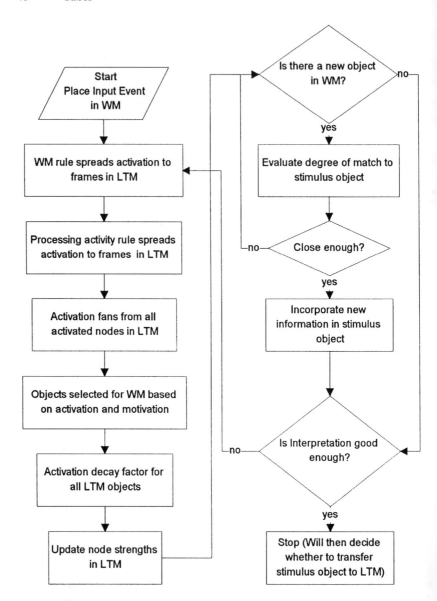

Figure 3.4. Process flow.

frame, an "international aggression" frame, and an "international police action" frame); our hypothetical citizen has no existing knowledge of Kuwait. Activation fans from these frames to linked frames (e.g., some activation spreads from the Iraq frame to a simple Iran frame). Six memory objects are transferred to slots in WM probabilistically according to levels of activation. For our example, these include the Iraq frame, the mugging frame, a "crime in the subways" frame that received activation across a link from the mugging frame, and three totally unrelated frames.

After updating activation and node strengths in LTM, working memory processes start by assessing the relevance of the six new objects in WM for interpreting the attack on Kuwait, using degree of pattern match. (The specific pattern matcher used is not important for the current description; in fact, we are experimenting with several different pattern matchers, ranging from one that focuses exclusively on similarity of components to one that measures the overall similarity of arrangement of components.) The actor slot within the stimulus object is updated to include the entire Iraq frame pulled from LTM, including the beliefs that Iraq is militaristic and has oil and a very slightly negative affective tag. The possible matches to "attack" – mugging and subway crime – are discarded. Because the interpretation is incomplete, processing iterates back to LTM in a search for more relevant information. Our citizen may also seek information from the environment if highly motivated, although unless strong motivation comes from the environment (e.g., lurid media reports), this seems unlikely here because the only current motivation is a slightly negative impression of Iraq. The stop-rule, which determines when an interpretation is satisfactory, is a function of the size and complexity of the stimulus object, whether anything new has been added to the stimulus object in recent processing rounds, and the strength of motivation.

On the second round of interpretation, activation is again sent to the Iraq frame and linked frames and to the remaining possible matches for "attack," according to the rules described in the preceding section. This ultimately moves the more helpful "international aggression" and "police action" frames from LTM into WM (along with a steady stream of irrelevant material). "International aggression" is judged a good match, and the verb attack is interpreted by reference to it. This yields stronger motivation, because the "aggression" frame carries a strong negative affective tag. After several further iterations of search through LTM and selection in WM, the stimulus object becomes reasonably elaborate. Iraq is interpreted as a bully (from the aggression frame); Hussein is interpreted as Hitler (from the Munich/World War II case, which was linked in LTM to the international aggression frame); attack is interpreted as aggression; Kuwait is interpreted as the innocent victim (its role in the aggression/bully frame); and motivation has become strongly negative toward Iraq.

Of course, one could imagine many other possible interpretations of this event. In the EVIN model, processes remain constant; differences of interpretation are determined by the differing content of LTM as EVIN represents different individuals.

Conclusion

How foreign policy decision makers (and citizens in a democracy) interpret international events and the behavioral impact of these perceptions have interested IR scholars for decades. Several theoretical conceptualizations exist in this line of research, including perceptions and misperceptions, images, belief systems, cognitive maps, operational codes, problem representations, and paradigms, but the basic theoretical premise is the same: In explaining foreign policy, individuals and their mental states matter.

This chapter has reviewed the cognitive science literature on the construction of mental understandings, developed a theory of foreign policy event interpretation, and briefly described a model of the theory (EVIN). Much remains to be done – EVIN must be completed and tested, its individual-level behavior must be explored, and it must be embedded within a social structure to study foreign policy cognition in context – but it promises to be an interesting and important journey. To understand how we understand the world, despite its complexity, remains one of the central puzzles of the social sciences.

Author's Note: For helpful comments and suggestions on this work, I thank Ken Rona, Rich Timpone, and Milton Lodge at Stony Brook, and Robert Billings, Katherine Gannon, Margaret Hermann, Charles Hermann, Donald Sylvan, and Michael Young at the Mershon Center. This research is based on work supported by the National Science Foundation under Awards No. SES-9102901 and SES-9310351 to the author and DIR-9113599 to the Mershon Center Research Training Group on the Role of Cognition in Collective Political Decision Making at Ohio State University.

References

Abelson, Robert P. (1973). "The structure of belief systems." In Roger C. Schank and K. Colby (eds.), *Computer Models of Thought and Language*. San Francisco: W. H. Freeman.

Alker, Hayward R., Jr., Gavan Duffy, Roger Hurwitz, and John C. Mallery (1991). "Text modeling for international politics: A tourist's guide to RELATUS." In Valerie M. Hudson (ed.), *Artificial Intelligence in International Politics*. Boulder, CO: Westview Press.

Anderson, John R. (1983). *The Architecture of Cognition*. Cambridge, MA: Harvard.

Anderson, Paul A. (1981). "Justification and precedents as constraints in foreign policy decision making." *American Journal of Political Science, 25:* 738–761.

Baddeley, A. D. (1986). *Working Memory*. Oxford: Oxford University Press.

Baddeley, A. D., and G. Hitch (1974). "Working memory." In *The Psychology of Learning and Motivation* (Vol. 8). London: Academic Press.

Banerjee, Sanjoy (1991). "Reproduction of perception and decision in the early Cold War." In Valerie M. Hudson (ed.), *Artificial Intelligence in International Politics*. Boulder, CO: Westview Press.

Belmore, Susan (1986). "Determinants of attention during impression formation." *Journal of Experimental Psychology: Learning, Memory, and Cognition, 13:* 480–489.

Bennett, W. Lance (1981). "Perception and Cognition: An Information Processing Framework for Politics." In Samuel Long (ed.), *The Handbook of Political Behavior*. New York: Plenum.

——— (1982). "Rethinking political perception and cognition." *Macropolitics, 2:* 175–202.

Boulding, Kenneth E. (1956). *The Image: Knowledge in Life and Society*. Ann Arbor: University of Michigan.

Bower, G. H., J. B. Black, and T. J. Turner (1979). "Scripts in memory for text." *Cognitive Psychology, 11:* 177–220.

Bruner, J. S. (1957). "On perceptual readiness." *Psychological Review, 64:* 123–152.

Carbonell, Jaime G., Jr. (1978). "POLITICS: Automated ideological reasoning." *Cognitive Science, 2:* 27–51.

Collins, Allan, and Edward E. Smith (eds.). (1988). *Readings in Cognitive Science: A Perspective from Psychology and Artificial Intelligence*. San Mateo, CA: Morgan Kaufmann.

Cottam, Martha L. (1986). *Foreign Policy Decision Making: The Influence of Cognition*. Boulder, CO: Westview Press.

Deutsch, Karl W. (1964). *The Nerves of Government*. New York: Free Press.

Doran, Jim (1985). "The computational approach to knowledge, communication, and structure in multi-actor systems." In G. Nigel Gilbert and Christian Heath (eds.), *Social Action and Artificial Intelligence*. Aldershoot, GB: Gower.

Duffy, Gavan, and Seth A. Tucker (1995). "Political science: Artificial intelligence applications." *Social Science Computer Review, 13:* 1–20.

Ensign, Margee M., and Warren R. Phillips (1991). "Decision making and development: A 'glass box' approach to representation." In Valerie M. Hudson (ed.), *Artificial Intelligence in International Politics*. Boulder, CO: Westview Press.

Eysenck, Michael W. (1984). *A Handbook of Cognitive Psychology*. Hillsdale, NJ: Lawrence Erlbaum.

Eysenck, Michael W., and Mark T. Keane (1990). *Cognitive Psychology: A Student's Handbook*. Hillsdale, NJ: Lawrence Erlbaum.

Feigenbaum, Edward A., and Julian Feldman (eds.). (1995). *Computers and Thought*. Cambridge, MA: MIT Press.

Fiske, Susan (1980). "Attention and weight in person perception: The impact of negative and extreme behavior." *The Journal of Personality and Social Psychology, 38:* 889–906.

Galambos, J. A., R. P. Abelson, and J. B. Black (1986). *Knowledge Structures*. Hillsdale, NJ: Lawrence Erlbaum.

Geva, Nehemia, Karl DeRouen, and Alex Mintz (1993). "The political incentive explanation of Democratic peace: Evidence from experimental research." *International Interactions, 18:* 215–229.

Gibson, J. J. (1979). *The Ecological Approach to Visual Perception*. Boston: Houghton-Mifflin.

Gregory, R. L. (1972). "Seeing as thinking." *Times Literary Supplement*, June 23.
—— (1980). "Perceptions as hypotheses." *Philosophical Transactions of the Royal Society of London, Series B., 290:* 181–197.
Haney, Patrick J. (1995). "Structure and process in the analysis of foreign policy crises." In Laura Neack, Jeanne A. K. Hey, and Patrick J. Haney (eds.), *Foreign Policy Analysis: Continuity and Change in Its Second Generation.* Englewood Cliffs, NJ: Prentice-Hall.
Holsti, Ole R. (1962). "The belief system and national images." *Journal of Conflict Resolution, 16:* 244–252.
—— (1967). "Cognitive dynamics and images of the enemy: Dulles and Russia." In David Finlay, Ole Holsti, and Richard Fagan (eds.), *Enemies and Politics.* Chicago: Rand McNally.
Jervis, Robert (1970). *The Logic of Images in International Relations.* Princeton: Princeton University Press.
—— (1976). *Perception and Misperception in International Politics.* Princeton: Princeton University Press.
Kelman, Herbert C. (1965). *International Behavior: A Social-Psychological Analysis.* New York: Holt, Rinehart and Winston.
Khong, Yuen Foong (1992). *Analogies at War: Korea, Munich, Dien Bien Phu, and the Vietnam Decisions of 1965.* Princeton, NJ: Princeton University Press.
Kolodner, Janet L. (ed.). (1988). *Proceedings of the First Case-Based Reasoning Workshop.* Los Altos, CA: Morgan Kaufmann.
Kunda, Ziva (1990). "The case for motivated reasoning." *Psychological Bulletin, 108:* 480–498.
Larson, Deborah Welch (1994). "The role of belief systems and schemas in foreign policy decision-making." *Political Psychology, 15:* 17–33.
Lazarus, R. S. (1982). "Thoughts on the relations between emotion and cognition." *American Psychologist, 37:* 1019–1024.
Leake, David B. (1991). "Goal-based explanation evaluation." *Cognitive Science, 15:* 509–545.
Lebow, Richard Ned (1981). *Between Peace and War: The Nature of International Crisis.* Baltimore: Johns Hopkins.
Lippmann, Walter (1922). *Public Opinion.* New York: Harcourt.
Lodge, Milton (1993). "Toward a Procedural Model of Candidate Evaluation." Political Psychology Working Paper, Department of Political Science, SUNY at Stony Brook.
Mallery, John C. (1991). "Semantic content analysis: A new methodology for the RELATUS natural language environment." In Valerie M. Hudson (ed.), *Artificial Intelligence in International Politics.* Boulder, CO: Westview Press.
March, James, and Herbert Simon (1958). *Organizations.* New York: Wiley.
Masuch, Michael, and Massimo Warglien. (eds.). (1992). *Artificial Intelligence in Organization and Management Theory: Models of Distributed Activity.* Amsterdam: North-Holland.
Mefford, Dwain (1987). "Analogical reasoning and the definition of the situation: Back to Snyder for comments and forward to artificial intelligence for method." In Charles F. Hermann, Charles W. Kegley, Jr., and James N. Rosenau (eds.), *New Directions in the Study of Foreign Policy.* Boston: Allen and Unwin.
Miller, D. T., and M. Ross (1975). "Self-serving biases in attribution of causality: Fact or fiction." *Psychological Bulletin, 82:* 213–225.

Miller, George (1956). ''The magical number seven, plus or minus two: Some limits on our capacity for processing information.'' *Psychological Review, 63:* 81–97.

Minsky, Marvin (ed.). (1968). *Semantic Information Processing.* Cambridge, MA: MIT Press.

Neisser, U. (1967). *Cognitive Psychology.* New York: Appleton-Century-Crofts.

Newell, Allen, and Herbert A. Simon (1972). *Human Problem Solving.* Englewood Cliffs, NJ: Prentice-Hall.

Nisbett, R. E., and L. Ross (1980). *Human Inference: Strategies and Shortcomings of Social Judgement.* Englewood Cliffs, NJ: Lawrence Erlbaum.

Petty, R. E., and J. T. Cacioppo (1986). ''The elaboration likelihood model of persuasion.'' In L. Berkowitz (ed.), *Advances in Experimental Social Psychology* (Vol. 19). New York: Academic Press.

Powell, Charles A., James W. Dyson, and Helen E. Purkitt (1987). ''Opening the 'black-box': Cognitive processing and optimal choice in foreign policy decision making.'' In Charles F. Hermann, Charles W. Kegley, Jr., and James N. Rosenau (eds.), *New Directions in the Study of Foreign Policy.* Boston: Allen and Unwin.

Pyszczynski, T., and J. Greenberg (1987). ''Toward an integration of cognitive and motivational perspectives on social inference: A biased hypothesis-testing model.'' In L. Berkowitz (ed.), *Advances in Experimental Social Psychology* (Vol. 20). New York: Academic Press.

Ram, Ashwin, and David B. Leake (eds.). (1995). *Goal-Driven Learning.* Cambridge, MA: MIT Press.

Reichgelt, Han (1991). *Knowledge Representation: An AI Perspective.* Norwood, NJ: Ablex Publishing.

Riesbeck, Christopher K., and Roger C. Schank (1989). *Inside Case-Based Reasoning.* Hillsdale, NJ: Lawrence Erlbaum.

Ripley, Brian (1993). ''Cognition in Context: Revitalizing Bureaucratic Politics in Foreign Policy Analysis.'' Paper presented at the APSA annual meeting, Washington, D.C.

(1995). ''Cognition, culture, and bureaucratic politics.'' In Laura Neack, Jeanne A. K. Hey, and Patrick J. Haney (eds.), *Foreign Policy Analysis: Continuity and Change in Its Second Generation.* Englewood Cliffs, NJ: Prentice-Hall.

Rosati, Jerel (1984). ''The impact of beliefs on behavior: The foreign policy of the Carter administration.'' In Donald A. Sylvan and Steve Chan (eds.), *Foreign Policy Decision Making: Perception, Cognition, and Artificial Intelligence.* New York: Praeger.

(1995). ''A cognitive approach to the study of foreign policy.'' In Laura Neack, Jeanne A. K. Hey, and Patrick J. Haney (eds.), *Foreign Policy Analysis: Continuity and Change in Its Second Generation.* Englewood Cliffs, NJ: Prentice-Hall.

Schank, Roger C. (1975). *Conceptual Information Processing.* Amsterdam: North-Holland.

Schank, Roger C., and Robert P. Abelson (1977). *Scripts, Plans, Goals, and Understanding: An Inquiry into Human Knowledge Structures.* Hillsdale, NJ: Lawrence Erlbaum.

Schrodt, Philip A. (1991). ''Pattern recognition of international event sequences: A machine learning approach.'' In Valerie M. Hudson (ed.), *Artificial Intelligence in International Politics.* Boulder, CO: Westview Press.

(In press). *Patterns, Rules, and Learning: Computational Models of International Behavior.* Ann Arbor, MI: University of Michigan.

Shimko, Keith L. (1995). ''Foreign policy metaphors: Falling 'dominoes' and 'drug wars.' " In Laura Neack, Jeanne A. K. Hey, and Patrick J. Haney (eds.), *Foreign Policy Analysis: Continuity and Change in Its Second Generation.* Englewood Cliffs, NJ: Prentice-Hall.

Snyder, Richard C., H. W. Bruck, and Burton Sapin (1962). *Foreign Policy Decision Making: An Approach to the Study of International Politics.* New York: Free Press.

Sowa, John F. (1984). *Conceptual Structures: Information Processing in Mind and Machine.* Reading, MA: Addison-Wesley.

Spellman, Barbara A., and Keith J. Holyoak (1992). "If Saddam is Hitler then who is George Bush? Analogical mapping between systems of social roles." *Journal of Personality and Social Psychology, 6:* 913–933.

Sylvan, Donald A., Thomas M. Ostrom, and Katharine Gannon (1994). "Case-based, model-based, and explanation-based styles of reasoning in foreign policy." *International Studies Quarterly, 38:* 61–90.

Taber, Charles S. (1992). "POLI: An expert system model of U.S. foreign policy belief systems." *American Political Science Review, 86:* 888–904.

Taber, Charles S., Milton Lodge, and Jill Glathar (In press). "The motivated construction of political judgements." In James Kuklinski (ed.), *Political Psychology.* Cambridge: Cambridge University Press.

Taber, Charles S., and Kenneth S. Rona (1995). "EVIN: A Computational Model of Event Interpretation." Paper presented at the Annual Conference of the International Studies Association, Chicago, IL.

Taber, Charles S., and Richard Timpone (1994). "The policy arguer: The architecture of an expert system." *Social Science Computer Review, 12:* 1–25.

(1996a). *Computational Modeling* (Sage University Paper Series on Quantitative Applications in the Social Sciences, 07-113). Newbury Park, CA: Sage.

(1996b). "Beyond simplicity: Focused realism and computational modeling in international relations." *Mershon International Studies Review, 40:* 41–79.

Tetlock, Philip E. (1983). "Policy-makers images of international conflict." *Journal of Social Issues, 39.*

Vertzberger, Yaacov Y. I. (1990). *The World in Their Minds: Information Processing, Cognition, and Perception in Foreign Policy Decisionmaking.* Stanford: Stanford University Press.

Zajonc, R. B. (1984). "On the primacy of affect." *American Psychologist, 39:* 117–123.

CHAPTER 4

Problem Identification in Sequential Policy Decision Making: The Re-representation of Problems

Robert S. Billings and Charles F. Hermann

It is our contention that most foreign policy problems continue over an extended period of time and that policy makers often find themselves returning again and again to the task of coping with an issue they have addressed before. Problems that have been addressed on a number of previous occasions will present a different decision task than those newly faced. Our goal here is to continue our analysis of sequential decision making in foreign policy groups, building on the model outlined in Hermann and Billings (1993). We focus on one specific piece of the overall puzzle of sequential decision making – the conditions that foster a reexamination of the nature of the problem. We assume that the way in which the problem is represented affects much of the subsequent decision-making process, along with the resulting action. Accordingly, a complete model of sequential decision making requires an understanding of how and why problems may become ''re-represented.''

Despite the frequency of sequential decision making in the actual conduct of foreign policy, many analytic studies of decision are narrowly constructed episodes that focus on one major decision or a set of decisions that occur in only a short period of time. A study typically characterizes a challenge facing a government and the manner by which it decides on a response. Laboratory studies on sequential decision making are also rare.

Of course, there are exceptions. Game theory has explored the implications of iterative games (e.g., Axelrod 1984), and cybernetic models have featured feedback loops (e.g., Steinbruner 1974). Psychologists have explored the escalation of commitment (e.g., Staw 1981; Brockner 1992), frequently invoking American decision making on Vietnam as an example. Recently, several researchers have begun to examine the effects of past decisions on decision biases (e.g., Kleinmutz 1985) and risk taking (e.g., Hollenbeck, Ilgen, Philips, and Hedlund 1994; Thaler and Johnson 1990), often using the term *dynamic decision making* to refer to a sequence of decisions on the same issue. But the vast majority of decision-making studies have keyed on a single decision

or episode. A recent review (Stevenson, Busemeyer, and Naylor 1990) concluded that sequential decision making is one of the most complex and least
understood topics in the literature on decision making.

There are a number of consequences that flow from our tendency to treat
each decision-making episode as an isolated event, but the most important is
that the impact of prior history is ignored. Most models of decision making
(e.g., rational choice, prospect theory) examine how policy makers will weigh
the future, but they neglect the past. It is perhaps noteworthy that even in
experimental applications of game theory where there is a series of trials or
games, the focus is still on what will be the effect of future iterations on the
present game, leading to the concept of "the shadow of the future." But in
sequential decision making there also is a powerful "legacy of the past."

As used in this chapter, sequential decision making occurs when policy
makers engage in a series of decisions across a period of time about the same
issue or problem area. In an initial occasion for decision, a problem is recognized within that issue area, and after deliberation initial decisions are made
(to take certain actions or to do nothing at present). With these initial decisions, a momentary sense of closure is reached for the policy makers. They
turn their attention to other matters. The decision making becomes sequential
when policy makers subsequently find that they must reconsider the problem
or some variant of it. In some problems, reconsideration occurs repeatedly
over a period of months or years. The result is a sequence of *n* occasions for
decision with respect to a single problem or a series of highly interrelated
problems.

Although there are various types of decision units in foreign policy (see
Hermann and Hermann 1989; Hermann, Hermann, and Hagan 1987), our
focus is on decision-making groups – the frequent body for decisions in all
types of governments, at all levels. For groups, as for individuals, problem
representation constitutes a central feature of decision making.

On the Nature of Problem Representation

Although problem representation is generally recognized as the foundation
for decision making, different schools of thought exist about the nature of
this construct. Some authors (e.g., Voss and Post 1988) take an information-
processing approach and assume that decision makers represent problems in
terms of goals, current states, operators, barriers, consequences, and so forth.
This perspective seems to view the cognitive representation as a reference to
something ("the problem") that can exist independent of cognition. Alternatively, a discursive-practices approach, of particular interest to some in political science (e.g., Doty 1993), views the referents of politics as grounded in
the language of users that defines a discursive space and comprise the "real-

ity'' of political phenomena. By extension, a ''problem'' exists in the language of a community of policy makers, but not independently in some objective sense.

As we use the concepts, both problem and representation require separate specification. For the individual, a problem is a cognitive construct about a perceived discrepancy between some preferred or valued state of affairs and the perceived current or anticipated state of nature. In this context, discrepancy involves a sense of potential loss (producing a perceived threat) or gain (resulting in a perceived opportunity), regarding something that is valued. The state of nature may be tangible (e.g., the existence of an atomic bomb, the presence of troops near the border) or intangible (e.g., legitimacy, status). Intangible states are likely dependent on meanings and valuation attached to them by a community of language users; even tangible states are characterized by language that establishes boundaries and may not be neutral (e.g., an enemy nuclear weapon of mass destruction).

But most problems also have an assumed empirical referent in that the existing or anticipated state of nature usually has consequences that are observable directly or indirectly (e.g., the bomb may be detonated, status may be lost). Not only does the detonation of a nuclear weapon have observable effects; so does the loss of status or change in legitimacy (e.g., others respond differently). Thus, in our judgment problem is a cognitive construct for individuals that is shaped and bounded by the language community of the individual, but which makes reference to consequences that usually can be intersubjectively observed as having occurred or not occurred in the manner anticipated by those who identify the problem.

Problem representation also refers to both the cognitive process and the resulting product. We assume that the cognitive process occurs in two stages: *location* and *diagnosis*. Location (generally assumed to be the first stage; see Cowan 1986) involves two interrelated processes: (1) detecting a gap between one's goals and the perception of the state of nature and (2) placing the problem into cognitive categories, which might be generic (e.g., threat, opportunity) or content-specific. The other stage, diagnosis, involves a more thorough assessment of the causes and consequences of the problem. The product of problem representation is the result of these two stages, and is a complex cognitive representation, consisting of a gap between a desired state and the perceived situation, which is categorized (and thus labeled) and embedded in a more or less well-developed causal network.

Empirical studies of problem representation generally examine some manageable piece of this complex cognitive representation. For example, a study of problem identification by Pounds (1969) focused on problems as gaps. Others, such as Axelrod (1976) and Shapiro and Bonham (1973), have emphasized the causal network, using a cognitive mapping approach to problem representation. Some psychologists (e.g., Dutton and Jackson 1987) have examined the nature of issue categories, such as threat and opportunity.

Groups, and the larger organizational and institutional settings in which they are embedded, can have a significant effect on both the process and product of problem representation. It may well be that the organization has created the issue areas into which members classify policy problems. There also may be organizational norms and accepted types of explanation for certain problems that strongly influence the individual. Among group members there may be different problem representations initially, but it is most unlikely that the group can move to closure on a decision without tacit acceptance, if not total agreement, among most members on the problem representation. Depending upon the group's norms and decision rules, members may continue to disagree about the means of coping with a problem and the likely results, but they will have more or less agreed on the problem categorization – the first part of representation – if they remain in the group. For that reason, recasting the problem representation in sequential decision making becomes a major occurrence in the life of a policy group.

A General Scheme for Sequential Decision Making

Key Stages in Sequential Decision Making

Having discussed our approach to problem representation, we can set forth the larger framework that guides our examination of sequential decision making. Figure 4.1 provides a highly simplified representation of key stages in sequential decision making by a policy group. The imposition of these analytical constructs on any decision process can create a number of widely acknowledged difficulties: Not every stage occurs in every occasion for decision; certainly the order is not necessarily linear; and the "rationality" implied by the categories is often not apparent. Furthermore, the collective processes in groups can complicate the simplicity suggested by these stages. Despite these caveats, conceptualizing decision making in these terms reveals various processes important to sequential decision making.

The first five stages in the process, from determination of goals to choice, are described in detail by many other authors (e.g., Cowan 1986; Mintzberg, Raisinghani, and Theoret 1976). We do not dwell on these five stages but do make a few observations about the processes leading to an initial choice. Notice that Stages 2 and 3 comprise what we define as *problem representation*. Stage 4, option development, involves the identification and description of a procedure or action that advocates believe could prevent, correct, or reduce the problem. For someone to conclude that an action will have some effect on the problem, they must engage in some kind of analysis (implicitly

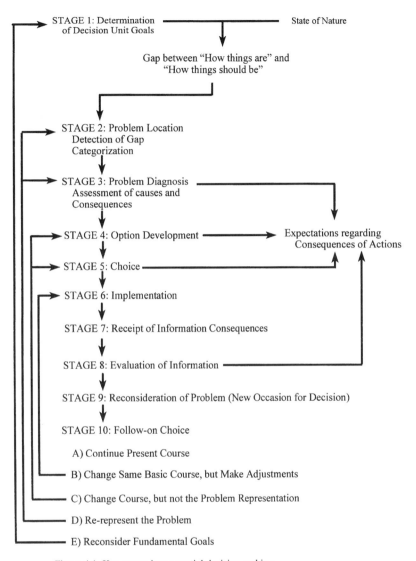

Figure 4.1. Key stages in sequential decision making.

or explicitly) linking the proposed option to the cause of the problem. Thus, option development is an extension of development of beliefs about the cause of the difficulty that occurs in problem representation.

The choice or actual decision (Stage 5 in Figure 4.1) has been the focal point of much of the research on decision making. We wish to emphasize that when a group adopts an option or approach to the problem, the members are accepting – perhaps with varying degrees of confidence – that the actions will have certain effects. As is elaborated later, the type of expectation created depends on the type of action. In brief, group expectations are created during problem diagnosis, option development, and choice. The mutual effects of these three stages and expectations concerning the consequences of action are shown in Figure 4.1.

Implementation (Stage 6) involves the execution of the decision. In the study of bureaucracies and other organizations, the point has often been made that considerable discrepancy can sometimes emerge between the course of action intended by the decision group and the actual implementation. Therefore, the decision group may have an inaccurate understanding about the nature of the action resulting from their choice.

Stage 7 involves the receipt of information from the environment about the results that appear to have followed after the implementation of the decision. For sequential decision making, this feedback of information is critical. The only other stimulus for the reexamination of a prior decision is internal, that is, when the policy makers themselves change (e.g., when the membership of the group is reconstituted). Feedback, which may not be distorted and which can be misperceived or ignored, forms the basis for evaluation of the previous decision and implemented actions (if any).

Evaluation (Stage 8) depends upon the comparison between the feedback and the expectations associated with the prior decision. The "fit" between the prior expectations and the reported results determines whether a new occasion for decision arises and sequential decision making occurs. Feedback can in principle confirm expectations, disconfirm expectations, or appear ambiguous. (Although feedback that the decision makers regard as ambiguous and not interpretable is an important class of information, we disregard it for the purpose of outlining the general perspective in this chapter.)

When we exclude changes in the composition of the decision unit (not considered here), the process of sequential decision making is triggered by a perceived discrepancy between prior expectations and recognized feedback. Unmet expectations – and thus reconsideration of the problem – generally are a result of disconfirming feedback, but they can also occur when undesirable side effects are detected or when the action succeeds far better than expected.

When a new occasion for decision results from the discrepancy between expectations and feedback, the decision group's reconsideration of the problem (Stage 9 in Figure 4.1) will lead to a follow-on choice, which can take one of five forms (Stage 10): The choice may be to continue on the present course. Alternatively, the choice may involve making some adjustments (e.g., to commit more resources, to assign implementation to another unit). A third alternative is to change course by selecting another option, without a change in the problem representation. A fourth alternative is to reconsider the nature of the problem itself by reconsidering either the problem location or altering the problem diagnosis. These processes constitute problem re-representation, which presumably would lead to the development or choice of new actions. The final alternative is the most fundamental: reconsideration of one's goals (e.g., abandoning a goal such as maintaining a separate South Vietnam). Rejecting a goal would result in a total re-representation of the problem and a dramatic change in course.

We assume that if any change in the approach to a problem occurs during a group's reconsideration, the magnitude of that change will be reflected in the comparable stage of the decision process. In other words, if the change is limited to some adjustments, then the group will devote most of its energy to reviewing implementation. ("Our basic approach is correct, but we need to modify how we are doing it.") More serious changes are likely to follow from reconsideration of options. ("This approach is not working, we need to try something else to achieve what we want.") The most basic changes, however, are associated with a re-representation of the problem or a reconsideration of fundamental goals. When the group questions their fundamental goals, reconsiders how they have categorized the problem or alters their diagnosis of the problem, then fundamental restructuring can occur and with it major redirection in policy. These predicted effects are represented in Figure 4.1 as a series of feedback loops.

Before discussing the factors that affect the likelihood of problem re-representation, we need to further elaborate three crucial pieces of our model: (1) types of actions, (2) the structure of expectations, and (3) feedback.

Types of Actions

We argue that in sequential decision making, the nature of the prior action (or inaction) affects the likelihood of problem re-representation. Therefore, we need a classification of actions differentiating among features particularly relevant to reconsideration of the problem. Our proposed set of categories includes search, provisional, conditional, and definitive actions. These types of actions fall along a continuum of the decision makers' relative certainty in how to interpret and cope with the problem they are facing – with search reflecting the greatest uncertainty and definitive the least. Associated with increased certainty is the tendency to undertake actions that are more difficult to revoke because of the nature of the action or the costs in reversing the decision.

Search: Actions of this kind are intended to gather information that may resolve some uncertainty about an aspect of the problem or possible responses to it. It may concern an attempt to collect further insight into any aspect of the problem including the definition of the problem, an appraisal of the consequences of a particular response, or the confirmation of a particular diagnosis. Search routines do not seek to respond to the problem directly, but to acquire insight that will enable such action. When the initial expectations of American policy makers about the Korean invasion appeared to be incorrect, they initiated a search routine. President Truman directed General MacArthur to fly to Korea and evaluate the situation.

Provisional: In contrast to search routines, provisional actions are intended to affect the problem directly, although in some tentative and limited manner. The decision makers believe that some commitment or signal is desirable or necessary at present, and they speculate that their action may influence the problem in a preferred way. They remain uncertain, however, about its effectiveness and assume that the present action keeps a number of their options open, including the possibility of terminating the activity or limiting its consequences if it proves to be inappropriate. The small incremental stages associated with provisional actions are associated with an approach Lindblom (1959) termed "muddling through." Again, the 1950 Korean invasion offers an example. On learning of the South Korean army's retreat, Truman ordered U.S. aircraft to fly protective cover for evacuating American citizens. It was a relatively small commitment. When the Americans were out, the action would end. Even if all U.S. citizens did not get out safely, the government could claim that everything that could be done from the air had been done, thus limiting the consequences of the decision.

Conditional: An action of this kind takes the form of a signal that stipulates or implies that future action will be contingent on the response of others. It announces, "We will do x, if you do (or fail to do) y." Threats and promises are of this nature. Such actions usually assume that the decision makers believe they have a reasonably clear understanding of the cause and effects of the problem and a means of coping with it. In 1986, President Reagan threatened trade sanctions against the European Community if they did not reverse new barriers against the export of U.S. feed grains to Spain and Portugal. The American directive specified that the penalties would go into effect automatically on a specified date unless the Europeans backed down. In this classical example of a conditional action, the United States policy makers intended to structure the situation so only two outcomes were possible – which one would occur depended on the response of the European Community.

Definitive: These actions are undertaken when the decision makers believe they have a good diagnosis of the problem and have identified the possible means for coping with it under present circumstances. In some cases, they may be confident that the initiative will successfully deal with the problem; in others, they may have much less confidence that the outcome will be favorable. In either case, however, there is an irrevocable commitment made in the action. When the Panamanian dictator Noriega repeatedly interfered with American drug interdiction efforts, the Reagan administration set aside the niceties of international law. American armed forces went to Panama, grabbed the general, and threw him in a Florida jail. Regardless of whether it settled the drug problem in Panama, the action of the United States ended any major role by Noriega and was clearly an example of a definitive action.

Several further observations are in order about types of actions. First, a decision-making group in response to a current problem may undertake several different actions simultaneously. For example, they might undertake search on one aspect of the problem while initiating provisional action with regard to another. (The United States did exactly this in its early response to the 1950 invasion of South Korea.)

Second, international relations is a highly interactive system. Governments are constantly initiating or responding to actions addressed to one or more other actors from whom they expect a response. A more complete typology of actions – with implications for expectations – might take into account the nature of the other party toward whom action is addressed (e.g., ally, enemy) and the nature of the situation (e.g., crisis or noncrisis). Although we acknowledge that these features could also affect the structure of expectations, we focus initially on the more limited set of four categories.

The Structure of Expectations

When decision makers undertake one of the types of actions mentioned previously, they tend to form a set of expectations about what it will likely do. Table 4.1 summarizes the expectations that follow from each type of action. Also included are some of the effects of confirmation versus disconfirmation of these expectations, which is the focus of the next subsection.

Feedback – Confirmation versus Disconfirmation: New information is regarded here as any signal from the environment perceived by the decision makers after their most recent decision on a given problem and seen by them as relevant to it. The detection of such information in the first place is an important and problematic process, as we have discussed elsewhere (Hermann and Billings 1993). For our present purposes, however, we assume that new information has been detected by the policy group, and that what is problematic is the interpretation of such information.

The way in which feedback is interpreted is critical in understanding the group's reconsideration of the problem. The interpretation of outcomes has

Table 4.1. *Confirmation/disconfirmation of expectations for different actions*

Prior action	Expectation	Confirmation	Disconfirmation[a]
Search	New information will reduce uncertainty and create new occasion for decision.	Information obtained that answers questions posed or substantiates predilections. (New Action: Convene group for decision.)	No information is found, or it is ambiguous, or it disconfirms a hypothesis.
Provisional	Action may (or may not) make a situation more favorable from perspective of policy makers.	Situation improves. (New Action: If improvement is continuing, continue status quo; if effect has ended, extend same action – more effort.)	Situation is unchanged or worse.
Conditional	Response of others (compliance expected) will determine future behavior.	Compliance received. (New Action: If others comply with threat, no further action is required. If others comply with promise, initiate reward action.)	No compliance or behavior of others is ambiguous.
Definitive	Problem will be solved by actor's irrevocable commitment.	Problem disappears. (New Action: No action required.)	Problem continues; unexpected effects occur.

[a] No new actions are suggested in cases of disconfirmation in this table because such choices are the subject of much of the remainder of this chapter.

profound implications for the choices that a group makes. "If a decision is framed as a certain loss, then people tend to abandon a failing project. However, if a decision is framed as an attempt to recoup an investment, then people tend to escalate their commitment to a project" (Uhler 1993: 8). Prospect theory (e.g., Farnham 1992) and theories of escalation (e.g., Staw and Ross 1989) point to the significance of interpreting feedback as negative and indicating a high probability of loss for future decisions.

If feedback is interpreted as confirming the prior decision, it tends to substantiate for the decision makers that their previous comprehension and framing of the problem was correct. With the possible exception of some search routines (e.g., those that confirm threatening situations), confirmation of prior action tends to frame the current situation quite differently than disconfirmation. Provisional actions perceived as successful may be regarded either as having settled the problem or as creating new occasions for decision that are framed as opportunities. Similarly, framing seems likely with conditional actions (e.g., when compliance eliminates the need to execute a threat or when compliance triggers the obligation to fulfill a promise). If confirming feedback is received after definitive actions, it supports their expectation that the problem is settled.

On the other hand, disconfirming feedback may produce a variety of reactions, including continuation of the status quo, intensified monitoring of the environment, increases in the level of effort, reconsideration of specific approaches or tactics, and possibly re-representation of the nature of the problem itself. The remainder of this chapter explores factors that influence the reexamination of a problem and increase the likelihood of its re-representation as a result of disconfirming feedback.

When Re-representation Occurs in Sequential Decision Making

Given the existence of negative feedback on a previously chosen course of action, what factors affect the likelihood that the group will: (1) reexamine the problem (i.e., create a new occasion for decision), and (2) re-represent the problem? In other words, the policy-making group can react in many different ways to evidence of failure, and our goal in this part of the chapter is to describe some of the conditions that make re-representation more likely than other possible reactions. This analysis is organized in four sections: (1) group processes, (2) prior actions, (3) failure and the role of causal attributions, and (4) time and the number of decisions in the sequence.

Group Processes

We have suggested that the discrepancy between expectations and feedback is an essential element for a group to reexamine a problem. One difficulty in practice is the tendency not to recognize negative or disconfirming information. Potentially disconfirming information can be neglected, interpreted as ambiguous, or offset by the discovery of positive feedback. A group that previously reached closure and decided on a course of action might be expected to become advocates of the chosen position and engage in wishful thinking about its success, thus completely failing to recognize negative feedback or defining it in a positive manner. How are these potentialities avoided, at least under some conditions?

Two broad categories of actors are more likely to recognize negative feedback with respect to a group's prior decisions. The first are all those individuals and collectivities external to the decision unit that have some incentive to detect and report information suggesting the group's decision is not working. Swept into this external category are political opposition, adversely affected interest groups, media interests, and others. The importance of such external opposition on decision groups in foreign policy or any other governmental group cannot be minimized. We exclude further consideration of them in this chapter, however, and concentrate on the second category of actors, those within the decision group itself.

The counterparts within a decision group are any opponents of the group decision enacted by the majority. Of course, on some problems there may be no continuing disagreement among the members after the problem is initially discussed. On complex policy problems, however, there is a good possibility of disagreement on the causes of the problem, the means of dealing with it, and the conditions necessary for success. When a group has one or more members who constitute an opposing minority to the previously taken position, they can be an important influence on the reexamination of an issue.

Minority Influence and Re-representation: Since Asch's (1956) famous experiment, an enormous amount of research has demonstrated the effectiveness of group pressures on individuals to conform. Beginning in the 1970s, however, Moscovici (1985) led a challenge to the view that influence processes in groups are only one-way. Based on the premise that influence between group majorities and minorities is reciprocal, researchers have explored the causes and consequences of minority influence.

Moscovici contends that minorities use different processes to influence majorities than majorities use on minorities. He sees majorities using social pressure and coercion to get minorities to comply (whether they agree privately or not), whereas minorities must persuade members of the majority to rethink the problem and engage in new cognitive processes. Thus, if a member of the majority switches his or her view to that of the minority, it results in an actual change of position – a conversion – rather than the public acceptance or compliance forced on consenting minorities.

Empirical evidence confirming these two distinctive influence processes (one used by majorities, the other by minorities) remains ambiguous, and alternative interpretations have been advanced. (For a review, see Levine and Russo 1987.) Some evidence suggests, however, that the impact of the minority views on a majority usually take time to develop and that the minority often precipitate "divergent thinking" among majority members (Nemeth 1986). That is, after hearing the minority repeat their views and challenge the majority interpretation, members of the majority may begin over time to reappraise the entire situation and develop new perspectives – not necessarily those advocated by the minority, but different from their own prior view. (This reappraisal process is particularly likely when the group receives negative feedback on the prior decision.) Other findings suggest that minorities are more likely to influence majorities when the former are persistent but not rigid, and when they are consistent in their argument over time (Levine and Russo 1987; Moscovici 1985).

The studies of majority–minority group influence can shed important light on change in sequential decision making. Suppose the majority in a group, when faced with a foreign policy problem, interpret it in a particular way but other members of the group challenge aspects of that analysis or the strategy for coping with it. If the person or persons opposing the majority position have a strong commitment to their own position and believe that it is valid and the majority is wrong, they are less likely to forgo their interpretation (at least privately) and conform to the majority position. This is particularly so if there is one or more others who join them in dissent. Further, assume that the majority in this group prevails and the group follows their prescribed course of action despite the reservations of the minority.

Subsequently, if the group's minority continues in their dissent and is convinced that their own perspective is correct, they will be keen to monitor the environment for new supporting information. Should that feedback be interpretable as indicating that the action initiated by the majority appears not to be working or is causing adverse side effects, the minority will likely find it. Given a chance, they will present the disconfirming discoveries to the group on a new occasion for decision. In short, a persistent minority can force the group's attention to the stimulus and negative (or ambiguous) new information. Should one or more members of the majority not be fully confident of the correctness of their position (a condition that can be affected by the ambiguity and difficulty of the problem; Tajfel 1969), then they are more susceptible to informational influence by the minority. If the minority succeeds in converting just one of the former majority, group research suggests that the convert will add significantly to the effectiveness of the minority argument with others.

This discussion has suggested that the presence of active dissent in a decision group following its prior decision can have several possible effects. First, a minority perspective that has reservations about the merit of the prior action is most likely to recognize discrepant information about that action's subsequent effects, particularly in comparison to earlier expectations expressed in the group. By assuming that postdecision-monitoring function, minorities increase the likelihood that the group will be forced to acknowledge negative feedback and reconsider the problem.

Second, across time – perhaps after multiple reexaminations – a minority may have an effect on the thinking of some members of the majority. In particular, a persistent, consistent, and yet nonrigid minority may create divergent thinking in the majority. In turn, the group's active engagement in considering new perspectives can result in new decisions involving substantial change. As noted previously, the majority's new representation may not necessarily resemble that advocated by the minority, but it is likely to differ from the old majority representation.

It seems likely that the nature of the minority's disagreement also will affect the kind of changes that may result in the group's subsequent decisions. A minority who favor an adjustment in the relative level of effort devoted to the problem may have more success in achieving converts from the majority than opponents who wish to see the goals emphasized by the majority dropped in favor of some other purposes.

Minority effectiveness may also depend on the nature of the majority and the strength of their convictions. If some group members went along with the majority originally but had serious questions, then those persons may be more receptive to the arguments of the minority, because feedback shows that the action advocated by the majority is at variance with their earlier expectations. Moreover, in subsequent deliberations, if a member of the majority is willing to assume the role of broker or mediator between the majority position's strongest advocates and the minority advocates, then an added legitimacy for alternative views is created, and more ''space'' is established for deliberation. Possibly conditions such as these, which must be researched further, will determine whether persistent minority advocates of fundamental change in problem representation will be successful.

Prior Actions

Uncertainty and Prior Actions: Two characteristics of a decision group's prior action appear to influence the group preparedness to re-represent the problem in the face of negative feedback – the degree of uncertainty the action reflects and the level of commitment. The degree of uncertainty or lack of confidence that the action will effectively treat the problem can result from several sources. Policy makers may be more or less doubtful about the causes of the problem. They also may lack confidence about how the adopted option or ''solution'' may successfully affect the problem under ideal circumstances; that is, they may regard the causal connection between solution and problem as questionable. Members of the policy group may also be uncertain about the ability of the implemented solution to work effectively under the conditions that prevail in the present circumstances.

As previously noted, our four types of prior action (search, provisional, conditional, and definitive) are intended to reflect different levels of collective uncertainty existing in the decision-making group. We assume that search occurs when there is some uncertainty about some aspect of the problem, which might include how to classify the problem (e.g., Is it a threat or opportunity?) or what the correct diagnosis is (in terms of the linkage among causes, consequences, and solutions). Confirming feedback is likely to solidify the tentative classification and the preliminary causal map (the two parts of problem representation). Disconfirming information, given the uncertainty driving the search, is very likely to change either or both of these aspects of problem representation.

Provisional action indicates a higher level of certainty among the group as a whole than does action that is a search routine. Policy makers are confident enough to try some direct action aimed at the problem. But they remain quite uncertain as to the effects of the action. Therefore, the move is selected that appears to preserve such future options as terminating the activity or limiting the scope of the consequences. Disconfirming evidence of the effects of the action should not surprise members of the group. They may be receptive to an entirely new representation of the problem if their current action appears clearly to be failing.

By contrast, both conditional and definitive actions imply greater certainty in the minds of the policy makers. Definitive actions occur when there is a high level of certainty about the nature of the problem and the group's approach to it. Conditional actions may involve some degree of uncertainty about the environment (e.g., how others will react) but reflect a relatively high level of certainty about the assessment of the problem and selection of an action. For both of these types of actions, the policy group is confident of its categorization of the problem and believes that it has an accurate map of the causes and effects of the problem and the means of coping with it. Disconfirming feedback is therefore unlikely to challenge the existing problem representation but may lead to decisions by the group for some less far-reaching changes (e.g., in the level of effort).

In sum, the greater the collective uncertainty the policy group has about its approach to the problem, the more likely it is to engage in major reconstruction of its initial characterization of the problem, resulting in problem re-

representation. Furthermore, this relative uncertainty (about the problem categorization or the diagnosis) is captured by the type of prior action on which the group agreed.

Commitment to Prior Actions: Foreign policy actions also can be characterized by the level of commitment they entail. Commitment can be understood as the degree to which a person, group, or organization invests itself or its resources in an action or a course of behavior. Actions vary in degree of commitment, whether represented by level of resources or some other mechanism linking the actor's well-being or value states to the action.

The literature on commitment to a prior course of action suggests that negative feedback often leads to an escalation of commitment in subsequent considerations of the problem (e.g., Brockner 1992; Ross and Staw 1986; Staw 1981). Although the phenomena of escalation of commitment to a failing course of action has been widely studied, multiple causes have been advanced for this behavior. One explanation that is relevant to the present discussion is psychological in nature. It rests on the need to maintain a consistency between previous actions and subsequent decisions. In essence, escalation of commitment is a matter of putting more resources into the present course of action in order to justify (to oneself and to others) that the previous decision was correct. The need to justify and defend past actions makes it exceedingly difficult to consider problem re-representation.

Commitment to a prior course of action may also be explained as more than the psychological process of becoming attached to it in order to justify previous effort and decisions. Ross and Staw (1986) argue that programmatic considerations as well as social and institutional forces may act in concert with psychological factors to cause a decision group to maintain and escalate commitment in the face of negative feedback. Program considerations (that is, the belief that a course of action is the best option based on an analysis of costs and benefits) are presumed to be the most important in the early stages of sequential decision making. After negative feedback is experienced, psychological forces may take over and produce escalation. Over time, however, social and institutional forces reinforce the ongoing course of action, making a change in direction – not to mention re-representation of the problem – even more difficult and unlikely.

In summary, escalation of commitment to a failing course of action may be produced by a combination of psychological, programmatic, social, and institutional forces. No matter what the reason for escalation, the increased commitment to the ongoing behaviors makes re-representation of the problem very unlikely.

The effects of longevity and institutionalization of commitments with the accompanying rigidity of problem representation may be illustrated by the difficulties the U.S. Army experienced in Vietnam. For decades, the most critical mission of the army and its NATO allies was to defend Europe against an armored attack. Wilson (1989: 44) explains:

> Most of the units sent to Vietnam had been organized and trained with this in mind. What might work on the plains of Bavaria would not necessarily work in the remote highlands of Vietnam. Interestingly, the one American armed service that tried hard to develop a village defense program was the Marine Corps, a force not organized and trained to fight massive armored battles in Europe.

In other words, the army's representation of the problems of warfare was long-held and institutionalized, producing a high level of commitment and an inability to change the representation, even in the face of repeated failures.

Studies of commitment to organizations, however, suggest that the resolve to sustain a prior commitment may depend on the basis of that commitment. Recent work on organizational commitment (e.g., Becker and Billings 1993; O'Reilly and Chatman 1986) has introduced the idea that there may be different bases for commitment. These authors used the well-known bases of social influence first articulated by Kelman (1958) – namely, compliance, identification/norms, and internalization.

When we extend these ideas to sequential decision making, we suggest that there may be different types of commitment to a previous course of action. Our prediction is that re-representation of the problem is somewhat more likely when commitment to the prior action is based on compliance ("We did it because we were instructed to do so") or identification/norms ("We did it because traditions or practices obliged us to"), as compared to commitment based on the internalization of goals and values ("We did it because we thought it was the best thing to do").

In both compliance and identification, the decision makers may be able to recognize, after receiving evidence of failure, that their initial representation was "imposed" on them. As such, it may be easier for them to separate themselves from the prior course of action and its commitments. An earlier commitment based on compliance with the wishes of others can be dismissed as not really of their own choosing. If commitment to an action is based on identification with another social entity, then the action is undertaken due to the belief that the other party desires that action. Therefore, disconfirming feedback about the impact of prior commitment may not constrain reconsideration of the representation of the problem, if policy makers believe the action that failed was based on the other party's representation in the first place. Instead, it causes the policy makers to question the other party's definition of the problem or their own interpretation of the other's representation.

The changes in American policy in Somalia may be illustrative. The Bush administration initially introduced American ground forces in Somalia with the humanitarian intention of providing safety for the distribution of food to starving civilians. The plan called for gradually turning this assignment over to the U.N. peacekeeping forces, a process that was in progress when a number of Pakistani troops committed to the U.N. effort were attacked and killed by Somalia militia loyal to a regional leader. This incident and others like it led to a redefinition of the task by the United Nations Security Council (with full U.S. support): The regional leader should be tracked down and held accountable for crimes against the peacekeepers. The U.S. committed Army Rangers to the new effort. But the situation changed again when American troops, now engaged in offensive actions against a Somalia warlord, were attacked and experienced casualties. The U.S. policy makers quickly returned to the original definition of the American military task, halted offensive actions, and scheduled a date for their complete withdrawal from the country. The re-representation of this problem back to the more limited humanitarian mission after negative feedback (killed and captured U.S. troops) can be interpreted in terms of the compliance and identification effects. American policy makers interpreted the escalation of the original mission as a decision of the United Nations, not one they had made.

Failure and the Role of Causal Attributions

Basic Tenets of Attribution Theory: So far, we have discussed the likelihood of re-representation as a function of minority influence, the degree of uncertainty in the decision, and level and type of commitment to the course of action. Another major variable in our framework entails the way decision makers attribute responsibility for failure. Attribution theory is concerned with how a person "comes to attribute events to one or more of their possible causes" (Ross and Fletcher 1985). Certain circumstances, such as unexpected events or failure, lead people to attempt to figure out what is happening and why, and subsequent actions are based on these attributions.

Heider (1958), one of the early attribution theorists, suggested that an individual's level of performance on a certain task could be attributed to factors either within that person (internal) or within the person's environment (external). Further, Heider suggested such sources of causation could be regarded as either stable (permanent) or variable (transitory). The resulting two-by-two typology results in causes that are internal and permanent (e.g., ability), internal and transitory (e.g., effort), external and permanent (e.g., task difficulty), or external and transitory (e.g., luck). This classic version of attribution theory is only somewhat helpful in understanding when the re-representation of the problem occurs. For example, one of the actions consistent with an external, permanent attribution (e.g., task difficulty) is to defer action until the task is better understood, which might lead to a change in one's representation of the problem. However, not all permanent external attributions imply re-representation. For example, an attribution that the task is too difficult may lead to giving up and accepting failure. In order to make predictions concerning the effects of causal attributions on problem re-representation, we need to extend the basic attribution model to decision making on complex issues.

Extension of Attribution Theory to Sequential Decision Making: Our attempt to design such an extension is shown in Table 4.2. In that table we have retained the distinction between internal (within the group) and external causes. We have replaced the differentiation between permanent and transitory factors with a set of elements common in the analysis of the complex, multidimensional problems that foreign policy decision groups face.

We suggest that in reconsidering a problem, the policy makers in a group may single out particular elements of their prior analysis that may be seen as the root cause of the failure of a policy action. Many attributions concerning aspects of the problem analysis are possible, but we have selected four because they may enable us to distinguish among possible future actions: (1) lack of goal clarity, (2) incorrect problem diagnosis, (3) incorrect solution, and (4) insufficient tactical effort and/or resources.

In Table 4.2, we propose that if the group believes that failure occurred because goals were not clear, subsequent effort will be put into clarifying interests, goals, and objectives. If they question the previous diagnosis, they will want to examine the nature of the problem, its sources, and the effects it produces. Concern with the previous solution leads to a review of strategy and alternative treatments. If they question the tactical effort, then attention will turn to the amount of resources and commitment involved. It should also be noted that for each of these elements, the attribution can be internal or external. In summary, we hypothesize that the type of action in sequential decision making depends on the attributions for failure.

The predicted effects of attributions for failure on re-representation are clear. Attributing failure to a lack of goal clarity will affect that part of the problem representation that includes goals and constraints. If new goals are created, new standards for how things ought to be are quite likely. Since problems are defined (in part) by a gap between how things are and how they ought to be, the problem may be represented differently and may even switch categories (e.g., from an opportunity to a threat).

Re-representation is also quite likely when the attribution for failure concerns an incorrect problem diagnosis. The resulting reanalysis of the problem is likely to result in a new causal map of the problem, which, in turn, may

Table 4.2. *Possible effects on subsequent action of attributing failure to elements in prior problem analysis*

| Effort has failed because: | Attributed source | |
	Internal (group)	External (others)
Our goals and objectives were not clear enough.	Not clear what goals the action was to address (unstated purpose).	Other actors did not understand that our serious interests were affected and how they have affected them.
	Goal priorities are confused; what we wanted to do is not worth it.	Other actors were deceptive in assurance of respect for our interests (goals).
	Action: Clarify or change goals – realign policy accordingly.	Action: Warn others of importance we attach to goals (make them understand).
The nature of the problem is not as it appeared.	Our interpretation of what is happening and why it was defective. (Who is doing what to whom for what reason?)	The problem is so complex; little information is available; so complicated that it defies resolution.
	We performed poor analysis.	Someone is deliberately concealing the nature of their actions, their motives, and the consequences.
	Action: Change strategy based on new analysis.	Action: Either disengage because problem is unknowable or too hard, or change initiative so that nature of the behavior of others is more visible and condemned.
The specific approach used to deal with the problem did not work.	We chose the wrong approach; it is inappropriate and cannot work.	The problem (nature) changed causing the approach to be ineffective.
		Another actor engaged in countermoves (deliberately or accidentally) that caused our approach to fail – there has been obstruction by others.
	Action: Change to a different treatment approach.	Action: Change strategy or supplement it so as to offset interference.

Table 4.2 (*cont.*)

Effort has failed because:	Attributed source	
	Internal (group)	External (others)
There was insufficient tactical effort and/or the quantity or quality of resources was inadequate.	We misjudged the needed quantity or quality or implemented them poorly.	An accident or change factors overwhelmed our efforts – unforeseeable circumstances. Other actors increased their cfforts to offset the effec tiveness of our efforts.
	Action: Increase (or otherwise adjust) level of effort resources (human and otherwise) applied.	Action: Repeat effort if failure was caused by accident; strengthen effort if others interfered.

alter the other elements of the problem representation. On the other hand, representation of the problem is unlikely when the attributions for failure involve selection of the wrong solution or the application of insufficient effort or resources. The actions here would be to change the treatment or increase effort and other resources.

For a number of years after the Americanization of the Vietnam War in 1965, American policy makers appear to have illustrated these characteristics in their explanations for why the efforts to get North Vietnam to negotiate on favorable terms failed. The bombing of North Vietnam was supposed to signal them that American air power could destroy their country and would gradually be escalated if they did not negotiate. When they showed little interest in negotiations, the assumption was that a more convincing demonstration was needed, that is, more effort. The basic representation of the problem for the American government did not change.

It should be noted that re-representation is also unlikely when any of the attributions discussed here are external in nature. The actions implied by external attributions are detailed in Table 4.2 and do not involve rethinking the nature of the problem. In the Vietnam bombing case, there was an increasing tendency by the U.S. policy community to attribute to the North Vietnamese the reasons why bombing did not produce negotiations. The resulting explanations included such things as "Asians do not value individual lives the way we do." That type of external attribution made it very unlikely that the representation of the problem would be revisited.

In summary, we are predicting that failure will lead to re-representation of the problem only when the attributions for failure are directed toward the group itself and not to the environment or to other actors. In addition, those internal attributions must be directed toward a failure of goal articulation or problem diagnosis, and not toward mistakes in the selection of alternative actions or the application of resources.

Biases in Causal Attributions: There is considerable evidence of biases in attributions, with success being credited to oneself, but failure being blamed on the environment. Several studies (e.g., Salancik and Meindl 1984; Wong and Weiner 1981), however, suggest circumstances when the traditional attributional bias may not apply. When individuals or groups are in a position where it is important to appear to be in control of their environment, to blame a failure on external factors is to seem to acknowledge they are not effective managers. Thus, Salancik and Meindl (1984) found that CEOs of business firms tended to accept responsibility for poor corporate performance and then outline steps they were initiating to correct the difficulty. Foreign policy managers, accountable to legislatures and the public, might be expected to act similarly.

However, acceptance of responsibility for failure does not necessarily mean that policy makers are more inclined to engage in problem re-representation. They could, for example, blame failure on internal opposition and use the poor performance as a reason to dismiss troublesome minority members of the decision group. (A step that we would argue reduces the likelihood of re-representation!) Alternatively, the internal attribution might be focused on the choice of the wrong tactic or on insufficient effort.

Although we see reason for caution in assuming that policy-making groups will demonstrate the traditional form of attribution bias (blaming failure on the environment), we detect the possibility of another kind of bias. Our analysis implies a tendency to attribute failure to selecting the wrong solution or to not applying enough resources, versus questioning how the problem was conceptualized in the first place. In other words, when acknowledging failure as internally caused, there may be a predisposition to attribute it to those stages in problem solving that are (1) easier to adjust and (2) demand the least modification of collective beliefs about the nature and diagnosis of the problem. To our knowledge, this version of an attributional bias has not been discussed in the attribution literature.

Time and the Number of Decisions in the Sequence

In this chapter, we have considered the role of time in only an indirect and limited way. For most of our analysis, it would appear that the critical step is reconsideration of a problem after a prior action. But many foreign policy problems are considered again and again, as has been the case for many of the examples used throughout this chapter. Does it make any difference for problem representation whether it is the group's first or second reconsideration of a problem rather than their nineteenth or fifty-third? We believe time, or more precisely the relative decision point in a continuing sequence of problem management, does make a difference.

As an initial hypothesis for future exploration, we suggest a group's resistance to problem re-representation will follow the profile of an inverted "U" if charted over time. That is, a group might be relatively receptive to problem re-representation on the first few reconsiderations and then gradually increase their resistance. Their resistance to considering problem re-representation might be expected to diminish gradually, however, after having reached a plateau sometime later. Several factors contribute to this interpretation.

On the first encounter with a new problem, we might expect the decision group's categorization and diagnosis of the problem's causes to be rather tentative. Their initial actions, other things being equal, are likely to be characterized as search or provisional. Beliefs about the new problem are not likely to be well established. Negative feedback can be more easily accepted, and it may be easier to shift perspectives. In fact, early in the sequence, new information (even if negative) is likely to be eagerly sought and used to shape the policy makers' emerging views.

As noted in our discussion of prior commitments, once such investments are made, different factors (programmatic comparisons of costs and benefits, personal esteem, institutional practices) may kick in to encourage a policy group to stay the course and either maintain the commitment or even escalate it. Such decisions, often expressed as conditional or definitive actions, make reconsideration of the problem very unlikely.

Why, then, can we suggest that impact of such effects may eventually plateau and even decline? In the face of continuing negative feedback, we postulate that policy makers will first modify those things that are easiest to do and disrupt beliefs the least (e.g., change effort level, alter tactics). They will gradually exhaust these options, but if negative feedback continues, they may be driven to a deeper examination. This is particularly so if dissenters in the decision group remain active. Recall that studies of minority effects on majority positions suggest that their influence is more likely if the minority persists over time in a consistent manner.

Referring back to Figure 4.1, we are suggesting that five alternative actions under Stage 10 ("Follow-on Choice") will be tried in the order shown. If continuing the present course leads to negative feedback after several decision cycles, the first change is to make some adjustments in the basic course. If this does not work after more cycles, then alternative actions are tried. The more fundamental changes (re-representing the problem or reconsidering fundamental goals) will eventually occur if failure feedback continues after many iterations of the decision cycle.

In summary, we suggest that re-representation is "lumpy." In other words, viewed over the entire history of the management of an issue (assuming that feedback is continually negative), changes in the representation of a problem either occur quickly or are not seen for some considerable time.

Summary and Implications

Major shifts in courses of action due to problem re-representation (and in the absence of changes in group membership or regime change) are not commonplace; they are dramatic and important when they do occur. Examples from the domain of international relations (discussed in Herman 1990, and Hermann and Beasley 1992) include Egypt's change in policy toward Israel following Sadat's visit to Jerusalem, the shift in policies and goals toward Vietnam by the Johnson administration, the British cabinet's change in position toward Germany immediately before the invasion of Czechoslovakia, and the shift in U.S. policy toward China under Nixon.

The framework presented in this chapter may be useful in the analysis of cases of major policy changes, such as those previously listed. Our framework demands that decisions be viewed as embedded in a series of action–feedback–sense-making cycles. Case studies and laboratory experiments must move beyond the study of single, isolated decision events.

Beyond focusing attention on sequential decision making, our framework provides the language for the analysis of decision cycles. Concepts presented here include prior actions (search, provisional, conditional, definitive), the level and type of commitment to prior actions, differential expectations for different types of actions, causal attributions for failure of group decisions, and the dynamics of minority opinion within the group.

Furthermore, we have focused attention on the re-representation of problems, arguing that major changes in courses of action occur only when problems are restructured. Finally, we have presented some specific hypotheses that can be tested through comparative case studies or in laboratory experiments. Specifically, we have argued that the likelihood of problem re-representation in sequential decision making is increased:

1.   When feedback on the effects of the action disconfirms rather than confirms the initial expectations
2.   When there are repeated, consistent failure messages
3.   When a persistent, nonrigid minority has an alternative representation to offer

4. When the prior action reflects relatively more uncertainty, which tends to be more characteristic of search or provisional actions than of conditional or definitive actions
5. When the level of commitment to the prior action is low and is based on compliance or identification rather than internalization
6. When causal attributions for failure are internal to the group and focus on a lack of goal clarity or incorrect problem diagnosis
7. During the first few reconsiderations of the problem or after many occasions for decision making on the same issue

Perhaps, in an uncertain and imperfect world, it is not necessarily unfortunate that major policy changes due to problem re-representation are the exception rather than the rule. Nonetheless, the consequences when they do occur – or fail to occur at a critical juncture – is of such significance that their fuller investigation deserves more attention than has yet occurred.

References

Asch, S. E. (1956). "Studies on independence and conformity." *Psychological Monograph, 70:* 9.

Axelrod, R. (1976). *Structure of Decision: The Cognitive Maps of Political Elites.* Princeton: Princeton University Press.

——— (1984). *The Evolution of Cooperation.* New York: Basic Books.

Becker, T. E., and R. S. Billings (1993). "Profiles of commitment: An empirical test." *Journal of Organizational Behavior, 14:* 177–190.

Brockner, J. (1992). "The escalation of commitment to a failing course of action." *Academy of Management Review, 17:* 39–61.

Cowan, D. A. (1986). "Developing a process model of problem recognition." *Academy of Management Review, 11:* 763–776.

Doty, R. L. (1993). "Foreign policy as social construction: A post-positivist analysis of U.S. counterinsurgency policy in the Philippines." *International Studies Quarterly, 37:* 297–320.

Dutton, J. E., and S. E. Jackson (1987). "Categorizing strategic issues: Links to organizationsl action." *Academy of Management Review, 12:* 76–90.

Farnham, B. (ed.) (1992). "Prospect theory and political psychology: Special issue." *Political Psychology, 13:* 167–329.

Heider, F. (1958). *The Psychology of Interpersonal Relations.* New York: Wiley.

Hermann, C. F., and R. S. Billings (1993). "Sequential Decision Making in Foreign Policy Groups." Paper presented at the Annual Meeting of the American Political Science Association, Washington, D.C.

Hermann, M. G., and C. F. Hermann (1989). "Who makes foreign policy decisions and how." *International Studies Quarterly, 33:* 361–387.

Hermann, M. G., C. F. Hermann, and J. D. Hagan (1987). How decision units shape foreign policy behavior. In C. F. Hermann, C. W. Kegley, Jr., and J. N. Rosenau (eds.), *New Directions in the Study of Foreign Policy* (309–336). London: Allen and Unwin.

Hollenbeck, J. R., D. R. Ilgen J. M. Phillips, and J. Hedlund (1994). "Decision risk in dynamic two-stage contexts: Beyond the status-quo.'' *Journal of Applied Psychology, 79:* 592–598.

Kelman, H. C. (1958). ''Compliance, identification, and internalization: Three processes of attitude change.'' *Journal of Conflict Resolution, 2:* 51–60.

Kleinmutz, D. N. (1985). ''Cognitive heuristics and feedback in a dynamic decision environment.'' *Management Science, 31:* 680–702.

Levine, J. M., and E. M. Russo (1987). ''Majority and minority influence.'' In C. Hendrick (ed.), *Review of Personality and Social Psychology* (Vol. 3, 13–54). Newbury Park, CA.: Sage.

Lindblom, C. E. (1959). ''The science of muddling through.'' *Public Administration Review, 19:* 79–88.

Mintzberg, H., D. Raisinghani, and A. Theoret (1976). ''The structure of unstructured decisions.'' *Administrative Science Quarterly, 21:* 246–275.

Moscovici, S. (1985). ''Social influence and conformity.'' In G. Lindzey and E. Aronson (eds.), *Handbook of Social Psychology* (3rd edition, Vol. 11, 347–412). New York: Random House.

Nemeth, C. J. (1986). ''Different contributions of majority and minority influence.'' *Psychological Review, 93:* 23–32.

O'Reilly, C., III, and J. Chatman (1986). ''Organizational commitment and psychological attachment: The effects of compliance, identification, and internalization on prosocial behavior.'' *Journal of Applied Psychology, 71:* 492–499.

Pounds, W. F. (1969). ''The process of problem finding.'' *Industrial Management Review, 11:* 1–19.

Ross, J., and B. M. Staw (1986). ''Expo 86: An escalation prototype.'' *Administrative Science Quarterly, 31:* 274–297.

Ross, M., and G. J. O. Fletcher (1985). ''Attribution and social perception.'' In G. Lindzey and E. Aronson (eds.), *Handbook of Social Psychology* (3rd edition, Vol. II, 73–122). New York: Random House.

Salancik, G. R., and J. R. Meindl (1984). ''Corporate attributions as strategic illusions of managerial control.'' *Administrative Science Quarterly, 29:* 238–254.

Shapiro, M. J., and G. M. Bonham (1973). ''Cognitive processes and foreign policy decision making.'' *International Studies Quarterly, 17:* 147–174.

Staw, B. M. (1981). ''The escalation of commitment to a course of action.'' *Academy of Management Review, 6:* 577–587.

Staw, B. M., and J. Ross (1989). ''Understanding behavior in escalation situations.'' *Science, 246:* 216–220.

Steinbruner, J. D. (1974). *The Cybernetic Theory of Decision.* Princeton: Princeton University Press.

Stevenson, M. K., J. R. Busemeyer, and J. C. Naylor (1990). ''Judgment and decision making theory.'' In M. D. Dunnette and L. M. Hough (eds.), *Handbook of Industrial and Organizational Psychology* (pp. 283–374). Palo Alto, CA: Consulting Psychologists Press.

Tajfel, H. (1969). ''Social and cultural factors in perception.'' In G. Lindzey and E. Aronson (eds.), *Handbook of Social Psychology* (2nd edition, Vol. 3. 315–394). Reading, MA: Addison Wesley.

Thaler, R. H., and E. J. Johnson (1990). ''Gambling with the house money and trying to break even: The effects of prior outcomes on risky choice.'' *Management Science, 36:* 643–660.

Uhler, B. D. (1993). *The Escalation of Commitment in Political Decision-making*

Groups. Pittsburgh: Unpublished doctoral dissertation in psychology, University of Pittsburgh.

Voss, J. F., and T. A. Post (1988). "On the solving of ill-structured problems." In M. T. H. Chi, R. Glaser, and M. Farr (eds.), *The Nature of Expertise* (pp. 261–285). Hillsdale, NJ: Lawrence Erlbaum.

Wilson, J. Q. (1989). *Bureaucracy: What Government Agencies Do and Why They Do It*. New York: Basic Books.

Wong, P. T., and B. Weiner (1981). "When people ask 'why' questions, and the heuristics of attributional search." *Journal of Personality and Social Psychology, 40:* 650–663.

CHAPTER 5

Collective Interpretations: How Problem Representations Aggregate in Foreign Policy Groups

Ryan Beasley

The idea that the way people characterize or represent a situation or problem is important in the solving of that problem has been proposed by various researchers (Snyder, Bruck, and Sapin 1954, 1962; Simon 1981; Voss, Green, Post, and Penner 1983; Pennington and Hastie 1986; Purkitt and Dyson 1988; Premkumar 1989; Voss, this volume). These studies indicate in various ways that people establish representations and explanations of phenomena about which a decision is required, and that these representations vary not only according to individual and circumstance but also according to the actual choice or choices made.

Some empirical studies focusing on group decision making in foreign policy have suggested that how a group defines a problem significantly affects how it chooses to deal with that problem (Purkitt 1992; Sylvan and Thorson 1992), yet the processes involved in coming to some representation of a foreign policy decision problem in a group setting have not been addressed. What factors shape and influence the interaction of different individual perspectives on a foreign policy problem is an important research question if we are to understand the policy-making process and the influences on policy decisions.

The implications of adopting a problem-representation perspective on group decision making in foreign policy are many. It might reveal, for example, implications about the actual processes involved in the formation of foreign policies, or it might provide new perspectives on the centrality of alternatives and preferences in that decision-making process. Further, as problem representations are generally considered as being *prior to* the generation of solutions, findings suggesting a prominent or central role for representations at the group level may suggest that defective or poor decision making may reside not with the way preferences and alternatives are handled but with the assumptions that guide the generation, evaluation, revision, and selection among those preferences and alternatives. Indeed, various remedies for defective decision making may miss the mark in that they are ways of avoiding pathologies that are caused not by conflict among preferences but by competing, conflicting, or complementary problem representations. Understanding the role of problem representations and their interaction and aggregation in the foreign policy group could provide alternative ways of understanding such phenomena.

A Conception of Problem Representations

The conception of problem representation developed here is essentially based on the problem-solving conception of problem representation (see Voss, this volume). A problem-solving approach focuses on the way in which elements of a problem are set in relation to one another by the solver. The essential aspects of a problem are the objects and their relationships, the rules for transformation, the criteria for solution, and the operators that are available. In this approach, the way in which these factors are characterized by an individual is considered a *problem representation*. In other words, a problem representation under this perspective is essentially a mental model held by a problem solver that has some correspondence with a problem in the environment. In foreign policy problems, which are here considered to be ''ill-structured'' problems (Voss et al. 1983; Voss and Post 1988; Voss, this volume), it is not always clear what goals are involved, what constraints are faced, what a solution would look like, and what the effect of various operators (such as military force or economic aid, for example) would be. Indeed, ''ill-structured'' implies that the problem facing the decision-making body is one for which goals and constraints are not specified or are at least incompletely specified. Part of the process of solving the ill-structured problem is to develop constraints within which solutions can be found.

One important factor that Voss et al. note as influencing the way in which an ill-structured problem will be represented involves the beliefs and knowledge of the individual problem solver. As beliefs vary from individual to individual, so may representations based on those beliefs. Because individual beliefs with regard to a policy domain will play a potential role in the nature of any problem representation that is developed for that domain, it is necessary to specify the nature of those beliefs and how they affect the representation of a decision problem developed by an individual.

Although a number of approaches have been developed for examining the beliefs of political actors, one approach seems particularly appropriate and useful for the current research effort. Cognitive mapping was developed by Axelrod (1976) and has been modified and applied by many scholars (Walker 1977; Shapiro and Bonham 1982; Bonham, Shapiro, and Heradstveit 1988). This technique content analyzes statements made by policy makers for causal assertions regarding a particular issue or problem. Such assertions are then represented as nodes (objects, actors, or ideas) with causative associations between them.[1] In this way, a causal "map" of an individual's beliefs regarding causal associations between objects or events can be established (Axelrod 1976; Bonham and Shapiro 1976). Axelrod indicates that a cognitive map is "a mathematical model of a belief system [that] is designed to capture the structure of the causal assertions of a person with respect to a particular policy domain, and generate the consequences that follow from this structure" (Axelrod 1976: 58).

The cognitive-mapping approach seems to provide a foundation for establishing "individual understandings" of a policy domain at a level specific enough to predict decision-making behavior and differentiate between and among individuals within a group. Two main modifications to the causal mapping technique, however, will be adopted in order to utilize it within a *problem-solving* perspective for examining *group* decision making. First, causal mapping focuses on utility, whereas problem solving is concerned with desired problem states and does not explicitly deal with the abstract notion of utility.[2] Further, because this research is concerned less with predicting policy preferences for individuals than with understanding the dynamics of interaction between different interpretations of a foreign policy problem between and among group members, the focus on utility in terms of providing a mechanism for predicting individual policy preferences is less central.[3]

Second, causal mapping also focuses on only one type of relationship between cognitive elements or beliefs, namely, causal relations. The interaction of individual problem representations is a central focus of this research; hence, ability to establish key differences between individually expressed representations is important. This means that using a cognitive-mapping technique that either ignores noncausal assertions or translates multiple types of assertions into causal assertions may not be adequate. Further, approaches to the way people organize their political beliefs suggests different types of relationships. Schema theory takes as its premise that people actively construct reality. The notion of "schema" has been pivotal in terms of understanding how people make sense of their environments and has been utilized in various studies across several fields of inquiry (see, for example, Axelrod 1973; Tversky and Kahneman 1980; Conover and Feldman 1984; Crocker, Fiske, and Taylor 1984; Fiske and Taylor 1984; Taber, this volume). Schema provide for some hierarchy in terms of class membership and also provide for a number of different types of relationships between elements. For example, a "hat" may be a type of clothing (a categorical association), or it may prevent coldness (a causal association). The inclusion within the problem-solving approach of understanding a problem *state* (as well as the *causal impact* of operators on those problem states) must be taken into account. In

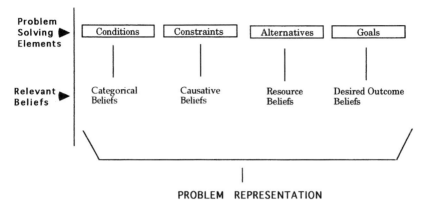

Figure 5.1. Problem representation.

other words, understanding problem solving requires the ability to distinguish characteristics of problem states that are relatively static (noncausal). The notion of categorical relationships between concepts, then, may enhance a conception of problem representation that includes causal relationships as well.

Moving to the ill-structured problem-solving domain of foreign policy making, examining actual decision makers in terms of their expressed problem representations, and focusing on group interactions with regard to those expressed problem representations necessitates the development of a specific conception of problem representation that is both consistent with the theoretical and empirical foundations of that concept and that can be applied in an empirical domain. Each conception of how an individual understands a problem, in other words, carries with it its own assumptions and implications about the nature of decision making. Figure 5.1 provides a concrete formulation of the ''problem-representation'' concept as it will be used in subsequent analysis. This development of problem representation associates different types of beliefs with different aspects of problem solving in an effort to have a conception that provides for analysis of both content of beliefs and structure of those beliefs relative to problem solving. The main elements of a problem-solving perspective are represented by the boxes labeled ''Conditions,'' ''Constraints,'' ''Alternatives,'' and ''Goals.'' These correspond to those elements that a problem-solving perspective indicates must be more or less specified in order to develop or arrive at solutions to a problem.

Associated with each component of problem solving are the types of beliefs that are here proposed to be relevant to that specific aspect of a problem representation (shown beneath each box in Figure 5.1). In other words, the relation between the beliefs and the problem-solving components is that specific types of beliefs define certain aspects of the problem for the decision maker, thereby providing content to the overall problem representation. This does not imply that actual decision makers distinguish between their beliefs according to the components of problem solving. Rather, this yoking of certain types of beliefs to the proposed aspects of problem solving provides an analytic tool for evaluating the nature of the problem representations that are based on those beliefs.

Categorical beliefs are beliefs about the nature of specific actors, objects, or events and are associated with specific conditions of the world relevant to a given problem. *Causative beliefs* are beliefs about causal relationships between actors, objects, or events and are associated with constraints within the world regarding a given problem.[4] Resource beliefs and desired outcome beliefs are associated with "alternatives" and "goals," respectively. Resource beliefs are directly relevant to those actions or policy options that might be taken by the decision maker(s). Desired outcome beliefs would pertain to the type of outcome envisioned that would productively address the problem. In other words, desired outcome beliefs refer to the beliefs the decision maker holds with regard to what needs to be accomplished in order to resolve a given problem situation.[5]

Problem Representation and Groups: The Aggregation Issue

Scholars working in the area of foreign policy making in groups have taken a variety of approaches, from understanding group structure and its effects (George 1980), to examining group processes (Anderson 1983, 1987; Purkitt 1992), to examining cognitive factors (Bonham et al. 1988; Walker and Watson 1989, 1992; Purkitt and Dyson 1990), to examining several types of variables in combination (Janis 1982; Stewart, Hermann, and Hermann 1989; 't Hart 1990).

One of the issues that has confronted those studying groups and group decision making is the nature of the relationship between the individual and the group. Axelrod proposes that public policy is frequently the product of collectivities, and thus "the understanding of how the beliefs and assertions of individual decision makers aggregate in decision-making groups is vital to a more complete understanding of how policy is formed" (Axelrod 1976: 239). This sentiment is echoed by Gaenslen, who argues that in the domain of information processing, there is abundant research at the individual level but a relative lack of attention to how groups perform such activities (Gaenslen 1992).

Another way of looking at this question is to ask, What is the nature of the aggregation of individuals in the group? In other words, how do individuals combine their various attributes within the group setting. Several approaches to this question have been taken. In psychology, the phenomenon of ''risky shift'' and later ''group polarization'' examined this issue in terms of individual choices as they compared to the extremity (riskiness) of group choices (Stoner 1968; Minix 1982; Isenberg 1986). There is also a rich tradition in group decision making dealing with ''social decision schemes.'' Social Decision Scheme (SDS) models look at individual group members' preferences among alternatives and often utilize members' first preferences in an aggregation to predict the group decision (Davis, Hornik, and Hornseth 1970; Crott, Szilvas, and Zuber 1991).[6] Game theory is essentially premised on individual preferences and interdependence between players, such that individuals choosing courses of action that maximize their own benefits will often reach collectively suboptimal outcomes when actions are interdependent (Oye 1986). Various studies on the effect of decision rules on decision making also address the issue of aggregation of individuals to groups (Hastie, Penrod, and Pennington 1983; Miller 1989; Kameda 1991).

On closer examination, we can see that most areas of research dealing with the aggregation of the individual to the group level in terms of decision making have focused primarily on preferences and on some maximization principle that utilizes those preferences in order to move to group choice. Even a bureaucratic politics perspective eventually comes to settle on the issue of who's *preferences* prevail, or how two or more *preferences* combine to form a ''resultant'' (Allison 1971; Halperin 1974). When we move our focus to individual understandings of a decision-making situation, we begin to see the group setting as more than the forum for bargaining among divergent and competing preferences. Axelrod indicates that ''there is more to a group than the static aggregation of its members. What lies beyond the formal theory of group belief is the study of how beliefs and decisions emerge from the actual functioning of a group'' (Axelrod 1976: 274–275).

Indeed, the premise of this study is that only a small portion of what decision-making groups do involves preferences; hence a sharper focus on the beliefs and understandings individuals carry into a collective decision-making setting can provide an alternative and fruitful explanation of the policy-making process. How different interpretations of a foreign policy problem interact and influence group decision making has, however, received little attention in the literature, deferring to the questions of how *preferences* aggregate, or (to a lesser extent) how *individuals'* problem representations influence choices outside the forum of the group. One of the themes repeated by those who do examine groups and problem representations is that of differences or disagreements between and among group members. Moreland and Levine propose that ''people can develop very different representations of the same problem, leading to further arguments about why the problem occurred, how it might be solved, and so on" (Moreland and Levine 1992: 21). Similarly, Sylvan and Thorson (1992) observe that understanding decision making as involving socially constructed "representation" may lead to conflict between competing representations. They state that "politics involves the selective privileging of representation," thereby introducing the issue of competing or divided representations and the way in which one representation may become "dominant" over another.

More than simply allowing for disagreements, competition, or conflict between representations, those focusing on groups propose that the problem representation itself may influence the group decision process, "because the kinds of alternative solutions that are developed for a problem and the ways in which those solutions are evaluated and implemented depend on how the problem is diagnosed by group members" (Moreland and Levine 1992: 21). This suggests that problem representation is an *integral part of the group processes involved in dealing with that problem.* The question becomes one of ascertaining how problem representations interact with or influence that *process.*

Group Process

Several studies have examined aspects of the relationship between how a problem is understood by individual group members and the way the group goes about dealing with that problem. Hastie et al. (1983) examined the construction of "stories" by jury members and suggest that different stories or understandings may influence the degree to which different jury members participate in the deliberation process. In other words, different understandings of a situation may directly lead to different types of interaction within a decision-making group. Similarly, in a study that attempted to address the issue of the interplay between knowledge structures and political processes in a group, Walsh, Henderson, and Deighton (1988) found that who participates is an important predictor of group performance. In other words, which problem-relevant schema are actually *employed* in decision-making groups is more important than the potential number and variety of schema *available* among the group members. This suggests that participation may be central to the way a problem is dealt with by a group. Finally, Purkitt and Dyson (1990) indicate the basic nature of interaction between problem representation or understanding and group interactions in ExComm during the Cuban missile crisis by stating, "Group interaction patterns became important because it was the inputs of group members rather than verifiable information that guided the individuals across the various aspects of the problem" (Purkitt and Dyson 1990: 363).

In sum, it seems that two important points emerge from the preceding

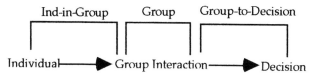

Figure 5.2. Components of aggregation.

review of literature related to the role of problem representations in group decision making. First, how a problem is defined or represented by individual group members can play a role in the group process of decision making, particularly in terms of how different individuals participate in that process. In other words, there may be a relationship between how a problem is understood and the nature of the participation in the decision process. Second, the different problem representations that are expressed in the decision-making process may significantly interact with that process and ultimately define the "problem" that the decision-making group is addressing. Stated differently, there is a complex relationship between individual understandings of a foreign policy problem, the group process involved in dealing with that foreign policy problem, and the types of decisions that can emerge based on that process. An examination of this complex relationship should focus on both the nature of the expressed problem representations in group decision making – that is, the nature of the group discussion in terms of representational elements – and the way group members participate and interact in that decision-making process.

Aggregation Principles

The term *aggregation* can have a variety of meanings with regard to the relationship of individuals to the group and group decision making. (See Figure 5.2.) Aggregation is here considered to be comprised of three main aspects: how individuals and their characteristics impinge on or influence the group interactions (Individual[Ind]-in-Group); the nature of the group interactions (Group); and how the group interactions impinge on or influence the group decision (Group-to-Decision).

The notion of "aggregation," then, is taken to indicate the way in which individuals' problem representations interact at the group level and affect decision making. As Moreland and Levine (1992) have indicated, only an individual can have a representation of a problem. A group, however, does have a potential for interaction and exchange of information and perspective between and among its constituents. In this sense, instead of talking about a mentalistic representation of a problem *held by a group*, we can talk about the nature of discourse in the group setting as it relates to the representations held by individual group members.

An aggregation principle for problem representations, then, is a particular pattern of relationship between problem representations and group decision making in terms of the way individuals influence the decision process, the characteristics of the decision process, and the decision process's effects on decisions. Questions can be asked with this conception of aggregation. For example, how do group members interact during the decision-making process? How do arguments progress through the problem-solving process? What is the nature of the content of the group discussion? Although the variety of interaction patterns of group decision makers with regard to problem representations may be quite large, I propose that these variations can be categorized according to a few dominant characteristics. In other words, although there is nearly infinite variation in the patterns of possible problem-representation aggregations, it is possible to classify certain dominant patterns according to their implications about aggregation and the aggregation process.

Variables

To observe how closely group decision making corresponds to any proposed aggregation principles, it is, of course, necessary to measure relevant variables of group decision making. In terms of the role of problem representation in collective decision making, several variables are considered to be central to understanding how a group goes about solving a foreign policy problem and how problem representations relate to that problem-solving process. The proposed variables of importance for the aggregation of problem representations involve both the *content* of expressed representations in the decision-making group and the *processes* by which individuals interact and involve themselves in decision making. (See Table 5.1.) These variables have been developed for current purposes from extant theories upon which the aggregation principles are based; they also reflect various approaches to group problem solving from psychology dealing with aspects of beliefs and representations (Walsh et al. 1988; Gruenfeld and Hollingshead 1993).

The idea that principles of aggregation might exist has long been of interest to those studying *preferences*. The study of decision rules in small groups parallels this idea, and many of these studies have examined the relationship between distributions of preferences, decision rules, and group decisions (Miller 1989). Other studies have explicitly looked at the group decision *process* under different decision rules (cf. Hermann, Hermann, and Hagan 1987). Still other studies address the relationship of individuals, group processes, and decision making. Laughlin and Ellis (1986) proposed that, for example, ''truth wins'' or ''truth supported wins'' are possible principles that

Table 5.1. *Variables for problem representation aggregation*

Individual-in-Group	
Content	Type of individual problem representation (PR) that dominates decision process
	Frames or agendas introduced by individual
Process	Centrality of specific individual
	Dominance of an individual in discussion
Group interaction	
Content	Complexity of group discussion
	Type of PR-concepts discussion oriented toward:
	Number of topics discussed
	Dominance of any topic
	Extent of agreement/disagreement
	Amount of conflict
Process	Distribution of contributions among members
	Degree of alternation between speakers
	Timing of conflict
	Discussion continuity
Group-to-decision	
Content	Degree of compromise vs. one side prevails
	Degree of relationship between problem solving and decision
Process	Degree of emergence of solutions vs. a priori solutions
	Degree of explicit vs. implicit agreement on decisions

guide a group to a decision, although this is primarily for problems with an identifiable ''correct'' answer.

The idea of examining aggregation principles with regard to *problem representations* is relatively unexplored.[7] Several aggregation principles can be asserted based on literature pertaining to group decision making, particularly in foreign policy. These aggregation principles reflect a number of factors or dimensions that have been suggested as important in terms of group decision making, particularly within the foreign policy–making realm and, thus, represent a broad base from which to compare observations of collective foreign policy decision making. In essence, they represent different potentially observable patterns from which actual observation may conform or deviate, and they are based on the limited literature regarding problem representations and group decision making. They are not an exhaustive list of possible patterns, but they represent a wide variety of factors that may be pivotal in the aggregation process and as such should be taken as a starting point for comparison to empirical observation.

Six Aggregation Principles

Simplicity: The complexity of individuals' understandings of a foreign policy problem may well be significant for the way in which that problem is confronted by the group. Some of the propositions of groupthink (Janis 1982) clearly suggest that group members may seek to avoid complex analysis and decision-making procedures that could introduce potentially disrupting information into the decision-making process. Indeed, the groupthink phenomena is proposed as "a mode of thinking that people engage in when they are deeply involved in a cohesive in-group, when the members' strivings for unanimity override their motivation to realistically appraise alternative courses of action." Janis goes on to state that "groupthink refers to a deterioration of mental efficiency, reality testing, and moral judgment that results from in-group pressures." Walker and Watson (1989, 1992) explicitly relate groupthink to various aspects of cognitive complexity of individual group members. In terms of the aggregation of problem representations, we can propose that the representation that has the fewest necessary components, or the fewest steps involved to solve the problem potentially, could be the ultimate focus of group discussion. Articulation of the problem in group discussion, in other words, could be biased toward those explanations that are simplest and most easily grasped by all or most group members. If a simple conception of the decision problem drives decision making, then the group discussion itself should be fairly simple and should not explore a wide variety of issues or topics with regard to the problem. Indeed, a simple representation should focus the group on a particular aspect or topic, such that that topic comes to dominate the group discussion. Further, conflict and dissension within the group would necessarily be minimal – as divergent points of view tend to foster debate and analysis. Thus, the group may be particularly solution-oriented rather than dealing with an analysis of causes and constraints. As group discussion would not be oriented toward trying to develop alternative conceptions of the problem, there would probably be little alternation in group discussion, and discussion contributions would likely be skewed around a few individuals who are clearly expressing the problem. Finally, there should be little in the way of compromise, because the group is essentially following the simple representation that has been presented, and little conflict has occurred. This, however, should produce a strong relationship between the discussion and what is actually decided, because the group is particularly focused on one or a few aspects of the problem. There should be little in the way of solutions emerging from the group discussion, because that discussion is relatively narrow and simplistic. Rather, the solution should be introduced with the simplistic representation itself. In this sense, we should expect implicit agreement rather than explicit statements of support for the solution the group adopts.

Single Representation Embellishment: Often what drives group decision making may not be what is said but who is doing the talking. At times, a single individual – perhaps a group leader, or someone who is perceived as an expert on a particular problem – may be the focus of the decision process. The groupthink phenomenon also suggests the importance of a strong leader (Janis 1982) in terms of guiding the group through the decision problem. Indeed, strong leadership seems to be particularly important in terms of the overall dynamics of group interaction (cf. Hermann, Hermann, and Hagan 1991). In terms of problem representations, we could expect a single individual's representation to be central and other group members to support or embellish this representation. Thus, this aggregation principle involves taking one representation as dominant and then contributing to that expressed representation by finding supporting arguments or simply supporting a course of action advocated by the leader. Agreement should be high and conflict should be minimal, because the group would strive to support the individual's understanding of the problem. Individual participation would be skewed toward the dominant individual, who would be central and dominant in the discussion. There may be some alternation between group members as they attempt to embellish the leader/dominant individual's characterization of the problem; for the same reason, the discussion continuity would also be high. There would be little need for compromise, and there should be a high degree of correspondence between the group's discussion and the content of decisions that are made. The leader, however, would probably also introduce the course of action or solution to the problem, which the group would obediently and explicitly support.

Factionalism: Group members are not always so ready to adopt a particular perspective on a given problem, nor are they always willing to follow the lead of a particular individual. Often groups will form factions regarding a decision issue, and the group decision process will reflect this divided and potentially conflictual state of affairs. Under such circumstances, "bureaucratic politicking" may occur, where individuals attempt to form winning coalitions; failing that, they will turn to side payments and compromise (Valenta 1979; Hermann et al. 1991). In terms of problem representations, this aggregation principle would entail a group developing various subgroups or factions based on common or similar representations of the decision problem.

This type of aggregation process would be characterized by these subgroups' supporting their constituent members and then pushing discussion to focus on and ultimately "resolve" the differences between such groupings. A particularly powerful faction may attempt to set the agenda or to frame the debate, but no particular individual would be central or dominant in the group discussion. Indeed, individuals would participate in group discussion according to their support for competing interpretations, and the group would focus on both points of agreement within factions, but particularly on points of disagreement and conflict between factions. We would suspect that once clear differences emerge within the group, specific solutions would be the focus of contrast. When various factions are competing for their interpretation to prevail, no particular topic should be dominant. The factions may be driven by concerns other than the solving of the problem per se; therefore a high degree of alternation and even distribution among group members trying to productively interact would probably be absent. Compromise would be minimal, because the factions would continue to compete in order to have their side prevail. When decisions are taken, they may simply paper over differences and, thus, have a low correspondence to what was actually the focus of discussion for the group. The competition to prevail would probably prevent interactively generating solutions to emerge from the decision-making process, but any expressions of agreement with or disagreement with solutions would be quite explicit.

Common Decomposition: Conflict need not drive collective decision making, just as an excessively centralized and directed type of interaction need not necessarily emerge in a decision group. Groups may interact in a more "collegial" fashion and may attempt to construct an understanding of the foreign policy problem based on different individual understandings. This in some ways is the antithesis of groupthink, in that individuals are making contributions based on their own interpretation of the problem, and the group is interacting in an effort to find or develop a viable solution. This also is distinct from bureaucratic conflict in the sense that group members are not necessarily factionalized and are attempting to evaluate and integrate different perceptions of the problem. In terms of problem representations, the group as a whole may operate by attempting to decompose individual representations and then construct a cogent and commonly acceptable understanding of the foreign policy problem. Thus, there would be no dominant representation and no individual would attempt to set the agenda or frame the problem. As groups are attempting to find the best solution to the problem, excessive disagreement should not occur. Points of disagreement, however, would not be shunned, and conflicting points of view would be discussed. We should also observe a broadly encompassing discussion that uses several different aspects of individuals' representations. Possible solutions should be debated in terms of their impact on the problem. Group discussions, in their efforts to be inclusive and integrative, should be relatively complex and should focus on the relationship between various aspects of the problem as opposed to being extensively oriented toward different solutions. No individual should be excessively central or dominant, and contributions should be evenly distributed. The group discussion should progress toward a decision directly based on the group problem-solving efforts. Individuals should be both willing and able to recognize potential compromises between different solutions being advanced, based on their extensive examination of the problem. Group members should also be explicit with regard to their willingness to support a particular course of action.

Common Alternatives: Groups may not be as interested in coming to a clear understanding of a problem as they are in finding some acceptable solution. As such, groups may tend to focus their decision energy on alternatives and spend much less time attempting commonly to comprehend the nature of the foreign policy problem they are confronting. Paul Anderson's conception of "decision making by objection" is, in principle, similar to such a process. He indicates that group decision making can be a social process and that decisions may result from a series of choice points between noncompeting alternatives wherein possible courses of action die for lack of a second alternative (Anderson 1983, 1987). Indeed, other researchers have suggested that foreign policy groups are often more concerned with alternatives than with other aspects of the decision problem (Purkitt 1992). In terms of problem representations and aggregation, we might expect that commonly shared alternatives (resource beliefs) would dominate group discussion and that other suggested alternatives would be quickly abandoned, thereby allowing the shared alternative to frame the debate. The group discussion would be focused on alternatives and their consequences, with less attention to the causes and constraints of the foreign policy problem. In this sense, group discussion may not reflect high degrees of integration and, thus, may be less complex. Discussion would tend toward having little conflict, as group members pursue commonly shared alternatives for action. Disagreement between members could exist but may be manifest as alteration of proposals rather than their negation through explicit argument. Participation may be somewhat evenly distributed, particularly among those with commonly held solutions, and no individual would be expected to be excessively central or dominant in the group interactions. Because the group is focused simply on finding a solution that is commonly shared, at least among some subset of the group members, there would be little need for compromise. The group will simply go with the solution that enough members support. Because that solution should dominate the discussion, there should be a strong relationship between what is discussed and what is decided. The solution would probably be introduced; there would be little group interaction in the way of constructing a new solution. The group members should be explicit, however, in advocating or supporting the final group decision.

Expertise: Finally, groups may not be driven simply by finding solutions, nor by focusing on one individual's or one type of representation. Further, they may not divide into factions or attempt to integrate across individuals. They may, in fact, divide responsibility for problem solving according to individuals' expertise.[8] The aggregation principle developed here focuses more on the division of responsibility rather than on the resolution of conflict (which might be more characteristic of "factionalism"). In this sense, groups may turn to various group members to understand aspects of the foreign policy problem according to their area of expertise. Thus, group problem-solving activities would involve individual group members offering contributions within given domains, while other members attempt to utilize those in developing a problem response. No particular type of representation should dominate the group discussion, nor should any individual be central or dominant in the discussion. Group discussion would involve little direct disagreement. Discussion complexity may be moderately high as various perspectives are introduced and utilized in coming to a decision, but it would not be exceptionally high because the integration of different perspectives would not be central. This also would result in less continuity in the group discussion. As experts, however, group members should focus on explaining various aspects of the problem to other group members rather than focusing on solutions; this should foster a relatively wide variety of topics for the group discussion. Further, this would prevent extensive conflict or disagreements, because domains of expertise are recognized. Participation may be diverse, but some individuals may be more central as they attempt to utilize their various expertise in problem solving. There may need to be some compromise between advocated courses of action, and the decision should essentially emerge from the contributions of the various experts. This need not indicate, however, that all individuals would be explicit with regard to their support for a decision. Indeed, all group members may not be called upon equally to endorse a particular course of action.

Method

The aggregation principles outlined previously are not an exhaustive list of possible observable patterns. Indeed, although they are based on extant literature dealing with group decision making in foreign policy and the relationship of individual beliefs and representations in group decision making, they may not fully capture the dynamics involved between individually expressed problem representations and foreign policy decision making in groups. The nature of those dynamics is a subject that is open to empirical investigation. The design of this study is to evaluate comparatively decisions made by politically authoritative groups regarding foreign policy problems in an effort to determine the extent to which the aggregation principles can be observed and to determine any important factors or contingencies that may help to explain the aggregation phenomenon.

One proposition made by examiners of the Munich crisis is that a pattern of activities within the cabinet suggest that a sort of "cabinet revolt" occurred in the latter stages of the crisis, wherein one of the members of the executive began to doubt the wisdom of the course advocated by Prime Minister Chamberlain (Colvin 1971; Middlemas 1972). Walker and Watson (1989, 1992) systematically examined the Munich crisis from the standpoint of groupthink and concluded that groupthink may have actually varied across different stages of group decision making. Their examinations focused on the cognitive complexity of a limited number of participants in the decision-making group. Thus, the Munich case provides some potential in terms of observing variation in aggregation principles. *We should expect to observe the simplicity or the single representation embellishment aggregation principles – the two developed from and most parallel to groupthink – in the meetings proposed to be characterized by the presence of groupthink.*

The representation of a decision problem is not here considered a single, well-defined activity that can be located at a particular point in time. Representation may indeed be *developed* through time, and the processes associated with different "stages" of development may be quite different (see Hermann and Billings, this volume). For this reason, a series or sequence of decision-making episodes are examined. Twelve meetings of the British cabinet during the Munich crisis have been examined using a content-analytic technique – based in part on modified causal mapping – designed to measure aspects of individually expressed problem representations and group interactions.[9] The meetings occurred between August 30 and September 27, 1938. (See Table 5.2.) These minutes, originally highly classified, can be taken to represent group discussion without concern for public-image maintenance. The meetings' minutes retain much of the original language used by the speakers, and they include individual arguments, questions, and stated preferences, as well as recording the group's decisions. Further, they indicate who is speaking and maintain the temporal order of the arguments that were made. As indicated, these cabinet minutes have been used in earlier research to measure individual cognitive complexity and seem to be of sufficient quality for current purposes.

Table 5.2. *Munich case meetings by episode, date, and topic*

Meeting #: date	Topic
Episode 1 (groupthink)	
#1: 8/30/38	Meeting called to inform ministers of recent developments with regard to German plans to invade Czechoslovakia.
Episode 2 (groupthink)	
#2: 9/12	Meeting held in response to various provocative statements made by Hitler, pressure by France for clarification of Britain's attitude toward Czechoslovakia, and anticipation of that evening's speech by Hitler.
#3: 9/14	Meeting held after Hitler's speech to discuss a proposal made by Chamberlain that he personally visit Hitler ("Plan Z").
Episode 3 (groupthink)	
#4: 9/17 11:00 A.M.	Meeting held to inform the cabinet of recent efforts and events and to provide information regarding Chamberlain's meeting with Hitler.
#5: 9/17 3:00 P.M.	Meeting to continue discussions on issue of self-determination for the Sudeten-Germans, the possible plebiscite, and the British relationship to the French.
#6: 9/19	Meeting held to inform cabinet members of the nature of the meetings with the French ministers.
#7: 9/21	Meeting held to update the situation with regard to Czechoslovakia's reaction to the joint message from Britain and France and developments in the international situation generally.
Episode 4 (nongroupthink)	
#8: 9/24	Meeting held to give account of Chamberlain's meeting with Hitler at Godesberg.
#9: 9/25 10:30 A.M.	Meeting held to continue discussions regarding Hitler's proposals for dealing with the Sudeten-German issue in Czechoslovakia.
#10: 9/25 3:00 P.M.	Meeting held to continue discussions regarding Hitler's proposals for dealing with the Sudeten-German issue in Czechoslovakia.

Table 5.2 (*cont.*)

Meeting #: date	Topic
#11: 9/25 11:30 P.M.	Meeting held to update the situation with regard to the French attitude regarding Hitler's proposals.
Episode 5 (groupthink) #12: 9/27	Meeting held to update the situation and to hear an account of the delivery of the warning message to Hitler.

Reliability and Validity

Reliability of a content-analytic technique can be measured in a number of ways (Krippendorf 1980). Stability involves the same coder coding the same material two or more times with a given time delay and then comparing the codings. This procedure was followed for the concept-mapping technique by randomly sampling text from across the twelve meetings of the Munich case and recoding using the concept-mapping coding technique. Eight samples were drawn and compared. Overall, the agreement between the total number of codes (i.e., concept-concept relationships) was 94 percent (Pearson r = .737, $p < .05$), and 95 percent between the total number of concepts (Pearson r = .891, $p < .05$). In only those cases where the concepts were equivalent between the initial coding and the subsequent coding, 83 percent of the relationships between the concepts were coded exactly the same way. This suggests that there is a fairly high degree of stability for the coding procedure in terms of the coding of concepts and relationships between concepts. Other variables can be similarly evaluated in terms of stability. One of the meetings was randomly selected and recoded, with a time delay between the initial coding and the recoding. This procedure showed a similarly high degree of stability for the coding procedure.[10]

Finally, some of the findings for this study are consistent with findings from other studies using the causal-mapping technique. For example, the overall amount of disagreement across all the decision episodes is relatively low, averaging less than 2 percent of total concepts. This is similar to a finding by Axelrod (1977) in his evaluation of argumentation in foreign policy settings utilizing the causal-mapping technique. Axelrod found that only about 4.5 percent of all asserted relationships by decision makers working in small groups were disagreed over across three foreign policy making settings.

Table 5.3. *Hypothesized and observed aggregation principles*

	Meeting number											
	1	2	3	4	5	6	7	8	9	10	11	12
Observed Best Fit[a]	CD	SRE	SRE	**Exp**	<u>CD</u>	<u>CD</u>	**CD**	<u>CD</u>	Fct	<u>CD</u>	SRE	Exp
Observed Worst Fit	Smp	CA	Exp	Fct	SRE	Exp	Fct	CA	CA	SRE	Exp	Smp
Groupthink	SRE	SRE	SRE	SRE	SRE	SRE	SRE	–	–	–	–	SRE
Hypothesis (Either)	Smp	Smp	Smp	Smp	Smp	Smp	Smp	–	–	–	–	Smp

[a] **Boldfaced** aggregation principles exhibited a particularly strong match between the aggregation principle indicated and the coded variable values for the meeting. <u>Underlined</u> aggregation principles exhibited a weak match in this regard. Abbreviations for the aggregation principles are: CD = Common Decomposition, CA = Common Alternatives, Exp = Expertise, Fct = Factionalism, Smp = Simplicity, and SRE = Single Representation Embellishment.

Results

In examining the different aggregation principles observed in the twelve cabinet meetings for the Munich case (see Table 5.3), one of the most striking aspects is the wide variety of aggregation principles across the meetings. Indeed, four of the six aggregation principles are approximated, with Common Decomposition occurring six times, Single Representation Embellishment three times, Expertise two times, and Factionalism occurring once. The Simplicity aggregation principle and the Common Alternatives aggregation principle were not evident in any of the meetings. Moreover, only two of the meetings (numbers 4 and 7) exhibit a strong match between an aggregation principle and observation, while five meetings (numbers 5, 6, 8, 9, and 10) exhibit a weak match between an aggregation principle and observation. In other words, taken as a whole, the patterns of variable values as hypothesized in the six aggregation principles are only moderately strongly evidenced in the twelve meetings of the Munich case. With this in mind, it is possible to compare the observed aggregation principles to those hypothesized by the groupthink hypothesis. The groupthink hypothesis was supported in five of the twelve meetings (numbers 2, 3, 8, 9, and 10).[11] This moderately weak support of the groupthink hypothesis is consistent with the rather extensive degree of variation in the types of aggregation principles observed across the twelve Munich case meetings.

Aggregation Principles and Other Factors

The fact that the groupthink hypothesis did a fairly poor job in predicting the types of aggregation principles that were observed, combined with the fact that there was rather extensive variation in the observed aggregation principles, leads to an examination of any other factors that might account for the pattern of aggregation principles across the twelve meetings. There does not seem to be any systematic trend with regard to the division among the five decision-making episodes utilized by Walker and Watson in terms of the observed aggregation principles. (See again Table 5.2.) There does, however, seem to be some tendency for the middle periods of the crisis to exhibit the Common Decomposition aggregation principle. In fact, in five of the six meetings beginning with meeting 5 in the afternoon of September 17 and ending with meeting 10 in the afternoon of September 25, the Common Decomposition aggregation principle is at least weakly approximated.

Rather than focusing on the episode or the particular stage of the crisis, it is possible to examine the actual nature of the decision or decisions that were taken in each meeting. Some of the cabinet meetings resulted in decisions to commit resources toward resolving the problem confronting the regime, while other meetings essentially resulted in decisions to delay making any important decisions. Interestingly, of the four meetings where no significant decision was taken regarding British policy, two (2 and 8) showed aggregation principles in line with the groupthink hypothesis. Indeed, half of the meetings in the nongroupthink episode were characterized as *nondecisions* (decisions to delay making a significant decision), while only 25 percent of the meetings in the groupthink episodes were characterized as a *nondecision*. In other words, when the cabinet did not commit itself to a particular policy choice, the pattern of problem-representation aggregation was more consistent with the groupthink prediction. The groupthink hypothesis, in other words, was supported more often when the group was not making a significant foreign policy decision.

Other Patterns through Groupthink/Nongroupthink

In further examining the groupthink (GT) and nongroupthink (NGT) episodes in terms of specific variables (not using the aggregation principles as a whole), several differences become apparent.[12] In other words, dividing the decision-making meetings along the lines proposed by Walker and Watson (1992) – following the analysis by Middlemas (1972) and Colvin (1971) – provides some leverage in terms of differentiating specific decision-making variables. For instance, of the twelve meetings examined, the only one that was characterized by compromise between two or more advocated courses of action was one in the NGT episode (meeting 10). In this sense, an important decision-making variable showed some variation between GT and NGT episodes.

Another variable that seemed to distinguish between the proposed GT and NGT episodes was the degree of emergence with regard to possible solutions. Emergence is the extent to which potential solutions seemed to emerge from the group interaction as opposed to having been asserted by a single individual or small subset of individuals. In other words, the degree to which decisions seem to emerge from the decision process may indicate the extent to which the group is collectively solving a problem. *The degree of emergence was coded "moderate" in all four NGT episodes and "low" in all but two of the eight GT meetings.*

Finally, the degree of disagreement and conflict exhibited in the group discussions also seems to differ according to the GT/NGT classification, with more disagreement and conflict coming in the NGT meetings. *The overall degree of disagreement within the group discussion varies significantly between the GT and NGT episodes, with more overall disagreement among group members in the NGT than in the GT meetings* ($t = 1.849$, $p < .1$). There is, however, an associated rise in overall agreement among group members in the NGT meetings as well. (See Figure 5.3.) In other words, both disagreement and agreement increased in the NGT meetings, although this was more pronounced for disagreement. Across all twelve meetings, there was a positive correlation between overall agreement and overall disagreement (Pearson $r = .798$, $p < .05$).

An examination of the data reveals that most of the disagreements in the NGT meetings involved expressed preferences for actions, whereas the agreement, though dominated by expressed preferences, also included consensus regarding causal and categorical relations between concepts. In other words, the agreement in the NGT meetings was more diverse in terms of problem-representation elements than the disagreement, which tended to focus mainly on preferences.

The data also indicate that the number of instances of conflict between group members increased during the NGT episodes (Mean NGT = 7.5; Mean GT = 4.75).[13] Examining the nature of the conflict in terms of "problem conflict" (conflict about aspects of the problem itself) and "solution conflict" (conflict about courses of action) reveals a similar division between the GT and the NGT episodes (Mean problem conflict NGT = 2.5; Mean problem conflict GT = 1.63; Mean solution Conflict NGT = 5; Mean Solution Conflict GT = 3).

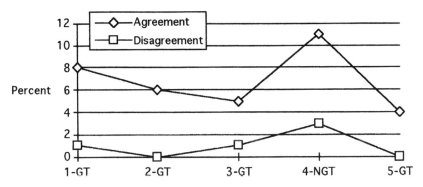

Figure 5.3. Agreement and disagreement by episode as a percentage of total concepts.

Other Patterns and Observations

When we examine the correlations among the variables used to differentiate the aggregation principles across all twelve meetings, a few interesting observations can be made. Cognitive complexity is one variable used to examine both individuals and the group as a whole. In the six cabinet meetings where Chamberlain's representation was dominant (meetings 3, 4, 6, 7, 8, and 11) – that is, where his assertions about the problem went relatively unchallenged and played a central role in the group discussions – Chamberlain's cognitive complexity (as measured by General Integration) varies from low to high.[14] However, across all twelve meetings, his general integration did not correlate with the group general integration ($r = .376$, $p > .1$). *Although the group meetings were often dominated by Chamberlain, and Chamberlain frequently played a central and dominant role in the interaction patterns, variations in his cognitive complexity (as measured by general integration) did not seem to correlate with the complexity of the group discussion as a whole.*

The decision episodes offered in the Walker and Watson (1992) study correspond to distinct phases of decision making by the group in terms of dealing with significant events in the environment. With regard to these decision episodes, the first meeting in a new decision episode was almost always more oriented toward categorical relations between concepts than causal relations, and they all exhibited "low" solution orientations. In fact, *four of the five meetings that mark the beginning of a new decision episode were more oriented toward categorical relations between concepts, and all five meetings were lower in regard to the degree of expressed preferences (preference orientation)* ($t = 3.029$, $p < .05$). Further, in the five meetings that mark the beginning of a decision episode, the average amount of conflict is 3.5,

Table 5.4. *Overview of groupthink/nongroupthink findings: Munich*

Groupthink	Nongroupthink
No "Compromise" meetings	One "Compromise" meeting
25% "nondecision" meetings	50% "nondecision" meetings
"Low" Emergence in most meetings	"Moderate" Emergence in all meetings
Lower Disagreement and Agreement	Higher Disagreement and Agreement
Types of Agreement not diverse	Types of Agreement diverse
Less Conflict	More Conflict

whereas in the seven other meetings, the average amount of conflict is 7.3. Finally, in three of these five decision episodes, the initial meeting resulted in no significant decision being taken. These patterns are consistent with the idea that the group begins by evaluating the problem and only subsequently turns toward discussion and argument regarding how to solve that problem.

In terms of the nature of the interaction patterns between and among group members, as the percent of people attending the meeting who made contributions to the group discussion rises, so does the group's causal integration scores ($r = .683$, $p < .05$). Looking at the data, this appears to be due in part to a general tendency for group meetings with a greater percentage of members contributing to focus more on causal relations between concepts, although the causal order of this cannot clearly be discerned. In essence, *there is a positive relationship between the number of members participating in the discussion and the extent to which the discussion focuses on causal aspects of the problem.*[15] Similarly, there is a positive correlation between the percent of people attending the meeting who made contributions to the group discussion and the overall group agreement ($r = .755$, $p < .05$). In other words, *there is a positive relationship between the number of group members in attendance contributing to the discussion and the amount of agreement between group members regarding various aspect of their expressed problem representations.*

If we limit our examination to only those members who contributed to group discussion, the degree to which those members alternated in their contributions between one another is negatively correlated with overall group agreement ($r = -.648$, $p < .05$), somewhat negatively correlated with overall group disagreement ($r = -.551$, $p < .1$), and negatively correlated with preferences expressed as a percent of total codes ($r = -.766$, $p < .05$).[16] *There is a negative relationship between alternation between contributing group members and both expression of agreement and disagreement, and expression of preferences in the group discussion.* This is consistent with an interpretation of group interaction that suggests the greater the degree to which contributors punctuate group discussion, the more they are attempting to elaborate the nature of the problem rather than agree or disagree with other members or express preferences regarding a course of action, although again the causal order cannot be certain with the correlational analysis alone.

As the number of questions asked in a meeting increased, there was an increase in the Broadness measure ($r = .63$, $p < .05$).[17] There was, in other words, a more extensive range of topics in meetings where more questions were asked. Interestingly, as more cabinet attendees made contributions in a meeting, there was an associated decrease in Broadness ($r = -.67$, $p < .05$). There was no significant correlation between the number speaking in a meeting and the number of questions in a meeting ($r = -.25$, $p > .1$). There was, however, a negative correlation between the number of questions asked and the amount of conflict ($r = -.599$, $p < .1$). To the extent that question asking indicates the seeking of information in order to develop or modify understanding of the problem, and conflict indicates some confrontation between understandings of a problem (as manifest by either advocated courses of action or propositions about the nature of the problem; see Table 5.5) we might suspect the existence of markedly different tasks in which the group engages – namely, information gathering and information exchange or integration.

Dividing the meetings according to this information-gathering/information-exchange dimension, some differences seem to emerge. Meetings 1, 2, 4, 6, 7, 8, and 12 represent meetings that can be characterized as "information" meetings – wherein significant new events were presented by one or two members to the rest of the group. Meetings 3, 5, 9, 10, and 11 were more characterized as continuing deliberations, wherein significant new information was not a dominant issue ("noninformation" meetings). The average number of questions during the "information" meetings was 4.43; in the "noninformation" meetings, it was lower, at 1.2. The amount of conflict in the "information" meetings was 3.14; in the "noninformation" meetings, it was much higher, at 9.2.[18] Thus, it seems that the types of interaction between and among the decision makers were markedly different contingent upon the nature of the task they were confronting – that is, whether or not they were attempting to receive new information.

Turning to the actual content of discussion in these meetings, it is possible to examine patterns of topics through time. The Munich case shows the cabinet initially dealing most extensively with the topic of the intentions of Germany as well as Britain's position regarding Czechoslovakia. Although Germany's/Hitler's intentions declines through time, it remains a relatively prominent topic of discussion in each subsequent meeting. Similarly, British-French relations and interactions is a frequent topic across meetings. Britain's

Table 5.5. *Overview of findings for Munich case*

=====

• The initial meeting in each decision episode (following Walker and Watson 1992) is usually more oriented toward categorical relations between concepts.

• The initial meeting in each decision episode (following Walker and Watson 1992) is lower in degree of expressed preferences.

• The initial meeting in each decision episode (following Walker and Watson 1992) is low in expressed conflict between cabinet members.

• As the number of contributors to group discussion rises, so does the group's causal integration and focus on causal relationships between concepts.

• As the number of contributors to group discussion rises, so does the extent of agreement between group members.

• As the number of contributors to the group discussion rises, so does the broadness of the group discussion.

• As alternation between speakers rises, so does agreement, disagreement, and expression of preferences.

• As the number of questions rises, so does the broadness of the group discussion.

• As the number of questions rises, conflict between cabinet members goes down.

• "Information" meetings were higher in number of questions asked and lower in the amount of conflict between cabinet members than were "noninformation" meetings.

=====

position regarding Czechoslovakia, however, is a prominent topic until meeting 9, whereafter it drops off completely, while at the same time, British-Czech relations/interactions increases significantly (see Figure 5.4).[19]

This examination of the various topics as discussed in each cabinet meeting offers some specific insights into the nature of the problem representation as it was expressed through the group. It is interesting, for instance, to note a general transition in the way the cabinet dealt with Britain's relationship to Czechoslovakia through time. At the morning meeting on September 25 (meeting 9), the cabinet discussed possible "advising" of Czechoslovakia and the issue of "accepting Hitler's terms," but this remains unclearly articulated. Does accepting Hitler's terms mean pressuring Czechoslovakia, or perhaps the French? Foreign Secretary Halifax – reflecting on his growing concern that the Franco-British proposals for transfer of territory and Hitler's current proposals represented, in fact, a marked change – stated that "he did not feel that it would be right to put pressure on Czechoslovakia to accept. We should lay the case before them. If they rejected it he imagined that France would join in, and if France went in we should join with them" (CAB

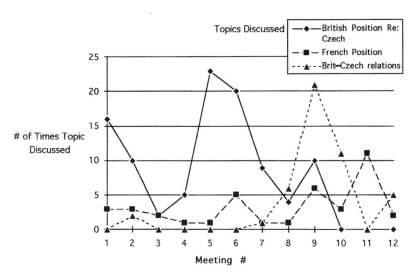

Figure 5.4. Frequency of British and French position, and British-Czech relations/ interactions across cabinet meetings.

23/95, p. 5). Secretary of State for Air Sir Kingsley Wood's comments further exemplify this uncertain quality to "accepting the terms" and "advising" Czechoslovakia.

> Continuing, the Secretary of State for Air said that he shared the feelings expressed by the Chancellor of the Duchy of Lancaster. We had suffered a humiliation for which we must all take the responsibility – a responsibility extending back over many years. It was necessary, however, to look at the matter from the practical point of view, and the present circumstances would show a weak Russia and a doubtful France. He agreed with the President of the Board of Education and the Minister for Co-ordination of Defence that the terms should be accepted. He reached this conclusion notwithstanding his intense disgust at the terms. . . . He thought that the matter had been put very well by the Minister for Co-ordination of Defence, and it was both fair and honourable, as well as our duty, to put the facts of the case before Czechoslovakia. (CAB 23/95, p. 11)

It seems that the idea of "putting the facts" before Czechoslovakia served as a proxy for the issue of standing up to Hitler. When the cabinet resumed the discussion regarding Hitler's proposals for dealing with the Sudeten-German issue in Czechoslovakia at the 3:00 P.M. meeting on September 25, Chamberlain stated:

> The first point he [Chamberlain] wished to make was that he was sure that even those of his colleagues who did not see matters in precisely the same

light as himself would be the last to wish to magnify differences. They were faced with a critical situation, and it was important that the Cabinet should present a united front. When he came to the position we were in today, and to the immediate decision which had to be taken, he did not think he would find any real differences. In the course of the discussion certain of his colleagues had spoken somewhat loosely of "accepting" or "rejecting" Herr Hitler's proposals. It was, of course, clear that it was not for us to accept or reject them, or, indeed, to feel any humiliation in regard to these terms. The proposals were not addressed to us, and we were only acting as an intermediary. The final responsibility for acceptance or rejection lay with the Czechoslovak Government. (CAB 23/95, p. 29)

He continued momentarily:

There had also been talk of "pressure" on Czechoslovakia. What did this mean? Nobody suggested that if the Czechs rejected the terms we should go to war against them. The assumption was ridiculous, but it served to illustrate the point that there was no pressure which we could exert in the literal sense. He felt sure that those who talked about "pressure" did not suggest that we were debarred from putting before Czechoslovakia all the consideration which should properly be borne in mind in reaching a decision. We owed it to them to do no less than this, and not to let them make a decision without knowing what was involved. (CAB 23/95, p. 30)

This move on the part of the prime minister was actually quite remarkable, considering the extent to which previous discussions in the cabinet had turned on what position Britain would take with regard to the German demands on Czechoslovakia. Additionally, it was remarkable because the British had indeed been applying pressure on the Czech president, Benes.[20] This further illustrates the extent to which the move on Chamberlain's part was a recasting of the problem as opposed to a genuine commentary on a particular course of action.

In essence, Chamberlain seemed to have reframed the debate by extricating Britain from its previously assumed central role in the relationship between Germany and the Czech government and moved Britain into an "intermediary" role instead. In consequence, this allowed the cabinet to unpack the idea of potential "pressure" being applied on Czechoslovakia and to subsequently address the more specific issues of Britain's relationship and interaction with Czechoslovakia. This is reflected in the extent to which the topic of "British Position regarding Czechoslovakia" declines in frequency in the coded meetings and is replaced by an increase in references to British-Czechoslovak relations/interaction, which is virtually absent prior to the meeting on September 24. (See again Figure 5.4). This also helps to explain an observed return to a focus on the French position/attitude regarding the

German proposals, as Britain seems to be removing itself from the most central position.

A second point that this illustrates is the relationship between the way in which a problem is defined or represented and the nature of the solutions that are generated to deal with that problem. The solutions can be understood only in the context of the definition of the problem. The issue of ''pressure'' on Czechoslovakia makes sense if Britain is attempting to assert a particular attitude toward Germany. This same option, however, has an entirely different meaning if Britain is attempting to establish a mediating role between two other actors (Germany and Czechoslovakia). The cabinet minutes support this observation. The discussion of this option and the conflict that it generated between the group members – this meeting was coded as High Agreement, High Disagreement, and High Conflict – seems to have been rather effectively addressed by Chamberlain's articulation of the idea of ''pressure'' and his associated move to place Britain in a mediating position.

Discussion

The fact that this study focused attention not only on the concept of problem representation but also on the group level of analysis is significant in developing an understanding of the complex nature of the foreign policy–making process. One of the critiques of groupthink is the confusion it has generated with regard to its definition (Longley and Pruitt 1980; 't Hart 1990; Walker and Watson 1992). Sometimes groupthink is considered an ''individual mode of thinking''; at other times, it is considered ''excessive concurrence seeking'' by a group. In reference to some of the results of this study, this distinction can be significant. Although Chamberlain's cognitive complexity, for example, may have varied in some forms across the proposed ''groupthink'' and ''nongroupthink'' meetings, an examination of the group and its discussion complexity reveals that his complexity alone may not necessarily predict to the group complexity. Examining groupthink in terms of individual complexity – although consistent with Janis's ''mode of thinking'' definition – may miss important aspects of the *group* in terms of decision making.

The group interaction dynamics, however, were highly volatile across both GT and NGT episodes. Overall, the Munich case exhibited some aggregation principles consistent with the groupthink hypothesis and only limited approximations (in terms of exact matches to the predicted patterns of variables) of most of the aggregation principles observed. This begins to suggest that characterizing a series of decision-making episodes on a single dimension – such as groupthink/nongroupthink – may miss important variation *within* the case. In other words, the rather extensive variation in the patterns of decision making observed in the Munich case tends to suggest that the way decision makers deal with a problem through time may be more important than more general qualities characterizing the decision setting – such as perceived threat or stress, both of which are often associated with the groupthink phenomenon.

It seems, however, that subsequent iterations of dealing with a foreign policy problem alone do not offer a clear pattern of decision-making dynamics within the group setting, but that there is some evidence for different decision-making *tasks* having differential impact on the nature of the decision-making process. This is supported by the different patterns observed in the "decision" and "nondecision" meetings, as well as the more and less "provision of information" meetings. Further, the first meeting in the decision episodes showed more categorical relations, lower solution orientation, and lower conflict than the other meetings, and these meetings were often "nondecision" meetings. Thus, both time and task seem to be more significant to the nature of the decision-making process in terms of problem representations and their interactions than are more gross characterizations such as "groupthink" or a more linear "progression through time" conception.

With regard to the specific content of group discussion and problem representation, it seems that the group's emphasis on particular aspects of the problem drove their decision making regarding the problem. In terms of framing the group discussion, for example, if the issue of Britain's relationship/role vis-à-vis Czechoslovakia is presented as central, then the nature of discussion is shaped by the emphasis on this aspect of the problem rather than on, say, British military preparedness or on the general policy with regard to standing up to Hitler. The consequence of such differential focus on aspects of the problem is that the problem seems to become defined by the group *in terms of* the particular element or elements under consideration. The coded group meetings show that there are not frequently explicit differences in terms of asserted relationship between aspects of the problem, such as disagreements regarding whether X increases or decreases Y, or whether or not Q is an instance of R. It seems that differences between group members as manifest in group discussion pertains more to the emphasis they place on different aspects of the problem. For example, some individuals considered Hitler's intentions or trustworthiness of central concern to the overall situation, whereas others considered it more peripheral. The group discussion tended to be concerned initially with the intentions of the Germans and Hitler and the nature of the proposals with regard to the actual transfer of territory from Czechoslovakia. When the issue of the Czech reaction, as opposed to the British reaction, to the German proposals entered the discussion, then the entire nature of the problem seemed to shift from one of defining a British response to the proposals to defining the relationship Britain would have with Czechoslovakia and whether to pressure Czechoslovakia into accepting. Arguments being made by group members that did not clearly fit within the dominant aspects of the group discussion in terms of problem elements being discussed did not tend to be effective in terms of motivating particular decisions.

Conclusions

Foreign policy studies focusing on individual decision makers have flourished, branching into areas such as individual personalities, motivations, information-processing tendencies, world views, operational codes, and "definitions of the situation." We have systematically investigated how different individuals are from "economically rational beings," and our investigations have increased in their complexity, taking into account more variables and different contexts. Studies of groups and foreign policy, however, have retained an excessive focus on preference-centered concepts, such as decision rules, compromises, bargaining, and the evaluation of alternatives. This has left an empirical and theoretical gap concerning the role of nonpreference-centered concepts at the group level. We need to consider the group as a complex forum for the interaction of decision makers and to begin to apply our insights regarding individuals to the collective level. This research has attempted to address this gap by examining the role of problem representations and their interaction and aggregation in foreign policy decision making groups.

I would argue, however, that foreign policy decision making (FPDM) is a misnomer for future research. "Decision making" has historically focused extensively on choices. But analysts have increasingly identified foreign policy making to be much more than choosing among options. If we take seriously such insights, then perhaps we would be better served by the appellation "foreign policy problem solving" (FPPS), which, in my view, more appropriately reflects what "decision makers" do when they "make a decision." The problem-solving perspective recognizes the external environment as being relevant and allows for the psychological construction and social communication of "the problem" to be a significant influence on the way it is addressed. The question of what problem is being solved may be at least as important as that of how predisposed a person is toward a particular solution.

Notes

1 See Axelrod (ed.) (1976), for an extensive treatment of the cognitive-mapping approach.
2 Bonham and Shapiro (1976) used four types of concepts relevant to their cognitive-mapping technique: affective, cognitive, policy, and value. These concepts referred, respectively, to immediate policy objectives, beliefs about events,

possible alternatives or options, and abstract values that decision makers try to satisfy (Bonham and Shapiro 1976: 115).

3 The focus on utility also creates problems for the cognitive-mapping approach in that it can lead to indeterminate results, in that one causal path in an individual's belief system may increase utility while another path may decrease utility, and these paths may share policy elements, thereby creating a situation of indeterminacy.

4 Causal beliefs are here considered to be very similar to causal-mapping associations, such that an increase or decrease in A leads to, corresponds to, or promotes an increase or decrease in B. Constraints are those aspects that limit or direct the potential actions that might be pursued regarding the solving of a problem. In this sense, the causal beliefs of an individual may operate as constraints on action, as certain actions may lead to consequences that are undesirable, or certain causally related phenomena in the perceived world may constrain the types of solutions that could be applied. This is a more specific meaning of constraint than that proposed by Voss (this volume), although conceptually the two are similar.

5 Each of these types of beliefs and their associated types of relationships can be further differentiated for purposes of coding materials. Each set of beliefs associated with the components of the problem representation has various associated measures that help to characterize the nature of the problem representation. See Beasley (1996).

6 Other SDS models focus on several ranked preferences, but functionally these models focus on a given preference ordering and offer various mathematical or statistical techniques to predict group decisions.

7 Although not entirely. Lyles and Mitroff (1980) present four possible ''methods of inquiry'' for problem solving in terms of problem formulation. They are principally, however, concerned with the individual level. Shapiro, Bonham, and Heradsveit (1988) present an aggregation principle related to shared discursive spaces and the power of an explanation in group discussion. Although fairly narrow, their conception is used to some extent to inform the ''expertise'' aggregation principle.

8 The approach of Shapiro, et al. (1988) to the power of arguments parallels this conception of group decision making. They develop what is essentially a principle of aggregation based on the concept of the power of a path in a collective discursive space. Power involves the *control* over an explanatory path (such as ''A leads to [causes] B'') and the *interest* in that path. Control scores are derived by obtaining decision makers' ''confidence'' ratings in their fellow group decision makers regarding a particular linkage between concepts – essentially a presumed ''expertise'' rating. Interest scores involve the ranked value of each component in an explanatory path by supporters of that path. They hypothesize that the most powerful explanations in a discussion will survive, thereby predicting policy choices.

9 For a more complete description of the coding procedure, see Beasley (1996).

10 The number of people attending and the number of people contributing to the group discussion were coded exactly the same way, as were the number of speaker changes, the amount and type of conflict, and the number of questions asked. The total number of topics for the meeting differed by four between the two codings.

In terms of the number of topics per speaking turn, twelve of the seventeen speaking turns had the exact same number of topics, and two more were off by only one topic. The correlation between the two codings in terms of number of topics discussed per speaker was $r = .837$ ($p < .01$). The most dominant topic was the same for both codings. Finally, the degree of compromise, the relationship between the process and the decisions, the emergence of solutions, and the agreement on solutions were all coded the same way.

11 Support is here considered as showing either of the most groupthink-like aggregation principles in the groupthink meetings and *not* showing the most groupthink-like aggregation principles in the nongroupthink meeting. This is because nongroupthink does not necessarily imply *least like groupthink* – although the common decomposition aggregation principle here considered the least like groupthink was weakly evident in two meetings in the nongroupthink meetings.

12 Due to the limited number of group meetings in the "nongroupthink" episodes ($n = 4$), it is difficult to perform any statistical tests of significance across the groupthink conditions. Where appropriate, trends in a particular direction are noted.

13 "Conflict" and "disagreement" are conceptually similar variables but take into account different aspects of member–member interactions. "Disagreements" might be one individual stating that "*A* increases *B*" while another states that "*A* decreases *B*" or one stating "We should do *X*" while another states "We should not do *X*." "Conflict" includes these types of disagreements between members but also examines arguments as a whole to determine if there is conflict between two or more members even though they may have no "disagreement" in terms of expressed concepts or concept–concept relationships. The correlation between the "disagreements" variable and the "conflict" variable is .77, with both measures indicating a high number of preferences and solutions, respectively.

14 General integration is measured as the number of links between concepts divided by the total number of unique concepts. This gives an indication of the extent to which concepts are associated with other concepts (categorically and causally). Chamberlain's general integration measure is calculated using only statements attributed to Chamberlain, whereas the group's general integration measure is calculated by using the group discussion as a whole.

15 Although group general differentiation is a percentage, the total number of persons in attendance across the group meetings had very little variance, ranging from 19 to 22, with a mode of 21.

16 Preferences are a type of resource concept wherein an individual expresses a preference for or against a particular course of action.

17 This measure indicates the variety of topics discussed in a meeting relative to the number of times any topic was mentioned summed across a meeting. In other words, Broadness gives an indication of how varied the discussion was relative to how much discussion there was.

18 The type of conflict (problem conflict, solution conflict, or general conflict), however, was similar in both "information" (problem = 32%, solution = 68%) and "noninformation" (problem = 33%, solution = 65%, general = 2%) meetings.

19 "British position regarding Czechoslovakia" generally refers to what attitude or position Britain will take with regard to the Czechoslovakia situation. In other words, what will Britain do or what attitude should Britain take about German actions/demands regarding Czechoslovakia? This is distinguished from "British-Czechoslovak" relations/interactions in that the latter refers more to communication and interaction between Britain and Czechoslovakia, not what attitude Britain should (or has) adopt(ed) more generally.

20 Oliver Harvey, the private secretary to Lord Halifax, noted in his diary on September 19 (some five days *prior to* Chamberlain's remarks) "P.M. also sent a message to Hitler proposing to return to Germany on Wednesday – which Hitler has now accepted. Meanwhile every pressure is being applied to Benes to accept and to accept quickly" (Harvey 1970: 186–187).

References

Allison, Graham T. (1971). *Essence of Decision*. Boston, MA: Little, Brown and Company.

Anderson, P. (1987). "What do decision makers do when they make a foreign policy decision? The implications for the comparative study of foreign policy." In C. F. Hermann, C. W. Kegley, and J. N. Rosenau (eds.), *New Directions in the Study of Foreign Policy*. Boston: Allen & Unwin.

Anderson, Paul A. (1983). "Decision making by objection and the Cuban missile crisis." *Administrative Science Quarterly, 28:* 201–222.

Axelrod, Robert (1973). "Schema theory: An information processing model of perception and cognition." *American Political Science Review, 67:* 1248–1266.

(ed). 1976. *Structure of Decision*. New Jersey: Princeton University Press.

(1977). "Argumentation in foreign policy settings." *Journal of Conflict Resolution, 21:* 727–756.

Beasley, Ryan K. (1996). *Collective Interpretations and Foreign Policy,* Unpublished doctoral thesis, The Ohio State University.

Bonham, G. Matthew, Michael J. Shapiro, and Daniel Heradstveit (1988). "Group cognition: Using an oil policy game to validate a computer simulation." *Simulation & Games, 19:* 379–407.

Bonham, Matthew, and Michael J. Shapiro (1976). "Explanation of the unexpected: The Syrian intervention in Jordan in 1970." In Robert Axelrod (ed.), *Structure of Decision*. New Jersey: Princeton University Press.

CAB 23/95, Cabinet Minutes and Conclusions, 1938–1939.

Colvin, Ian (1971). *The Chamberlain Cabinet*. London and New York: Gollancz.

Conover, Pamela Johnston, and Stanley Feldman (1984). "How people organize the political world: A schematic model." *American Journal of Political Science, 28:* 95–126.

Crocker, Jennifer, Susan T. Fiske, and Shelley E. Taylor (1984). "Schematic bases of belief change." In J. R. Eiser (ed.), *Attitudinal Judgement*. New York: Springer.

Crott Helmut W., Klaus Szilvas, and Johannes A. Zuber (1991). "Group decision, choice shift, and polarization in consulting, political, and local political scenarios: An experimental investigation and theoretical analysis." *Organizational Behavior and Human Decision Processes, 49:* 22–41.

Davis, James H., John A. Hornik, and John P. Hornseth (1970). "Group decision schemes and strategy preferences in a sequential response task." *Journal of Personality and Social Psychology*, Vol. 15, 397–408.

Fiske, S. T., and S. E. Taylor (1984). *Social Cognition*. New York: Random House.

Gaenslen, Fritz (1992). "Decision-making groups." In E. Singer and V. Hudson (eds.), *Political Psychology and Foreign Policy*. Boulder, CO: Westview Press.

George, A. (1980). *Presidential Decisionmaking in Foreign Policy: The Effective Use of Information and Advice*. Boulder, CO: Westview Press.

Gruenfeld, Deborah H., and A. B. Hollingshead (1993). "Sociocognition in work groups: The evolution of group integrative complexity and its relations to task performance." *Small Group Research, 24:* 383–405.

Halperin, Morton H. (1974). *Bureaucratic Politics and Foreign Policy*. Washington, D.C.: The Brookings Institution.

Harvey, John (ed.). (1970). *The Diplomatic Diaries of Oliver Harvey*, 1937–40. London: Collins.

Hastie, Reid, Steven D. Penrod, and Nancy Pennington (1983). *Inside the Jury*. Cambridge, MA: Harvard University Press.

Hermann, C. F., M. G. Hermann, and J. D. Hagan (1991). "How Decision Units Shape Foreign Policy: Development of a Model." Paper presented at the annual meeting of the International Society of Political Psychology, Helsinki.

Hermann, Margaret G., Charles F. Hermann, and Joe D. Hagan (1987). "How Decision Units Shape Foreign Policy Behavior." In Charles F. Hermann, Charles W. Kegley, Jr., and James N. Rosenau (eds.), *New Directions in the Study of Foreign Policy*. London: Allen and Unwin.

Isenberg, Daniel J. (1986). "Group polarization: A critical review and meta-analysis." *Journal of Personality and Social Psychology, 50:* 1141–1151.

Janis, I. L. (1982). *Groupthink*. Boston, MA: Houghton Mifflin Company.

Kameda, Tatsuya (1991). "Procedural influence in small-group decision making: Deliberation style and assigned decision rule." *Journal of Personality and Social Psychology, 61:* 225–245.

Krippendorf, Klaus (1980). *Content Analysis: An Introduction to Its Methodology*. London: Sage Publications.

Laughlin, Patrick R., and Alan L. Ellis (1986). "Demonstrability and social combination processes on mathematical intellective tasks." *Journal of Experimental Social Psychology, 22:* 177–189.

Longley, J., and D. G. Pruitt (1980). "Groupthink: A critique of Janis' theory." *Review of Personality and Social Psychology, 1:* 74–93.

Lyles, Marjorie A., and Ian I. Mitroff (1980). "Organizational problem formulation: An empirical study." *Administrative Science Quarterly, 25:* 102–119.

Middlemas, Keith (1972). *Diplomacy of Illusion*. London: Weidenfeld and Nicolson.

Miller, Charles E. (1989). "The social psychological effects of group decision rules." In Paul B. Paulus (ed.), *Psychology of Group Influence*. Hillsdale, NJ: Lawrence Erlbaum.

Minix, Dean A. (1982). *Small Groups and Foreign Policy Decision-Making*. Washington D.C.: University Press of America.

Moreland, Richard L., and John M. Levine (1992). "Problem identification by groups." In Stephen Worchel, Wendy Wood, and Jeffry A. Simpson (eds.), *Group Process and Productivity*. London: Sage Publications.

Oye, Kenneth A. (1986). *Cooperation under Anarchy*. New Jersey: Princeton University Press.

Pennington, Nancy, and Reid Hastie (1986). "Evidence evaluation in complex decision making." *Journal of Personality and Social Psychology, 51:* 242–258.

Premkumar, B. (1989). "A cognitive study of the decision-making process in a business context: Implications for design of expert systems." *International Journal of Man-Machine Studies, 31:* 557–572.

Purkitt, H. E., and J. W. Dyson (1988). "An experimental study of cognitive processes and information in political problem solving." *Acta Psychologica, 68:* 329–342.

——— (1990). "Decision making under varying situational constraints." In Katrin Borcherding, Oleg I. Larichev, and David M. Messick (eds.), *Contemporary Issues in Decision Making.* Amsterdam: North-Holland.

Purkitt, Helen E. (1992). "Political decision making in small groups: The Cuban missile crisis revisited – One more time." In E. Singer and V. Hudson (eds.), *Political Psychology and Foreign Policy.* Boulder, CO: Westview Press.

Shapiro, Michael J., and G. M. Bonham (1982) "A cognitive process approach to collective decision making." In Christer Jonsson (ed.), *Cognitive Dynamics and International Politics.* New York: St. Martin's Press.

Shapiro, Michael J., G. Matthew Bonham, and Daniel Heradstveit (1988). "A discursive practices approach to collective decision-making." *International Studies Quarterly, 32:* 397–419.

Simon, H. A. (1981). *The Sciences of the Artificial.* Cambridge, MA: MIT Press.

Snyder, Richard C., H. W. Bruck, and B. Sapin (1954). *Decision-making as an Approach to the Study of International Politics.* Princeton: Princeton University Press.

——— (1962). *Foreign Policy Decision Making.* Glencoe, IL: Free Press.

Stewart, Philip D., Margaret Hermann, and Charles F. Hermann (1989). "Modeling the 1973 Soviet decision to support Egypt." *American Political Science Review, 83:* 35–59.

Stoner, J. A. F. (1968). "Risky and cautious shifts in group decisions: The influence of widely held values." *Journal of Experimental Social Psychology, 4:* 442–459.

Sylvan, Donald A., and Stuart J. Thorson (1992). "Ontologies, problem representation, and the Cuban missile crisis." *Journal of Conflict Resolution, 36:* 709–732.

't Hart, P. (1990). *Groupthink in Government: A Study of Small Groups and Policy Failure.* Amsterdam: Swets & Zeitlinger.

Tversky, Amos, and Daniel Kahneman (1980). "Causal schemas in judgments under uncertainty." In Martin Fishbein (ed.), *Progress in Social Psychology.* Hillsdale, NJ: Lawrence Erlbaum Associates.

Valenta, J. (1979). *Soviet Intervention in Czechoslovakia, 1968: Anatomy of a Decision.* Baltimore, MD: Johns Hopkins University Press.

Voss, James F., Terry R. Greene, Timothy A. Post, and Barbara C. Penner (1983). "Problem solving skill in the social sciences." In G. H. Bower (ed.), *The Psychology of Learning and Motivation: Advances in Research Theory (Vol. 17),* New York: Academic Press.

Voss, J[ames] F. and T. A. Post (1988). "On the solving of ill-structured problems." In M. T. H. Chi, R. Glaser, and M. J. Farr (eds.), *The Nature of Expertise.* Hillsdale, NJ: Lawrence Erlbaum.

Voss, James F., Christopher R. Wolfe, Jeanette A. Lawrence, and Randi A. Engle (1991). "From representation to decision: An analysis of problem solving in international relations." In R. J. Sternberg and P. A. Frensch. *Complex Problem Solving* (119–158). Hillsdale, NJ: Lawrence Erlbaum.

Walker, Stephen G. (1977). "The interface between beliefs and behavior: Henry Kissinger's operational code and the Vietnam war." *Journal of Conflict Resolution, 21:* 129–167.

    (1987) "Personality, situation, and cognitive complexity: A revisionist analysis of the Israeli cases." *Political Psychology,* Vol. 8, No. 4, 605–621.

Walker, Stephen G., and George L. Watson (1989). "Groupthink and integrative complexity in British foreign policy-making: The Munich case." *Cooperation and Conflict, 24:* 199–212.

    (1992). "The cognitive maps of British leaders, 1938–1939: The case of Chamberlain-in-Cabinet." In E. Singer and V. Hudson (eds.), *Political Psychology and Foreign Policy.* Boulder, CO: Westview Press.

Walsh, James P., Caroline M. Henderson, and John Deighton (1988). "Negotiated belief structures and decision performance: An empirical investigation." *Organizational Behavior and Human Decision Processes, 42:* 194–216.

CHAPTER 6

Image Change and Problem Representation after the Cold War

Martha Cottam and Dorcas E. McCoy

International political trends after the Cold War have raised many important questions for image theory. First, there are questions concerning image change. The Cold War worldview was composed of some very clear images of international actors. How has that worldview been restructured, if at all? Have new images been formed? Are new tactics associated with emerging images? What has stayed the same in images and policy prescriptions?

Second, were the images in the Cold War worldview only one variation of those particular images? For example, were the enemy and ally images of the Cold War era different from enemy and ally images before and after the Cold War? Were they different from those images in arenas outside of the Cold War conflict during the Cold War? Are there different subtypes of these and other images? Much of image analysis has explored images and resulting policies in the worldview of policy makers deeply involved in the Cold War. Do we now need to look for new images that restructure a changed world and different variations of the images that we knew so well in the Western worldview during the Cold War?

Third, are policy makers who lived through and dealt with the Cold War beginning to recognize, if only implicitly and intuitively, that the nature of conflicts after the Cold War reflects perceptions of opponents that are different in important ways from those they were so familiar with during the Cold War? Has their "problem representation" – that is, the definition, explanation, and interpretation – of the causes of violence and war changed as the conflicts changed?

The first set of questions was theoretically derived and not unanticipated before the end of the Cold War. The second and third sets, however, are a direct result of the kinds of conflicts occurring in the post–Cold War era. Catastrophes like those in Bosnia and Somalia suggest that the enemy image Americans associated with their U.S.-Soviet perceptions was only one type

116

of enemy image. Post–Cold War conflicts also lend credence to the criticism that cognition-based political frameworks treat human beings as computers, and affect must be incorporated into the model (Walker 1988; Jervis 1986, 1989).

This chapter explores the first and third set of questions with reference to the Clinton administration's response to the crisis in Somalia. It explores the second set of questions as well, but primarily through a tentative theoretical discussion of the relation between affect and cognition.

Image Change

The Cold War was associated with a clear and powerful worldview composed of clearly defined images, scripts, and schemata and a repertoire of tactics that derived from containment. Without the Cold War, that cognitive worldview is no longer as efficient as it once was in organizing the international environment. (Whether or not the tactics have been questioned is a different issue.) Cognitive studies indicate that the process of change involves abandoning fixed images when they no longer "work" and using piecemeal evaluation patterns until new images firmly replace the old (Fiske and Neuberg 1989). Piecemeal information processing would involve an assessment of the same politically relevant attributes as were found in the discarded images (e.g., assessments of capability, intentions), but without full images perceivers cannot lock into the basket of information, responses, and predictions that the image offered them. Therefore, piecemeal evaluation is more short-term, situation-specific, goal-oriented, and ad hoc tactical than long-term, multidimensional goal-oriented, and strategic.

Without the Soviet Union, the United States does not have a good candidate for the enemy image.[1] That image may still exist in the worldview of American policy makers, but it currently has no occupants. However, not all images held during the Cold War are going to be inefficient organizing devices because of the end of the Cold War. The end of the Cold War does not necessarily entail a reason to expect change in American policy makers' dependent images of many Third World states. Situations that were previously defined in Cold War terms (such as insurgencies, instability, and revolution) are likely to be seen differently. Those that were typically divorced from Cold War concerns (such as bilateral trade conflicts) are likely to be defined in the same terms after the Cold War as during the Cold War.

This brings up the issue of when and why images change. As mentioned, images change when they no longer structure the world for perceivers, enabling them to respond to that world satisfactorily (achieving desired goals, avoiding deleterious events, etc.). The categorization of a country in an image changes when the perceiver receives undeniable information that disconfirms the country's membership in the image. The stronger the image and the more important the image to perceivers in terms of the values it entails, the more resistant it is to change. Any image that is value-laden and important to perceivers' values becomes important to self-image, and people will strive to maintain a positive self-image. Thus, such an image will be extremely resistant to disconfirming evidence (Hogg and Abrams 1988).[2]

The dependent image is likely to be such an image. It involves social comparison in which each perceiver's country (or ingroup) is considered vastly superior to and beneficent toward the dependent. To dismantle the image would involve recognizing that one's own society is not superior to those deemed childlike and incompetent. To change the dependent image of others, Americans would not only have to question their own superiority, but some may even have to face the idea that the actions taken toward dependents in the past were harmful. These together are tremendous threats to self-image. Not surprisingly, psychological studies find that individuals resist this assault on self-image (Hogg and Abrams 1988). Hirshberg's (1993) study of political perceptions indicates that a positive self-image is linked to American perceptions of their country's foreign policies. He argues that the conception of the United States as the "in-nation and as such, virtuous" is central to the "American patriotic self-image" (p. 79). American interventions in the Third World that have destroyed the very values Americans think their country upholds on a global scale, such as democracy and liberty, are rarely interpreted or remembered in this way by most Americans.

There is also the question of whether American policy makers have received significant amounts of image-disconfirming evidence since the end of the Cold War. Complaints about American imperialism did not result in ruptures of relationships between the United States and Third World states. Moreover, the Desert Storm episode would have provided image-confirming evidence to many Americans. For all of these reasons, it is likely that the dependent image of Third World countries would not have disappeared with the end of the Cold War.

Of course, not all American policy makers had a strong dependent image of the Third World during the Cold War, but they often demonstrated evidence of a moderate dependent image (M. Cottam, 1992). Those with weaker dependent images tended to be more aware of Third World nationalism as a strong political force. They understood that nationalism would produce undesirable results for the United States if dealt with through tactics ordinarily applied to the Third World by those with strong dependent images (M. Cottam, 1986, 1992, 1994). This perceptual element should be maintained after the Cold War. In general, those with weaker dependent images also should be more receptive to change.

Image Change, Tactics, and Problem Representation

This leads to some important analytical questions regarding the relation between images, tactical preferences (what instruments should be applied and how), and problem representation. The relationship was very formulaic during the Cold War: See an insurgency; define the problem as one of enemy subversion; send in military aid and advisors. The psychological representation of a policy problem, including both its identification and its definition as a problem, was derived from the image of the countries causing the problem. During the Cold War, conflicts in the Third World were usually interpreted as containment problems requiring containment tactics. These tactics typically included an American takeover of decision making in the crisis, a result of the perception that dependents were too childlike and incompetent to know how best to handle the problem. Bargaining for mutual accommodation (such as power-sharing solutions to civil war) was not considered an option. And the United States used whatever degree of coercion was deemed appropriate for the situational degree of threat, usually without hesitation.

It is logical to expect change in image to be followed by changes in tactics and problem representation. How, and how quickly, this would happen is an open question. If the image of a country changes suddenly, tactical preferences and problem representation should change fairly quickly as well. But how often does this actually occur? There are some extraordinary cases in international politics, for example, China's 1972 perceptual transformation from a barbaric enemy to a complex country in terms of motives, political realities, and culture, or the sudden disintegration of the Soviet Union and the Communist governments of Eastern Europe, which made their peoples nonenemies practically overnight. But these kinds of events are relatively rare. Ordinarily, change must come through a series of tough lessons in discovering that disconfirming evidence has been ignored and has caused policy embarrassments or disasters (e.g., the war in Vietnam).

In these cases, the target country is likely to be seen as less and less of a good fit in an image until it is eventually removed from the image altogether. In the process, tactical preferences will shift as tactics fail to work. The analytical problem is that tactical failure is often the first source of evidence that the image is inadequate. It is unlikely that change in one will follow change in the other. Rather, incremental adjustments of tactics would occur as the image gradually shifts. Problem representation may not be as confounded as images and tactics are, however, and change there may follow change in image more clearly. The identification and definition of a problem is derived from the image itself. For example, during the war in Vietnam, those who argued that the conflict was a civil war and those who argued that it was a case of international aggression had very different images of the combatants to begin with (R. Cottam 1977). Problem representation is more likely to be the subject of political debate than image placement because the latter is a nonconscious process. Such a debate may be taken as an indicator of the operation of different images. Nevertheless, problem representation, debated or not, is still contingent upon the operative image.

There are other reasons to expect change in image, tactics, and problem representation to occur unevenly. Disconfirming evidence does not necessarily cause a massive change in images of other countries. Unless challenge to the image comes from multiple cases at the same time, it is more likely that subimages will be developed to accommodate countries that do not fit the old dependent image well (Hewstone 1989). In short, the mind is reluctant to give up an image it has found useful. Even when an image is no longer useful, tactics and problem representation take time to change. Studies of stereotyping offer some evidence in this regard. Prejudicial behavior does not simply disappear once the stereotyped beliefs are changed. The behavioral responses must be both inhibited and replaced by new behavioral options (Monteith, Devine, and Zuwerink 1993). In other words, people must change their beliefs as well as learn how to treat people differently.

When an image is no longer seen as adequate, the short-term effect is an inability to develop a comprehensive, integrated, long-term policy approach to another country. People revert to piecemeal evaluation, which is narrowly focused on immediate circumstances. In the long run, however, given the inherent drive to perceive through images and the heightened attention to information about the specific situation involved in piecemeal evaluation, problem representation and tactical preference should eventually evolve, because people should be more attentive and receptive to evidence disconfirming their use. It would seem that change in tactics would have to be a result of a revised definition of the problem at hand, in the absence of an overall guiding image.

In summary, in the case of the dependent image, we anticipate post–Cold War image change to be slow and on a case-by-case basis. Cold War tactics should be applied to the dependent, although the intensity of the interaction should be lower, particularly in crisis circumstances because there is no longer an enemy to arouse high threat. The confusion starts when things begin to change. If tactics fail, the image may weaken. As the image weakens, tactics should shift. The question remains, however, as to when problem representation changes. It is possible that reconsideration of the nature of the problem at hand is a central element in developing a new image of a country (either placing it in an existing image or developing a new image to add to the worldview).

Affect and Post–Cold War Conflict

This leads back to the second set of questions presented at the beginning of this chapter.[3] Bringing the theoretical discussion down from the abstract plane to political realities (and before moving on to another abstract theoretical dimension), it would appear at first glance that the majority of American policy makers have approached post–Cold War problems with debates about which of the typical Cold War tactics would be most appropriate in cost-benefit terms rather than fundamental questions about problem representation. The bad guys (e.g., the Serbs, Saddam Hussein) are quickly identified, and then the use of economic sanctions versus military intervention (as peace-keeping or as a means to reinvent political order) is debated. Critics of this policy pattern have emerged and have raised questions of problem represen-tation: Why are people fighting, and why are they doing it in the form of genocidal or near-genocidal behavior? How can the conflicts be understood, and, given that it is, what types of conflict-resolution tactics would work?

What is the difference between the critics and the traditional policy advo-cates? To address this question, it is necessary to diverge to a consideration of the relationship between affect and cognitive images in driving conflict in the post–Cold War era. The Cold War was very much a cognition-dominated conflict because it was an intellectual one. We did not fight the Soviets, we did not lose many lives over the forty-odd years, and we thought of war in terms of an imaginary nuclear conflagration that would be met with imaginary game-theoretic strategic doctrines.

But many post–Cold War conflicts are very different and involve deep, highly affective interactions among people who live cheek by jowl with their opponents, can see or imagine real losses in material and value terms as a consequence of that interaction, and dehumanize their opponents in ways far different from the Dr. Strangelove quality of dehumanization in the Cold War. To understand this analytically, the social functions of cognition must be examined, which in turn leads to a more detailed consideration of affect.

Social categorizations, the formation of images of one's ingroup and out-groups, are inevitable. According to Hogg and Abrams (1988):

> Categorization and social comparison operate together to generate a specific form of behaviour: group behaviour. This involves intergroup differentiation and discrimination, ingroup favouritism, perceptions of the evaluative su-periority of the ingroup over the outgroup, stereotypic perceptions of in-group, outgroup and self, conformity to social norms, affective preferences for ingroup over outgroup and so on. (p. 23)

These propensities need not lead to stereotyping, hostility, and group conflict, but sometimes they do, and when they do, the conflicts can become highly affective for a number of reasons. First, categorizations of self and others serve social-identity needs as well as personal-cognitive needs. Social identities are a central element in personal self-esteem. People need not only to preserve and protect those identities – that is, they need that group to continue – they also need to maintain the positive elements of those social identities. Moreover, individuals are not directly responsible for the identities available to them. The delineation of groups, particularly politically relevant groups, is attributable to broader sociohistorical conditions, the structure of political systems, and channels of access to participation (Jalali and Lipset 1992–93).

It is at this stage that the social functions of social categories become so important. To the extent that images serve social-identity roles, they produce group behavior that differs from individual behavior in important ways. Perceived threat to social identities leads to the transformation of images into negative stereotypes. These, in turn, serve important social functions including social causality (the identification of a group responsible for the difficulties of one's own group – scapegoating); social justification (the elaboration of the negative characteristics of the responsible group, which leads to the justification of its exploitation and maltreatment – dehumanization); and social differentiation (the enhancement of the characteristics of one's group, which maintains the group, supports positive self-esteem, and further condemns the group blamed for injustice) (Hogg and Abrams 1988: 77).

Many patterns found in studies of affective intensity have implications for social and political group conflict. The intensity and quality of emotion is influenced by the perceiver's outcomes, including alternative future or past outcomes. Intensity is also influenced by the extremity of the image of another – the more simple and extreme the image, the more intense the affect (Fiske and Taylor 1991: 428). Finally, emotions, once aroused, can control cognitions. They can make people suddenly aware of goals or shift goals. They can also precede or replace cognition in that people may recall their emotional response to a person or event and respond accordingly, without being dependent on cognitions. The impact of these patterns in periods of sociopolitical stress can be easily imagined. Social comparison between one's ingroup and outgroup is an ongoing process. Frustrated goals for the future, and goals related to the prosperity and well-being of ingroups, should certainly elicit more highly charged affective reactions to outgroups perceived as responsible for those frustrations.

The implications are numerous. First, understanding the social functions served by images and some of the dynamics of group behavior makes it possible to understand better the forms of violence long observed in international politics (and largely ignored during the Cold War) – dehumanization and brutality. Second, given the role of social identity, conflicts among groups with long histories of interdependence are likely to involve extremely intense affect as well as simplification of the images of one another. Many ethno-nationalist conflicts in the post–Cold War world fit this description. They cannot be resolved by addressing the cognitive elements alone, that is, by breaking down the image with disconfirming evidence. Indeed, attempting to break down the image by providing disconfirming evidence about its cognitive content may backfire into a confirmation of the image instead.

A common technique used to do this is increasing contact between perceivers and members of the stereotyped group. But the affective elements play an important role in maintaining stereotypes and consequently must also be addressed if stereotypes are to be eliminated. Contact itself is affectively arousing. Both negative and positive affect have been found to increase the extent to which outgroup members are seen as having similar characteristics (Stroessner and Mackie 1993: 79). To be effective in breaking down stereotypes, contact must occur among people of equal status, must be intimate in a cooperative context in pursuit of superordinate goals, and must be sanctioned by external actors (Wilder 1993: 93). Moreover, when such contact takes place between people who are engaged in extreme conflict, affect can easily interfere with the cognitive processes involved in recognizing disconfirming evidence:

> Unfortunately, many aspects of the contact situation work against those factors that are important in ensuring its success as a means to alter more general evaluations of the outgroup. . . . [T]he prospect of contact with an outgroup member may be sufficient to provoke a variety of negative emotions: anxiety, loathing, fear, disgust, anger. . . . When applied to intergroup relations, the anticipation of contact with a member of a disliked outgroup should generate anxiety and reduce the likelihood for a successful contact experience. (p. 93)

Third, it is possible that the strong role of affect in such conflicts will produce an enemy image different from that associated with the U.S.-Soviet conflict during the Cold War. If emotions can override cognitive elements, in situations where groups in close proximity are in conflict, the social function played by dehumanization may suppress the cognitive attribute of cultural equality that was evident in the enemy image during the Cold War.[4] If so, enemy images in highly affective conflicts, unlike the Cold War, may have a slightly different set of attributes including the assumption that the enemy is equal in capability, but assessments of its cultural sophistication are diminished because of the powerful affective-elements operative. Thus, one would see the propensity to treat the enemy as insects rather than human beings.

The important question under consideration here is whether or not the major participants in the Cold War, instructed as they were by the Cold War enemy image and the dependent image, will recognize the differences in non–

Cold War conflicts. Because the Cold War was a highly cognitive conflict, and because the enemy was seen as equal in culture and capabilities, and as highly rational, it is quite likely that American policy makers would have few heuristics available for recognizing the intensity of affect in a highly affective conflict among enemies. Moreover, when the parties in conflict are perceived through the dependent image, the perceiver would regard the affective element as evidence of the irrationality and emotionality of the participants. This would be evidence that would confirm the image because they associate emotion with childlike behavior, cognition with rationality. Also, such a view would lead one to fail to understand threat to values as a basis for conflict, since the assumption is that the dependent's values are perceived as inferior and irrelevant.

In short, the dependent image is poorly suited to understanding the intricacies of ethnic and nationalistic conflict, because to understand those kinds of conflicts, one must understand the complexity of perceptions of others and of self as well as problems involved in conflict resolution. It is unlikely that those who continue to perceive states through this image will recognize the complexities of combat among these states or elements of these states who perceive each other as enemies.

Thus, to return to the question at the beginning of this section, there is a theoretically sound basis for expecting that those who are debating the continued application of Cold War tactics have not changed the operative image of the target country, whereas those who are seeking to redefine the problem are either in the process of change and are engaging in piecemeal information processing or have changed and are forming new images of ideal typical enemies and states formerly seen through the dependent image, as well as modes of conflict resolution.

This study now turns to an examination of image and problem representation in U.S. foreign policy. We first describe the conditions in Somalia and the evolution of U.S. policy there. Then we proceed to assess Clinton administration perceptions, policy consequences, and implications for image and problem-representation change evident in this case.

Somalia

Background

An assessment of the impact of Clinton administration perceptions of Somalia and the crisis there cannot be done without a description of Somalia's political context. The complexity of those characteristics can then be compared with the Clinton administration's perceptions and consequent policy prescriptions for Somalia.

It is well known that Somalia's polity is organized in terms of genealogical clans. Most clans trace themselves to a common ancestor, Samaale. Clan affiliation is the strongest identity in Somali society. At the same time, Somalis have a strong identity as Somalis, a common religion, Islam, and a common language. Today's crisis in Somalia can be traced directly to the dynamics of the dual and inextricably intertwined identities of clan and nation. On the one hand, strong national identity drove the creation of a legitimate Somali *nation* many centuries ago. On the other hand, strong clan identity undermined the creation of a legitimate *state* after independence (Laitin and Samatar 1987). Their interaction in the Cold War political context created the circumstances of today's crisis. Clan identity has constituted the "heart of the Somali social system and . . . the basis of the Somali collective predilection to internal fissions and internecine sectionary conflicts as well as the unity of thought and action among Somalis – a unity that borders on xenophobia" (Laitin and Samatar 1987: 29).

Nationalism resulting from the commonality of their identity as Somalis was a strong force in Somalia's independence movement, domestic political developments since independence in 1960, and foreign policy. Independence from Italian and British colonial authorities united only part of the Somali nation into a common territory. Strong nationalist sentiment produced irredentist demands for the incorporation into Somalia of portions of Ethiopia, Kenya, and Djibouti inhabited by Somalis. One consequence of this desire for the realization of a Greater Somalia was the disastrous war in the Ogaden in 1977–1978. The failure to realize Greater Somalia weakened the Siad Barre regime in many important respects.

At the same time, clan identity has formed the basis for political organization and competition for resources. As Touval argues, this should not be unfamiliar to Westerners:

> Politics in the Horn, like politics of industrial societies, consists of competition among groups for influence in the management of public affairs. The distinction lies in the character of the groups. In developed industrial societies the competing groups are made up of individuals united by common economic or social interests or perhaps a common ideology. Among the Somalis they are determined by common ancestry. (Touval 1963: 85)

Clan identity can thus circumvent national identity while not directly competing with it. Because each clan strongly identifies as Somali, clan and national identity need not necessarily conflict with each other. Therefore, pursuit of one would not necessarily cause any strong dissonance. When a trade-off must be made, however, clan identity would come first, because the clan is most immediate and the central source of security. For decades, Somali political leaders have both resisted and found irresistible clan influence and competition in the political system. Nationalist independence leaders fought to eradicate the clan influence on politics as the newly independent polity emerged. They recognized that clan loyalties and demands would make difficult a national approach to economic, social, and political problems. Yet as Touval notes (using the term *tribalism* in place of *clan loyalty*):

> Even . . . the most modern ardent nationalists who violently oppose tribalism, are not oblivious of their tribal connections. They cannot be, since their political careers depend essentially on the hard core of support they can generate "at home" – among their own tribe. To understand Somali politics, one must recognize the ambivalence of politicians toward tribalism – concessions to it as well as their struggle to eliminate it. (Touval 1963: 86)

The dilemma was no different for General Mohammed Siad Barre. His coup of 1969 set the stage for the establishment of a government based on "scientific socialism." Like others, Siad Barre intended to replace clan-based political loyalty with loyalty to the Somali (now socialist) state and nation. To that end, he tackled a number of aspects of clan influence in the political system (Makinda 1993: 19). His early cabinet appointments reflected merit considerations and drew from many different clans.

But when conditions deteriorated, Siad Barre turned to clan support to keep his power. He feared the Majerteen clan, which had dominated politics during the civilian years. His government relied primarily upon his own clan, the Marehan, his mother's clan, the Ogadeni, and his son-in-law's clan, the Dolbahante (together referred to as the MOD). This left the Majerteen, Hawiye, and Isaaq clans feeling relatively deprived in the distribution of political power (Laitin and Samatar 1987: 92). Siad Barre also played clans off against one another to divide potential opposition. Siad Barre's failure to win the Ogaden from Ethiopia in the 1977–1978 war exacerbated clan-based conflict. The failure to achieve Greater Somalia further undermined his efforts to project himself as the personification of a unified Somalia. The war had aroused intense nationalism in Somalia, and Siad Barre would inevitably be blamed for failing to deliver on the promise to achieve national grandeur goals. Because he had aroused intense suspicion among the clans he sidelined, they were the first to criticize his leadership. Moreover, in part as a consequence of the war and in part as a consequence of Siad Barre's use of repression in ruling, the army became highly politicized while the bureaucratic administrative machinery disintegrated. The army was torn by clan-based divisions as well, and much of the criticism of Siad Barre came from Majerteen officers (Laitin and Samatar 1987).

Siad Barre's regime became increasingly unstable. There was an attempted coup in 1978 involving Majerteen clan military officers. The coup failed, but they formed a guerrilla organization and went into rebellion, having been granted asylum by Ethiopia. Other clan-based opposition groups formed in the 1980s. Siad Barre's response to increasing instability was in part cooptation, an effort to expand the political arena through one-party elections. He also further surrounded himself with his own clan supporters. According to Laitin and Samatar (1987), Siad Barre did include members of other clans in his coalition. But he "made alliances with many Somalis from small, politically powerless subclans of the Majeerteen, Hawiye, and Isaaq, and he has rewarded them with jobs and contracts. This strategy makes the prominent members of the non-MOD clans even angrier" (p. 94). Another technique was to manipulate the clan nature of the army's officer corps, giving preference to the Marehan and Ogadeni clans. Soldiers were placed in units, under leadership, and in geographical proximity to their own clans. Consequently, by the late 1980s, there was "no clear difference between regular army units and clan militias" (Makinda 1993: 24).

By 1989, Siad Barre could no longer maintain control. Between late 1989 and 1990, Somalia slipped toward anarchy. Numerous clan-based opposition groups fought against Siad Barre, often in shifting alliances with one another, and were met with brutal response by the pro-regime military. Siad Barre was finally overthrown in January 1991, after which anarchy increased in Somalia. During the war, opposition groups had been united only by their desire to get rid of Siad Barre. Moreover, immediately after his downfall, the Hawiye clan assumed power even though the Hawiye had joined the opposition to Siad Barre only a few months earlier (Makinda 1993: 27). Thus, the stage was set for continued conflict among clans, militias, and various political and military figures in Somalia. Weapons acquired from the superpowers during the Cold War were numerous; militias abounded and were led by individuals called warlords who were not necessarily clan elders and did not necessarily have popular support. In addition, famine loomed as civil war and weather disrupted the agricultural process.

Fighting was particularly severe in Mogadishu, the capital, where Ali Mahdi Mohammed, leader of the Abgal (Hawiye) subclan-based military force, proclaimed himself interim president. This was resisted by the forces of General Mohammed Farah Aidid (from another Hawiye subclan, the Haber Gedir), which had in fact driven Siad Barre out of Mogadishu and thus considered Aidid the rightful interim president. Fighting continued, and even the so-called warlords had little control over roving bands of armed bandits. As one observer described the situation,

> Because Siad Barre had favored his own clan, the Marehan, so heavily and abused others so brutally, each rebel group vengefully sought to take Siad Barre's power for itself. . . . A Mogadishu businessman described the new

clan dynamic well: "Siad Barre dominates the psychology of this country. All clans want what his clan had." (Stevenson 1993: 142)

International Intervention

The United Nations finally recognized the growing famine and chaos in Somalia in late 1991. After the United Nations threatened to abandon Somalia completely, a ceasefire went into effect in March 1992. In April 1992, U.N. Secretary General Boutros Boutros-Ghali appointed an Algerian diplomat, Mohammed Sahnoun, as his envoy to Somalia. Sahnoun's diplomatic approach to the conflict was based on an understanding of clan politics and an effort to use clan politics to promote a negotiated settlement to the civil war. His first task was to get Somali acceptance of a peacekeeping force approved by the U.N. Security Council (which became UNOSOM I). This required delicate negotiations with clan elders and military leaders. Sahnoun was successful in getting approval for five hundred peacekeepers, but Aidid withdrew his approval in June when he became suspicious that the United Nations was favoring Ali Mahdi. By August, Sahnoun had convinced Aidid to resume approval.

The peacekeepers arrived in October but were never effective. They were supposed to establish a military presence that would ensure that food shipments from the port of Mogadishu would reach the starving. The task was impossible, given the fact that there were over one thousand armed gunmen loyal to five different subclans in the port area. They insisted on being paid to take food to the distribution points throughout Somalia. The peacekeepers were clearly outnumbered and were also prohibited from firing weapons except when fired upon, and their commander refused to deploy his forces, fearing for their safety (Stevenson 1993: 146).

Despite these many difficulties, Sahnoun's understanding of clan politics enabled him to make important progress. He "aimed to put the clan system to work for Somalia" (Stevenson 1993: 146), and by August he had the necessary cooperation from clan elders to get food delivered to many parts of Somalia. He continued to negotiate in this manner, attempting to get Aidid and other military and clan leaders to accept an additional three thousand peacekeepers, but ultimately was undone by Boutros-Ghali. In October, the United Nations announced that it would send in the additional personnel with or without consent from the Somalis, which prompted Aidid to threaten to send them home in body bags. The further alienation of Aidid in turn caused the relief operations to falter as violence again increased. Sahnoun resigned at the end of October and was replaced by Ismat Kittani, who did not have Sahnoun's understanding of the Somali clan politics.[5]

By December 1992, the Security Council approved a Unified Task Force

(UNITAF) for Somalia, to be led by the United States. After securing the ports for food deliveries and opening supply routes, this force would be replaced by a second United Nations multinational peacekeeping force that would constitute UNOSOM II. In announcing the policy to the public, President Bush stated that his goals were to create a secure environment so that food could be distributed. After that, American troops would be withdrawn. Bush insisted that U.S. troops would be there for a limited time and that the United States did not intend to "dictate political outcomes" (Bush 1992: 22). Despite these limited goals, disagreements emerged quickly about the mission. Boutros-Ghali believed that the United States had committed itself to the disarming of combatants in Somalia, whereas the U.S. commander of the UNITAF did not believe that this was a necessary element in establishing a secure environment (Makinda 1993: 71). The Bush administration also entered into the negotiating process in Somalia. Ambassador Robert Oakley was appointed special envoy in Somalia. His approach to negotiations resembled Sahnoun's in that he was determined to use the clan system as a basis for reconstruction of a political system. He also understood the importance of obtaining the agreement and working cooperation of clan elders in order to implement a stable food distribution system. He also sought to ensure every clan that no other clan would dominate. Although clan leaders agreed to this in principle in March 1993, they continued to compete for dominance, sucking the United States and the United Nations into the Somalian power game, and each major player attempted to increase his own group's power by getting the United States on his side. Aidid was notable in this respect, and for some time after the arrival of American troops, he had excellent access to the U.S. embassy.

In May 1993, UNOSOM II went into effect, and most American troops left Somalia. About four thousand U.S. soldiers remained as part of UNOSOM II. By that time, Bill Clinton replaced George Bush as president of the United States, Robert Gosende replaced Robert Oakley as special envoy, and a retired U.S. admiral, Jonathan Howe, took over as U.N. envoy.

Clinton-Administration Images

Self-Image

The national self-image evident in the Clinton administration during its first year was initially strongly positive. In fact, the similarity between early Clinton administration self-image and that of the early Cold War administrations is striking. In both eras, the United States was seen as the leading light of freedom and democracy and as having the moral obligation to promote those ideals globally. The administration explicitly recognized the parallel between the two eras. Clinton described America's global role as follows:

> Although the Cold War is over, the world remains a dangerous place. The United States cannot be the world's policeman, but we also cannot turn a blind eye to the world's problems, for they affect our own interests, and our own ideals. The U.S. must continue to play its unique role of leadership in the world. But now we can increasingly express that leadership through multilateral means such as the United Nations. . . . That was one of the lessons of Desert Storm. (Clinton 1993a: 26)

The administration also recognized that as the Cold War required a global strategy, so the post–Cold War era, beginning with Desert Storm, required a new global strategy. Anthony Lake proposed a strategy, a "strategy of enlargement."

> [Today] our interests and ideals compel us not only to be engaged, but to lead. . . . [W]e must promote democracy and market economics in the world – because it protects our interests and security and because it reflects values that are both American and universal. The successor to a doctrine of containment must be a strategy of enlargement – enlargement of the world's free community of market democracies. (Lake, 1993: 41)

Both statements reflect a very positive self-image. There is recognition that a new strategy is needed as well, and confidence that America should lead. As shown later, events in Somalia (and elsewhere) caused some decline in the strength of this positive self-image.

The Image of Somalia

Because the United States does not have a record of years of intense involvement in Somalia and because the Clinton administration is both the first post–Cold War presidency and an administration that had to make important decisions regarding Somalia during its first year in office, perceptual evidence must unfortunately be drawn from the same actions it will be used to explain. It is certainly preferable to have a separate source of perceptual information in order to avoid the dangers of tautology. A cursory examination of material from earlier American involvement in Somalia does suggest the existence of a dependent image of that country. Reports from American Public Safety Advisors in 1965, for example, described the average Somali police recruit as a primitive being, having

> no mechanical aptitude whatever and no appreciation of the value of things mechanical. . . . [Y]ou must teach them how to hold a firearm. . . . You must

not only show them how to cock and fire a pistol but must show them how to use their fingers and thumb so that this can be accomplished. To teach people with such a background how to use such things as modern firearms, cameras, tape recorders and similar equipment is a job that requires much patience and perseverance. (United States, Department of State, Airgram, Dec. 4, 1965)

The perceptual characteristics of members of the Clinton administration, including the president himself, are not as extreme but still demonstrate the central elements of the dependent image of the Third World in general and Somalia in particular: a simple, childlike culture; an ineffectual, incompetent people who must be guided by their superiors; a people who have insignificant power and can be dealt with easily; a people for whom nationalism is not important and whose political characteristics are uncomplicated, making it possible to shape and reshape their political system for them. A recent article by National Security Advisor Anthony Lake describes the current international system as a world in which the United States "has a special responsibility to nurture and promote . . . core values" including democratic institutions, free markets and the peaceful resolution of conflicts (Lake 1994: 45). After describing America in the paternalistic role, he proceeds to describe the various "problem-children" that America must deal with – the "backlash" states such as Cuba, North Korea, Iran, Iraq, and Libya. These states "choose to remain outside the family [and] assault its basic values" (p. 45). Lake describes these states as having remarkably similar characteristics. He is, in short, describing and promoting a stereotype of the dependent child gone bad, transformed into the juvenile delinquent that must be dealt with strictly and immediately.

Clinton administration perceptions of the Somali culture, political characteristics, capability, and intentions also demonstrate the elements of the dependent image. For example, although there are contrasting views concerning America's continued involvement in Somalia, there is much evidence that the Clinton administration and many U.N. officials view the indigenous Somalis as backward, uncivilized, and inferior. In a September 1993 *New York Times* article headed "U.S. Troops Fire on Somalis; Death Toll May Reach 100," Major David Stockwell, an American and the chief U.N. spokesman in Mogadishu, described the actions of the Somali soldiers as savage, uncivilized, and barbaric. "We saw all the people swarming on the vehicles as combatants," he stated. "We've seen this before. If they reach our soldiers they tear them limb from limb." The killing of Somali women and children by U.N. troops, on the other hand, was justified as a "last-ditch, last resort effort to protect the United Nations troops" (Gordon, *New York Times*, Sept. 10, 1993). Stockwell, however, admitted there was a great deal of uncertainty surrounding the attack, particularly regarding the issue of whether the Somali women were actually armed.

Peacekeeping actions are described as necessary responses, whereas the actions of the Somali troops are viewed as beastlike and ruthless. Moreover, American policy makers are frequently slow to comment on U.N. and American actions, often calling for a more careful evaluation of the events. Assessments of Somali actions, on the other hand, are usually spontaneous, reflecting a strong and simple image of the Somalis. In response to the killing of women and children by fire from U.S. helicopters in Mogadishu, Defense Secretary Les Aspin was careful to avoid expressing any criticism of American actions. "Let's wait until I know more about what actually happened," he told reporters. Responses to reports of Somalis parading the remaining body parts of Americans, however, were not as reserved. In essence, it appears that such actions actually helped to confirm the existing, uncivilized image of the indigenous people. "If they are bragging and boasting, if it's true, these people are barbaric and animalistic," Stockwell asserted (Schmitt, *New York Times*, Sept. 26, 1993).

This perception of Somali culture tends to be thematic among U.S. policy makers. Senator Robert Byrd, a West Virginia Democrat, openly expressed his disdain concerning American involvement in Somalia. Arguing that Congress never approved of U.S. participation in the African conflict, he describes the crisis as unworthy of American military sacrifice. "I find it difficult to believe it is possible to muster a consensus here, or in the country at large, that such an effort is worth any price in American blood" he stated (Gordon, *New York Times*, Sept. 10, 1993).

Even those who advocate American involvement in Somalia express condescending motives for such intervention. Rejecting Congress's proposal to withdraw from Somalia, President Clinton's stated reasons for continued involvement there clearly indicated his desire to enhance America's prestige through its savior role in Somalia. "If the United States left Somalia now, our leadership in world affairs would be undermined at the very time when people are looking to America to help promote peace and freedom in the post–Cold War world, and all around the world, aggressors, thugs and terrorists will conclude that the best way to get us to change our policies is to kill our people," Clinton said (Apple, *New York Times*, Oct. 8, 1993). (The implication that Somalia's conflict is caused by some such ilk is also evident here.) Parallel to a parent rendering punishment on a child who explains his or her obligation to chastisement with the phrase, "it hurts me as much as it hurts you," Clinton asserted that the halting of United States operations in Somalia too soon would undermine his presidency and would be viewed as a sign of American weakness (Gordon, *New York Times*, Sept. 10, 1993). As the punishment of the child is expected to prevent or at least curtail future family disruptions, so Clinton contends that America's role in Somalia is necessary for international stability.

The Clinton administration's childlike image of Somalia's socioeconomic conditions, political structure, and resulting policies became clear as the events surrounding the crisis unfolded. The descriptions and explanations of the political situation in Somalia have not been founded on an assessment of central elements of Somali politics already described, nor has there been any public expression of an analysis of the impact of the Siad Barre regime on the political context. Rather than evaluating this as an extremely complex civil war, the administration described the crisis as the result of some bad behavior by some power-hungry individuals. As one official explained, a "constant resort to intimidation is the mother's milk of Somali politics" (Lorch, *New York Times*, Oct. 6, 1993). In June 1993, the President noted that the American effort to restore peace in Somalia had been largely successful, but "there remains a small but dangerous minority of Somalis who are determined to provoke terror and chaos" (Clinton 1993a).

A simplified perception of political conditions can also be seen in the administration's effort to determine who were the "good guys" and "bad guys" and the subsequent effort to remove the bad element from the scene. It was not long before General Aidid was picked out as the bad guy responsible for the mess in Somalia. A State Department spokesperson said, "what we are seeing is a very small faction of the Somalis led by General [Aidid]. He's not a hero; he's basically a thug" (United States, State Department press briefing, June 14, 1993). Having determined that Aidid was the problem, the administration sought to exclude him from negotiations for a political solution.

The administration's depiction of America's role and responsibility in this crisis adds evidence to the point that Somali political realities were viewed in a simplified and contemptuous way. Clinton adamantly advocated the presence of American troops in Somalia until there was more evidence that the Somalis were capable of independent government. To this end, he argued that the Somalis should be supported until they are in a position to "take control of their own affairs in peace and dignity and without starvation and murder" (Ifill, *New York Times*, Sept. 18, 1993). In June 1993, a number of Somali civilians were killed by U.N. forces, prompting widespread anger toward the United States and accusations that it was acting as an imperialist. Clinton's response reveals his dependent image: "I still believe that most people in the country think that we came in there, we ended starvation, we ended brutalization, we ended violence, *we opened up the country again to the beginnings of civilization*" (italics added, Clinton 1993b). American responsibilities required behavior modification of the bad elements in Somalia. President Clinton reportedly indicated that "the trick" to policing Somalia was learning "how to do it without in any way rewarding the kind of behavior that we have seen that could spread among all the other warlords who have been essentially playing by the rules" (Ifill, *New York Times*, Sept. 18, 1993). A solution to the conflict would presumably be one that teaches America's dependent children in Somalia and elsewhere the rules of behavior in the post–Cold War arena dominated by the United States. This sentiment is echoed in a *Newsweek* editorial that asserts that the Somalia campaign "was meant to be a test case for the post–Cold War world." The Somalia crisis is described as "localized violence quelled by a multinational force for which the United States provided the muscle" (Elliott, *Newsweek*, Oct. 18, 1993).

Having argued that the image of Somalia was a dependent image, a couple of caveats are in order. First, there were some individuals periodically involved in the policy process who did not share the dependent image. Both Mohammed Sahnoun and Robert Oakley (probably to a lesser extent) understood and operated in accordance with the extraordinary complexity of Somali politics. These two individuals were not involved in the development of Clinton administration policies, however, although Oakley was brought in to salvage that policy after seventeen American soldiers died on October 3, 1993.

Second, there is evidence that members of the Clinton administration are struggling to understand why they went wrong in Somalia. In the process, there appears to be some nonconscious questioning of the image of Somalia as well as the American self-image. This questioning may hold the key to long-term changes in problem representation.

The Impact of Images on Policy

The Bush administration left office in the midst of the humanitarian relief phase of UNITAF, thereby avoiding the inevitable question of what to do after food began to reach the starving but before peace returned to Somalia. These most difficult policy questions were dumped in the lap of the Clinton administration, which responded to them by expanding America's goals in Somalia. Viewing Somalia as the opportunity to set a precedent for America's post–Cold War international role, the United States pressured the Security Council to adopt Resolution 814, which committed the organization to pacify Somalia militarily and then to engage in nation building. According to the U.S. Permanent Representative to the United Nations, Madeline Albright, "with this resolution, we will embark on an unprecedented enterprise aimed at nothing less than the restoration of an entire country as a proud, functioning and viable member of the community of nations" (quoted in Bolton 1994: 62).

The United States and the United Nations were now committed to nation building in Somalia. In June 1993, the military arm of the policy increased in importance when twenty-three Pakistani peacekeepers were killed in an ambush attributed to the Aidid forces. The United Nations, again with American support, passed another resolution endorsing the arrest of General Aidid. The abstract goal of nation building was matched and eventually surpassed by the goal of catching Aidid. The search lasted for one hundred days, and in the process the United States was lambasted by Aidid and many other Somalis for the imperialist nature of its actions.

As the summer of 1993 proceeded, the hunt for Aidid often brought American troops into combat. In September, American troops killed a hundred Somalis, intensifying Somali anger toward the United States. Meanwhile, American and Italian officials disagreed about policy as America pressed for Aidid's capture and the Italians advocated a political solution through negotiations with Aidid's rivals (Sciolino, *New York Times*, Sept. 12, 1993c). Negotiations among various subclan leaders were under way, but without Aidid. In late September, the Clinton administration expressed satisfaction in the establishment of a number of local district councils to govern communities in Somalia (Schmitt, *New York Times*, Sept. 26, 1993). American military forces were supported by the introduction of Rangers and Delta Commandos in late August. U.S. envoy Gosende asked for more troops to enable them to conduct weapons searches. He also encouraged the administration not to negotiate with Aidid because he was a terrorist (Gordon and Cushman, *New York Times*, Oct. 18, 1993). Nevertheless, Congress was increasingly displeased with the continued presence of American forces, and the Clinton administration began to reconsider limitations on its future role in U.N. peacekeeping operations.

Disaster struck in late September and again in early October. In September, a Black Hawk helicopter was shot down, killing three Americans. On October 3, seventeen American servicemen were killed after a failed attack on a location where Aidid was supposed to be. In between these events, the administration began to move away from the goal of capturing Aidid and toward a new goal, a "political" solution that involved "isolating [Aidid] and creating a political structure without him" (Sciolino, *New York Times*, Sept. 28, 1993a).

It is clear that the Clinton administration was changing course before the loss of American troops on October 3. In late September, the State Department had completed a classified new policy paper that Secretary of State Warren Christopher presented to Boutros-Ghali. The paper suggested that a negotiated solution be sought but that Aidid be excluded from a conference on national reconciliation. The paper also suggested a number of public relations options that would reduce criticism of the United States by reducing the obviousness of its role in Somalia (Sciolino, *New York Times*, Sept. 28,

1993). At the same time, the administration insisted it was not abandoning the military policy. A State Department spokesperson stated, "a military presence in Somalia is necessary to maintain the type of security that will prevent Somalia from slipping back into the anarchy and chaos" (Sciolino, *New York Times*, Oct. 5, 1993b). Meanwhile, the Pentagon was reported to be upset at the abandonment of the goal of capturing Aidid.

After the October 3 raid, Clinton at once sent additional American forces to Somalia and set a six-month deadline for complete withdrawal. Robert Oakley was sent back to Somalia to broker a reconciliation, indicating another slight shift in policy in that Oakley had criticized the U.S. effort to keep Aidid out of a negotiated solution. The administration continued to insist that the United States would not hold direct talks with Aidid but did finally acknowledge that a solution was not possible without Aidid's participation. Nevertheless, the administration refused to state that Aidid would not be arrested. The administration also advocated a "regional" solution that consisted of an African investigative force to assess Aidid's culpability in the peacekeepers' deaths as well as an African and Islamic coalition to devise strategy for preventing a return to chaos in Somalia after the U.S. departure.

The direction of American policy toward Somalia can be understood as a result of the image of Somalia and the Clinton administration's self-image. First, the desire to continue and expand the task set forth by the Bush administration is clearly an outgrowth of self-image. Combined with the recognition that a post–Cold War strategy was needed, and using Desert Storm as a model, the Clinton administration followed a pattern of action that could have come straight from the Cold War policies of the 1950s. America, being superior, would use its strength – that is, military power – to rescue the needy and would then teach them the democratic way.

One of the most interesting aspects of this process is the unreflective adoption of military power as the instrument with which goals would be achieved. And the choice was truly unreflective. Reviewing policies throughout the spring and summer of 1993, it is clear that the United States devoted itself to the capture of General Aidid. It pushed for the Security Council resolution to arrest Aidid; Clinton's public remarks on Somalia emphasized the goal of capturing Aidid; and the United States had no political strategy for negotiations. That is evident in the dispute between the United States and Italy during this time. Moreover, U.S. envoy Gosende was a supporter of the effort to capture Aidid, and he did not take on the mediator role adopted by Robert Oakley.

In October, when the administration was called to task for pursuing a purely military policy in Somalia, it appeared confused and quite defensive in its justification of that policy. It seemed that the administration itself had not recognized the extent to which it had no policy other than military defeat (i.e., capture) of General Aidid. A State Department spokesman tried to explain U.S. policy as being both military and political, saying ''a military presence in Somalia is necessary to maintain the type of security that will prevent Somalia from slipping back into the anarchy and chaos'' (Sciolino, *New York Times*, Oct. 5, 1993b). A flurry of finger pointing erupted in the administration as various individuals tried to blame others for the policy. Secretary of Defense Aspin blamed Jonathan Howe for insisting on more and more military force; Howe responded that he had ''never asked for anything that American and Turkish leadership did not want'' (Gordon and Cushman, *New York Times*, Oct. 18, 1993). Christopher claimed that policy details were the responsibility of subcabinet officials, yet other officials claimed that Clinton, Aspin, and Lake had approved sending the Rangers to Somalia for the purpose of capturing Aidid. Clinton blamed the United Nations for the policy, conveniently ignoring the fact that the United States helped draft it (Friedman, *New York Times*, Oct. 15, 1993).

The change in the administration's approach to Somalia in late September may have reflected a diminution of the strongly positive self-image, at least for some officials. After the October fiasco, there was more evidence of such a change. News reports indicated that Somalia was supposed to be the test case for a post–Cold War policy that had now failed. The failure would reduce American activity in international crises (Engleberg, *New York Times*, Oct. 11, 1993). It was also reported that Clinton's team saw themselves as ''pioneers groping their way toward new principles,'' hardly the gang-buster self-perception evident in earlier statements (Apple, *New York Times*, Oct. 13, 1993b).[6] One State Department official explained: ''It's not easy to define our national interests, to decide when to intervene, to see all the consequences of intervention, to know when to declare victory and end the intervention. And there's no up side. You win, and nobody in the general public cares much; you lose American lives and the country demands that you pull your horns in'' (quoted in Apple, *New York Times*, Oct. 13, 1993b).

American policy is also consistent with the dependent image of Somalia. The idea that the cause of the conflict was a single bad warlord, Aidid, is one outcome of seeing Somalia's political realities in a simplified way. The administration's approach to a ''political'' solution, once one was attempted, also bore the impact of the dependent image. Christopher's proposal for a political solution consisted of negotiations between different clans with help from other Africans. Christopher requested the United Nations to convene a meeting of the various faction leaders in a move toward national reconciliation. The proposal excluded Aidid from those negotiations and, presumably, from the political process after reconciliation. The United States would search for a political solution that would permit it to create a political structure without Aidid. In fact, his arrest was still a goal. The U.S. refusal to bring

Aidid and his people into the negotiations indicates that U.S. officials still did not understand the essence of clan politics or of Aidid's position as a militia leader but not a clan elder. The proposal also failed to acknowledge the extent to which Aidid's popularity had increased *because of* the American efforts to exclude him from the political process and to capture him.

The inclusion of other Africans in the negotiating process is another result of the dependent image of Somalia and Africa. Christopher said, "We're going to try to use African leaders' assistance to provide an African solution to what is really an African problem" (Engleberg, *New York Times*, Oct. 11, 1993). Why and how is this an African problem? It appears that this characterization is a result of similarities in complexion rather than an assessment of the implications of the Somali crisis for the rest of Africa. The idea was not explained in terms of the impact of decades of poverty on conflict in Africa. The poverty, in turn, was not explained as a result of the global inequality that has prevented an expanding resource pie and, consequently, the luxury of political stability. Nor was Somalia's war explained as a long-term result of efforts to realize the goal of a Greater Somalia combined with superpower competition. All of these explanations would have related Somalia's crisis to problems throughout Africa, but these arguments were not the basis for identifying this as an African problem.

Moreover, had Christopher developed his political plan with Somali political realities in mind, he hardly would have included Ethiopia as a mediator in Somalia's tragedy given Ethiopia's status as Somalia's enemy and a country responsible for denying the realization of Greater Somalia. In short, the administration's September movement from a military to a political solution was only a tactical change. It did not reflect any new and improved understanding of the fundamentals of the causes of this conflict nor other Third World conflicts.

On the other hand, after the October killings, the administration did reconsider its exclusion of Aidid and may have started down the long path of image change. Oakley was no doubt influential in this, and Oakley's image had always been different from the prevailing one in the Clinton administration. Shortly after October 3, Oakley argued that it was not possible to pursue political negotiations and Aidid's capture at the same time. Clinton asked Oakley to return to Somalia as envoy and apparently gave him permission to negotiate as he saw fit. By October 11, Oakley had conducted meetings with Aidid's clan elders and argued "you do not conduct any kind of diplomacy without meeting with all the clans" (Engleberg, *New York Times*, Oct. 11, 1993). By October 15, Clinton was also expressing a new view of Somalia: "We have no interest in keeping any clan or sub-clan or group of Somalis out of the political process affecting the future of their people. *The clan structure seems to be the dominant structure in the country*'' (Friedman, *New York Times*, Oct. 15, 1993, italics added).

Post–Cold War Images and Problem Representation

The final questions we must consider here are: Has image change occurred in this case? If so, has it resulted in problem-representation change? As noted, some indicators of image change are evident. As the image weakened, the administration's tactics shifted. A policy that resembled the typical American approach to Third World crises during the Cold War eventually turned into a policy in which the United States appeared to be willing to permit Somalis to restructure their own polity. Similarly, the Clinton administration has become more cognizant of and concerned about Somali hostility to Americans and America. This too indicates image slippage in that they have moved from assuming that Americans are viewed as saviors to understanding that they may be despised as imperialists. American policy today appears to be most strongly affected by the diminution of the positive self-image. That would explain the decision to get out of Somalia rather than change tactics and try again. The perception seems to be that we cannot fix this and we cannot see why we should try, not that our approach was wrong and that we can and should develop a winning approach. This case offers some opportunity to speculate about questions raised at the beginning of this chapter concerning the order of change in image, tactic selection, and problem representation. What we see here is that images and tactical-preference change seems to go together. But change in problem representation is not yet evident. The Clinton administration has not explained Somalia's tragedy in terms that reflect a new post–Cold War interpretation of ethno-nationalist conflicts. Where are the policy papers asking how it is possible that a people with intensely held national identity, an identity strong enough to produce wars to achieve Greater Somalia, could end up in a civil war such as this? Where are the policy papers examining dual identities strong enough to both create and destroy a nation? Who is wondering what the impact of the Cold War was on this kind of conflict? If the administration had developed a new problem representation for conflicts such as this, it would be asking those questions.

The U.S.-backed approach to negotiations and reconciliation appears to focus on cognitive elements alone, another indication of little change in problem representation. Talks centering around institution building and power sharing through elections do not address the central affective dynamics. Those dynamics could be addressed by using the identity characteristics of Somali society. The common identity, Somali nationalism, may still be an affectively viable foundation for national reconciliation. In comparison with wars such as that in the former Yugoslavia, the prospects for Somalia should be quite favorable because there is a strong national identity. Instead, affective elements in this conflict appear to be regarded as another outgrowth of Somali inferiority.

American policy makers have not publicly discussed the complexities of Somali politics nor have they used this case as a basis for a post–Cold War analysis of the causes of violence and war. There is no evidence of a debate, internal or otherwise, about whether all enemies are perceived the same, comparing the Cold War conflict between the United States and the Soviet Union with conflicts between Somali clans or Bosnian Muslims and Serbs. Instead, there appears to be an intellectual vacuum. Americans can no longer explain instability and war as a consequence of Soviet subversion. That is not a problem as long as they have not lost the dependent image of Third World countries. Through that image, they can explain instability as a consequence of anything other than the tendency of the dependent image state to behave irrationally and foolishly.

In general, there is little in this case to indicate that American policy makers have developed a complex assessment of post–Cold War conflicts. The clearest indicator of such change would be the identification of the potential for similar conflict in the United States, and that kind of analogy has not been made. In fact, it may be that American policy makers are incorporating ethno-nationalist conflicts into the dependent image as another behavioral pattern to be expected. Meg Greenfield's recent assessment of American perceptions of post–Cold War violence describes this nicely. She argues that the American view of current conflicts is largely one

> of condescension and nowhere is that more the case than when we speak of "ethnic conflicts." People in Washington believe those words alone dispose of the argument. To say a dispute (or a war) is an "ethnic conflict" in this city is akin to saying the children are fighting again (exasperated smile) or . . . that any conflict among women is a "catfight." The implication is that there cannot possibly be a rational or moral basis for the dispute or any dimension to it that should engage us on one side or the other. (Greenfield, *Newsweek,* March 14, 1994)

In the case examined here, the image started to disintegrate, and Somali politics appears to be better understood as a consequence. But there is no indication that a general lesson is being learned and that policy makers are engaged in problem-representation change. It may be that problem representation is unlikely to change without the complete removal of a country from the image, which has not happened in Somalia and will not happen, because the U.S. forces have left the country. Moreover, this case may reveal another possible pattern – one in which, with a weaker self-image, there is less incentive to change problem representation, because it is easier psychologically and politically to pack one's bags and go home than it is to understand reality.

Notes

1 This argument must be considered in the context of the theoretically based definition of an enemy image (see R. Cottam 1977; Herrmann 1985; and M. Cottam 1986). This is an image of a type of state *equal* to the perceiver's state in capabilities, harmful in terms of intentions and motivations, equal though reprehensible in cultural sophistication, and monolithic in domestic decision-making structure.

2 This may also help us understand why so many Americans never considered the possibility that the Soviet Union was not an "evil empire" during the Cold War given the enormous peace overtures and internal changes when the Soviet Union called for an end to the Cold War. Instead of suspecting that their perceptions of the Soviets may have been incorrect, they assumed that the United States forced the Soviets to change their stripes and become different people.

3 According to Fiske and Taylor, "affect subsumes preferences, evaluations, moods, and emotions. Preferences and evaluations are simple, long-term positive or negative reactions to a target, whereas moods are simple, long-term positive or negative feelings without a specific target. Emotion refers to the richer variety of affective states, which may be intense and short-term. Various efforts to reflect the richness of emotion have used dimensional analysis, prototype models and social role approaches" (1991: 415).

4 This requires further elaboration. Image models have described the ideal-typical enemy image as that of a state perceived as equal in capability, equal (although different and disliked) in culture, evil and harmful in intentions, and ruled by a monolithic cabal of policy makers. Both the Soviet Union and Hitler's Germany fit the image in the extreme. Japan, during the Cold War, did not, however. It was perceived to have many of the enemy attributes, but the American perception of the Japanese was filled with cultural contempt (see Dower 1986). The same could be said of China during the 1960s. This could be an indication that each was placed in a different image, for example, the dependent image of the enemy. Or it could mean that there are either variations in the enemy image or a natural perceptual cross-section where the enemy and dependent images of the enemy merge. Today's image may be significantly different, in any case, and the enemy image in these conflicts may be different in the combination of attributes evident.

5 The conflict between Sahnoun and Boutros-Ghali was multidimensional. On the one hand, Boutros-Ghali was eager to establish U.N. leadership in this conflict and envisioned a military intervention under U.N. control that would convince those Western countries that continued to ignore Somalia that a military response was necessary as well as establish a post–Cold War role for the United Nations. Sahnoun, on the other hand, saw all things in the context of Somali politics and believed that any step taken without consent from the Somali factional leaders would be a mistake. Sahnoun also blamed the U.N. bureaucrats for undermining his negotiating efforts, and Boutros-Ghali, faced with a critical Sahnoun and threatened

bureaucracy, got rid of Sahnoun. At the same time, Somalis were highly suspicious of Boutros-Ghali, in part because Aidid had helped spread the rumor that Boutros-Ghali was using his position as Secretary General to further alleged Egyptian ambitions concerning Somali territory. Sahnoun's removal could only have fed these suspicions. See Stevenson (1993) and Makinda (1993) for further details.
6 Anthony Lake, on the other hand, appears not to have changed at all.

References

Apple, R. W., Jr. (1993a). "Clinton Doubling U.S. Force in Somalia." *New York Times,* Oct. 8.
   (1993b). "Policing a Global Village." *New York Times,* Oct. 13.
Bolton, John, "Wrong Turn in Somalia." *Foreign Affairs,* January–February, 56–66.
Bush, George (1992). Speech to the Nation, December 4, 1992. *Foreign Policy Bulletin, 3,* 21–23.
Clinton, Bill (1993a). President's Weekly Radio Address, June 12, 1993. *Foreign Policy Bulletin, 4,* 26–27.
   (1993b). Excerpts from President's Press Conference, June 15, 1993. *Foreign Policy Bulletin, 4,* 27.
Cottam, Martha (1986). *Foreign Policy Decision Making: The Influence of Cognition.* Boulder: Westview Press.
   (1992). "The Carter Administration's Policy toward Nicaragua: Images, Goals and Tactics." *Political Science Quarterly, 107,* 123–146.
   (1994). *Images and Intervention: United States' Policies Toward Latin America.* Pittsburgh: University of Pittsburgh Press, 1994.
Cottam, Richard (1977). *Foreign Policy Motivation.* Pittsburgh: University of Pittsburgh Press.
Dower, John (1986). *War without Mercy: Race and Power in the Pacific War.* New York: Pantheon Books.
Elliott, Michael (1993). "The Making of a Fiasco." *Newsweek,* Oct. 18.
Engleberg, Stephen (1993). "U.S. Envoy Meets Clan Leader's Kin in Somali Capital." *New York Times,* Oct. 11.
Fiske, Susan, and Steven Neuberg (1989). "Category-based and individuating processes as a function of information and motivation: Evidence from our laboratory." In Daniel Bar-Tal, Carl F Graumann, Arie W. Kruglanski, and Wolfgang Stroebe (eds.), *Stereotyping and Prejudice: Changing Conceptions.* New York: Springer-Verlag.
Fiske, Susan, and Shelley Taylor (1991). *Social Cognition* (2nd ed.). New York: McGraw Hill.
Friedman, Thomas (1993). "Somalia Buzzwords: 'Constructive Ambiguity'." *New York Times,* Oct. 15.
Gordon, Michael (1993). "US Troops Fire on Somalis; Death Toll May Reach 100." *New York Times,* Sept. 10.
Gordon, Michael, and John Cushman Jr. (1993). "After Supporting Hunt for Aidid, U.S. Is Blaming U.N. for Losses." *New York Times,* Oct. 18.
Greenfield, Meg (1994). "Falling Back on Fatalism." *Newsweek,* Mar. 14.
Herrmann, Richard (1985). *Perceptions and Behavior in Soviet Foreign Policy.* Pittsburgh: University of Pittsburgh Press.

Hewstone, Miles (1989). "Changing stereotypes with disconfirming information." In Daniel Bar-Tal, Carl Graumann, Arie Kruglanski, and Wolfgang Stroebe (eds.), *Stereotyping and Prejudice: Changing Conceptions*. New York: Springer-Verlag.

Hirshberg, Matthew (1993). "The Self-Perpetuating National Self-Image: Cognitive Biases in Perceptions of International Interventions." *Political Psychology, 10,* 77–98.

Hogg, Michael, and Dominic Abrams (1988). *Social Identifications: A Social Psychology of Intergroup Relations and Group Processes*. New York: Routledge.

Ifill, Gwen (1993). "President Calls American Role in Somalia Necessary for Stability." *New York Times,* Sept. 18.

Jalali, Rita, and Seymour Martin Lipset (1992–93). "Racial and Ethnic Conflicts: A Global Perspective." *Political Science Quarterly, 107:* 585–606.

Jervis, Robert (1986). "Cognition and political behavior." In Richard Lau and David Sears (eds.), *Political Cognition: The 19th Annual Carnegie Symposium on Cognition*. Hillsdale, NJ: Lawrence Erlbaum.

———— (1989). "Political psychology – Some challenges and opportunities." *Political Psychology, 10,* 481–495.

Laitin, David, and Said Samatar (1987). *Somalia: Nation in Search of a State*. Boulder, CO: Westview Press.

Lake, Anthony (1993). Speech at Johns Hopkins University, Sept. 21, in *Foreign Policy Bulletin, 4:* 39–46.

———— (1994). "Confronting Backlash States." *Foreign Affairs*, March/April.

Lorch, Donatella (1993). "Somali General Denounces Talks." *New York Times*, Oct. 6.

Makinda, Samuel (1993). *Seeking Peace from Chaos: Humanitarian Intervention in Somalia*. Boulder, CO: Lynne Reinner.

Montieth, Margo, Patricia Devine, and Julia Zuwerink (1993). "Self-Directed versus Other-Directed Affect as a Consequence of Prejudice-Related Discrepancies." *Journal of Personality and Social Psychology, 64,* 198–210.

Schmitt, Eric (1993). "U.S. Vows to Stay in Somalia Despite an Attack." *New York Times,* Sept. 26.

Sciolino, Elaine (1993a). "Pentagon Changes Its Somalia Goals as Effort Falters." *New York Times,* Sept. 28.

———— (1993b). "Somalia Puzzle: What Is the American Strategy?" *New York Times,* Oct. 5.

———— (1993c). "Somali Warlord Is Reported to Want Peace Talks." *New York Times,* Sept. 12.

Stevenson, Jonathan (1993). "Hope Restored in Somalia?" *Foreign Policy, 91,* 138–154.

Stroessner, Steven, and Diane Mackie (1993). "Affect and perceived variability." In Diane Mackie and David Hamilton (eds.), *Affect, Cognition, and Stereotyping: Interactive Processes in Group Perception*. New York: Academic Press.

Touval, Saadia (1963). *Somali Nationalism: International Politics and the Drive for Unity in the Horn of Africa* (pp. 85–86). Cambridge, MA: Harvard University Press.

United States (1965). Department of State. Airgram from USAID Mogadiscio, U-513 Report (End of Tour). Public Safety 649-11-710-018. Dec. 4.

———— (1993). Department of State. Excerpts from Department of State press briefing, Jun. 14. *Foreign Policy Bulletin, 4:* 27.

Walker, Stephen (1988). "The Impact of Personality Structure and Cognitive Processes upon American Foreign Policy Decisions." Paper presented at the American Political Science Association Meeting, Washington, D.C., September.

Wilder, David (1993). "The role of anxiety in facilitating stereotypic judgments of outgroup behavior." In Diane Mackie and David Hamilton (eds.), *Affect, Cognition, and Stereotyping: Interactive Processes in Group Perception*. New York: Academic Press.

PART III

EMPIRICAL ANALYSIS

Problem Representations and Political Expertise: Evidence from "Think Aloud" Protocols of South African Elite

Helen E. Purkitt

Introduction

The main focus of this study is cognitive processes of political elite with particular emphasis on the ideas of expertness and problem representation. Generally speaking, political expertise is ascribed to policy makers – elected, appointed, or anointed – but few efforts are made to map the cognition of these people, including their problem representations. As Beasley (this volume), Dyson and Purkitt (1986a), Voss (this volume), Purkitt (1991), and Sylvan and Thorson (1989, 1992) note, public policy decision making emanates from a "pre-decision" phase – a phase in which policy makers develop an initial representation of a problem and use the representation to understand and solve the problem. During this pre-decisional phase, an understanding of the form and structure of a problem is developed (Paige 1958; Pruitt 1965; Snyder and Paige 1958). This understanding affects subsequent stages of decision-making activity.

In politics, decision activity is often described as a function of experience where decision makers and analysts are seen as experts while those not meeting some minimal criteria are seen as novices. Research on problem-solving behavior and studies of differences between experts and novices in a variety of judgment and decision tasks provide a body of findings about the relative abilities of experts and novices in subjective decisional tasks. The standard practice in these decisional-task studies is to compare experts with novices. While controversy remains regarding the alleged superior performance of experts in comparison with novices (see for example, Anderson 1988; Chan 1982; Einhorn, 1974; Einhorn and Hogarth 1978, 1981; Gaeth and Shanteau 1984; Purkitt and Dyson 1990; Shanteau 1987, 1989; Slovic, 1972; Tetlock, 1992), a comparison of experts and novices is largely absent from political science research.

Although attentiveness to the importance of the differential knowledge, cognitive schemata, experiences, and cultures of different types of "experts" for understanding variation in political analysis and choice behavior exists (see, e.g., George 1980, 1993), the nature of political expertise seen in terms of variations in cognitive activities and problem-solving abilities has received little attention. (For exceptions to this general trend, see Anderson 1987, 1988; Beasley, this volume; Dyson and Purkitt 1986a; Sylvan, Ostrom, and Gannon 1994; Sylvan and Haddad, this volume; Purkitt and Dyson 1988, 1990; Voss and Dorsey 1992; Voss, Greene, Post, and Penner 1983; Voss and Post 1988). This deficiency may derive from a belief about the superiority of expertness in political problem solving. Unfortunately for the assumption, if political choice is ideologically driven, the effects of expertness may be ambiguous.

Whereas an elite may disagree among themselves, they unite to formulate and implement public policies on behalf of a larger group. To a great extent, elite discussions and decisions about political policies evolve from argumentation (see, e.g., Boynton 1991; Gannon, this volume; Voss, Wiley, Kennet, Schooler, and Silfies, this volume). Each particular elite view is often based on prior beliefs and the views of selected special interests. To understand political choices, researchers increasingly focus on how elite represent or frame political issues; the ideas elite consider to make decisions become the basic intellectual fodder of public choice.

A common assumption of cognitively grounded political decision studies recognizes that social, informational, and contextual processes help form a nexus of shared representations for solving society's political problems. Humans, however, are error-prone information processors, even while they exude supreme confidence about their cognitive and judgmental abilities in their problem-solving quests. Humans maintain high levels of confidence in the merits of their problem-solving abilities, despite error-proneness, by holding preferred "framing" of political issues, bolstered by shared scripts about political reality.

Elite use shared "frames" and associated scripts to formulate beliefs and preferences about policy and the role of government in society. The frames apply symbolic thinking to public policy making by stressing cultural values to highlight a culture's virtue and focus attention away from issues; this helps elite gain support for a policy preference without factual analysis. The adversarial-advocacy style of political problem solving occurs mainly because elite differ about the root characteristics of problems and their solutions. Adversarial-advocacy allows ideology and bombastic diatribes to substitute for issue analyses. Consequently, discourse reflects disagreements over preferred framing of key political issues, framing that determines activity during subsequent stages of choice processes – from information search to a final decision (see, e.g., Boynton 1991, 1987; Burstein and Berbaum 1983; Gannon, this volume).

Political scientists summarize the content and structure of relevant cognition by using concepts such as belief systems, operational codes, or schema. Researchers understand that while prior convictions play a key role in structuring the framing of problems in specific decision contexts, the evidence indicates that people are also responsive to the demand characteristics of the task (see, e.g., Carroll and Payne 1976; Hayes 1964, 1981; Hayes and Simon 1976, 1977; Larson 1994; Kahneman, Slovic, and Tversky 1982; Nisbett and Ross 1980; Nisbett and Wilson 1977; Nygren, this volume; Payne, Bettman, and Johnson 1993; Simon and Hayes 1976; Sylvan and Haddad, this volume; Tversky and Kahneman 1974, 1981, 1983).

The malleability of humans as adaptive decision makers is readily apparent in experimental task settings. In experimental contexts, people acting alone or as members of a group repeatedly demonstrate that, if asked, they will solve a problem or reach a decision. But the experimental research also documents that subjects often function more like domain-specific novices than experts in seeking to solve the types of ill-structured problems found in political-choice settings. This image of individuals as highly adaptive decision makers suggests that people from a variety of backgrounds will often proceed to find a "solution" to a problem without first developing a representation of the problem and often do so with only minimal understanding of the problem or task (Dyson and Purkitt 1986a,b; Voss et al. 1983; Voss and Post 1988).

The process of finding a solution or solving a complex problem under conditions of uncertainty often involves a messy and murky problem-solving process characterized by cycles or a series of verbal loops more approximate to trial-and-error learning than to logical reasoning (Burstein and Berbaum 1983; Gallhofer, Saris, and Schellenkens 1988; Purkitt and Dyson 1988). As Voss (this volume) notes, problem solvers grappling with ill-structured problems typically employ a number of weak methods to develop a problem representation and solution. An ill-structured problem representation frequently emerges from an effort to generate options or reach a decision. It is difficult to determine whether the ill-structured representations derive from a lack of requisite knowledge, belief interference, lack of relevant experience, or an inadequate domain-specific data base. What we do know is that problem representations do not lead a decision maker to apply an appropriate problem-solving logic or to develop a fully useful problem solution.

In my study, reported on later in the chapter, a "think aloud" exercise was used that asked each subject to construct an initial problem representation and solution to a vague problem of interest to the participants. The subjects had to form responses on the basis of working memory. The task, like other "advise and recommend" situations in politics, required subjects to develop a cognitive representation of a complex political reality using on-line processing capabilities.

By examining the concurrent verbalizations, which are assumed to be valid indicators of the on-line processing of twelve individuals, it was possible to obtain data about similarities and differences in the problem-solving behavior of these individual members of a political elite. This data was designed to address two related questions about the problem-solving behaviors of political elite: (1) Does the degree of experience with similar cognitive tasks (i.e., domain expertise) influence subsequent problem-solving behavior? (2) Are there commonalities in the structure of these individual problem representations that are tied to the basic information-processing constraints affecting everyone when they engage in on-line information processing within the confines of working memory?

By empirically examining rather than asserting the linkages among such fundamental concepts as social class, ethnicity, substantive expertise, and cognitive processes, we may begin to enhance understanding of how shared background characteristics and personal experiences relate to shared mental representations of specific political problems. Because problem representations in political decision-making settings are socially constructed products (Sylvan and Thorson 1992), we need to understand better exactly how, if at all, background characteristics like class and ethnicity affect the structure and content of an individual's cognitive representation. Once we have a more thorough understanding of the linkages between individual characters, personal experiences, political beliefs, and the construction of problem representations by individuals, we should be able to understand better how and why a certain problem representation gets accepted as an adequate representation of the immediate problem at hand among political decision-making groups.

When policy makers meet in small groups to reach agreement on a shared representation of the problem and a preferred course of action, each participant operates under similar information-processing constraints. These cognitive constraints are created by the limited amount of information that may be processed and retained in working memory. Evidence suggests that information-processing constraints of working memory affect how political problems are analyzed and decisions made both individually and in a group context (see, e.g., Hever 1978; Purkitt 1991, 1992; Simon 1973, 1983, 1985; Sylvan and Haddad, this volume; Rubino-Hallman, this volume, 1993; Taber, this volume; Wallsten 1980). Because information-processing constraints influence the structure and content of problem representations, from these results we should be able to generalize to other political contexts where the nature of the task requires individuals to use on-line processing of information in order to construct a representation of an ill-structured problem. Research over a number of domains, however, may assist in comprehending political problem-solving activity.

Experts as Problem Solvers

In studying experts and expertness in problem-solving activities, a population may be divided into experts (elite, policy makers, or their advisors) and novices (citizens or mass publics). Typically, experts and expertness represent the people and the decision behavior one expects to find in important places within social, political, and economic systems.

In politics, experts are differential from novices on cognitive or knowledge grounds and by position. Political scientists ask whether a person has knowledge of local or national affairs, and whether they think of politics in abstract terms or mainly on the basis of personal experiences. Thus, cognitive complexity, social awareness, and minimalism provide standards for differentiating experts (Dawes 1988; Fiske and Taylor 1984; Sniderman, Brody, and Tetlock 1991).

To understand the relationship between cognitive processes, prior knowledge, and ability to apply knowledge and experiences in specific situations, cognitive psychologists study how experts and novices solve various types of problems. The research indicates differences in the problem-solving activities of experts and novices: (1) Experts have a more extensive and better-organized knowledge base than novices; (2) experts deal more effectively with problems that have structure and known ''best solutions''; (3) experts tend to work from problem understanding to problem solution (novices tend to work from solutions to solutions problem-understanding); and (4) experts draw upon a larger set of heuristics than novices during problem solving (see Anderson 1988; Chi, Glaser, and Farr 1988; Dyson and Purkitt, 1994; Larkin et al. 1980; Shanteau 1987, 1989; Taber and Steenbergen 1993; Voss, this volume).

Generally speaking, experts are better prepared than novices: Experts have better organized memories containing more interrelated cognitive elements. But theorists have conceptual differences about the fundamental units in long-term memory. The main differences pertain to describing the units as cognitive schemata, scripts, cognitive maps, and some other elements (Taber, this volume). Prior problem-solving research has documented that experts in a number of fields have precompiled subroutines, frame an issue more efficiently, and wait until they gain problem familiarity before seeking solutions. These patterns of operations allow experts to direct search activities more effectively than novices because they tend to produce more reasonable solutions. But there is a nested point here: Problems with known best solutions tend to have developed algorithms, whereas problems without known best solutions do not – hence, satisficers, muddlers, rational actors, and ideological thinkers may not be so effective (Chi et al. 1988; Dyson and Purkitt, 1994; Voss and Post 1988; Voss, this volume).

Some researchers suggest that in intuitive fields (i.e., fields without known best solutions), experts organize their knowledge base into a large number of specialized perceptual patterns or domain-specific cognitive schema. This type of process requires a long time to develop expertise (Shanteau 1987, 1989). Chase and Simon (1973a,b), for example, estimate a chess expert's repertoire of patterns at about fifty thousand. This leads Simon to conclude that at least ten years are required to develop the requisite specialized knowledge base to be an expert in such fields as chess, art, and music. Similarly, Shanteau and Phelps (1977) note that "expert" livestock judges have more than thirty years of judging experience. Yet the time frame needed to develop expertise does not concomitantly mean that experts are effective problem solvers. Time frames for learning do not tell us if differences in knowledge bases affect the quality of choice.

Since the knowledge base of experts is domain specific, expert-novice differences are most apparent with domain-specific tasks. As Anderson (1982) noted, with experience, trial-and-error "search becomes more selective and is more likely to lead to rapid success." But by stressing the idea that experts possess and use a knowledge base of long-term knowledge to distinguish experts from novices, we may underestimate the limitations imposed by working memories' information-processing constraints of both experts and novices attempting to solve ill-structured political problems.

Moreover, as Voss and Post (1988: 264–265) have cautioned, ill-structured problems, lacking an agreed-upon solution, are likely to evoke a range of different solutions because many more differences in the memory structures of respective solvers are likely to be exposed, regardless of level of expertise. When the concept of "expertise" is viewed within the broader context of research on problem solving of ill-structured problems, it becomes apparent that a number of basic questions about the nature of political experience and performance in solving complex but poorly structured political problems have not been adequately addressed.

Research Questions

This study examines in detail the structure and content of the problem representations developed by diverse members of political elite in the highly polarized political system of South Africa. The interviews were undertaken before agreement was reached on the rules governing the transition to majority rule.

Thus, the data base is the verbalizations of twelve South African participants who were among the country's political elite. Through in-depth interviews and "think aloud" virtual protocols, each subject was asked to engage in a "think aloud" analysis of current political trends in South Africa and make recommendations to former President de Klerk to facilitate progress toward a transitional government in South Africa. Although the results from such a small convenience sample are only illustrative, the twelve individuals represented different political points of view, occupational roles, and subcultures within South Africa's political elite.[1]

The data are of interest because this information was collected at a time of maximum political uncertainty, August 1992, about the timing and nature of fundamental changes in the status quo in South Africa – before the historic agreement to hold national elections in April 1994 to guide a peaceful transition to majority rule in South Africa. The protracted, multiparty negotiation process known as CODESA II, which was designed to forge agreement on transition procedures, had broken down months before the interviews were conducted: The African National Congress (ANC) had walked out of the negotiations in April 1992 to protest the Bobetang massacres and lack of response by South African police and security forces and to register a formal protest at what it perceived to be intentional intransigence and backsliding on the part of government negotiators.

The data were collected toward the end of the ANC's national campaign of rolling protests and strikes. These political protests were designed to demonstrate the depth and breadth of the ANC's popular support. Few doubted that the major parties would return to negotiations, but there was uncertainty during the interview period about when the multilateral negotiations would be resumed. South Africans of all persuasions increasingly voiced long-held concerns about whether "time would run out" for a negotiated settlement. The race was against time: Would the level of violence and social unrest spiral out of control before agreements could be reached?

During this period of increased incidence of political violence, it was announced that South Africa was experiencing its third year of negative growth. Unemployment rates in urban areas were running between 40 and 60 percent. Daily reports of worsening economic conditions and about the adverse effects of an unprecedented drought seemed to produce added strains toward separatism in the country.

In this context, participants were asked to "think aloud" about the key actors and issues involved in the effort to make progress toward a new political status quo in South Africa. Each respondent was asked to consider current political conditions and to make policy recommendations to then-President F. W. de Klerk. This approach generated data on five main topics:

1. Who is an "expert" when confronted with the task of developing a representation of a complex problem under uncertainty?

2. Does the degree of experience with similar cognitive tasks (i.e., domain expertise) influence subsequent problem-solving behavior?

3. Do individuals from diverse backgrounds manifest commonalities in the way they structured their problem representations?

4. What are the important components of a problem representation of current political conditions? Does the content of the problem representation developed by the individuals reflect a shared "frame of reference" of distinct social classes, subcultures, or rival elite within the current political status quo?

5. Are there any structural similarities in these cognitive representations of a complex political problem related to information-processing constraints of working memory?

Operationalization

By examining in detail what each of these individuals did after receiving task instructions, it was possible to make some preliminary generalizations about the usefulness of the "representation" construct as an analytical device. By comparing the structure and content of each of the problem representations, it is possible to reach some preliminary conclusions about whether this cognitive construct requires some minimal amount of prior knowledge (i.e., pre-existing cognitive representation or domain-relevant schema) or experience with similar verbal tasks. This exploratory analysis was designed to provide some empirical data relevant to the question of political "expertise" in the context of analyzing current political conditions.

Although many background factors have been cited as important determinants of political orientation, few empirical studies have included attempts to link personal characteristics and experiences to commonalities and differences in problem representations or problem-solving behavior of political novices and elite. One of the most interesting findings from my study was the generalization that the subjects participating in this "think aloud" exercise who had the most experience with similar cognitive tasks were also the most articulate subjects. This finding, discussed in detail later, offered a basis for comparing the structure and content of each subject's problem representation. The length of each verbal protocol was used as an indicator of "verbal skill" so that each individual could be placed along a continuum of "verbosity."

The structure and content of each verbal protocol was then analyzed using coding conventions developed by Ericsson and Simon (1984/1993) and Dyson and Purkitt (1986a; see also Purkitt and Dyson 1990). Thematic content analysis and cognitive maps drawn freehand were used to represent the principal concepts mentioned in the verbal protocol. These summaries were compiled in order to compare similarities and differences in the problem-solving logic of politically experienced subjects, called "the experts" in this study, with that of the relatively inexperienced and inarticulate political novices. The verbal protocols for four individuals – the most articulate subject, an "expert" whose verbal protocol was of medium length, and the two least articulate subjects – are summarized and discussed in detail in the "Results" section of this chapter.

Each participant differed on one or more indicators of social class or ethnicity. Therefore, these comparisons are useful for investigating possible linkages between factors related to social class, ethnicity, prior experiences, and problem-solving behaviors. Because each individual brought to the task a distinct set of cognitive, social, and cultural frames of reference, individual verbalizations could be used to assess differences in cognitive representations and how differences linked to subcultures within the existing political elite of South Africa. The apartheid structure of South African society created distinct ethnically based elite and counterelite united by a willingness to resist, or to seek, change in the status quo. Thus, we may analyze whether shared frames of references among different elite influence initial framing of contemporary conditions, the process of identifying key actors and issues, and policy preferences.

Finally, by analyzing the structure of each verbal protocol, I could assess whether the individuals evidenced common characteristics in how they structured the task; that is, were they "limited information processors"?

My study falls within a general framework of political decision making as a form of problem-solving behavior under an uncertainty condition. Through the study, I focused on how twelve South African political "experts" from different ethnic, educational, employment, and experiential backgrounds used their prior experiences and knowledge to understand and make recommendations about a political problem (issue). I hoped to learn what people do when asked to assess and make recommendations about ending a political stalemate. Although the participants varied widely in terms of political expertise, each was personally involved in the politics of South Africa and, therefore, would qualify as a "political expert."

Experts and Majority Rule in South Africa: Sample Set and Task

The "think aloud" verbalizations of twelve individuals occupying a diverse set of roles in South Africa's political elite were collected during August 1992 – a period of high uncertainty about the probable success of negotiations to achieve a peaceful transition to majority rule. Each expert, while very familiar with the politics of South Africa, was also unique in terms of political viewpoint (e.g., political ideology and partisan affiliations), prior experience, formal educational experience, and current occupational role. This sample included three senior political leaders,[2] a senior political editor of a major newspaper, four political scientists working at major universities that historically served ethnically distinct student bodies, a colonel in the South African Defense Force currently working in a teaching billet, two policy analysts working at research institutions that had reputations for being sympathetic to the policies of either the ANC or Inkatha, and a former political activist employed as a senior administrator at a nonpartisan organization dedicated to facilitating communication and negotiations among the various political parties in South Africa.

The backgrounds of these experts reflect personal experiences of individuals based on their ethnicity and prior political activities under the apartheid system. In terms of ethnicity, 9 of these experts would be classified as "white," 1 as "colored," and 2 as "African" (e.g., one Cosa and one Zulu) under the old apartheid system. Among the whites, 3 were Afrikaaners and 6 were English-speaking. All of the whites in this sample had obtained advanced degrees (e.g., Ph.D.) at major universities in South Africa or abroad. All of the nonwhites had obtained advanced degrees (e.g., typically a master's degree), but these graduate experiences represented a diverse range of learning experiences and environments. For instance, one of the participants in this study designated as a political "novice" obtained a second advanced degree while under an official banning order. Another "novice" in this sample obtained his degrees by correspondence during a decade spent in prison. This formal education was supplemented by years of participation in informal political discussion sessions led by Nelson Mandela and other ANC leaders held on Robbins Island.

Because this study focused on making a systematic identification and description of the content and structure of problem-solving activity of a diverse set of "experts," each participant was asked to engage in the same "think aloud" exercise, which involved analyzing contemporary politics in South Africa and making recommendations to then-President de Klerk about how to facilitate progress toward a transitional government in South Africa. Before starting this exercise, each participant read the following task statement:

> Assume you are a policy advisor to the President. The President asks you to draft a viable policy that will lead to a new government in South Africa. He indicates that a number of factors must be considered in some way or another, including the future of the Nationalist Party, the need to maintain political order and economic growth, proposed reforms of police and security forces, the current and future demands of key economic and political forces in society, regional security issues, and current and future actions by key actors in the international community. How would you develop such a

policy and what would be the nature of the policy? *Be sure to think out loud* as you consider the development of the policy.

The directions contained a number of cues related to key aspects of the overall political situation in South African politics. The general wording aimed to allow respondents to supply their own interpretation or framing of the current political situation and to avoid framing effects triggered by specific wording in the task statement. By asking each respondent to complete the same "assess and recommend" task using a common task statement, a number of situation constraints imposed by time, task, decision environment, and problem difficulty were held constant.

Each respondent was given time to read the task statement and to ask questions. The verbal statements made by respondents during their "think aloud" sessions were tape recorded. A virtual (unedited) written transcript of these thoughts was made at a later date. These verbalizations constitute the raw data used in the protocol analysis reported later in this chapter.[3] The procedures used to parse the transcripts for data coding followed procedures and principles outlined in Ericsson and Simon (1984/1993). The verbal statements for each participant were divided into segments. Each segment became an independent datum of the information attended to sequentially in short-term memory as each respondent verbalized during the "think aloud" session. Usually, segments were relatively easy to identify because they typically coincided with a grammatical statement (e.g., a sentence or phrase). Occasionally, a segment contained only a word or an incomplete sentence, delineated by such cues as a pause in speech. Each segment was assumed to represent a separate "idea" or informational unit, which was heeded or attended to in working memory as the individual "thought aloud" (Ericsson and Simon 1984/1993).[4]

The data were coded using a category scheme based on a problem-centered information-processing perspective of political decision making developed in earlier experimental studies of how people process information to make political choices (see Dyson, Godwin, and Hazlewood 1974; Dyson and Purkitt 1986a; Purkitt and Dyson 1988). This coding scheme combined categories similar to a Bales (1950, 1953) interaction scheme with categories germane to the types of problems used in specific political tasks.

A modified version of a problem-centered information-processing perspective was used to analyze the deliberations of the ExComm group during the Cuban missile crisis (Purkitt 1992), U.S. foreign policy initiatives toward Africa during the Carter and Reagan administrations (Purkitt and Dyson 1986), and the political rhetoric of top-level policy makers in the Bush administration just prior to the Gulf conflict (Francis and Purkitt 1993). Most of the major categories used in my study (see Table 7.1) also were evident in other task settings (e.g., noise, references to information, identification of a problem).[5] Some additional categories as well as subcategories were added to reflect individual problem-solving actions (e.g., "Describe past, current, future states"). One additional category, "Reject task assumption," may be unique to this specific problem-solving task.[6]

To describe and compare the content of the problem representation developed by each expert, both the structure and the semantic content of each segment was retained in a relatively direct fashion. First, the objects and relations used to define the problem space and operators used in subsequent verbalizations were coded. On a second pass, sequences that referenced key problem factors and recommendations were coded.

On a third pass through the protocols, the objects mentioned in each segment in terms of the semantic content and the level of abstraction, when these objects were references to "key actors" (i.e., individuals, groups, or aggregates), were coded. Because considerable lexical variability was found, Actors as a generic category were coded, when referred to, by means of a common noun or a name (e.g., a proper noun). When no explicit reference (e.g., a noun or pronoun) was verbalized, an actor reference was not coded.[7]

A more global approach was used to identify segment sequences related to specific topics or problem factors. Pauses, hesitations, and changes in intonation could often be used to mark shifts in processing about a specific topic. Using this convention, the length and number of analytical topics or dimensions used in each protocol were identified.

From a theoretical perspective, each of the analytical dimensions represented a central feature of problem representation. Identification of problem dimensions was a critical step in coding because research does not suggest how to represent "chunks" of heeded information in working memory. Sequences of heeded information or "problem-solving episodes" were identified and analyzed to determine whether there were detectable patterns of solution steps (e.g., working toward a solution or working backward from a solution).[8]

A key research question related to the structure of the problem-solving logic of experts pertained to whether they manifested a modal pattern of problem solving or whether variations in their verbal statements reflected individual differences in an "ease of verbalizing thoughts" and differing degrees of familiarity and practice with similar verbal tasks. Although verbal ability is a characteristic of political experts, it is unknown whether verbal skill reflects fundamental differences in problem-solving abilities or merely differences in prior experience with verbal tasks. Experts may be highly verbal and project an image as a highly articulate analyst but still look remarkably similar to a novice in terms of the problem-solving behaviors used to understand or "solve" complex and unstructured political tasks.

No a priori hypothesis about the nature of the variation in the content of the problem dimension or the level of abstraction used for actor references was developed, because past research clearly indicated that problem representations may vary on a number of dimensions, including the degree of abstraction (see Young, this volume). There was a weak expectation that more highly educated individuals would use more abstract terms. This intuitive notion was bolstered by at least one past study, which found that more experienced problem solvers in the domain of teamwork used fewer and more abstract cognitive schema than less experienced novices (Rentsch, Heffner, and Duffy 1993). There was also an expectation that a certain degree of patterning in these problem representations would be related to such background characteristics as social class and ethnicity.

Results

Political Expertise, Verbal Skill, and Prior Experience with Similar Cognitive Tasks

Given the context of this "think aloud" exercise, the task was not a sterile academic exercise. The verbalization task tapped aspects of the political issues that were uppermost in the minds of most South Africans. Although generalizing from a small, nonrandom sample of political experts is hazardous, we still may look for patterns in the verbalizations. Table 7.1 summarizes the verbal segments for each political expert using the problem-centered categorization scheme. The summaries (columns) for each subject are rank ordered from left to right on the basis of the total number of segments. The wide range of total statements made by these twelve persons (e.g., 14 to 207 segments) supports an initial proposition that political expertise falls along a verbal ability continuum.

Rank ordering by "verbosity" indicates a breakpoint in the number of verbal statements provided by the eight most verbal and the four least verbal participants in this study. Individual variations in verbalizing thoughts about political change in South Africa were strongly correlated with two powerful attributes of social class: race and level of formal education. Looking first at race, there is a strong correspondence between race and verbosity: Subject numbers 1–8 were white, whereas subject numbers 9, 10, and 12 were not. A similar pattern is apparent when the variable used is either "level" or "quality of formal education" (e.g., numbers 1–3 and 5–8 all had Ph.D.s in political science or a related field).

There was complete correspondence between the number of verbal statements made during this exercise and prior experience (practice) and familiarity with similar verbal tasks. This correspondence suggests that "verbal abil-

Table 7.1. *Protocol summary – Ranked by length of segment (in %)*

	#1	#2	#3	#4	#5	#6	#7	#8	#9	#10	#11	#12
Noise	0	1	0	5	8	4	19	2	7	8	4	0
Seek clarification	1	0	2	0	0	0	3	0	0	0	0	0
ID unknown	0	1	4	1	0	0	0	0	0	0	0	0
Reference-Personal Information	5	1	5	0	0	2	0	3	7	0	0	0
Reference-Other Information	3	6	2	6	2	2	0	2	0	0	0	0
Reference-Task statement	2	0	3	2	8	6	9	3	22	0	8	7
Reject-task assumption	2	0	2	0	0	2	0	5	0	12	0	0
Describe	31	21	27	36	12	15	23	5	15	8	21	14
Predict	3	11	7	2	5	1	4	5	0	4	0	14
Evaluative	15	32	25	20	28	28	19	23	19	32	17	0
Classify	1	0	1	0	1	0	0	0	0	0	0	0
Compare	1	0	2	1	0	0	0	0	0	0	0	0
Explain	10	14	8	10	9	12	14	3	0	8	0	0
Recommendation	25	14	13	18	26	27	9	51	30	28	50	64
	99%	101%	100%	101%	99%	99%	100%	102%	100%	100%	100%	99%
Number of segments	207	139	130	104	85	82	74	65	27	25	24	14

ity," measured by sheer "verbosity," which may be gained by practicing one's public-speaking skills about politics, is a principal characteristic distinguishing political experts from novices. In this sample of "experts," the cognitive reflection of political expertise corresponded completely with prior experience, or familiarity with similar verbal tasks.

Despite considerable individual differences in terms of ethnicity, level and type of advanced education, current occupational roles, and prior experiential knowledge, the four who acted most like political novices in terms of their verbal behavior, all had little or no prior experience with similar verbal tasks.

Expert number 9 had earned several master degrees while under a formal banning order for her political activities and had a varied background, having worked as a community activist and computer programmer for a major public policy institute.

Expert number 10 had no prior experience with similar verbal tasks but had extensive, informal training in political education and discussions of politics in South Africa while serving a ten-year prison sentence for his political affiliation and activities in support of the ANC. Although he had earned a correspondence-school master's degree in prison, had discussed South African politics extensively with Nelson Mandela and other ANC leaders during his incarceration, and had headed a well-known public-policy institute, this individual, as a black South African dissident, had been seriously disadvantaged by the limitations placed upon him in terms of access to a quality formal education and to political information throughout the 1980s.

Subject number 11 was an Afrikaaner colonel in the South African Defense Force who had an advanced degree in politics but little prior experience with political decision tasks.

Subject number 12 was a black South African with a strong ethnic identity who had served as both a senior official in the KwaZulu government and the Inkatha Freedom Party prior to his current role as head of a policy institute.

Types of Reasoning, Verbosity, and Political Expertise

From Table 7.1 we may infer that the least verbal subjects in this sample, along with the senior politician in this sample (Expert number 8) focused more of their attention on making recommendations and evaluating the current situation. The least verbal subjects were similar in verbal behavior to novice subjects in political experiments (see, e.g., Dyson and Purkitt 1986a; Voss et al. 1983). Thus, these subjects did not focus on the current situation by using descriptive or explanatory statements, but rather they (e.g., subjects numbers 8–12) focused immediately and nearly constantly on problem recommendations and evaluations without considering concomitant descriptions or explanations. Thus, more than half of all of the verbal segments of three of the least verbal experts (numbers 8, 11, and 12) consisted of policy recommendations, whereas the most verbal experts (numbers 1–4) referenced descriptive ideas more than recommendations.

The differential use of description and explanation compared to evaluative statements and policy recommendations may also reflect certain ideological or partisan differences among members of the sample. For instance, it was clear both from the transcripts and from postprotocol interviews that the wording of the task statement affected those participants who objected to what they felt were incomplete or incorrect implicit assumptions in this description of current political conditions in South Africa. The effect of the initial task statement was most evident in the protocol of the more ideologically liberal members of this sample, experts numbers 9 and 10. Both these individuals explicitly rejected the wording and premises of the task statement, and more than 20 percent of all the verbalizations made by expert number 9 centered on the task statement per se. Expert number 10 had similar problems with the implicit framing of the problem and sought to redefine the current political status quo by repeatedly returning to the task statement in a novice-like fashion. (See Table 7.1, Refer-task statement and Reject-task assumption.)

Types of Actors, Level of Abstraction for Actor References, and Individual Differences

Individual variation in the semantic content (e.g., objects, relations, and operators used) of the protocols appeared to be related to certain life experiences, level of social class, current occupation, and political orientations or beliefs of subjects. Although all of the subjects focused their attention on societal and governmental actors, there were individual differences in attentiveness to different types of actors that seemed to relate to occupational or personal experiences. For instance:

1. The four academicians working in the field of international relations were the only individuals for whom external actors comprised an important response category – external actors represented a fifth or more of their actor references (i.e., see actor references in Table 7.2 for Expert Subject [ES] numbers 2, 3, 6, and 7).

2. The two subjects who had the most to lose in terms of their current occupational and social status (e.g., the senior politician and the professional Afrikaaner soldier) focused much of their attention on the composition and structure of the future government (i.e., see Future government in Table 7.2 for ES numbers 8 and 11).

3. The three subjects who had long been committed to the struggle against apartheid, and who had to cope on a daily basis with the recent violence,

Table 7.2. Type of actor references

	#1	#2	#3	#4	#5	#6	#7	#8	#9	#10	#11	#12
Societal	**57%** **(109)**	**49%** **(98)**	**38%** **(41)**	21% (31)	26% (24)	**38%** **(34)**	13% (7)	23% (15)	**57%** **(13)**	**53%** **(18)**	**35%** **(11)**	29% (6)
Security/Military	13% (25)	2% (4)	1% (1)	9% (14)	3% (3)	**14%** **(13)**	21% (11)	3% (2)	9% (2)	26% (9)	0% (0)	**38%** **(8)**
Government	21% (41)	10% (21)	35% (37)	**42%** **(62)**	**33%** **(30)**	24% (22)	29% (15)	30% (19)	26% (6)	12% (4)	6% (2)	33% (7)
Future government	5% (9)	15% (30)	2% (2)	27% (40)	25% (23)	4% (4)	6% (3)	**34%** **(22)**	4% (1)	0% (0)	**58%** **(18)**	0% (0)
External	4% (8)	**24%** **(49)**	**24%** **(26)**	1% (2)	13% (12)	**19%** **(17)**	**31%** **(26)**	9% (6)	4% (1)	9% (3)	0% (0)	0% (0)
	100%	100%	100%	100%	100%	99%	100%	99%	100%	100%	99%	100%
Number of actor references	(192)	(202)	(107)	(149)	(92)	(90)	(62)	(64)	(23)	(34)	(31)	(21)

tended to define the key actors and issues in this communal conflict using very similar terms (see Table 7.2) (ES in columns numbers 9, 10, and 12).

4. The one subject who had intimate knowledge about the current thinking and reactions of police to recent efforts to reform the police and security establishment spent a significant amount of time analyzing the forces placed on de Klerk's negotiating position (i.e., see actor references for ES number 6 in Table 7.2).

The means used to point up a linkage between background factors and cognitive processes focused on the content and structure of the problem representation. By comparing similarities and differences in the cognitive representations of subjects from a variety of political viewpoints and life experiences, we may see in greater detail how certain types of background characteristics affect problem-solving behaviors.

Individual Profiles: A Comparison of the Structure and Content Cognitive Representations of Four Members of the South African Elite during the Summer of 1992

The "continuum of verbal ability" described in Table 7.1 was used to classify individuals by similarities and differences in their problem-solving logic. Overall, qualitative, in-depth analyses of these verbal protocols indicated certain similarities in terms of the structure and content of the problem-solving behaviors of the more experienced and articulate subjects when compared to the least articulate subjects. Similarly, patterns corresponding to life experiences, occupations, and political orientations identified in Tables 7.1 and 7.2 were noted. Although verbal protocols were coded for all twelve of these subjects, it is difficult to summarize concisely the coded protocols. Consequently, the approach adopted here is to summarize and compare the problem-solving behavior of two highly experienced political problem solvers (ES numbers 1 and 8) with that of the two least experienced and least verbal problem solvers in order to illustrate some of the expert-like and novice-like characteristics of the problem-solving behavior of four members of South Africa's political elite.

The Political "Experts"

Subject Number 1: An Academician and Community Activist. Our qualitative analysis begins with the verbal protocol of ES number 1, the most verbose subject in this sample. Some reasons why number 1 was so articulate are suggested by his background, current profession, and recent experiences. As an English-speaking, white South African with a Ph.D. degree in public administration, he had years of experience as an academic, community planner, and political activist. His current position as the director of public affairs at a major, historically black university, while also serving as the local representative for the ANC, afforded him many opportunities to develop the verbal ability he had gained in similar cognitive tasks in the past. This university, located in Natal province, was at the center of some of the worst community violence experienced in South Africa in recent years.

Originally founded as a university to train Indians, 90 percent of the student body consists of Africans. Most students at this university had lost one or more family members in recent community violence. The majority of student activists there were pro-ANC. During the week prior to this interview, demonstrations and a riot on campus occurred in response to an effort to form a campus chapter of Inkatha, the national organization claiming to represent Zulu in South Africa. Thus, with English as his native language, an advanced degree in politics, a job requiring extensive public speaking, and years of experience as a community activist and politician, number 1 had extensive experience and practice discussing issues related to current and future politics in South Africa. This extensive experience with similar verbal tasks may also explain the well-developed ends-means approach he used to discuss politics in South Africa. Such an approach has been identified as a common problem-solving logic employed to solve ill-structured problems across a number of domains (see Voss, this volume). Table 7.3 summarizes the number of segments, steps, and key points made at each step by number 1 during the "think aloud" exercise. In chronological order, his verbalizations involved:

1. Identifying general goals
2. Referencing the task statement, including reformulating the nature of the problem as one involving three factors
3. Identifying and describing the three problem dimensions created by South African apartheid, including the consequences of these problem dimensions and constraints for reaching a negotiated agreement
4. Identifying and analyzing a three-dimensional solution that flowed from this problem representation
5. Concluding – including a descriptive summary and prescriptive and predictive statements

The freehand-drawn cognitive map summarizing number 1's problem representation and solution (see Figure 7.1A) provides evidence suggesting that he manifested some of the same expert-like characteristics in problem-solving approaches as did novices documented in other fields. First, the initial problem representation consisted of only a few, highly abstract problem dimensions. This is remarkably similar to the results of Rentsch et al. (1993) in a

Table 7.3. *Summary of problem-solving behavior of ES #1 – Most Verbal Subject*

(English-speaking, white South African, Ph.D. in public administration. *Profession:* director of public affairs at a historically black university. *Politics:* regional ANC official.)

Number of segments	Steps	Key points
1–30	Step 1: Identify goals.	• Must establish democratic processes. • Must analyze constraints and change processes in current society. • Must ensure inclusive, phased-in process of change.
31–53	Step 2: Reference task statement.	• Reject linkage of economic growth and democracy. • Assert racism worse in America than South Africa, and reformulate task. • Must look at South African society in simpler way than the twelve factors listed on the task statement.
54–130	Step 3: Identify and analyze *three* dimensions of current South African society.	
(54–86)	Identified and described the current problem dimensions and *constraints* caused by apartheid's fragmentation of control.	• Territorial fragmentation • Control of military and security • Civilian authority
(87–126)	Identified and described *consequences* of apartheid in terms of creating particular cultures.	• Culture of entitlement • Culture of violence • Culture of unequal standards
(127–130)	*Goal* must be to promote nonracial, nonsexist, unitary society while promoting peoples' pride in their culture.	
131–196	Step 4: Identify and analyze *three*-dimensional *problem solution* for reversing control and fragmentation created by apartheid.	
(131–133)	General recommendations to target geographical, military, and government level.	

Table 7.3 (*cont.*)

Number of segments	Steps	Key points
(134–159)	Geographical level:	
		• Increase awareness among whites of impact of apartheid.
		• Reverse separation in housing, education, and welfare in order to promote unity and diversity.
		• Develop effective planning programs.
(160–175)	Establish effective control mechanisms over military.	
		• Key future issue will be how to reintegrate fragmented military and security apparatus.
		• Future state president should eliminate homeland forces.
		• Nationalize regional police force.
(176–184)	Make effective some discipline within government.	
(185–193)	Describe current system and constraints.	
		• Most complex process given current patronage, corruption, government structure.
		• Must create single authorities (education, housing, welfare).
		• Must create single municipalities (relates personal experiences; a complex process to create single entity and tax base).
(194–196)	Goals – Ensure democracy after election; effect social politics while also controlling the military.	
197–202	Step 5: Conclusion – Summarize, prescribe, predict.	
		• These are the most difficult three levels of complexities.
		• Easy to create social welfare, education, and housing policies.
		• A democratic government will have difficulty exercising control over the military.
		• Gaining control over government apparatus will be the most difficult tasks facing the new government.

Figure 7.1: Background Characteristics and Problem Representations of Four South Africans.

A. ES #1 – Most Verbal Subject

Background Characteristics: English-speaking, white South African, Ph.D. in public administration. *Profession:* director of public affairs at a historically black university. *Politics:* regional ANC official.

Problem Representation: A threefold problem resulting from apartheid's fragmentation and control.

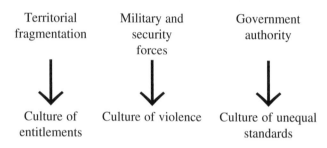

| Territorial fragmentation | Military and security forces | Government authority |

| Culture of entitlements | Culture of violence | Culture of unequal standards |

Problem Solution: Reverse fragmentation of control.

| Territorial fragmentation | Military and security | Government authority |

B. ES #8 – Moderate Verbosity

Background Characteristics: English-speaking, white South African, Ph.D. in political science. *Profession:* former academician, current politician and delegate in parliament, making a career shift to international business. *Politics:* leader of small, liberal party in parliament.

Problem Representation: A multiparty negotiating task about the twofold problem of source of legality versus source of legitimacy. Key procedural and substantive issues.

Establish multiparty "think tank." ⟶ *Process goals* (advise, complement leaders, get chairman)

⟶ Establish agenda

Figure 7.1 (*cont.*)

Problem Solution: *Issues* (ranked in terms of priority).
Stop current violence. → Work with U.N. and other monitors.
Establish interim government. → Urge de Klerk to accept.
Adopt Constitution. → Accept CODESA Working Group #2 principles.
Focus on economy once political transition is in place. → Use same combined, multiparty approach.

C. ES #11 – Ranked 11th in Verbosity

Background Characteristics: Afrikaans-speaking, white South African; M.A. in politics from elite Afrikaaner university. *Profession:* professional army colonel in former South African Defense Force (SADF); combat tours in Angola before current assignment as lecturer at military academy. *Politics:* not disclosed but probably sympathetic to views of then all-white Nationalist or Conservative parties. However, he stressed during the postprotocol interview that career SADF officers were willing to perform any task, including police functions, for any future government.

Problem Representation/Problem Solution

Two problem dimensions and three concepts were identified while making recommendations in a listlike fashion:
Need federal or confederal system   Need capitalist free-market system.
  (decentralized, power at regional
  level).
                    ← a multiethnic society
Establish a confederal system.

D. ES #12 – Least Verbal Subject in Sample

Background Characteristics: multilingual, black South African with Zulu as first language; worked as high school teacher and principal before obtaining Ph.D. in education at prestigious English-speaking university. *Profession:* worked several years for Inkatha Freedom Party (IFP) trying to resolve political conflicts between IFP and the United Democratic Front (UDF), a broad-based umbrella organization that existed prior to the unbanning of the ANC; currently director of UDF, which was funded primarily by Western donors. *Politics:* Inkatha Freedom Party (IFP).

Figure 7.1 (*cont.*)

Problem Representation/Problem Solution

Five themes were identified in a listlike fashion as recommendations:
1. National Party should promote political tolerance and freedom of association now.
   A bill of rights will ensure political stability.
2. Implement market-driven economic policy with a social conscience.
   The majority have been excluded from economic participation and must be reintegrated.
3. Composition of police and security should reflect composition of society.
   Need central command but regional organization.
4. Business community will play key role in advising on economic issues.
5. Need to promote foreign trade and export-oriented manufacturing.
   (No conclusion)

---

comparison of the conceptual schema of teamwork used by high-experience and low-experience individuals.

Second, as is often the case when a problem solver develops a relatively well-organized problem representation with explicit problem dimensions, the solution or solution path flows easily from the initial problem representation (Chi et al. 1988; Hayes and Simon 1976; Larkin, McDermott, Simon, and Simon 1980; Voss, this volume; Voss et al., 1983; Voss, Tyler, and Yengo 1983). The structure of number 1's problem representation and solution is summarized in Figure 7.1A. After identifying a threefold problem, he proceeded in an uninterrupted fashion to identify and discuss a solution set that followed from the three dimensions developed in the initial problem representation (e.g., territorial fragmentation, the military and security forces, and government authority).

Finally, it should be noted that the labels given to each problem dimension reference abstract concepts. The use of abstract concepts is another feature that distinguishes expert from novice problem solvers (see Rentsch et al. 1993; Voss et al. 1983; Voss et al. 1983). A common explanation for the greater use of abstract concepts by experts offered by cognitive psychologists is that experts have a well-developed and highly organized set of schemata or cognitive maps residing in long-term memory that can be accessed and used during the course of developing a problem representation in working memory (see Taber, this volume; Young, this volume).

Additional evidence suggesting the existence of a set of well-developed schemata or scripts residing in long-term memory is also provided by the key points mentioned at each problem-solving stage. (See Table 7.3.) These statements suggest that number 1's problem-solving behavior had a scriptlike character to it. This characteristic suggests that large portions of his problem representation and solution were retrieved from cognitive scripts or schemata stored in long-term memory. In one sense, it is hardly surprising to find that a professional spokesperson and political official for a national party in a highly charged partisan atmosphere used a "canned" or precompiled cognitive script to interpret current politics and policy prescriptions. The scriptlike nature of his verbalizations, however, may have a wider import if his verbal protocol is illustrative of the characteristic political problem-solving behavior or analyses developed by political experts across a variety of tasks and contexts when discussing contemporary and future political problems. (See Dyson and Purkitt 1994.)

Thus, while number 1's verbal protocol consists of a relatively well-organized set of statements for an on-line information-processing task, a critical review of the content and structure of his problem representation and solution suggests a rather superficial representation of a complex reality. After all, the representation involved little more than the identification of three problem dimensions. There was little specificity in terms of identifying causal linkages, specific evaluations, or solution paths. Instead, the underlying structure mirrored the simple structure found in a number of other studies of the problem-solving logic used by political experts engaged in on-line information processing in "real world" contexts (see, e.g., Rubino-Hallman, this volume). If this interpretation is correct, it suggests that even the most extensively developed problem representation in this sample was based on a relatively simple and superficial representation of the current political situation. This interpretation is certainly consistent with our initial finding that verbal ability is a central dimension of political expertise.

Subject Number 8: A Career Politician. ES number 8 had a medium-length verbal protocol (e.g., 64 segments) and represented the breakpoint in this data between experienced and inexperienced political analysts. Table 7.4 summarizes this subject's problem-solving steps, and Figure 7.1B is a freehand drawing of the cognitive map developed by number 8 during this exercise. He shared certain background characteristics with number 1, including native English-speaking, South African, Ph.D. in politics, and experience working as a political scientist. In recent years, however, number 8 had worked as the leader of a small liberal party in parliament.

At the time of this interview, he was a prominent national figure involved in negotiations to reach agreement on a political transition to majority rule.

Table 7.4. *Summary of problem-solving behavior of ES #8 – Moderate Verbosity*

(English-speaking, white South African, Ph.D in Political Science. *Profession:* former academician, current politician in parliament, making a career shift to business. *Politics:* leader of small, liberal party in parliament.)

Number of segments	Steps	Key points
1–8 Step 1:	Reference task statement Reject task statement Reformulate task	• Not President de Klerk's job alone. • Now a multiparty negotiating task.
9–15 Step 2:	Identify twofold problem (i.e., What is source of legality? What is source of legitimacy?)	
16–29 Step 3:	Identify a series of related *process* goals in establishing a "think tank" representing all political viewpoints.	
		• Seek advice across political spectrum.
		• Study all political viewpoints.
(25–29)		• Compliment leaders for doing most important thing – establishing trust.
(26–29)		• Get international chairperson.
30–37 Step 4:	Establish agenda.	• No. 1 issue is the violence.
	First stop violence.	• Goldstone Commission most effective exiting body.
		• Support U.N. Secretary General proposals regarding violence and a general amnesty.
		• Work with U.N. and other monitors.
38–58 Step 5:	Move quickly to establish interim government.	
		• Accept idea of Transitional Executive Council.
(47–51)	Adopt constitution.	• Accept principles already formulated by CODESA Working Group #2.
		• Universal franchise.
		• Proportionate representation.
		• Independent judiciary.
		• Separation of powers.
		• Devolution of function to region.
(52–58)	Urge de Klerk to accept an elected assembly.	

Table 7.4 (*cont.*)

Number of segments	Steps	Key points
59–63 Step 6:		Focus on economy once political transition process is in place using similar combined-leader approach.
		• Appeal to lift international sanctions.
		• Involve international community.
		• Encourage foreign investment.
64 Step 7:		Concluding statement: "That is all the procedural steps and some of the substantive steps that I want to see happen in implementing the assignment which you have given me."

Despite his active current political role, number 8 had recognized that there would be few prospects for a small liberal party led by whites in the new South Africa. Consequently, he was in the process of making a career shift to business by expanding his consulting business designed to aid international investors interested in investing in South Africa and the wider African continent.

Perhaps number 8's high level of education or political beliefs as an opponent of the government's helps explain why he, like number 1, chose to reformulate the problem task from one of advising then-President de Klerk to a problem of how to advise a multiparty negotiation team, which would include Nelson Mandela, Chief Buthelezi, and other key African leaders in addition to de Klerk. Also, similarly to number 1, he redefined the nature of the problem dimension using simpler yet more abstract terms than those listed on the problem sheet. For number 8, the key issues centered around the dual issues of the source of legality and source of legitimacy in South Africa. (See Figure 7.1B.)

Unlike number 1, number 8 did not go on to develop the analytical dimensions in his initial problem representation. Instead, he focused on a combination of procedural and substantive goals. After identifying the principal goal as one of establishing a multiparty "think tank," which would include all relevant political viewpoints and leaders, he identified and briefly described a number of *process goals* including: a recommendation to seek advice from across the political spectrum, the suggestion to compliment the major national leaders for recognizing that the most important aspect of their task was to increase interparty trust, suggesting specific individuals who might be asked to serve as the "think tank" chairperson, and stressing the importance of establishing an agenda. (See Table 7.4.)

After describing several major procedural issues, number 8 discussed in rank order the critical issues he felt should be addressed by this "think tank." He argued that attention must first be directed toward stopping the current violence and offered a number of specific solutions involving international aid and monitors. He discussed the need to establish an interim government and adopt a constitution, and he stressed the importance of adopting the principles already agreed to by the Conference on Democracy in South Africa (CODESA II) forum. Once progress had been made in effecting a political transition, he urged, the national leaders should focus on the economy, even before the formal transition occurred. He ended with a statement indicating that these were the procedural and substantive issues he would stress to current national leaders.

Subject number 8's verbal protocol is interesting because his problem-solving behavior seems to be a hybrid of (1) the more typical two-stage problem representation–to–problem solution developed by "expert" number 1 and (2) the more listlike specification recommendations and problem solutions using more concrete terms that was manifested by the least verbal and least experienced "novice" participants (see next section). Although number 8's verbal protocol suggests the use of a variety of schemata stored in long-term memory, the content of his problem representation focused more on the procedural and nuts-and-bolts issues of effecting a political transition after a very cursory "framing" of the problem.

The detailed analysis of the structure and content of these individual cognitive representations indicates that individual differences in cognition are linked to life experiences, current occupations, and political orientations evident in the earlier analysis of the relative attention paid to different types of actors. (See Table 7.2.) It is not surprising that an academic working in a university setting would tend to develop a relatively academic problem representation, whereas an experienced politician would tend to stress a mixture of both procedural and substantive aspects of the task. The individual differences in structure and content underscore the fact that the cognitive representations of members of any political elite, operating as either individual problem solvers or members of a group, are patterned in predictable ways that link to a shared experience such as occupation.

These individual variations tied to personal experiences, education, occupation, and political orientation replicate the pattern of variations in the semantic content or differential attention paid to different types of actors. (See Table 7.2.)

The Political "Novices"

It is possible to discern certain novice-like qualities in the problem-solving behaviors of the two least verbal subjects in this sample. An analysis of the protocols of the four political "novices" suggest that some aspect of social class, whether defined in terms of education, income, or aspects of South African society, was a critical determinant of individual differences in level of abstraction of the concepts. Certain novice-like characteristics and class-based individual differences can perhaps be illustrated by examining in detail the verbal protocol of the two least verbal subjects in this sample.

Subject Number 11: A Colonel in the Formal South African Defense Force. ES number 11 is a native-born Afrikaans speaker who had recently completed an advanced degree in politics at an elite Afrikaaner university while serving as a career officer in the former South African Defense Force (SADF). Prior to his current assignment, he spent most of his recent tours of duty in Angola and township areas in South Africa. He only recently assumed his current responsibilities as a military instructor at a South African military academy. Number 11 did not volunteer his political affiliation but comments during his postprotocol interview suggest that his political allegiance was given to either the National Party of F. W. de Klerk or the former Conservative Party. This colonel also emphasized during the postprotocol interview that he and other SADF career officers would be willing to perform any duties, including continuing policing activities in the townships and homelands, after the transition. Recent deterioration in military wages and benefits, rather than politics, was the most salient feature of recent politics for number 11.

Several characteristics in this subject's background may account for the limited verbosity of his verbal protocol. Although fluent in English, number 11, like most well-educated native Afrikaaner speakers, spoke English much more slowly and in a more deliberate style than native English speakers. As a career army officer who spent most of his time in operational billets, he lacked prior experience with cognitive "think aloud" tasks. Unlike some of his colleagues, however, he was a very outgoing person who was enthusiastic about the challenge presented by the task.

Number 11's lack of experience with similar tasks and his more severely limited verbal ability in English compared to the "experts" in this sample may also help to explain why his problem-solving behavior more closely approximated the behavior of "novices" attempting to solve problems in other settings. Unlike the more experienced and articulate "expert" subjects in this study (i.e., numbers 1 and 8), number 11 did not initially develop a problem representation. Instead, he accepted the task as outlined in the problem statement and offered specific recommendations to then-President de Klerk in a listlike fashion. These recommendations referenced two basic problem dimensions – the need for a federal system with decentralized power and authority vested at the regional level, and the need to establish a capitalist, free-market system. Neither dimension was developed in detail. Instead, number 11 first identified each of these dimensions as specific recommendations that de Klerk should implement in the future.

After pausing and referring back to the problem statement, number 11 returned to the concept of the structure of the future government and enumerated several reasons, mainly tied to the multicultural or multiracial nature of the society, why the next government should not be a strong central government. (See Figure 7.1C.) After discussing the multiracial nature of the society, he recommended that de Klerk ''propagate a confederate system while at the same time promoting a unity government capable of operating in the face of deep societal cleavages.''

The fact that number 11 relied heavily on the problem statement, rather than developing his own problem representation, and immediately made specific recommendations is characteristic of the problem-solving behavior of novices (e.g., undergraduates) (Dyson and Purkitt 1986a; Voss et al. 1983). The tendency to jump immediately to specific solutions has been observed across a number of domains and is often explained in terms of the lack of domain-relevant schema or precompiled problem-solving routines that may be available to develop a problem representation in the minds of ''experts.''

Although number 11 evidenced characteristic novice-like problem-solving behaviors, he nonetheless used highly abstract concepts in developing his solution (i.e., the need for a federal or confederate political system). This use of abstract concepts suggests that social class may be a more important predictor of the level of abstraction used in developing a problem representation rather than experience with similar cognitive tasks.

Subject Number 12: A Zulu Nonpartisan Activist and Former Politician. ES number 12, the least verbal of our twelve subjects, used many more concrete concepts than number 11. Some of the factors that may explain number 12's limited verbosity and use of concrete ideas are suggested in his background profile. (See Figure 7.1D.)

Subject number 12 is a multilingual, black South African whose native language is Zulu. He worked as a high school teacher and principal before obtaining a Ph.D. degree in education at a prestigious English-language university. He worked closely for several years with Chief Buthelezi and officials representing the former homeland of KwaZulu for the Inkatha Freedom Party

(IFP). Subject number 12 said that his main activity as an IFP official was to try to resolve the political conflicts between IFP and the United Democratic Front (UDF), a broad-based umbrella organization that existed prior to the unbanning of the ANC.

Number 12 observed during the postprotocol interview that he had quit the IFP in order to start a nonaligned institution dedicated to peaceful change and reconciliation in South Africa. He remarked with heartfelt intensity that he had been stunned by the level of intolerance evidenced by members of both the IFP and UDF and hoped as director of this nonpartisan organization to make a contribution to peace and reconciliation especially in Natal province and KwaZulu. This organization was one of many funded by Western donors during the late 1980s and early 1990s in an effort to promote civic society and conditions conducive to a peaceful political transition.

Although number 12 is fluent in English, he spoke in a deliberative style similar to the one used by number 11 and the other non-native English speakers who engaged in this exercise. The structure and content of his verbal protocol is summarized in Figure 7.1D. Unlike number 1 but similar to number 11, he did not develop a problem representation. Instead, number 12 accepted the problem task as provided and immediately began to offer specific recommendations to then-President de Klerk. He verbalized five themes in the course of listing recommendations for President de Klerk. As can be seen in Figure 7.1D, none of the themes was developed in detail. Instead, he used a listlike verbal style similar to that of number 11 and ''novice'' problem solvers.

Individual differences are apparent when comparing the content and structures of numbers 11 and 12. Although number 12, as director of an organization dedicated to political reconciliation and negotiation, had a great deal of prior experience discussing current and future politics, he lacked formal educational experiences. Instead, he struggled as one of the few members of the modern elite in Zululand to obtain formal training at a prestigious South African university. His university training had come late in life, and his current level of verbal ability and fluency in English seemed lower than that of number 11. Hence, although it is impossible to disentangle the different effects of language, education, and life experiences of someone living as a privileged or a disenfranchised member of South Africa's apartheid system, it is apparent that these two individuals had very different life experiences. Differential life changes seemed to show up in terms of different levels of abstraction of key concepts and the presence of a few linkages in the cognitive map of the white South African army colonel. Whereas number 11 had some minimal structure in his cognitive representation, number 12 had none. (See Figure 7.1.)

If these two cases are representative of larger groups of white and black members of South Africa's political elite, they suggest that formal education, class, and race are important determinants distinguishing the level of abstraction of the concepts used by different political "novices." Although both of these subjects were less articulate and used a listlike approach to problem solving when compared to the political "experts" in this sample, they nonetheless manifested important individual differences seemingly tied to class or race. Thus, experience with, or practice at, a similar task may help predict "verbosity" and the degree to which an individual develops an explicit problem representation before offering solutions, but the data suggest that social class (though perhaps only the level and quality of formal education) operates as an important differentiating variable, especially in terms of explaining differences in the content of the mental representations of political problem solvers.

Commonalities in Problem Structuring Tied to Information-Processing Limitations

The most fundamental reason why even the most elaborate problem representation in this sample (i.e., ES number 1) evidenced a simple, three-part structure is tied to a limitation of humans attempting to process and verbalize about complex political problems within the confines of working memory. Thus, despite the many important and interesting differences in the semantic content and the structure and content of the problem representations that were developed by these subjects, they nonetheless shared commonalities in how they processed information and verbalized about complex political problems.

Table 7.5 underscores this pattern by showing that each of the subjects used only a few analytical dimensions in developing problem representation and in analyzing the situation intuitively. Although the participants mentioned several analytic factors in their task statements, they were able to address only two to four factors in detail. The two subjects who did reference five factors did so in a listlike manner. The more articulate and experienced subjects were more systematic in their discussions of a few analytical factors, but none of the subjects was able to bring to bear more than a few factors in trying to understand this complex and uncertain situation. This pattern once again supports a well-known proposition in the information-processing literature: Individuals use only a few factors to achieve problem understanding and to analyze complex but uncertain problems without the aid of an explicit algorithm.

Table 7.5. *Number of analytical dimensions discussed (mentioned)*

	#1	#2	#3	#4	#5	#6	#7	#8	#9	#10	#11	#12
Number of problem dimensions discussed	3	4	4	4	3	4	4	4	2	5	2	5
(mentioned)	(5)	(6)	(6)	(6)	(6)	(6)	(6)	(7)	(6)	(6)	(6)	(5)

Conclusion

The results of these verbal protocol analyses underscore the conceptual and empirical murkiness of the concept of "expertise" as used in political science. The results indicate that expertise in solving complex but ill-structured political problems is closely coupled to verbal ability and a person's social status rather than to problem-solving successes or cognitive abilities. This may seem self-evident, but researchers indicate an abiding faith in the adequacy of the intuitive judgments of political experts, especially when analyses and judgments conform to a researcher's own script or political ideology. Contrary to conventional wisdom, and under a condition of uncertainty, these results suggest that a healthy dose of skepticism is needed regarding the adequacy of the problem-solving logic of experts who rely on prior experiences or intuition to make choices about complex political problems. The results confirmed that diversity of expressed ideas at varying levels of abstractions prevails, but the data also indicated that both experienced and novice political problem solvers use only a few analytic dimensions in developing their problem representations. As Simon (1955) and Miller (1956) documented while working in different contexts and using different research traditions nearly forty years ago, people are "boundedly rational" at their very best because of limitations in their information-processing capacity – working memory places serious constraints on what people can accomplish in their attempts to solve complex problems under uncertainty.

These basic information-processing limitations may explain why nearly every study that looked at cognitive processes used in political-choice settings (Snyder and Paige 1958) found that individuals rely heavily upon perceptions of the immediate task at hand to develop a subjective definition of the problem and to make recommendations. Viewed from a limited information-processing perspective, both expert and novice problem solvers used a limited number of problem dimensions. In fact, we might expect an analogous simple structuring in the shared problem representations of both experts and novices on similar on-line information-processing tasks, whether they work as individuals or in a small-group context.

The simple qualitative methods used to compare the structures and contents of individual political problem solvers, the problem-centered classification scheme used to classify verbal segments (Table 7.1), the coding conventions used to classify the level of abstraction of referent objects such as actors (see Table 7.2), and the summaries of problem-solving steps (Table 7.3 and 7.4) indicate important similarities and differences in the structures and contents of problem representations. (For descriptions of these methods see Dyson and Purkitt 1986a; Purkitt and Dyson 1990; Ericsson and Simon 1984/ 1993.) Viewed collectively, the results of this line of research suggest that the methods may be used with either individual or small-group units of analysis as these units attempt to represent and solve political problems.

There are substantial variations in the problem-solving approaches used to understand and formulate solutions to a complex political situation, and in the content and structure of individual problem representations. Certain characteristics such as social class and similar political beliefs help to explain certain patterns in the data – why, for instance, the individuals holding the more liberal or radical political views when compared to the political status quo were the subjects who most intensely rejected the initial framing of the immediate task at hand. Yet the diversity of problem-solving behaviors, structures, and contents of subjects' problem representations and solutions developed in response to a common task statement may provide a strong warning to researchers attempting to use single-part or static frameworks either to explain the cognitive process of political decision makers or to demonstrate the superior cognitive performance of political experts. The reported results indicate that both political novices and experts are highly adaptive problem solvers who will construct a problem representation or a set of policy prescriptions when asked to ''solve'' a complex but ill-structured political problem. Individual understandings and solutions for these problems will reflect certain individual characteristics, some prior knowledge and beliefs, incoming information that is perceived to be relevant to the immediate task at hand, and the individual's or group's perceptions of the immediate task at hand. Specification of the conditions and ways in which these determinants of problem representation may combine reflect a principal intellectual challenge for the next generation of problem-representational and choice scholars.

Author's Note: This research was supported by travel funds from the Dept. of Political Science of the U.S. Naval Academy, and grants from the Naval Academy Research Council during 1992 and 1993. Subsequent support was also received from a National Science Foundation grant (DIR-

9113599) to the Mershon Center Research Training Group on the Role of Cognition in Collective Political Decision Making.

Notes

1 It should be noted that small samples have long been used extensively to study expert–novice differences and to evaluate cognitive schema differences in past cognitive and problem-solving research.

2 I promised the participants anonymity in exchange for their cooperation. Because South Africa has a small political system, the background characteristics and current occupational roles of the subjects are not described in detail. The three politicians included a senior member of the Democratic Party, which was represented in the former all-white chamber of parliament; a senior former official of the KwaZulu government; a former ranking member of Inkatha; and a regional leader and member of the National Executive Council of ANC.

3 In-depth interviews were completed after each "thinking aloud" exercise. No substantive topics were discussed before the exercises, however, because there is substantial evidence that prior questions will influence the responses to subsequent questions (see, e.g., discussion in Ericsson and Simon 1984/1993).

4 There is substantial evidence that "think aloud" instructions do not significantly alter the thought processes of individuals and that concurrent verbalizations offer a nearly complete record of the information heeded in short-term working memory during a session. (For a review of these studies, see Ericsson and Simon 1984/1993, Chapters 2 and 3.) These concurrent verbal segments are assumed to reflect closely the cognitive processes actually used as successive states of "heeded" information in short-term memory. Thus, each segment represents an indicator of the successive states of "heeded" information in working memory from either external cues or long-term memory (Ericsson and Simon 1984/1993; Simon 1978).

5 It should be noted that the convention used here of coding certain segments as "noise" is a departure from the procedures often employed in problem-solving protocol coding. (See, e.g., 2 or 3 cited in Ericsson and Simon 1984/1993.) In many protocol analyses, meaningless verbal utterances are excluded on the assumption that they reflect spontaneous internal speech rather than meaningful cognitive processes. However, past political experimental research has found that "noise" is a relatively frequent type of verbal interaction, especially in the context of small-group problem solving. (See, e.g., Dyson and Purkitt 1986a.) Because I was interested in comparing the relative frequency of certain types of verbal behavior, I chose to include the "noise" category.

6 Although the terminology and theoretical perspective of humans as limited information processors outlined by Newell and Simon (1972) is used in this analysis, it should be noted that similar phasing procedures are used by researchers working with alternative theoretical perspectives of the organization of memory (e.g., Anderson 1983). See Ericsson and Simon (1984/1993) for a further discussion of the assumptions underlying the phasing procedures and a discussion of the evidence

that there is limited effect from mediating processes present in such concurrent verbal reports.

7 Coding judgments were made for each segment independently. Context cues were used to identify the reference (e.g., subject or object) of a segment. Many segments approximated the grammatical structure of a sentence with a verb, subject, and object reference. Thus, verb and verb tenses could often be used to distinguish statements about current, past, or hypothetical system states with minimal references to context cues. Distinctions between evaluative and descriptive, predictive, and explanatory statements were the most problematic to classify, but most ambiguities could be resolved on the basis of the linguistic content of the segment (e.g., evaluative statements had to reference explicit normative judgments).

8 Copies of these coded protocols and details of the coding conventions and break points associated with a detectable sequence related to the specific "problem dimensions" are available from the author upon request.

References

Anderson, John R. (1982). "Acquisition of cognitive skill." *Psychological Review, 89:* 369–406.

(1983). *The Architecture of Cognition.* Cambridge, MA: Harvard University Press.

Anderson, Paul A. (1987). "What do decision makers do when they make a foreign policy decision?," In Charles Hermann, Charles Kegley, and James Rosenau (eds.), *New Directions in the Study of Foreign Policy* (pp. 285–308). Boston, MA: Allen and Unwin.

(1988). "Novices, Experts and Advisers." Paper presented at the meeting of the International Studies Association, March 29 – April 2, St. Louis.

Bales R. F. (1950). *Interaction/process Analysis: A Method for the Study of Small Groups.* Cambridge, MA: Addison-Wesley, 1950.

(1953). "Some uniformities of behavior in small social systems." In G. E. Swanson, T. M. Newcomb, and E. C. Hartley (eds.), *Readings in Social Psychology.* New York: Holt.

Boynton, G. R. (1987). "Telling a Good Story: Models of Argument: Models of Understanding in the Senate Agriculture Committee." In Joseph W. Wenzel (ed.), *Argument and Critical Practices.* Annandale, VA: Speech Communication Association.

(1991) "The expertise of the Senate Foreign Relations Committee." In V. M. Hudson (ed.), *Artificial Intelligence and International Politics* (pp. 291–309). Boulder, CO: Westview Press.

Burstein, Eugene, and Michael L. Berbaum (1983). "Stages of group decision making: The decomposition of historical narrative." *Political Psychology,* Vol. 4(3): 531–557.

Carroll, J. S., and J. W. Payne (eds.). (1976). *Cognition and Social Behavior.* Hillsdale, NJ: Lawrence Erlbaum.

Chan, S. (1982). "Expert judgments under uncertainty: Some evidence and suggestions." *Social Science Quarterly, 63:* 428–444.

Chase, W. G., and H. Simon (1973a). "Perception in chess." *Cognitive Psychology, 4:* 55–81.

(1973b). "The mind's eye in chess." In W. G. Chase (ed.), *Visual Information Processing*. New York: Academic Press.

Chi, M. T. H., Glaser, R., and Farr, M. J. (eds.). (1988). *The Nature of Expertise*. Hillsdale, NJ: Lawrence Erlbaum.

Cottam, M. (1986). *Foreign Policy Decision Making: The Influence of Cognition*. Boulder, CO: Westview Press.

Dawes, Robyn (1988). *Rational Choice in an Uncertain World*. San Diego: Harcourt Brace Jovanovich.

Dyson, James W., H. B. Godwin, and L. Hazlewood (1974). "Group composition, leadership orientation and decisional outcomes." *Small Group Behavior*, Vol. 1: 114–128.

Dyson, J[ames] W., and Helen E. Purkitt (1986a). "An experimental study of cognitive processes and information in political problem solving." Final Report to the National Science Foundation, Florida State University and U.S. Naval Academy.

(1986b). "Review of experimental small group research." In S. Long (ed.), *Political Behavior Annual* (Vol. 1, pp. 71–101). Boulder, CO: Westview Press.

Einhorn, H. J. (1974). "Expert judgment: Some necessary conditions and an example." *Journal of Applied Psychology, 59:* 562–571.

Einhorn, J. J., and R. M. Hogarth (1978). "Confidence in judgment: Persistence of the illusion of validity." *Psychological Review, 85:* 395–416.

(1981). "Behavioral decision theory: Processes of judgment and choice." *Annual Review of Psychology, 32*: 53–88.

Ericsson, K., and H. A. Simon (1984). *Protocol Analysis: Verbal Reports as Data*. Cambridge, MA: MIT Press. (Rev. ed., 1993.)

Fiske, Susan T., and Shelley E. Taylor (1984). *Social Cognition*. Reading, MA: Addison-Wesley.

Francis, Shaun, and H. E. Purkitt (1993). "Foreign Policy Rhetoric of the Bush Administration During the Persian Gulf Crisis." Unpublished manuscript.

Gaeth, G. J., and J. Shanteau (1984). "Reducing the influence of irrelevant information on experienced decision makers." *Organizational Behavior and Human Performance, 33:* 263–282.

Gallhofer, Irmtraud N., Willem E. Saris, and Maarten Schellekens (1988). "People's recognition of political decision arguments." *Acta Psychologica, 68:* 313–327.

George, Alexander (1980). *Presidential Decisionmaking in Foreign Policy: The Effective Use of Information and Advice*. Boulder, CO: Westview Press.

(1993). *Bridging the Gap: Theory and Practice in Foreign Policy*. Washington, D.C.: United States Institute of Peace.

Hayes, J. R. (1964). "Human data processing limits in decision-making." In E. Bennett (ed.), *Information Systems, Science and Engineering Proceedings of the First International Congress on the Information Systems Sciences*. New York: McGraw-Hill.

(1981). *The Complete Problem Solver*. Philadelphia: Franklin Institute Press.

Hayes, J. R., and H. A. Simon (1976). "Understanding complex task instructions." In D. Klahr (ed.), *Cognition and Instruction*. Hillsdale, NJ: Lawrence Erlbaum.

(1977). "Psychological differences among problem isomorphs." In N. F. Castellan, D. B. Pisoni, and G. R. Pottes (eds.), *Cognitive Theory* (Vol. 2). Hillsdale, NJ: Lawrence Erlbaum.

Heuer, R. J. (1978). "Do you think you need more information?" Mimeograph, October.

Kahneman, Daniel, Paul Slovic, and Amos Tversky (eds.). (1982). *Judgment under Uncertainty: Heuristics and Biases*. Cambridge: Cambridge University Press.

Larkin, J., J. McDermott, D. P. Simon, and H. Simon (1980). "Expert and novice performance in solving physics problems." *Science, 208:* 1335–1342.

Larson, Deborah (1994). "The role of belief systems and schema in foreign policy decision making." *Political Psychology, 15*(1): 17–33.

Miller, George A. (1956). "The magical number seven plus or minus two: Some limits on our capacity for processing information." *Psychological Review, 63:* 81–97.

Newell, Allen, and Herbert Simon (1972). *Human Problem Solving*. Englewood Cliffs, NJ: Prentice-Hall.

Nisbett, R. E., and L. Ross (1980). *Human Inference: Strategies and Shortcomings in Social Judgement*. New York: Wiley.

Nisbett, R. E., and P. P. Wilson (1977). "Telling more than we can know: Verbal reports on mental processes." *Psychological Review, 84:* 231–59.

Paige, Glen D. (1958). *The Korean Decision, June 24–30, 1950*. New York: Free Press.

Payne, John W., James R. Bettman, and Eric J. Johnson (1993). *The Adaptive Decision Maker*. Cambridge: Cambridge University Press.

Pruitt, D. G. (1965). "Definition of the situation as a determinant of interactional action." In H. C. Kelman (ed.), *International Behavior: A Social-psychological Analysis*. New York: Holt, Rinehart, and Winston.

Purkitt, Helen E. (1991). "Artificial intelligence and intuitive foreign policy decision makers viewed as limited information processors: Some conceptual issues and practical concerns for the future." In V. Hudson (ed.), *Artificial Intelligence and International Politics* (pp. 35–55). Boulder, CO: Westview Press.

  (1992). "Political decision making in the context of small groups: The Cuban missile crisis revisited – one more time." In E. Singer and V. Hudson (eds.), *Political Psychology and Foreign Policy* (pp. 219–245). Boulder, CO: Westview Press.

Purkitt, Helen E., and J. Dyson. (1986). "The Role of Cognition in U.S. Foreign Policy Toward Southern Africa." *Political Psychology, 7*(3): 507–532.

  (1988). "An experimental study of cognitive processes and information in political problem solving." *Acta Psychologica, 68:* 329–342.

  (1990). "Decision making under varying situational constraints." In Katrin Borcherding, Oleg I. Larichev, and David M. Messick (eds.), *Contemporary Issues in Decision Making* (pp. 353–366). Amsterdam: Elsevier Science Publishers B.V. (North-Holland).

Rentsch, Joan R., Tonia S. Heffner, and Lorraine T. Duffy (1993). "Teamwork Schema Representations: The Role of Team Experience." Paper presented at Eighth Annual Conference of the Society for Industrial and Organizational Psychology, San Francisco, CA, April 30 – May 2.

Rubino-Hallman, Silvana (1993). "Women in Combat: The Role of Representations in the Assignment of Women in the Military." Research proposal and presentation to the Fall Meeting of the Research Training Group (RTG), Burr Oak State Park, October.

Shanteau, James (1987). "Psychological characteristics of expert decision makers." In J. Mumpower, O. Renn, L. D. Phillips, and V. R. R. Uppuluri (eds.), *Expert Judgement and Expert Systems*. Berlin, Germany: Springer-Verlag.

(1989). "Psychological characteristics and strategies of expert decision makers." In Bernd Rohrmann, Lee R. Beach, Charles Vlek, and Stephen Watson (eds.), *Advances in Decision Research* (pp. 203–215). Amsterdam: North-Holland.

Shanteau, James, and R. H. Phelps (1977). "Judgment and swine: Approaches and issues in applied judgment analysis." In M. F. Kaplan and S. Schwartz, (eds.), *Human Judgment and Decision Processes in Applied Settings* (pp. 255–272). New York: Academic Press.

Simon, H. A. (1955). "A behavioral model of rational choice." *Quarterly Journal of Economics, 69:* 129–138.

——— (1973). "The structure of ill-structured problems." *Artificial Intelligence, 4:* 181–201.

——— (1978). "Information-Processing Theory of Human Problem Solving." In W. K. Estes (ed.), *Handbook of Learning and Cognitive Processes: Human Information Processing* (Vol. 5). Hillsdale, NJ: Lawrence Erlbaum.

——— (1983). *Reason in Human Affairs.* Stanford, CA: Stanford University Press.

——— (1985). "Human nature in politics: The dialogue of psychology with political science." *The American Political Science Review, 79:* 293–304.

Simon, H. A., and John R. Hayes (1976). "Understanding complex task instructions." In David Klard (ed.), *Cognition and Instruction* (pp. 269–286). Hillsdale, NJ: Lawrence Erlbaum.

Slovic, P. (1972). "Psychological study of human judgment: Implications for investment decision making." *Journal of Finance, 27*(4): 779–899.

Sniderman, Paul M., Richard A. Brody, and Phillip E. Tetlock (1991). *Reasoning and Choice: Explorations in Political Psychology.* New York: Cambridge University Press.

Snyder, Richard C., and Glenn D. Paige (1958). "The United States decision to resist aggression in Korea." *Administrative Science Quarterly, 3:* 341–378.

Sylvan, Donald A., Thomas M. Ostrom, and Katherine Gannon (1994). "Case-based, model-based, and explanation-based styles of reasoning in foreign policy." *International Studies Quarterly, 38:* 61–90.

Sylvan, Donald A., and Stuart J. Thorson (1989). "Looking Back at JFK/CBA: Considering New Information and Alternative Technology." Paper presented at the 13th annual meeting of the International Studies Association, March 27–April 2, London.

——— (1992). "Ontologies, problem representation, and the Cuban missile crisis." *Journal of Conflict Resolution, 38*(4): 709–732.

Taber, Charles S., and M. Steenbergen, (1993). "Computational experiments in electoral behavior." In Milton Lodge and Kathleen McGraw (eds.), *Political Information Processing.* Ann Arbor, MI: University of Michigan Press.

Tetlock, Philip E. (1992). "Good judgment in international politics: Three psychological perspectives." *Political Psychology, 13*(3): 517–539.

Tversky, Amos, and D. Kahneman (1974). "Judgment under uncertainty: Heuristics and biases." *Science, 185:* 1124–1131.

——— (1981). "The framing of decisions and the psychology of choice." *Science, 211:* 453–458.

——— (1983). "Extensional vs. intuitive reasoning, the conjunction fallacy in probability judgment." *Psychological Review, 90:* 293–315.

Voss, James F., and Ellen Dorsey (1992). "Perception and international relations: An overview." In Eric Singer and Valerie Hudson (eds.), *Political Psychology and Foreign Policy.* Boulder, CO: Westview Press.

Voss, James F., Terry R. Greene, Timothy A. Post, and Barbara C. Penner (1983). "Problem solving skill in the social sciences." In G. H. Bower (ed.), *The Psychology of Learning and Motivation: Advances in Research Theory*, Vol 17 (pp. 165–213). New York: Academic Press.

Voss, J[ames] F., and T. A. Post (1988). "On the solving of ill-structured problems." In M. T. H. Chi, R. Glaser, and M. J. Farr (eds.), *The Nature of Expertise*. Hillsdale, NJ: Lawrence Erlbaum.

Voss, James F., Sherman W. Tyler, and Laurie A. Yengo (1983). "Individual differences in the solving of social science problems." In R. F. Dillon, and R. R. Schmeck (eds.), *Individual Differences in Cognition* (pp. 205–232). New York: Academic Press.

Wallsten, T. (ed.). (1980). *Cognitive Processes in Choice and Decision Behavior*. Hillsdale, NJ: Lawrence Erlbaum.

CHAPTER 8

Reasoning and Problem Representation in Foreign Policy: Groups, Individuals, and Stories

Donald A. Sylvan and Deborah M. Haddad

Introduction

Since the early 1960s,[1] the results of work on intragroup dynamics (e.g., Stoner 1968; Wallach, Kogan, and Bem 1962) have consistently demonstrated that decision making in a group context does not result in an aggregation of individual group members' preferences (see Beasley, this volume), nor does it provide assurance that there will be superior decisional outcomes over such an aggregation (Levine 1989; Levine and Moreland 1987; Maass, West, and Cialdini 1987; Mullen 1987; Stasser 1992; Stasser, Kerr, and Davis 1989). How is it that a group context mediates individual cognition, and how does this mediation make a difference in foreign policy decision making?

A significant number of foreign policy decisions are made in a group environment. Even where a single actor will make the final decision, he or she often will solicit the advice of an ad hoc committee of experts or other interested persons. For instance, during the Gulf crisis during the Bush administration, James Baker assembled a group of academics and State Department representatives under the leadership of Dennis Ross to provide the president with strategy options. Similarly, during the Cuban missile crisis, President Kennedy charged ExComm with the task of generating alternative responses to the confirmation of the presence of Soviet offensive missiles in Cuba.

In these and many other decision-making events, collective decision making has been pivotal in the final decision. Of particular interest, however, is that seldom have the decisions exactly reflected a *single* individual's preferences.

Some of the more prominent explanations for deficient group decision making focus on a breakdown in collective information acquisition, exchange, and processing (Stasser 1992; Stasser et al. 1989). Among these, for instance, intragroup attitude polarization was the subject of research by

Burnstein and his associates in the early 1970s, leading to the Persuasive Arguments Theory (see also Mackie 1986; Turner 1987). Similarly, certain group environments may mediate individual cognition when a common "mode of thinking" emerges through group pressures to conform (Janis 1972, 1982; Vertzberger 1990). Other variables in the process of decision making in a group context that alter otherwise individual cognition have to do with the cohesiveness of intragroup minority subcultures (Moscovici 1976; Nemeth 1987), risk management (Dion, Baron, and Miller 1978; Vertzberger 1994), leaders' management of options and information (Hermann 1987), and so forth.

We conceptualize our work in collective decision making as an exploration of the intersection between cognitive processes and the social context of those processes. As Levine, Resnick, and Higgins (1993) note, there is excellent work in each of those two areas, but less that deals with the implications of the relationship. Generally, social influences have been shown to mediate cognition in a group context (Allen and Wilder 1980; Kaplan 1989; Mackie 1986; Moscovici 1976, 1980; Wallach et al. 1962; Wilder 1978). Our inquiry, however, emphasizes the implications of cognitive mediation for collective decisional outcomes.

This chapter advances our proposition that Pennington and Hastie's (1986, 1988) "Story Model" helps to synthesize much of this work. For a decision-making group, a "story" is a heuristic for members of that group; that is, it is a way for group members to economize on the mental effort required to reach a decision as a group. A "story" is a composite of a group's common social and substantive meanings that helps to delimit the group's problem space.[2]

According to Pennington and Hastie, the group's "story" is an explanation-based "intermediate summary representation," which is actively constructed in a group through social interaction. This "structure" provides a guide for decision making in the group because it conveys which information is important (acquisition constraints) as well as the organization of that information (causal connections). Although Pennington and Hastie were careful to limit their conclusions to the scope of their own work on jury deliberations, we propose that the group's story effectively serves as a collective problem representation in the domain of foreign policy decision making. The story becomes a guide for inferencing, and as it develops through group members' interactions, new information is understood in a way that will accommodate the story. After some time, the story (rather than new information) becomes the primary source for decisions and is used to guide decisions even to a fault.

We begin with a short discussion of problem representation. Next, we offer our explicit understanding of Pennington and Hastie's story model, after which we describe the protocol of our experimental approach and some of our results. We conclude with a discussion of our preliminary findings.

Problem Representation

Our conceptualization of problem representation is a fundamental assumption underpinning our work on collective decision making in the foreign policy domain. The way in which an individual represents an issue makes a difference as to how that individual will reason about and make decisions about that issue.[3] The elements of the issue that are salient and the causal connections between those elements are the temporal and spatial "reality" of the issue for the individual. Sylvan and Thorson (1992) say that this ontologically based understanding of representation "denies the universal separation between an object and its representations by rejecting the notion that objects can be viewed apart from structures of representation and interpretation."

This understanding of representation rejects as irrelevant dysfunctional communication labeled as *misperception;* such labels imply the existence of an objective, veridical "reality" against which the individual can check the representation for correctness (ibid.). A representation is the product of an individual's knowledge level, experiences, and beliefs, and the value and meaning of an object or phenomenon are fully embodied by a representation.

Hence, an individual's representation is a constraint on reasoning in that it limits understanding to a specific organization of conceptual knowledge. These "mental explanations" are complex sets of relations between concepts usually with a causal basis, and they provide consistency between individuals' concepts and their understanding of interacting objects and forces (Murphy and Medin 1985). In short, representations are a product of discrimination in information acquisition and causal interpretations.

The Story Model

Pennington and Hastie's Story Model has been described at length elsewhere (1981, 1986, 1987, 1988); however, we highlight some of that work here. Pennington and Hastie make four fundamental claims about the Story Model in the legal domain that distinguish it from other types of models that have been developed to explain the correspondence between group processes and collective decisional outcomes. First, from trial evidence, jurors construct explanations that take the form of stories. These "mental representations" are domain-specific causal models that organize evidence, expectations, other related world knowledge, and the causal connections among them. This explanation-based "intermediate summary representation" is interpositioned between the evidence and the decision and is stored in memory.

Second, decision alternatives are represented as categories. Pennington and Hastie posit that the active construction of these categories is a second activity (the first is the construction of the summary representation) engaging jurors. In the legal domain, the construction of these categories is apparently a minor activity because verdict alternatives are the results of the judge's instructions; that is, the defining characteristics of a category are given. Nonetheless, certain attributes of a category are doubtless given greater weight than others by different individuals (Barsalou 1983, 1985; Higgins and Bargh 1987; Kerlinger 1984; Murphy and Medin 1985), resulting in the potential for differentials among jurors in the "match" between summary representations and verdicts.

The third claim that distinguishes the Story Model from traditional models is that variability in stories corresponds to variability in decisions. Pennington and Hastie noted that differences in evidence strength as well as in story coherence and global clarity, when contrasted with alternative summary representations, affected juror confidence and, hence, jurors' decisions. Further, verdict decisions did not covary with verdict representations.

Finally, Pennington and Hastie present evidence that the summary representations, or stories, are spontaneously constructed, and that they play a causal role in determining verdict decisions. Some critics have suggested that experimental subjects are evaluating the plausibility of evidence rather than accessing memory representations, and that the stories are being used as justifications for decisions rather than guides for decision making. However, the authors point out that experimental subjects responded almost as fast in making false recognition judgments as they did in making "correct" judgments about what had been seen before as an evidence item, supporting the claim that subjects access memory representation rather than assess plausibility of the evidence item. In addition, their finding that the strength of one story over alternative interpretations affects decisions leads them to reject the argument that stories are "postdecision justifications."

According to Pennington and Hastie, the distinctive element of their explanation-based approach is their proposition that "decision makers construct an intermediate memory representation of the evidence and that this representation, rather than the original 'raw' evidence, is the basis of the final decision" (1988: 523). In other words, evidence is "explained" according to the causal connections of the model, or representation. The authors say that their research reveals that reasoning processes do not reflect continuous updating patterns or conventional probability theory, nor does it reflect unidimensional verdict categories (i.e., "guiltiness"). In short, where traditional models assume that cognitive structures accommodate new information as it becomes available, the explanation-based model has demonstrated that new information is made to accommodate cognitive structures.

Our own independent work on reasoning types supports the explanation-based approach. In a series of experiments that included decision making in the foreign policy domain, we found that explanation-based reasoning is dominant over case- and model-based reasoning cross-culturally, across experimental protocols, and independently of individual or group contexts (Ostrom, Sylvan, Harasty, and Haddad 1993). Further, we found that explanation-based reasoning predominates regardless of methods of graduate training and regardless of levels of education and expertise (Sylvan, Ostrom, and Gannon 1994). Our more recent research into the connection between types of reasoning and modes of problem representation in groups (Sylvan, Haddad, and Ostrom 1994) encourages our current inquiry.

In the present work on collective decision making, we make use of the notable parallels between the foreign policy domain and the legal domain. Pennington and Hastie suggest that the explanation-based model is more useful than traditional models of the decision-making process when there are large amounts of information that are interdependent and contingent, and when decisions involve motivated human behavior. Such conditions are descriptive of the foreign policy domain. Foreign policy decisions are the results of myriad amounts of information from numerous sources, including the more conventional intelligence sources, as well as from the media, special interests, and other sources outside of the policy-making apparatus.

Pennington and Hastie's reference to decisions involving motivated human behavior clearly parallels Voss, Wolfe, Lawrence, and Engle's (1991) description of ill-structured problems (see also Voss, this volume). Pennington and Hastie say that the explanation-based approach would not be necessary where the "decision is made on a relatively small set of independent evidence items, and where the required judgment dimension is unidimensional and known" (1988: 531). Like decision making for Voss's well-structured problems, these decisions do not require socially based judgment and seldom require reasoning about causal relations among relevant information items. Voss, as well as Pennington and Hastie, says that computational decisions (e.g., mathematics, geometry) are examples of this class of decisions.

An *ill-structured problem,* on the other hand, is Voss's label for the kinds of problems that Pennington and Hastie say lead to explanation-based intermediate summary structures. These kinds of problems are typical in the foreign policy domain. Constraints on problem solutions are variously recognized by different decision makers, and the goals themselves may be unclear. Decisions about ill-structured problems are the results of discrimination in information acquisition and processing, judgments about causal links among information items, and evaluations of the implications of the conceptual organization for decisional alternatives. Decisional outcomes are delimited by the decision maker's knowledge level, experiences, beliefs, and attitudes.

The parallels between the legal domain and the foreign policy domain in these terms, then, suggest that the Story Model is an appropriate construct for investigating collective decision making in foreign policy. There are differences between Pennington and Hastie's decisional environments and our own, however. Three of these differences are discussed here.

First, decision alternatives are seldom a "given" in a foreign policy decision-making environment. Although, for instance, an ad hoc group may suggest alternatives to an ultimate decision maker, these alternatives nonetheless have been socially constructed within the group. These alternatives also tend to be specified poorly in terms of categorical attributes; that is, the alternatives may be variously represented by different participants.

The decision-making process in the Cuban missile crisis provides an example. Against the perceived provocation that Soviet missiles in Cuba were offensive, President Kennedy sought advice from ExComm for his response. Among ExComm's suggested alternatives were an air strike, diplomatic negotiations, and a naval quarantine. First, the fact that more than one solution was offered to the same problem suggests that ExComm members had varying representations of the problem. Second, representations of each decision alternative varied as well. For instance, whereas some viewed the naval quarantine as a military maneuver, others viewed this same alternative as a form of communication to the Soviet government.

Pennington and Hastie say that decisional alternatives are actively constructed through social interaction. But because decisional alternatives are essentially given in the legal domain (through the judge's instructions on verdicts), the authors effectively ignore this aspect of the Story Model. In our own work, preliminary findings suggest that the emergence of an intragroup decision rule precedes the generation of intragroup decision alternatives.

As is discussed later, our experiments with three-person groups required a single group response (however, subjects chose to define "group response") for each of a series of questions. This externally imposed constraint resulted in a first occasion for reasoning within the group. That is, group members tended to focus more on the social interactions within the group than on the substantive task initially. Differences over meanings in the substantive task precipitated the establishment of intragroup "roles" as a social hierarchy emerged. This social hierarchy was pivotal for understanding decision rules and subsequently became the strategy the group used in coming to single group decisions.[4]

A second difference between the legal and foreign policy domains is in the presentation of "evidence." Pennington and Hastie say that in the legal domain jurors are presented with a "massive 'database' of evidence" and that "the evidence comes in a scrambled sequence; usually . . . pieces of a historical puzzle in a jumbled sequence" (1988: 521). Nonetheless, this information is bounded in that jurors can assume that it is all potentially relevant in one way or another to the verdict "choice set." In fact, jurors are often instructed to disregard any other information they may have that is not presented at trial.

In the foreign policy domain, such boundedness does not exist. Here, the "massive database" includes information that may or may not be potentially relevant to a decision. The extent of "scrambledness" is greater because it is indeterminate which pieces of information will be considered relevant. Which pieces of information are chosen as relevant depends on the attentiveness of the decision maker (i.e., the prominence of the issue itself), as well as which elements of the issue are salient.

In the present experimental research, we do not present subjects with information that is potentially irrelevant to the decision; that is, information deemed irrelevant to the group's decision is a function of the subjects' choice. In this sense, we have approximated the legal domain in terms of the boundedness of the information presented, and in terms of the attentiveness of the decision makers. "Information overload," a real effect on actual foreign policy decisions, is not specifically investigated here.

A third area where Pennington and Hastie's decisional environment differs from our own is more fundamentally a difference in research questions. Pennington and Hastie explore individual jurors' decisions rather than jury decisions. Our interest is in the cognitive underpinnings of collective decisions. In a group context, the prominence of a social dimension becomes critical in what Sylvan and Thorson (1992) say is a "socially oriented attempt to understand webs of representations." We surmise that Pennington and Hastie's work is limited to jurors' representations before they convene to deliberate in the jury room, because there is no discussion of the distinction between decisions made in an individual environment and those made in a group environment.

Our inquiry reflects an interest in how single decisions emerge from a collective decision-making environment despite the potential for multiple individual problem representations. In other words, do individual problem representations of an issue converge to create a collective problem representation of that issue? Preliminary findings from the experimental research presented here overwhelmingly suggest that they do, and that they take the form of an explanation-based intermediate summary representation, or story construct.[5] This is the subject of the next section.

Experimental Design

Thirty-six undergraduate students at The Ohio State University were the subjects for this research. All were students in an upper division course in foreign policy decision making, and the vast majority were either juniors or seniors. The experiments were undertaken with twelve groups, each composed of three students. Our study focused on two different aspects of their sessions: interactions within the groups in responding to foreign policy scenarios, and the strategy used by the group in coming to decisions. In short, we investigated what mode of problem representation best captured the way in which group members interacted with one another in order to answer the foreign policy questions.

The experimental protocol involved two types of data collection. Data from on-line decision processes in a collective environment and an on-line group self-report were gathered, as well as individual self-reporting through postexperimental questionnaires.

In the former instance, the medium for communicating questions and eliciting responses from subjects was not pen and paper but a computer monitor and keyboard. Each of the groups of three students interacted with the JESSE Computational Model (Sylvan, Goel, and Chandrasekaran 1990) by reading and responding to questions about Japanese energy supply security and foreign policy. The platform was a Sun Microsystems SPARCstation. In contrast with the other experimental settings, where subjects read printed scenarios and responded by writing or placing marks or numbers on printed pages, this new medium allowed for on-line processing. In other words, subjects read the scenarios and follow-up questions and simply touched a key on the keyboard to respond.

An increase in spontaneity is clearly more possible with this procedure. We believe this spontaneity enhanced our prospects for capturing styles of reasoning and ''strategies'' (or modes of problem representation) in reaching group decisions. Responses to each individual question were recorded, response times were generated, and the sessions were videotaped for later coding. In addition, an experimenter observed each session.

Subjects were asked to answer ''substantive'' questions concerning Japanese energy supply security and foreign policy that appeared on the screen. Sessions began with each subject's reading what we call a *situation sheet* – a printed version of two scenarios that provide equivalent referents for all subjects in all groups. The order in which the scenarios appeared depended on which JESSE classifier the group received first. After all subjects in a group had had ample time to read the situation sheet, video- and audiotaping began and the computer simulation was started. To illustrate the structure of the scenarios, the one that pertains to an increase in the price of oil reads as follows:

> Your country depends on oil imports for a large portion of its energy needs. An oil exporting country has increased the price of oil on the world market

and other countries are indicating that they will also increase prices. However, the supply of energy on the market is enough to meet current demand.

Each group responded to two scenarios. The initial question following the foregoing scenarios was, "Has an energy-related event that may concern the energy supply security of Japan occurred in the recent past?" The order of scenario presentation was counterbalanced across subjects using a Latin square design. Subjects were randomly assigned to the different questionnaire, thereby counterbalancing conditions.

On two occasions during the session, immediately after the subjects had answered the initial question of a classifier, a follow-up question dealing with how they had arrived at that response appeared on the screen. Subject response options contained six thoughts that were relevant to the decision. These thoughts were prepared by the experimenters and sampled the kinds of thoughts persons might have while considering the decision. The thoughts were generated to reflect six *a priori* types of decision-relevant thinking. Three of these thoughts supported a positive decision, and three supported a negative decision. The three thoughts in each of these two groups were constructed to represent either case-based, explanation-based, or model-based types of reasoning. One favorable and one unfavorable thought for each type was presented, for a total of six thoughts.

The instructions for this thought-checking task appeared on the screen, so that each member of the group could read them. The member of the group who had volunteered to be the "reader" also read all options aloud. Those instructions were as follows:

> We are interested in the thoughts you had while making the last decision. Below are different thoughts people may have when making this kind of decision. Select "y" if a similar thought occurred to you. Select "n" if a similar thought did not occur to you.

Following are the six statements provided for the scenario that related to an increase in the price of oil. The first three support a "yes" response, and the last three support a "no" response. Within each of these groups, the first statement is an example of case-based reasoning, the second is explanation-based, and the third is model-based.

1. "In 1973, despite an adequate supply of oil, price hikes produced an energy crisis."
2. "The high percentage of oil your country imports suggests that you have an energy problem."
3. "Resource management theory suggests that change-overs from one energy source to another can be difficult."

4. "Government supply regulations in 1973–1974 increased the effect of price hikes."
5. "The wide range of energy sources that your country uses suggests that no energy problem exists."
6. "Economic theory suggests that, as energy supplies become expensive, they will be replaced with cheaper alternatives."

Following the initial question and the thought-checking section, several other questions appeared for each classifier that were relevant for the context of the scenario from the situation sheet. A typical question from one scenario might deal with whether or not there was a serious problem with energy flow or supply routes or, in the case of the other scenario, whether or not a problem had recently arisen with Japanese-Asian relations.

The final question from the on-line aspect of the experiment contained the question on "story usage," or as we term it in our analysis, the group's *strategy* for answering questions.

> We are interested in how groups come to group decisions. In the course of discussion, groups often develop strategies for dealing with the questions they collectively face. Please thoroughly read all of the following possible group strategies. After thoughtfully considering each of them, choose one that is closest to the strategy that your group used in coming to group decisions.

A. We considered each question (or group of questions) on its own merit. The way we answered one question had no bearing on how we chose to answer subsequent questions. Each question was a new problem to consider.

B. The more questions we considered, the more the group seemed to know how to collectively answer the next question. By the end of the session, we were responding to questions according to a "story" that we had developed.

C. Part way through the session, we realized that we kept returning to the same historic event to understand the questions and to come to a group decision. By using the historic "case," we really didn't have to use much other information for the remainder of the session.

D. If your group used a strategy, but you feel that it was unlike any of those above, please describe the strategy that you followed. Be sure to comment on the ways in which it was similar and different from options A, B, and C.[6]

This question is important to our research design in that it elicits a *group* self-report and reflects our attempt to capture whether or not a Story Model of the type described by Pennington and Hastie is the prevalent mode of a group's problem representation in the foreign policy domain.

Option A allows the group to characterize their strategy for coming to a single decision in a way that is similar to what Pennington and Hastie call a *computational process*, or to what Voss et al. (1991) refer to as a *solution process*, for well-structured problems. This option implies that information was treated by the group as independent evidence items. Only one of the twelve groups chose this option as similar to their strategy for answering questions in the simulation.

Option B allows the group to characterize their strategy as Pennington and Hastie's "intermediate summary representation," or Story Model. Here the group treats information as interdependent evidence items and uses the creation of a unique story as a filter between information and decision. Nine of the twelve groups (75%) chose this option.

For Option C, information is treated as interdependent evidence items; however, rather than creating a unique representation of information, groups choosing this option would be suggesting that a historic "case" guided their decisions. We had expected that case-based or model-based reasoners would most likely choose this option. They didn't. Four groups used some case-based reasoning, and ten of the groups used some amount of model-based reasoning. None of these groups chose Option C. Only one group of the twelve chose this option, and this group offered only two reasoning responses, both of which were explanation-based. Based on the videotape and the experimenter's observations, our initial impressions are that members of this group interacted in a way in which they were able to "work out" a common understanding about elements of the scenario, and these elements matched those of a commonly understood "case." Nonetheless, more work needs to be done to understand this phenomenon.

Only one group chose Option D. The group's description of their strategy was as follows: "One [group member] proposed an answer & [*sic*] then the group agreed or disagreed on the proposed answer by the individual." This presents another puzzle for us. On the postexperimental questionnaires, two of the group members independently said that a "group perspective" emerged for answering the computer questions as a group, whereas the third group member said that the group had an "unspoken way" of coming to decisions. Hence, individuals perceived the group strategy to be Option B, whereas Option D was chosen in the group context. This result suggests that individuals may be able to hold independently both individual and collective representations, invoking whichever is considered "ecologically appropriate" (Sylvan and Thorson 1992).

This group self-reporting test is supplemented by our analysis of group interaction in the experiment through videotape coding and is discussed later.

The second type of data collection for each group session followed completion of the computer-interaction portion of the experiment. Subjects were administered written questionnaires in an attempt to capture details of individual reasoning, as well as the way in which the individual perceived his or her group's reasoning processes. The chapter-end appendix contains the questions that attempted to get at the way in which the group functioned. We posed these questions for two reasons. First, we wanted to see what kinds of connections might exist among the ways a group functions (e.g., participant roles), the type(s) of reasoning they employ, and the strategy that a group uses for coming to a single group decision. We also wanted to see if we could detect any elements of problem representation in the way in which experiment participants understood the functioning of the group and the tasks that the group faced.

Results

We began our analysis by comparing the overall profile of reasoning to results of our past studies. As Table 8.1 illustrates, the general profile of reasoning style usage is quite similar to that of experimental groups in our earlier studies. The groups participating in this experiment chose explanation-based thoughts most frequently (.83), with model-based thought next (.50), and case-based thoughts least frequently (.25).

Next, we undertook an analysis of variance to see under what circumstances the profile of reasoning differed. Table 8.2 summarizes our results. Of particular interest to the focal point of this chapter is the relationship between the responses to the mode of problem representation variable (''strategy'') and the type of reasoning employed by the subjects. As Table 8.1 notes, the results, $F(2, 18) = 4.58$, $p < .025$, show a relationship between the type of reasoning employed by the groups and the mode of problem representation.

To help understand this pattern, though, we should concentrate on the overall response to the strategy variable. As Table 8.3 shows, the dominant response to the strategy variable was a ''story'' mode of problem representation. Of the 38 responses, 28, or 73.7 percent, chose ''story'' as the most appropriate characterization of the way in which their group reached a decision. Further, 67 percent of the groups using case-based reasoning, 75 percent of those using model-based reasoning, and 75 percent of those using explanation-based reasoning chose the story mode of problem representation as most similar to the strategy used by their group. What this seems to signify is that *regardless of the type of reasoning employed by the group, the Story Model is seen by participants as the most appropriate way of capturing the manner in which their group represented problems.*

Another aspect of this research is our development of a coding system in order to analyze videotapes of group sessions. Our focus has been an attempt to ''translate'' Pennington and Hastie's alternatives to the Story Model into

Table 8.1. *Reasoning style usage.*

	Spring/Fall 1993			Winter 1994		
	C-1	C-2	Total	C-1	C-2	Total
Case (+)	.50	.20	.35	.33	.00	.16
(N)	(12)	(5)	(17)	(4)	(0)	(4)
Case (−)	.16	.04	.10	.08	.08	.08
(N)	(4)	(1)	(5)	(1)	(1)	(2)
Expl. (+)	.79	.58	.68	.91	.66	.79
(N)	(19)	(14)	(33)	(11)	(8)	(19)
Expl. (−)	.00	.12	.06	.00	.08	.04
(N)	(0)	(3)	(3)	(0)	(1)	(1)
Model (+)	.12	.75	.43	.08	.66	.37
(N)	(3)	(18)	(21)	(1)	(8)	(9)
Model (−)	.45	.25	.35	.00	.25	.12
(N)	(11)	(6)	(17)	(0)	(3)	(3)
Summary						
Case	.66	.25	.45	.41	.08	.25
Expl.	.79	.70	.75	.91	.75	.83
Model	.58	1.00	.79	.08	.91	.50

			Case	.38		
			Expl.	.77		
			Model	.69		

possible operationalizations. We continue to refine this system, but we describe the rudimentary code here and present the preliminary results.

One category assumes that no representation guides group decisions, a second category assumes the story mode of problem representation, and two of the categories reflect different types of "computational" strategies. The first category, *No Rep* (i.e., no problem representation), refers to collective decision processes where the group continually refers to the situation sheet for guidance as to how to respond to a question. Causal connections among information items are not articulated; hence, consistency with previous answers is a low priority.[7] Group interactions for this category are characterized by statements such as "What does the sheet say?" and by confusion when the situation sheet does not directly address the question that appears on the computer screen. Nonverbals include frequent shrugging of shoulders and avoidance of eye contact. There is little or no discussion of meanings, whether of the scenario, the question, or possible alternative decision choices.

Table 8.2. *Analyses of variance*

Thought-Checking

Analysis: 2 (order:c1 or c2 first) × 2 (Scenario) × 2 (Support/Nonsupport) ×
3 (Type: CBR, EBR, MBR)

	Trial I $N=24$	Trial II $N=12$
Order	$F(1,22) = 2.13, p = .158$	$F(1,10) = .55, p = .48$
Scenario	$F(1,22) = .93, p = .346$	$F(1,10) = 4.29, p = .06$
Support	$F(1,22) = 52.19, p = .0001$	$F(1,10) = 58.28, p = .0001$
Type	$F(2,44) = 4.58, p = .016$	$F(2,20) = 13.21, p = .0002$
Scen*Support	$F(1,22) = .41, p = .529$	$F(1,10) = .34, p = .57$
Scen*Type	$F(2,44) = 12.18, p = .0001$	$F(2,20) = 7.65, p = .003$
Scen*Type*Order	$F(2,44) = 7.12, p = .002$	$F(2,20) = .59, p = .56$
Support*Type	$F(2,44) = 6.87, p = .0025$	$F(2,20) = 11.82, p = .0004$
Scen*Sup*Type	$F(2,44) = 24.50, p = .0001$	$F(2,20) = 2.20, p = .136$

Counterbalanced

Order	$F(1,22) = 2.37, p = .138$	$F(1,10) = .27, p = .617$
Scenario	$F(1,22) = .71, p = .407$	$F(1,10) = 2.36, p = .156$
Type	$F(2,44) = 4.20, p = .021$	$F(2,20) = 12.21, p = .0003$
Scen*Type	$F(2,44) = 9.93, p = .0003$	$F(2,20) = 7.84, p = .003$
Scen*Type*Order	$F(2,44) = 6.98, p = .002$	$F(2,20) = .62, p = .545$

With Strategy

Order		$F(1,9) = .00, p = 1.00$
Strategy		$F(1,9) = 1.95, p = .196$
Scenario		$F(1,9) = 6.27, p = .034$
Scen*Strat		$F(1,9) = 3.80, p = .083$
Support		$F(1,9) = 1.52, p = .249$
Type		$F(2,18) = 4.58, p = .025$

Counterblanced with Strategy

Order		$F(1,9) = .05, p = .82$
Strat		$F(1,9) = 2.13, p = .178$
Scenario		$F(1,9) = 2.90, p = .123$
Type		$F(2,18) = 3.72, p = .044$

Strategy, no Order Var.

Strat		$F(3,8) = 1.93, p = .203$
Scenario		$F(1,8) = 3.64, p = .093$
Support		$F(1,8) = 25.29, p = .001$
Sup*Strat		$F(3,8) = 3.44, p = .072$
Type		$F(2,16) = 4.46, p = .029$
Scen*Type		$F(2,16) = 7.02, p = .006$
Sup*Type		$F(2,16) = 9.01, p = .002$

Table 8.2 (*cont.*)

	Thought-Checking	

Analysis: 2 (order:c1 or c2 first) $\times$ 2 (Scenario) $\times$ 2 (Support/Nonsupport) $\times$ 3 (Type: CBR, EBR, MBR)

	Trial I	Trial II
	N=24	*N*=12

Counterbalanced Strategy No Order Var.

Strat		$F(3,8) =$ 1.62, $p =$ .26
Scenario		$F(1,8) =$ 2.33, $p =$ .165
Type		$F(2,16) =$ 4.99, $p =$ .021
Scen*Type		$F(2,16) =$ 6.94, $p =$ .007

Logged Reaction Times

	Trial I	Trial II
	$N = 24$	$N = 12$

Order	$F(1,22) =$ 5.89, $p =$ .024	$F(1,10) =$ .68, $p =$ .43
Scenario	$F(1,22) =$ 4.69, $p =$ .041	$F(1,10) =$ 13.10, $p =$ .005
Type	$F(2,44) =$ 6.61, $p =$ .003	$F(2,20) =$ 1.37, $p =$ .276
Scen*Supp	$F(1,22) =$ 5.86, $p =$ .024	$F(1,10) =$ 7.09, $p =$ .024
Scen*Type	$F(2,44) =$ 2.80, $p =$ .071	$F(2,20) =$ 2.99, $p =$ .073
Supp*Type*Order	$F(2,44) =$ 2.91, $p =$ .065	$F(2,20) =$ 1.04, $p =$ .371

Counterbalanced

Order	$F(1,22) =$ 5.07, $p =$ .035	$F(1,10) =$ .63, $p =$ .445
Scenario	$F(1,22) =$ 3.39, $p =$ .079	$F(1,10) =$ 13.15, $p =$ .005
Type	$F(2,44) =$ 5.31, $p =$ .009	$F(2,20) =$ .21, $p =$ .81
Scen*Valence	$F(1,22) =$ 4.41, $p =$ .047	$F(1,10) =$ 5.91, $p =$ .035

With Strategy

Order		$F(1,9) =$ 1.92, $p =$ .20
Strat		$F(1,9) =$ 1.75, $p =$ .219
Scenario		$F(1,9) =$ 2.84, $p =$ .126
Scen*Order		$F(1,9) =$ 2.41, $p =$ .155
Type		$F(2,18) =$ .37, $p =$ .695
Scen*Type*Order		$F(2,18) =$ 5.56, $p =$ .013
Scen*Type*Order		$F(2,18) =$ 2.23, $p =$ .137

Counterbalanced with Strategy

Order		$F(1,9) =$ 1.85, $p =$ .206
Strat		$F(1,9) =$ 1.75, $p =$ .219
Scenario		$F(1,9) =$ 2.59, $p =$ .142
Scen*Type*Order		$F(2,18) =$ 3.52, $p =$ .051

Table 8.3. *Mode of problem representation*

	None	Story	Case	Other
Case (+)	0	3	0	1
Case (−)	0	1	0	1
CASE ALL	0	4	0	2
Expl (+)	1	13	2	2
Expl (−)	0	2	0	0
EXPL ALL	1	15	2	2
Model (+)	0	8	0	1
Model (−)	1	1	0	1
MODEL ALL	1	9	0	2

For these groups, response times are unstable, showing no pattern of increasing ability to respond to questions.

The underlying assumption for this category of group decision processes is that no collective problem representation emerges to guide group decision. Pennington and Hastie do not discuss the possibility that an alternative to the Story Model is one where no intermediate representation emerges. For our research, this category represents a null hypothesis.

We refer to the second category as *story*. Meanings, causal connections among information items, consistency, and group decision rules are highly important. A typical sequence of interaction begins with subjects' agreement on decisional responses. After the first few questions, however, differences over meanings of terms, questions, and the scenario emerge. The statement "It depends" is pivotal and seems to signal a challenge to another individual's interpretation. Working out common meanings becomes very important. The following quotations come directly from experimental sessions: "We need to decide what country we're talking about." "What do you mean by ...?" "Whatever we do, be consistent." "What do you mean by 'substantial'?"

At this point, group interaction is high and response times to questions increase. Individuals begin to draw on their own knowledge from outside the scope of the situation sheet, and the word "because" is used frequently. The confrontation over meanings appears to be a springboard for the emergence of a social hierarchy based on individuals' abilities to articulate causal reasoning for decisions, as well as on individuals' perceptions of their own knowledge levels vis-à-vis the knowledge levels of others.[8]

As subsequent questions are answered, a decision rule emerges. Questions are considered by the group in terms of the organization of previous answers. Consistency appears to be the primary motivation for this consideration. If the organization of previous answers provides no guidance, an attempt is made by the group to "explain" the new question in a way that is not inconsistent with previous answers. If both previous answers and efforts to explain fail, the group tends to use a majoritarian decision rule.[9] By the end of the session, this "strategy" for coming to decisions is sufficiently entrenched, and response times decrease.

For a group using the story strategy, then, we find high usage of the word "because," the phrase "it depends," and propositional "if . . . , then . . ." statements. The level of consistency seeking is pronounced, and the frequency of references back to the situation sheet declines significantly and rapidly. Nonverbals include high levels of eye contact and tendencies to lean toward the group and the computer screen. At least two of the group participants are highly verbal. Initial response times are small, followed by marked increases, then steady declines.

We refer to a third category for coding the way in which groups come to a single decision in the foreign policy domain as *Bayesian*. Pennington and Hastie summarize their understanding of Bayesian probability models as "decision process[es] as a sequence of multiplicative products of the prior opinion and diagnosticity of each evidence item" (1988: 523). They also note that some conditionality among evidence items may exist. In other words, if there is a conceptual structure between the "raw" information and the decision, it does not organize new information. Rather, new information is a source for revising the structure.

Note also that in these terms, a Bayesian probability model of decision processes assumes unidimensionality of decisional "choice sets." That is, new information either increases or decreases the likelihood of a single decisional alternative. In our efforts to operationalize these kinds of models, we look for words like "probably," "likely," and so forth. We also look for evidence of nonmonotonic belief revision due to new information. For example, the following would be coded for Bayesian probability decision models: "Let's assume that we're talking about a different country because [new information changed the likelihood that this country is relevant]," or "I think we screwed up on the basis for our answer [to the last question]. I think Mike's right; we got off base on that question."[10] Notice that in the first statement, the word "because" did not lead to a Story code for two reasons: First, reference back to an intermediate summary structure was not apparent, and second, the basis for the decision was changed rather than the interpretation of the information item.

The fourth category for our coding system reflects our attempt to capture a different type of "computational" decision process. We refer to this as the

Ledger Model of decision processes. The underlying assumption for Ledger is that subjects "weigh" the costs/benefits or advantages/disadvantages of new information. We consider this coding category to be an acceptable synthesis of Pennington and Hastie's Information Integration and Sequential Weighting models of decision processes.

Similar to our Bayesian category, we look for unidimensionality of decision choice sets and evidence of nonmonotonic belief revision. Key to coding Ledger decision processes, however, are words that indicate the salience of elements of the scenario, the questions, and new information. Information items may be contingent but not related causally. Hence, information items in a Ledger decision process are basically independent. A typical Ledger decision-process item would be the statement "This is more important than. . . ." or "That doesn't help us with this."

In summary, our coding system attempts to capture four different types of group decision strategies. "No Rep" processes are those where there is no intermediate cognitive structure (i.e., problem representation) between new information and collective decision. A Story coding is used where there is evidence that an intermediate summary structure guides decision. Unidimensional computational decision processes appearing as probability updating are coded as Bayesian, whereas those appearing as cost–benefit analyses are coded as Ledger.[11]

In our initial effort to apply this system, we coded 9 of the 12 videotaped group sessions on which we reported in this chapter. We found 194 instances of codable interaction. Of these, 12 percent (24) of the interactions provided evidence of the "No Rep" category of group decision processes, 69 percent (150) provided evidence of the Story category, 8 percent (19) provided evidence of the Bayesian category, and only one interaction (0.3 percent) provided evidence of the Ledger category.

Conclusion

There is ample evidence to suggest that decision making in a group context results in different decisional outcomes than those that obtain for individual decision making. In addition, these collective decisions reflect neither an aggregation of individual preferences nor an assurance of optimal decisions. Because a significant number of decisions in the foreign policy domain are made in a collective environment, we are interested in the cognitive mediation produced by the group context. Our investigation has focused on whether or not problem representation is useful for understanding group decisional processes and, if so, what mode of problem representation is employed by groups in coming to a single decision.

Our preliminary results overwhelmingly suggest that problem representation is an appropriate cognitive construct for understanding group decisional processes, and that the most frequently used mode of problem representation is approximated by Pennington and Hastie's intermediate summary representation, or Story Model. The results from twelve on-line group self-reports indicate that 75 percent of our experimental groups characterized the group strategy for coming to a decision as the Story Model. From the coding of nine videotaped group sessions, 69 percent of the group interactions provided evidence of the Story Model. From the postexperimental questionnaire, 69 percent (25/36) of individuals independently self-reported perceptions that a group perspective emerged.

In the area of reasoning style, these groups did not differ significantly from individuals and groups we had examined in previous work. Specifically, explanation-based reasoning was the most common type, but there is evidence that case- and model-based reasoning are also employed by subjects.

These conclusions must be viewed as preliminary, subject to both further systematic analysis of the videotapes from this study and other follow-up research. They can serve, however, as a baseline for further exploration of collective problem representation and its usefulness for understanding cognitive mediation in a group environment.

Appendix: Questions on Group Functioning

How clear and understandable were the instructions for this simulation?

1........2 .... 3 ....4........5........ 6 .... 7 ....8........9
Not at all   Extremely
clear   clear

How interesting did you find the simulation?

1........2 .... 3 ....4........5........ 6 .... 7 ....8........9
Not at all   Extremely
interesting   interesting

A. YOUR THOUGHTS ABOUT THE EXPERIMENT

We are interested in *how* people complete the simulation. Please answer the following questions as thoughtfully as you can.

1. What kinds of thoughts did you have while answering the computer's questions?

2. Did you think of any principles of international relations while answering the questions? If so, what were they?

3. Did your knowledge of current events and/or past energy-related problems in the world help you in answering the questions? If so, what were these events?

4. Can you give us any more information about how you completed the simulation that can help us understand your thoughts?

5. To what extent did the comments by other group members affect your thoughts while completing the simulation?

1........2 .... 3 ....4........5........ 6 .... 7 ....8........9
Not at all   Extremely
affected   affected

Brief explanation:

6. To what degree were your personal opinions taken into account in the group responses?

1........2 .... 3 ....4........5........ 6 .... 7 ....8........9
Not at all taken   Completely taken
into account   into account

Brief explanation:

7. How well did the group cooperate?

1........2 .... 3 ....4........5........ 6 .... 7 ....8........9
Very poor   Excellent
cooperation   cooperation

Brief explanation:

8. How pleased were you with the group's performance?

1........2 .... 3 ....4........5........ 6 .... 7 ....8........9
Not at all   Extremely
pleased   pleased

Brief explanation:

B. YOUR THOUGHTS ABOUT THE GROUP

We are interested in how your group interacted. Please answer the following questions as thoughtfully as possible.

I was: ( ) Keyboard operator   ( ) Reader   ( ) Neither

1. Take a moment to think about your group responding to the questions on the computer. Was there more agreement among group members earlier or later in the session?

What was important to the group as it considered the questions? What might have been the goal(s) of your group?

2. What was the most useful suggestion or thought provided by the other group members? Why was it useful?

Was this suggestion or thought offered early or late in the session?

3. How much did group members know about the subject of the questions?

Keyboard Operator

1........2 ....3 ....4........5........6 ....7 ....8........9
Not very much   Extremely
knowledge of the   knowledgeable
subject

Reader

1........2 ....3 ....4........5........6 ....7 ....8........9
Not very much   Extremely
knowledge of the   knowledgeable
subject

Third Group Member?

1........2 .... 3........4........5........ 6 .... 7 ....8........9
Not very much   Extremely
knowledge of the   knowledgeable
subject

---

   4. I felt like I fit in with this group
_____   right from the start.
_____   about halfway through the experiment.
_____   toward the end of the experiment.
_____   I never quite felt like I fit in with this group

   5. The following are some possible objectives of any group of people who might be trying to make a decision. Number them according to their order of importance for your group (1 = primary goal). Please include *only* the objectives that were relevant for *your* group.

_____ Consistent/logical answers   _____ The ''right'' answer
_____ Consensus on answers   _____ Cooperation
_____ Other (explain)

C. YOUR THOUGHTS ABOUT GROUP STRATEGY

We are interested in how groups come to group decisions. In the course of discussion, groups often develop strategies for dealing with the questions they collectively face. Please carefully read each of the following possible group strategies. After thoughtfully considering each of them, choose the one that is closest to the strategy that your group used in coming to its decisions.

   A. We considered each question [or group of questions] on its own merit. The way we answered one question had no bearing on how we chose to answer subsequent questions. Each question was a new problem to consider.

   B. The more questions we considered, the more the group seemed to know how collectively to answer the next question. By the end of the session, we were responding to questions according to a *Story* that we had developed about the scenario under consideration.

C. Part way through the session, we realized that we kept returning to the same historic event to understand the question and to come to a group decision. By using this historic *Case*, we really didn't have to use much other information for the remainder of the session.

D. Our group used a strategy, but it was unlike any of those above.

Please describe the strategy that you followed. Be sure to comment on the ways in which it was similar and different from options A, B, and C. Please begin your answer with double quotes, and end your answer with double quotes.

Notes

1 Interest in group process as a source of cognitive mediation may be dated to Sheriff (1935), Asch (1951, 1956), and Crutchfield (1955). Eagly and Chaiken (1993) provide a succinct and insightful overview.

2 The concept, problem space, is considered elsewhere in the volume (see Voss). For the seminal work, see Newell and Simon (1972).

3 Zhang (1991) refers to this as the *representational effect*; that is, different isomorphic representatives can cause different behaviors.

4 Our preliminary findings are that the "strategy" most often used was the explanation-based intermediate summary representation, or Story Model. These findings are discussed in the next section.

5 This is not to suggest that a collective problem representation displaces individual problem representations of an issue – only that a collective representation is created in order for a group to come to a single decision. Individuals may retain a different problem representation, but this and the reconciliation between individual and collective representations are not investigated here.

6 This option required more effort than the other three options. Because this extra effort might have induced subjects to avoid it, we decided that it should have two parts. Hence, this last alternative actually reads, "Our group used a strategy, but it was unlike any of those above." Only after this option is chosen does the following appear on the computer screen: "Please describe the strategy that you followed. Be sure to comment on the ways in which it was similar and different from options A, B, and C."

7 The experimental protocol provides two sources for evaluating the extent of consistency seeking by a group. The desire for consistency is verbalized by the group, is captured on videotape, and is among the experimenter's notes. Second, the postexperimental questionnaire (see the chapter-end appendix) asks subjects to rank certain factors affecting group decision. Among these factors is consistency.

8 This is supported by individuals' responses on postexperimental questionnaires.

9 The tendency toward majoritarian rule is supported by the postexperimental questionnaire.

10 These are actual statements from subjects in our Spring 1994 experiments.
11 Recall that these last two categories, Bayesian and Ledger, assume that a collective representation is revised according to new information items, whereas the Story coding assumes that new information is interpreted in a way to accommodate the collective representation.

References

Allen, V. L., and D. A. Wilder (1980). "Impact of group consensus and social support on stimulus meaning: Mediation of conformity by cognitive restructuring." *Journal of Personality and Social Psychology, 39*: 1116–1124.

Asch, S. E. (1951). "Effects of group pressure upon the modification and distortion of judgments." In H. Guetzkow (ed.), *Groups, Leadership, and Men* (177–190). Pittsburgh, PA: Carnegie Press.

(1956). "Studies of independence and conformity: A minority of one against a unanimous majority." *Psychological Monographs, 70*.

Barsalou, L. W. (1983). "Ad hoc categories." *Memory and Cognition 11*, 3: 211–227.

(1985). "Ideals, central tendency, and frequency of instantiation as determinants of graded structure in categories." *Journal of Experimental Psychology, 11*: 629–654.

Crutchfield, R. S. (1955). "Conformity and character." *American Psychologist, 10*: 191–198.

Dion, K. L., R. S. Baron, and N. Miller (1978). "Why do groups make riskier decisions than individuals?" In L. Berkowitz (ed.), *Group Processes* (227–299). New York: Academic Press.

Eagly, A. H., and S. Chaiken (1993). *The Psychology of Attitudes.* New York: Harcourt Brace Jovanovich College Publishers.

Hermann, M. G. (1987). "Leaders' policy orientations and the quality of foreign policy decisions." In S. Walker (ed.), *Role Theory and Foreign Policy Analysis.* Durham, NC: Duke University Press.

Higgins, E. T., and J. A. Bargh (1987). "Social cognition and social perception." *Annual Review of Psychology, 38*: 369–425.

Janis, I. L. (1972). *Victims of Groupthink: A Psychological Study of Foreign Policy Decisions and Fiascoes.* Boston, MA: Houghton Mifflin Company.

(1982). *Groupthink.* Boston, MA: Houghton Mifflin Company.

Kaplan, M. F. (1989). "Task, situational, and personal determinants of influence processes in group decision making." In E. J. Lawler and B. Markovsky (eds.), *Advances in Group Processes* (Vol. 6, 87–105). Greenwich, CT: JAI Press.

Kerlinger, F. N. (1984). "The criterial referents theory of attitudes." In *Liberalism and Conservatism: The Nature and Structure of Social Attitudes* (Ch. 3). Hillsdale, NJ: Lawrence Erlbaum.

Levine, J. M. (1989). "Reaction to opinion deviance in small groups." In P. B. Paulus (ed.), *Psychology of Group Influence* (187–231). Hillsdale, NJ: Lawrence Erlbaum.

Levine, J. M., and R. L. Moreland (1987). "Social comparison and outcome evaluation in group contexts." In J. C. Masters and W. P. Smith (eds.), *Social Comparison, Social Justice, and Relative Deprivation: Theoretical, Empirical, and Policy Perspectives* (105–127). Hillsdale, NJ: Lawrence Erlbaum.

Levine, J. M., L. B. Resnick, and E. T. Higgins (1993). "Social foundations of cognition." *Annual Review of Psychology, 44*: 585–612

Maass, A., S. G. West, and R. B. Cialdini (1987). "Minority influence and conversion." In C. Hendrick (ed.), *Review of Personality and Social Psychology* (Vol. 8, 55–79). Newbury Park, CA: Sage.

Mackie, D. M. (1986). "Social identification effects in group polarization." *Journal of Personality & Social Psychology, 50*: 720–728.

Moscovici, S. (1976). *Social Influence and Social Change*. London: Academic Press.

(1980). "Toward a theory of conversion behavior." In L. Berkowitz (ed.), *Advances in Experimental Social Psychology* (Vol. 13, 209–239). San Diego: Academic Press.

Mullen, B. (1987). "Self-attention theory: The effects of group composition on the individual." In B. Mullen and R. Goethals (eds.), *Theories of Group Behavior* (125–146). New York: Springer-Verlag.

Murphy, G. L., and D. L. Medin (1985). "The role of theories in conceptual coherence." *Psychological Review, 92*: 289–316.

Nemeth, C. (1987). "Influence processes, problem solving, and creativity." In M. P. Zanna, J. M. Olson, and C. P. Herman (eds.), *Social Influence: The Ontario Symposium* (Vol. 5, 237–246). Hillsdale, NJ: Lawrence Erlbaum.

Newell, A., and H. A. Simon (1972). *Human Problem Solving*. Englewood Cliffs, NJ: Prentice Hall.

Ostrom, T. M., D. A. Sylvan, A. Harasty, and D. M. Haddad (1993). "Reasoning Styles in Foreign Policy: Comparing Cultures, Processing Environments, and Individuals Versus Groups." Paper presented to the annual meeting of the International Studies Association, Acapulco (April).

Pennington, N., and R. Hastie (1981). "Juror decision making models: The generalization gap." *Psychological Bulletin, 89*: 246–287.

(1986). "Evidence evaluation in complex decision making." *Journal of Personality and Social Psychology, 51*: 242–258.

(1987). "Explanation-based decision making." *Proceedings of the Ninth Annual Meeting of the Cognitive Science Society* (682–690). Hillsdale, NJ: Lawrence Erlbaum.

(1988). "Explanation-based decision making: Effects of memory structure on judgment." *Journal of Experimental Psychology, 14*, 3: 521–533.

Sherif, M. (1935). "A study of some social factors in perception." In *Archives of Psychology*, 27:1–60.

Stasser, G. (1992). "Pooling of unshared information during group discussions." In S. Worchel, W. Wood, and J. Simpson (eds.), *Group Process and Productivity* (48–67). Newbury Park, CA: Sage.

Stasser, G., N. L. Kerr, and J. H. Davis (1989). "Influence processes and consensus models in decision-making groups." In P. B. Paulus (ed.), *Psychology of Group Influence* (279–326). Hillsdale, NJ: Lawrence Erlbaum.

Stoner, J. A. (1968). "Risky and cautious shifts in group decisions: The influence of widely held values." *Journal of Experimental Social Psychology, 4*: 442–459.

Sylvan, D. A., A. Goel, and B. Chandrasekaran (1990). "Analyzing political decision making from an information processing perspective: JESSE." *American Journal of Political Science, 34*: 74–123.

Sylvan, D. A., D. M. Haddad, and T. M. Ostrom (1994). "Reasoning and Problem Representation in Foreign Policy: Groups, Individuals, and Stories." Paper presented at the 35th Annual Meeting of the International Studies Association, Washington, D.C. (March).

Sylvan, D. A., T. M. Ostrom, and K. Gannon (1994). "Case-based, model-based, and explanation-based styles of reasoning in foreign policy." *International Studies Quarterly, 38*, 1: 61–90.

Sylvan, D. A., and S. J. Thorson (1992). "Ontologies, problem representation, and the Cuban Missile Crisis." *Journal of Conflict Resolution, 36*: 709–732.

Turner, J. C. (1987). *Rediscovering the Social Group: A Self-Categorization Theory.* New York: Basil Blackwell.

Vertzberger, Y. Y. I. (1990). *The World in Their Minds: Information Processing, Cognition, and Perception in Foreign Policy Decisionmaking.* Stanford: Stanford University Press.

——— (1994). "Collective Risk-taking: The Decisionmaking Group and Organization." Paper presented at the 35th Annual Convention of the International Studies Association, Washington, D.C. (March).

Voss, J. F., C. R. Wolfe, J. A. Lawrence, and R. A. Engle (1991). "From representation to decision: An analysis of problem solving in international relations." In R. J. Sternberg and P. Frensch (eds.), *Complex Problem Solving: Principles and Mechanisms* (119–158). Hillsdale, NJ: Lawrence Erlbaum.

Wallach, M. A., N. Kogan, and D. J. Bem (1962). "Group influence on individual risk taking." *Journal of Abnormal & Social Psychology, 65*: 75–86.

Wilder, D. A. (1978). "Perceiving persons as a group: Effects on attributions of causality and beliefs." *Social Psychology, 41*: 13–23.

Zhang, J. (1991). "The interaction of internal and external representations in a problem solving task." In *Proceedings of the Thirteenth Annual Conference of the Cognitive Science Society*, Chicago (954–958). Hillsdale, NJ: Lawrence Erlbaum.

CHAPTER 9

Representing Problem Representation

Michael D. Young

Introduction

> If we are ever to reconstruct the path to the Cold War's end and sort out the
> relative validity of rival theories concerning the impact of its many discrete
> contributing causes, we, thus, will need to map the cognitive terrain of the
> actors in the process first. In this way we could describe the decision calcu-
> lus of those who orchestrated the Cold War's end and trace the balance
> between "opportunity and willingness" in these policy makers' conceptu-
> alizations of the structural possibilities of their environments and their de-
> cision structures. From these data, we could estimate the accuracy of their
> images. And the images themselves could be placed into a dynamic process
> model that visualizes the contributing factors colliding and influencing one
> another at certain points and not at others, with some factors moving to-
> gether but not affecting one another and other factors in constant interaction.
> Such a map of the conceptual terrain would chart the ways in which the
> [factors] were perceived by Soviet leaders in the flow of changing circum-
> stances as the Cold War perished. – Charles Kegley (1994: 35)

In Part I of this volume, James Voss presents a discussion of problem representation as it fits into the problem-solving framework. Voss also discusses
several problems with the problem-solving model (the need for a metric, lack
of application to groups and organizations, defining constraints and assessing
their importance, how information is retrieved and used, the difficulty of
prediction), which, at their heart, point to the difficulty of building appropriate
models without knowing the content of particular problem representations or
the processes of reasoning used. To move forward, as Charles Kegley notes,
we need to "map the cognitive terrain" and build "dynamic process models." That is, we need to build carefully representations (models) of the
problem representations of individuals whose policy choices we seek to explain and predict. Furthermore, these representations provide one set of inputs
for dynamic process models, with other inputs coming from the policy mak-

213

ers' environment. Representing problem representations provides a basis for solving the "problems of problem solving" and provides meaning to discussions of change by suggesting mechanisms for change. A useful strategy for accomplishing these goals is a combination of careful content analysis and computational modeling, which also offers a reasonable hope of prediction in addition to understanding.

This strategy has been employed in various studies, including a study of Kennedy administration reasoning during the Cuban missile crisis (Thorson and Sylvan 1982; Sylvan and Thorson 1992), studies of national policy makers (Abelson and Carroll 1965; Carbonell 1978; Sylvan 1987; Davis 1987 Taber 1992), a study of U.S. policy making in the Caribbean (Job and Johnson 1989), and a study of Chinese foreign policy decision making (Tanaka 1984). The use of a computational model is considered appropriate because it provides distinct advantages over more mathematical treatments of belief systems (Hastie 1988) or cognitive maps (Maoz and Shayer 1987). Computational models have all the advantages of numeric simulations identified by Hastie (1988), that is, a clear public statement of the theory involved, expressive versatility, an increased deductive power over other techniques, a common medium for representation in the social sciences, and a readily testable form of theory, with the added flexibility of symbolic and numeric processing, and increased ease of counterfactual modeling (Schrodt 1988; Tamashiro 1989; Hudson 1992; Mefford 1992). In addition, computational models reflect the goals of the cognitively oriented research program in foreign policy decision making; as Howard Tamashiro (1989) suggests, "because mental processes might be postulated to be computational, computational methods can be represented as strong simulations. In this mode they seek to elucidate cognitive structure, processing, and outcomes in contrast to weak simulations such as probabilistic or regression models that seek to exhibit only accurate outcomes."

The purpose of this chapter is to outline one combination of careful content analysis and computational modeling called *WorldView* (Young 1994), which provides a small step toward representing problem representation and dynamic models. In this particular case, the use of computational techniques makes possible the on-line study of foreign policy reasoning and problem representation and allows different reasoning models to be tested quickly and compared directly. The chapter proceeds with a discussion of three functions WorldView performs: (1) the identification of beliefs, (2) their representation in a formal structure, and (3) the operationalization of models of the problem-representation process. The discussion of these functions is followed by comments on the implications of WorldView for the problems of problem solving and problem-representation change (cognitive restructuring).

Identifying Beliefs

The first function WorldView performs is the identification of source texts such as speeches, and the procedure used is hand-coded content analysis. In broad terms, the content-analysis system seeks to identify beliefs that take the familiar subject-relationship-object format often found in English and used in creating causal cognitive maps (Axelrod 1976), for example, "Cuba is-a communist-country." The types of relationships and concepts that make up the content-analysis coding system were derived from both cognitive psychology and the study of foreign policy; although the resulting coding system has parallels with Axelrod's (1976) coding system for causal beliefs, it allows for different types of relationships between concepts and beyond causal relationships, and it captures much more information from the text, including goals and logical relationships between concepts. (Beasley, this volume, has also developed categories for relationship types.)

The initial unit of analysis for content analysis is the sentence. But because texts are often arranged as a coherent whole, and may be self-referring, the sentence is taken in the context of either identifiable and distinct paragraphs or the entire source text. This allows for the replacement of pronouns and provides the coder with an opportunity to clarify ambiguous references. Therefore, the unit of analysis is expanded beyond the sentence as needed to capture the relationships expressed in the text. For example, paragraphs are often arranged with a thesis sentence and several supporting examples; to capture the supporting role of the examples, it is necessary to look at the paragraph as a whole rather than restrict coding to a single sentence.

The sources for the relationships used to identify beliefs include Jean Piaget's theory of cognitive development based on the empirical observation of children (Piaget 1982; Daehler 1985; Mayer 1992), advances in cognitive development that build on the legacy of Piaget (Carey 1985; Keil 1989), and previous work in events coding in international relations, including the Kansas Events Data System (KEDS) (Gerner, Schrodt, Francisco, and Weddle 1994). An example taken from President Carter's inauguration speech offered later in the chapter illustrates the generation of data statements from free text.

Although the set of relationships described later is not considered universal, it is believed to be useful for the foreign policy communities of English-speaking countries, and the definition of a restricted set of relationships provides a foundation for rules of inference and meaning. This is in contrast to the Relatus system, developed by Gavan Duffy and John Mallery, which takes a more linguistic-lexicalist approach (Mallery 1991) and builds a text model using the syntactic structure of the text. In the Relatus system, a model of the text is generated before any interpretation takes place. Once the model of the text has been generated, sets of primitives can be defined for particular research questions reflecting the background knowledge of the researcher.

Coding Relationships

Many different relationships are available to the coder, and each is considered independent, although some appear only in combination with others. Items coded using the policy relationship, for example, are not required to be consistent with items coded using the goal relationship; however, the strategy relationship does connect goal statements with means statements. The coding relationships can be broadly divided into two types, relationships between concepts and actions of agents. The relationships between concepts refer more particularly to the description of problem representations, whereas the actions are induced from foreign policy texts and the KEDS event categories. The use of these relationships, however, is not restricted to actors. The relationships discussed here are all relationships between concepts; a full discussion of all the relationships can be found in Young (1994).

Causal Relationships: Causal reasoning is prevalent in human reasoning and, as observed by Piaget (1982: 118–153), arises early in a child's life along with goals and instrumental reasoning, although all are predominantly egocentric in nature during early development. Causal reasoning has been of great interest to the field of psychology, where causal reasoning is assumed to assist people in constructing a coherent interpretation of the world (Piaget 1982: 198–241; Tversky and Kahneman 1980). The prevalence of causal reasoning has been demonstrated by Michotte (1963) and highlighted by Heider (1958) and has given rise to an area of study that focuses on causal attribution (Jones et al. 1972, cited by Tversky and Kahneman 1980). Spontaneous causal reasoning has also been observed in subjects confronted with novel data (Anderson 1983). Within the overall concept of cause, however, we can distinguish between negative and positive causes – causes that produce an increase in quantity, frequency, or likelihood in some effect and those that produce a decrease. For this reason, two categories are provided for the coding of causal relations: + to code causal relations, which are designations of positive causal relationships between concepts, and − to code negative causal relationships. The coding system also provides the *cause* relationship to code the discrete causal actions of actors in the international system.

Logical Relationships: The logical relationships used in identifying beliefs in the WorldView system include three comparison relationships: less than (<), greater than (>), equal to (=), and two deductive relationships *condition* and *if-then*. The coding categories *condition* and *if-then* are used to model conditional, or hypothetico-deductive, reasoning (Piaget 1982: 394–398, 434–444, and 461–477; Hothersall 1985; Mayer 1992). The *condition* relationship represents the context under which the subject concept is true or applicable. The object concept in a *condition* data statement can be a single concept or a subordinate data statement that must currently be true for the condition to be satisfied. An *if-then* relationship indicates that the object will become true (or can be performed) if the subject is true. *If-then* relationships have a relationship as both object and subject. The *if-then* coding is also designed to capture the expression of standard operating procedures (Allison 1969; Halperin 1974), or policies that are in place. These policies may take the form of *if-then* statements, or strategies that have been publicly pronounced or codified internally in the policy-making apparatus. The *if-then* relationship captures sufficient conditions, whereas the *condition* relationship captures necessary conditions; a combination of the two handles necessary and sufficient conditions.

Attributes: This group of coding relationships is used for the attributes of things in general and broadly corresponds to Piaget's observations on children's construction of reality (Piaget 1982: 250–294). The *attribute* coding category is provided to record the characteristics of represented concepts such as the color, throw weight, or tonnage of an item. The *attribute* relationship provides a mechanism for classification based on matching class attributes and for integration of new situations and actors into the modeled belief system based on their attributes. In addition to the attribute coding relationship, three additional relationships are provided for coding attributes that are used frequently in foreign policy texts and have implications for behavior: *possess, know,* and *part-of.*

The *possess* coding category is used to indicate control over, and physical possession of, resources – for example, material assets, including those that may be considered military capabilities. *Possess* is distinguished from the attribute relationship in that it indicates ownership of objects rather than innate qualities of objects. The *know* coding category is used to represent beliefs about other actors' beliefs. The *part-of* relationship indicates that the subject is a component or integral part of the object. In cases where a concept is said to be comprised of several other concepts, then each component becomes the subject of a separate *part-of* relationship.

Classification: Classification is another process potentially used by individuals to provide a coherent interpretation of the perceived world; it answers the question, What kind of thing is this? The ability to classify appears in some sense to be innate to human beings and develops in most children between the ages of seven and eleven (Piaget 1982: 359–394). Classification also plays

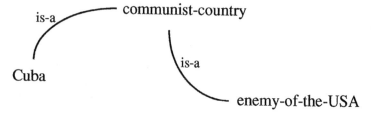

Figure 9.1. A Cold War example of inheritance: We know directly that Cuba is a communist country, and by the inheritance of the properties of communist-country, we also know that Cuba is an enemy-of-the-USA.

an important role in studies of problem recognition and problem solving (Jackson and Dutton 1988; Dutton and Jackson 1987; Kotovsky, Hayes, and Simon 1985; Kaplan and Simon 1990; Lamberti and Newsome 1989; Cowan 1986; Moreland and Levine 1992) and in artificial intelligence (Clancey 1984; Chandrasekaran and Punch 1988; Chandrasekaran 1986; Jackson 1990; Firebaugh 1988), where one of the techniques used to impart "intelligence" to software systems is to provide classification hierarchies for use in reasoning. Classification in the form of the *is-a* coding category captures classifications made by policy actors. The *is-a* coding category provides a mechanism for inheritance between concepts; for example, when the concept "Cuba" is encountered, and the relationships "Cuba *is-a* communist-country" and "communist-country *is-an* enemy-of-USA" are present in the represented belief system, then, by inheritance, we can quickly make the inference "Cuba *is-an* enemy-of-USA." (See Figure 9.1.)

Location: Given that foreign policy problems by most definitions involve some location other than a domestic location, and that people develop spatial reasoning ability innately (Piaget 1982: 576–642), the location coding category is provided to indicate the location of concepts – for example, the location of missiles in Europe, or ships on the high seas. Location becomes important in foreign policy reasoning in conjunction with the attribute and other coding categories. For example, Sylvan and Thorson (1992), in their reassessment of previous work on the Cuban missile crisis (Thorson and Sylvan 1982), suggest that the location of short-range missiles can change their classification from defensive to offensive; that is, short-range missiles that can reach domestic targets are offensive.

Strategy: The strategy coding relationship corresponds to statements that indicate a means to achieve a goal. This category is indicative of an assumption in the model of rationality in human action, to the extent that humans are considered to act in order to achieve goals. The concept of a strategy coding category also corresponds to Piaget's empirical observations of instrumental reasoning in children (1982: 215–249), and to the operator concept in a state space description of a problem from the information-processing perspective (Newell and Simon 1972; Mayer 1992). As such, a strategy relationship indicates that the subject of the data statement, a goal, has associated with it an object that is performable or achievable and is a cause of the subject. In effect, this coding category is an additional specialization of the causal relationship and indicates that this cause–action is the preferred means for reaching the goal.

Warrant-for: The last coding relationship discussed here, *warrant-for*, is derived from the structure of foreign policy texts, where often, as elsewhere, the relationship of the sentences to one another provides their meaning. Paragraphs are often arranged with a thesis sentence followed by a number of arguments or examples and concluded with a restatement of the thesis as a transition to the next paragraph. The *warrant-for* relationship is used to capture the relation of the supporting argument or example to the thesis. The subject of a *warrant-for* relationship is the example or support, and the object is the thesis. The number of warrants a proposition has is also used in addition to the frequency of the proposition as a measure of the proposition's salience for the author.

The content-analysis system is designed to use the set of defined coding relationships to produce data items that can be incorporated into the subject–relationship–object structure with as little interpretation as possible by the coder. These coding statements provide the basic subject–relationship–object structure. Two additional categories, *truth-value* and *relationship modifiers*, are provided to capture additional information from the text.

Truth-Values

The negation of relationships occurs with some frequency in foreign policy texts, and it is important to capture them in the coding system. In order to capture these negations with the greatest semantic fidelity, and for ease of computation, a truth-value is coded for each relationship and can have a value of either *true, false, partial, possible*, or *impossible*. The *true* truth-value indicates that the statement is true for both subject and object, and if either of these is a class of instances, then the statement is true of all instances of the class(es). The *false* truth-value indicates that the statement is not true for both subject and object, and if either of these is a class of instances, then the statement is not true of all instances of the class(es). The *partial* truth-value is a qualified indication of truth and is used when either the subject or object is a class of instances, but the statement is true of only some of the instances of the class(es). A *possible* truth-value indicates that the statement could become true at some unspecified time but it is not necessarily expected to become true, including statements of capabilities. An *impossible* truth-value indicates that the statement cannot become true at any time. *True* and *partial* take logical precedent over *possible*, and *impossible* takes logical precedent over *false*. If a statement cannot be true, it is false; and if it is true, it is also possible.

Relationship Modifiers

The content-analysis system recognizes six relationship modifiers, *past, present, future, goal, hypothetical*, and *normative*, which are used to code the circumstances under which the data statement indicated by the relationship and truth-value are true. A *past* relationship modifier indicates that the relationship referred to is in the past, or was true, partially true, or false in the past. If the relationship is an action, then the action is now complete. A *present* relationship modifier indicates that the subject, an actor, is performing some action, the object, that is ongoing, or that the indicated relationship is currently true, partially true, or false. The *future* relationship modifier is used to represent statements that the actor believes will be true at some future point in time, and it may have implications for the actor's policy behavior.

The *goal* relationship modifier is included in the coding scheme based both on the observations of Piaget and on an information-processing view of policy actors, which has benefited from the work of Herbert A. Simon and his many colleagues and collaborators (Newell and Simon 1972, 1976; Simon 1980, 1985, 1990). The information-processing perspective assumes that policy actors are goal-driven and are at some level aware of their goals, although they may not be aware of the conflicts between goals until presented with a conflict situation. Goal relationships coded from textual data provide the motivation for the policy behavior of the belief-system model, which in a very literal sense is goal driven. A *goal* relationship modifier indicates that the statement indicated by the relationship and the truth-value is a statement that the author of the text wants to become true. The *goal* relationship modifier combined with the strategy relationship provide a means for capturing goal hierarchies present in the text, because goal relationships can be both the subject and object of strategy relationships.

The *hypothetical* relationship modifier is used with the *condition* and *if-then* relationships to capture hypothetico-deductive reasoning (Piaget 1982: 394–398, 434–444, and 461–477; Hothersall 1985; Mayer 1992), where if a statement were to become true in the present, then another statement would be true or would express conditions for the first statement to become true.

The *normative* relationship modifier indicates that the relationship is normatively valued by the author of the text, or that there is a sense of responsibility or obligation. The *normative* relationship modifier is included because policy actors often state normative preferences about the state of the world, but these statements are made in an ideal sense, and the author demonstrates that he or she distinguishes between goals, which are to be acted on and striven for, and preferences. External support for this category comes from studies in developmental psychology (Piaget 1982; Hothersall 1985; Mayer 1992), which record the acquisition of an idealized reasoning ability during adolescence.

Conjunctions

In addition to previously discussed coding items, the WorldView system also recognizes two conjunctions, *and* and *or*, which are used with specific types of compound concepts. The *and* conjunction is used when two or more actors are engaged in joint action. The *or* conjunction is used primarily to indicate a set of alternatives to a decision.

With the inclusion of truth-values and relationship modifiers, data statements created by coders are composed of five parts: the subject concept, a relationship between the concepts, a relationship modifier, a truth-value, and an object concept. It is the coder's task to transform free text into five-part data statements ready for processing of the following form:

subject relationship truth-value relationship-modifier object

which is reduced in the formal representation of beliefs to a three-part relationship.

subject relationship object

with the relationship-modifier and truth-value information contained within the structure of the relationship.

As is true for all human coded content analysis, in this system the coder acts as the observer and interpreter of the text and brings to the text her or his own worldview and understandings of the world. Some degree of control over the impact of the natural interpretive role of the coder is attempted by generating coding rules that are specific enough to be understood commonly by coders, analysts, and the general readership, and which produce a high degree of reproducibility between coders. Although the vast majority of the data-collection content analysis has been performed by the author, the success of the coding system on these two points has been assessed by using two trained graduate-student coders for intercoder reliability on randomly selected passages. After approximately 12 hours of training, the two coders achieved reliability scores of .41 and .43 (using the author's coding as the standard).

Analysis of these results indicates a difficulty in coding across sentences, which caused cumulative errors. After review of this issue, the coders achieved reliability scores of .72 and .83.

Example of Content Analysis Applied to
President Carter's Inaugural Address

Our Nation can be strong abroad only if it is strong at home.
And we know that the best way to enhance freedom in other lands is to demonstrate here that our democratic system is worthy of emulation.

(united-states attribute true hypothetical strong-abroad)
condition true present
(united-states attribute true hypothetical strong-at-home)

(other-lands attribute true goal free)
strategy true present
(people-of-the-united-states demonstrate true present (united-states-democratic-system attribute true present worthy-of-emulation))

To be true to ourselves, we must be true to others.
We will not behave in foreign places so as to violate our rules and standards here at home, for we know that the trust which our Nation earns is essential to our strength.

(united-states attribute true hypothetical true-to-ourselves)
condition true present
(united-states attribute true hypothetical true-to-others)

(the-trust-which-our-nation-earns + true present united-states-strength)
warrant-for true present
(people-of-the-united-states violate false future united-states-rules-and-standards)

The data statements generated from the excerpt from Carter's address reflect the compound nature of many of the statements in free text. The excerpt also demonstrates *condition* statements

Our Nation can be strong abroad only if it is strong at home.

(united-states attribute true hypothetical strong-abroad)
condition true present
(united-states attribute true hypothetical strong-at-home)

as well as promises that are coded as present/future actions:

We will not behave in foreign places so as to violate our rules and standards here at home

people-of-the-united-states violate false future united-states-rules-and-standards

Table 9.1. *Complete list of coding*
relationships

=	*demonstrate*	*prefer*
<	*enforce*	*propose*
>	*enhance*	*purchase*
+	*feel*	*ratify*
−	*honor*	*reduce*
accept	*if-then*	*release*
allow	*ignore*	*request*
assert	*influence*	*restore*
assist	*intervene*	*sell*
attack	*invade*	*separate*
attribute	*is-a*	*share*
cause	*know*	*sign*
close	*lead*	*stop*
compete	*limit*	*strategy*
concern	*location*	*support*
condemn	*maintain*	*threaten*
condition	*meet*	*use*
confront	*monitor*	*verify*
consider	*negotiate*	*visit*
consult	*open*	*vote-on*
control	*order*	*warrant-for*
cooperate	*organize*	*withdraw*
decide	*part-of*	*yield-to*
defend	*perform*	
delay	*possess*	

Representing Beliefs

The second function WorldView performs is the representation of individual beliefs extracted from source texts into a memory model. As with all computer programming and computational modeling tasks, *the design of the data structures for beliefs and problem representations and their permissible interactions will have repercussions for the rest of the model*; therefore, insights from psychology about beliefs and memory structure should be taken into consideration in the design of belief data structures. Given the definition of a problem representation as a cognitive construct built from existing memory structures (see Voss, this volume), the associative network model of memory (Estes 1991) has been adopted to operationalize the problem representation. The structure of an associative network is a node and link structure, where a

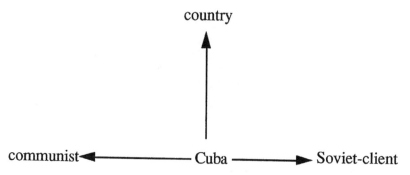

Figure 9.2. A fragment of an associative network. The network contains the following associations: Cuba is a country. Cuba is communist. Cuba is a Soviet client.

node is an idea (noun, object, or adjective), and each link represents a relationship between nodes. There are three important features of this model. First, links between nodes are associative (see Taber, this volume). The model stipulates that links between nodes refer to associations between concepts, and that links can be established and strengthened by the occurrence of these associations in experience – that is, when the links are activated by perception. Second, these links are directional; that is, any particular association is one-way between nodes, although a link in the opposite direction may exist. Third, the links between nodes in this model may be labeled; that is, there are types of relational links between concepts (class membership, etc.). In addition, activation or search through memory proceeds by spreading activation, whereby nodes in memory are activated or searched in a pattern spreading outward across all links from any previously activated nodes. Figure 9.2 illustrates the associative network concept with four nodes and three associative links.

This characterization of cognitive architecture leads to a "shoe box" model of a belief system, in which the connectedness of an individual belief (a node-link-node set) varies. The belief system is therefore clumpy, with structures of different complexity that may or may not be connected to other structures (Figure 9.3). For example, your beliefs about chocolate sundaes may have no connections to your beliefs about politicians. A problem representation is, therefore, a subset of the nodes and links in memory – that is, beliefs in the belief system – that are associated with one or more features of the problem. The problem representation, constructed by an individual from items in the individual's belief system, may include one or more of the unconnected structures in the belief system, and it may include nodes that are one or more links away from the activated node(s) – that is, those nodes directly associated with some feature of the problem. (As implemented in

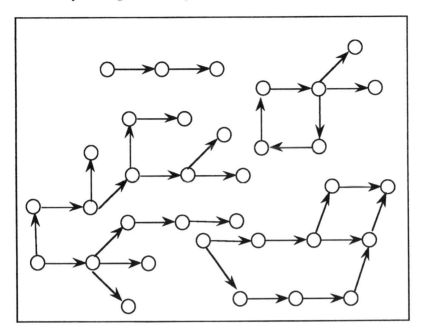

Figure 9.3. The "shoe box" model of a belief system. Cognitive structures of various size and connectedness populate the long-term memory of the subject and constitute the subject's belief system.

WorldView, memory is considered to have a very fine granular structure; see Taber's discussion of EVIN, this volume, for an alternative memory model with a frame-based structure.)

The data structures used for this model of problem representation are based on this associative network model but take advantage of the semantic network research in artificial intelligence (Lehman 1992). The structure of semantic networks is complementary to the graph structure of concepts and relations of the associative network model of memory.

In semantic networks, each node represents an object, concept, or situation, and each link represents a relationship between nodes. Semantic networks are very flexible data structures and can be used for deductive inference by inheritance, whereby the attributes of concepts (nodes, that is, Cuba) can be deduced from the attributes of class concepts (superordinate nodes, that is, communist-country) to which they are connected. (See Figure 9.2.) The data structure represents concepts, conjunctions, and relationships as data objects with pointers between them (Duffy and Tucker 1995) and is illustrated in Figure 9.4.

The compilation of individual data statements into a semantic network is

Simple Data Statement

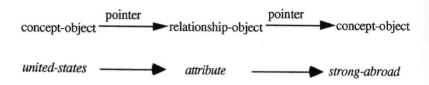

Compound data Statement

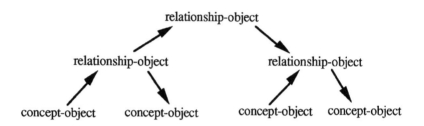

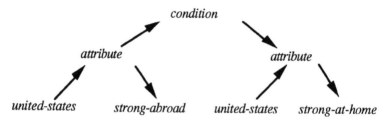

Figure 9.4. Data structure.

performed by a computer program written in Macintosh Common Lisp. The program takes as input the data statements created by a human coder, reading the items from text files, and then compiles them into "nodes" in the semantic network. The system also allows for the creation of a synonym list that will replace concepts with a preferred synonym; this process takes places at run time and *does not change the data*, but rather, allows the analyst to reduce the number of nodes in the semantic network by replacing redundant concepts. The synonym facility also allows the analyst to determine whether hypothesized redundancies in concepts will result in different policy choices when the concepts that are thought to be synonymous are combined.

Although the content-analysis example is not very complex and the information can readily be gained from a quick reading of the text, these structures are extremely useful because they provide a manipulable semantic network in memory that can be used to derive measures of problem representations, and to serve as the basis of dynamic simulations. The use of an automated system also allows us to examine the data in a variety of ways, including checking for differences in the semantic networks derived from texts aimed at different audiences, and to examine the implications this has for consistent policy behavior, a procedure that would be extremely costly without using a data structure and compiler like those described here. In addition, the system can combine the information from several texts consisting of hundreds of data statements to provide a composite and complex map, which is not readily amenable to unassisted analysis.

Problem Representation as Process

The last function WorldView performs is to provide a process model for the generation of problem representations and policy choices. For a study of President Carter (Young 1994), two similar but distinct models were used, a goal-based model, Policy-choice, and a simpler model, Directed-walk, that takes advantage of inheritance. (For an alternative model, see Taber's EVIN, this volume.) Policy-choice is patterned after the work of Bonham and his colleagues (Bonham, Shapiro, and Trumble 1979; Bonham, Heradstviet, Narvessen, and Shapiro 1978) on cognitive mapping. Policy-choice uses spreading activation to generate the problem representation, but it rejects spreading activation as a model for *reasoning* in a serial processing system (see Voss, this volume) and instead uses an explanation-based style of reasoning using a salience heuristic. The salience heuristic uses the strength of a proposition in a belief system to direct memory search. Starting from the first goal proposition located in the problem representation created by spreading activation, the search procedure selects the proposition with the highest salience to activate and carries out any indicated processing. Then it selects the most salient proposition leading from the conclusion of the just-processed proposition and repeats the process until no further progress can be made, that is, until a policy is output or new information is fully integrated into the semantic network. The choice of an explanation-based reasoning heuristic is by no means a rejection of case- or model-based reasoning; it is a tactical move. This tactic is designed to allow fairly rapid prototyping and an investigation into the ability of this style of reasoning to account for human foreign policy behavior. This model is fairly typical of descriptions of problem solving and is a simple means–ends procedure; as such, the Policy-choice process model (see Figure 9.8) provides a first estimation of the functional relationship between beliefs and policy.

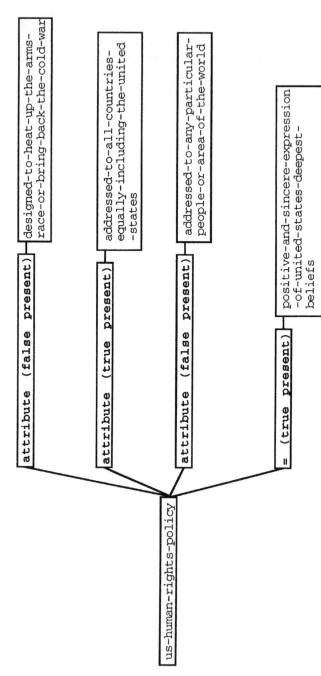

Figure 9.5. A Simple semantic network fragment.

228

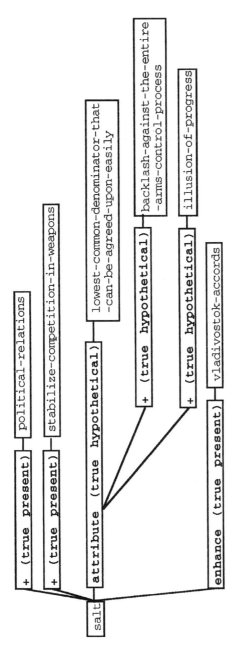

Figure 9.6. Semantic network fragment with relationships as objects of other relationships.

229

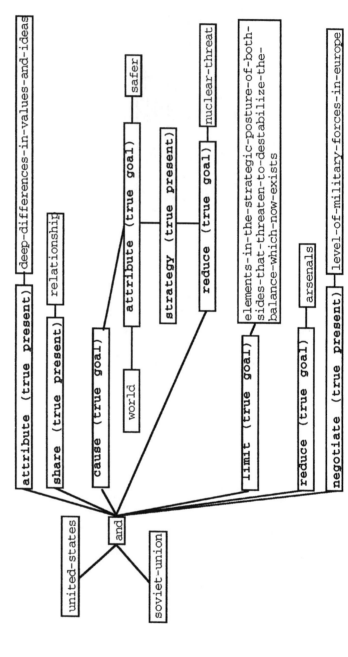

Figure 9.7. Semantic network fragment illustrating a conjunction and complex relationships.

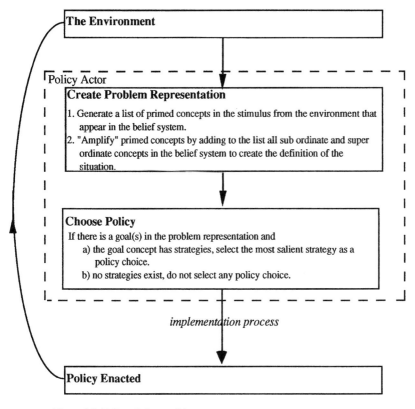

The Environment

Policy Actor

Create Problem Representation
1. Generate a list of primed concepts in the stimulus from the environment that appear in the belief system.
2. "Amplify" primed concepts by adding to the list all sub ordinate and super ordinate concepts in the belief system to create the definition of the situation.

Choose Policy
If there is a goal(s) in the problem representation and
  a) the goal concept has strategies, select the most salient strategy as a policy choice.
  b) no strategies exist, do not select any policy choice.

implementation process

Policy Enacted

Figure 9.8. Policy-choice model.

The second process model, Directed-walk, begins with the stimulus statement (for both models this is the Soviet invasion of Afghanistan, that is, soviet-union invade true present afghanistan), searches for information immediately related to the contents of the stimulus, and begins reasoning from this point forward. The main difference between the two models is that Policy-choice is strongly goal oriented while Directed-walk tries to elaborate the stimulus. These two routines produce quite different results when applied to a model of President Carter's beliefs.

Carter's Problem Representation

To analyze President Carter's problem representation during his years in office, twenty-two of his foreign policy speeches were coded using the procedures already described (Young 1994). Semantic networks were created

---

Goal found!
(soviet-union accept possible goal agreement-with-united-states-on-arms-exports-to-the-troubled-areas-of-the-world)

Goal not satisfied selecting strategy . . .
No strategies for this goal.

(soviet-union accept possible goal agreement-with-united-states-on-arms-exports-to-the-troubled-areas-of-the-world)
Is the object of:
(united-states cause true goal (soviet-union accept possible goal agreement-with-united-states-on-arms-exports-to-the-troubled-areas-of-the-world)

Figure 9.9. Policy-choice for cumulative speeches with "Soviet Union invade true present Afghanistan" as the initial input.

in a cumulative manner, with the two process models applied at each iteration to assess their performance. The test used was to predict Carter's response to the Soviet invasion of Afghanistan (December 27, 1979), a difficult test given the limited data available in the twenty-two speeches. This was done using the statement "soviet-union invade true present afghanistan" as the initial input for each reasoning routine. Examples from the results appear in Figures 9.9 and 9.10. Although at no time prior to Carter's own announcements does either model predict U.S. foreign policy response to the Soviet invasion, the results do demonstrate the ability of the coding and representation system to model the foreign policy reasoning of leaders. Both the Policy-choice routine and the Directed-walk routine demonstrate strengths that the other lacks.

The Policy-choice routine, while failing to "understand" the significance of the input statement, faithfully reports U.S. goals associated with its subject (the Soviet Union), such as the reduction of arms exports, enhancement of human rights, and the reduction of nuclear proliferation. This can be seen in the sample of output in Figure 9.9. Given the input statement, "soviet-union invade true present afghanistan," Policy-choice determines whether the goal is satisfied; then, on discovering the goal is not satisfied, the routine searches for strategies to accomplish the goal. When no strategies are found, Policy-choice reports any statement the goal is an object of, in this case: (united-states cause true goal (soviet-union accept possible goal agreement-with-united-states-on-arms-exports-to-the-troubled-areas-of-the-world)).

The Directed-walk routine, on the other hand, demonstrates the ability of the routine to generalize via the inheritance procedures described earlier. This can be seen in Figure 9.10. In the sample output, the Directed-walk routine first records a change in beliefs and then begins to reason about the input

Change in established belief!
From: (united-states cause true present mx-missile-system)
To: (united-states cause true past mx-missile-system)

(soviet-union invade true present afghanistan)

((soviet-union invade true present afghanistan) – true present the-careful-
balance-of-forces-in-a-vital-and-a-volatile-area-of-the-world)

((soviet-union invade true present afghanistan) – true present the-careful-
balance-of-forces-in-a-vital-and-a-volatile-area-of-the-world)
Warrant-for true present
((united-states cooperate true hypothetical moscow-olympics) condition true
present (soviet-invading-forces withdraw true goal afghanistan)))

((united-states cooperate true hypothetical moscow-olympics) condition true
present (soviet-invading-forces withdraw true goal afghanistan))

(soviet-invading-forces withdraw true goal afghanistan)

(afghanistan is-a true present sovereign-nation)

(soviet-invading-forces withdraw true goal sovereign-nation)

End of walk.

Figure 9.10. Sample output from Directed-walk.

statement. Directed-walk finds an immediately related belief ((soviet-union
invade true present afghanistan) – true present the-careful-balance-of-forces-
in-a-vital-and-a-volatile-area-of-the-world) and begins to reason from this
statement. The routine discovers that the statement is a warrant-for (supports)
the conditional United States participation in the Moscow Olympics *if* Soviet
forces withdraw from Afghanistan, ((united-states   cooperate true hypothetical moscow-olympics) condition true present (soviet-invading-forces withdraw true goal afghanistan)), which is a goal statement. Attempting to proceed from this goal, Directed-walk determines that Afghanistan is a sovereign
nation and substitutes this information into the goal statement. At this point
reasoning ends for lack of further information.

Although the Directed-walk routine appears to be more successful in coming to the conclusion that Carter's primary reaction to the invasion is to desire
the removal of Soviet invasion forces from Afghanistan, rather than persuasion of the Soviet Union to reduce arms sales (although they both may be
highly related), neither reasoning routine performed with prescience. The
main difficulty, however, may be not the routines themselves but the paucity
of information available for them. Although twenty-two speeches constitute a
respectable data set, they contain only a small portion of President Carter's

speeches, press conferences, radio addresses, and interviews both before and during his term in office. It is not unreasonable to assume that the inclusion of this material would provide much richer information on Carter's (public) beliefs and improve the performance of the model. At the same time, there are many assumptions about the world that might never be stated, such as which particular countries are members of the United Nations. This type of information may also be very important for the performance of the model. For example, had the information existed that the Soviet Union was also a sovereign nation, then the routine could have derived: (sovereign-nation invade true present sovereign-nation) – for which we may be able to predict Carter's response. In fact, a similar statement was made by Carter on March 17, 1978 (emphasis added):

> We've recently completed a major reassessment of our national defense strategy. And out of this process have come some overall principles designed to preserve our national security during the years ahead. We will match, together with our allies and friends, any threatening power through a combination of military forces, political efforts, and economic programs. We will not allow any other nation to gain military superiority over us. We shall seek the cooperation of the Soviet Union and other nations in reducing areas of tension. *We do not desire to intervene militarily in the internal domestic affairs of other countries, nor to aggravate regional conflicts. And we shall oppose intervention by others.* While assuring our own military capabilities, we shall seek security through dependable, verifiable arms control agreements wherever possible. We shall use our great economic, technological, and diplomatic advantages to defend our interests and to promote American values.

This excerpt produces data statements including the following:

united-states intervene false goal country
(country intervene true hypothetical country) if-then true present
(united-states resist true hypothetical (country intervene true hypothetical country))

The missing elements are a synonym mapping between *country* and *sovereign-nation*, a *sovereign-nation* designation for *soviet-union* in addition to that for *afghanistan*, and a mapping between *intervene* and *invade* as a more specific example of *intervene*. These modifications produce the following output:

(soviet-union invade true present afghanistan)
(soviet-union intervene true present afghanistan)
(soviet-union is-a true present sovereign-nation)

(sovereign-nation intervene true present afghanistan)
(afghanistan is-a true present sovereign-nation)
(sovereign-nation intervene true present sovereign-nation)
(sovereign-nation intervene true present sovereign-nation)
if-then true present
(united-states resist true hypothetical (sovereign-nation intervene true present
sovereign-nation))
(united-states resist true present (sovereign-nation intervene true present
sovereign-nation))
End of walk.

Evaluating WorldView

Broadly speaking, the appropriate criteria for evaluating simulations using computational models are outcome validity and process validity (Taber and Timpone 1996): Does the model predict the observed behavior or behavior consistent with the observed behavior? Is the process plausible as a model of the actual process? Both of the models used in this project, Choose-policy and Directed-walk, are very simple and clearly do not capture all of the important features of individual foreign policy decision making. However, each part of both routines is well grounded in psychology and information processing, and both do produce behavior that is at least consistent with the observed behavior. In particular, the expected resistance to the invasion produced by *the Directed-walk routine captures the broad outline of Carter's policy*, although not its details. This successful response by Directed-walk to the Soviet invasion provides strong support that President Carter's thinking can be approximated with a depth-first reasoning routine.

In addition, the difficulty of using spreading activation has also become apparent. As noted in Young (1993), because spreading activation is indiscriminate and potentially exhaustive, all concepts and relationships in the belief system become incorporated in problem representations generated in response to any situation with at least one concept in common with the belief system. The net result of simulations using spreading activation routines is that all policies contained within the belief system are suggested, providing no additional explanatory power than simply listing all options for all events present in the source documents. Spreading activation may correspond to background-memory activation processes (that is, priming); however it is clear from using this approach that more directed explanation-oriented routines are more appropriate for active reasoning. But explanation-based reasoning and spreading activation may occur in combination in cases where there is a great deal of ambiguity or uncertainty in the environment. For example, if an event in the external environment does not correspond to events in memory, or the concepts in the environment generate no clear line of reasoning, then spreading activation can be used. Spreading activation would allow the policy maker to consider a larger number of concepts and to determine if any of them match the input from the environment (e.g., free associating to try to determine where you met someone who looks vaguely familiar and whether you should talk to that person: Do I know this person socially? professionally? a relative?). Once a reasonable match has been made, directed processing can generate a coherent line of thought (ah, yes, I met her at the international studies meeting; she was on a panel on post-Soviet Russia; her talk was very interesting; she *is* someone I should talk to). It is also possible that people may reason in different ways – some may proceed from general goals (top-down processing), whereas others may respond more directly to events (bottom-up processing). Both these and other reasoning models can be implemented for comparison.

Finally, it is important to recognize that both Policy-choice and Directed-walk contain elements, such as goal-directed behavior and salience-driven reasoning, that are plausible processes that may prove more powerful in combination. In addition, the results from these simulations demonstrate the ability to model the foreign policy reasoning of leaders using the coding and representation system.

The Problems of Problem Solving

As noted at the beginning of this chapter, James Voss raises some issues in problem representation research, including how problem-representation change (cognitive restructuring) takes places. Voss also raises problems for problem representation and the problem-solving framework: the need for a metric, lack of application to groups and organizations, defining and constraints and assessing their importance, how information is retrieved and used, and the difficulty of prediction. Although WorldView does not resolve these issues or solve all the problems of problem solving, the modeling enterprise it represents does have implications for each of these issues.

Cognitive Restructuring

In many ways, cognitive restructuring is epitomized by President Carter's interview response to Frank Reynolds of ABC television following the Soviet entry into Afghanistan: "This action of the Soviets has made a more dramatic change in my own opinion of what the Soviets' ultimate goals are than anything they've done in the previous time I've been in office" (Sick 1986: 242). This quotation, taken at face value, indicates a dramatic change in Carter's beliefs about the Soviets. Yet, whereas a change of behavior is well established (Sick 1986: 242; Rosati 1991: 142–149), is the change in beliefs? One of the advantages of the approach taken by WorldView, in which beliefs are extracted from text at a very fine level, is that it can be set up to detect various types of changes in beliefs. When WorldView is asked to look for directly contradictory beliefs in the twenty-two speeches under examination, only two beliefs changed (Table 9.2), and both changed from "present" to "past." No other directly contradictory beliefs were recorded, although many new beliefs were added. (This is subject to some reservation. Change in belief is defined in the system only in terms of the same subject relationship and object. Other changes may exist, such as contradictory beliefs expressed in terms of two different relationships. For example, *withdraw* can be considered a change from *invade*.) Furthermore, as shown in the discussion of Carter's March 17, 1978, speech, the types of action Carter took following the invasion are foreshadowed in his previous speeches. In addition, Carter generally phrased comments about Soviet intentions in the conditional and did not directly link Soviet intentions to U.S. policy (emphasis added): "In the principles of self-restraint, reciprocity, and mutual accommodation of interests, *if these are observed*, then the United States and the Soviet Union will not only succeed in limiting weapons but will also create a foundation of better relations in other spheres of interest" (Carter, October 4, 1977). The impression left from a careful reading of twenty-two speeches is a complex view of the world with clear goals but with a highly conditional foreign policy that was adaptive to change in the environment, a view supported by Gary Sick's memoirs:

> In retrospect, it seems clear that the Soviet leaders committed a blunder of historic proportion when they misjudged the depth of the U.S. reaction to their aggression in Afghanistan. Jimmy Carter and Cyrus Vance represented an important but often invisible dimension of U.S. attitudes toward the Soviet Union. They believed deeply in the importance of dialogue and mutual accommodation between the two superpowers on vital issues of peace and international security. They were not starry-eyed idealists about the USSR, but they were profoundly convinced that the way to peace was through careful communication and persistent discussion of issues rather than threats and bluster. (Sick 1986: 342)

In his own memoirs, Carter says little about his reaction to the Soviet invasion, but it is clear that his beliefs about arms control remained unchanged.

> There were some things I did *not* want to do; one of the most important of these was scuttling the SALT II treaty. It was patently of advantage to the United States and vital to the maintenance of world peace. On January 3, I

sent a letter to Senator Robert Byrd, asking him not to bring it to the floor for a vote, but to leave it on the calendar for future action. Because of American disgust with the Soviet invasion, the treaty would have been defeated overwhelmingly, and to withdraw it from the Senate might have made it almost impossible to resubmit in the future or for most of its terms to continue to be observed. This action was the best I could do at the time to keep it alive. (Carter 1982: 475)

It is also clear that Carter reassessed the Soviet Union, as indicated by his comments to Hamilton Jordan on December 28, 1979, comparing the invasion to the hostage crisis with Iran:

This is more serious, Hamilton. Capturing those Americans was an inhumane act committed by a bunch of radicals and condoned by a crazy old man. But this is deliberate aggression that calls into question détente and the way we have been doing business with the Soviets for the past decade. It raises grave questions about Soviet intentions and destroys any chance of getting the SALT treaty through the Senate. And that makes the prospects of nuclear war even greater. (Jordan 1982: 99)

Carter echoed this sentiment in his diary entry for January 3, 1980:

This is the most serious international development that has occurred since I have been President, and unless the Soviets recognize that it has been counterproductive for them, we will face additional serious problems with invasion or subversions in the future. (Carter 1982: 473)

Other passages from his speeches suggest, however, that Carter was aware of Soviet intentions much earlier.

There also has been an ominous inclination on the part of the Soviet Union to use its military power to intervene in local conflicts, with advisers, with equipment, and with full logistical support and encouragement for mercenaries from other Communist countries, as we can observe today in Africa. (Carter 1978a)

To the Soviet Union, détente seems to mean a continuing aggressive struggle for political advantage and increased influence in a variety of ways. The Soviet Union apparently sees military power and military assistance as the best means of expanding their influence abroad. Obviously areas of instability in the world provide a tempting target for this effort, and all too often they seem ready to exploit any such opportunity. (Carter 1978b)

Other evidence from the most salient items in each speech supports a change in focus from human-rights/peace issues to security items. Human-rights/peace items are the most salient items in a 10:3 ratio before the invasion of Afghanistan and in a 2:1 ratio after the invasion (Young 1994). Although the small (22) and unequal sample size does not warrant definitive conclusions, the anecdotal accounts of Gary Sick, a member of Carter's staff, also tend to support this evidence:

> Carter, more than any recent U.S. president, was prepared to walk a second mile in pursuit of nonviolent solutions to security problems. For three years he stubbornly refused the advice of his more hawkish advisers in the hope that the USSR would respond to a historic opportunity to develop peaceful means of managing East–West competition. The Soviets, whose own historical experience provided scant basis to comprehend a policy founded on principles of mutual respect, chose to interpret U.S. policy as a policy of weakness, thus setting in motion a new round of confrontation and arms competition. (Sick 1986: 242–243)

That a change in Carter's beliefs and behavior did take place is not disputed here, but what was the nature of the change? Few specific changes of belief can be found in Carter's speeches, and in fact they contain statements that indicate a very cautious view of the Soviet Union. Yet Carter expressed profound surprise at Soviet actions, and a change in U.S. behavior occurred that included a reversal of foreign aid policy and an intensified, though not new, focus on modernizing the armed forces (Rosati 1991: 117–148). How can these behavioral changes be reconciled with the apparent constancy in expressed beliefs? The modeling exercise conducted with WorldView suggests four mechanisms that could produce behavioral change without producing detectable belief changes: a change in an assumption already existing in the belief system, changes in relative salience of beliefs, change in probabilities attached to beliefs, and the addition of a few new propositions to the belief system.

The first possibility is that there may not have been change in Carter's beliefs about Soviet intentions but a change in an existing assumption that he could convince the Soviets, with a policy of accommodation, that cooperation and international restraint was in their best interest. The apparent frustration of this belief over the course of three years, punctuated by the invasion of Afghanistan, may have changed only the premise behind Carter's policy, but this change had a profound effect throughout the belief system and transformed Carter's problem representation. For example, if the statement (soviet-union desire true goal ((and soviet-union united-states) cooperate true goal international-system)) were a *condition* for the United States to cooperate with the Soviet Union, then the invasion of Afghanistan would probably render this statement false – that is, (soviet-union desire false present ((and soviet-union united-states) cooperate true goal international-system)) – and thus fail to satisfy a necessary condition for cooperative U.S. behavior. In addition, if the statement (soviet-union desire false hypothetical ((and soviet-union united-states) cooperate true goal international-system)) were the subject of an *if-then* statement, the statement (soviet-union desire false present ((and soviet-union united-states) cooperate true goal international-system)) would satisfy the *if-then* and trigger noncooperative behavior.

The second possibility is that the invasion may have changed only the salience of certain propositions about Soviet actions. If reasoning is guided by salience, as in the Directed-walk and Policy-choice routines, then a change in the relative salience of some propositions would result in new chains of reasoning and different conclusions. For example, it is possible that the following two statements could coexist in the belief system: (soviet-union desire true present peace) and (soviet-union desire true present power). If a chain of reasoning begins with "soviet-union" and the first statement is more salient than the second, then reasoning will proceed down that chain, that is, to whatever follows from: (soviet-union desire true present peace). The invasion of Afghanistan could easily dramatically increase the salience of the second statement, (soviet-union desire true present power), such that a chain of reasoning beginning with "soviet-union" would proceed to (soviet-union desire true present power) and whatever follows from that.

An identical result could also be found with the third possibility suggested – that the change Carter experienced was a change in the probabilities attached to Soviet intentions. If Carter's estimates of the probabilities of the "bad" Soviet actions foreshadowed in his speeches were low, then the Soviet invasion of Afghanistan would indeed come as a great surprise and cause him to reassess the nature of Soviet leadership and increase his estimate that Soviet intentions were geared to acquiring power and not peace. Although probability information attached to beliefs is not captured by the current coding system, it could produce a change in behavior similar to that resulting from changes in salience without producing discrete changes in particular beliefs and therefore no measurable structural changes. In addition, optimism and pessimism can be phrased in terms of the probabilities attached to beliefs. If you believe the probabilities of "bad" outcomes are low ($<.50$), you are an optimist. If you believe them to be high ($\geq.50$), then you are a pessimist; this corresponds to Rosati's (1987: 136–150) characterization of a change in Carter's outlook from optimism to pessimism during 1979.

Finally, change in beliefs may not be noticeable if the change in behavior were the result of the addition of one or two new propositions. For example, if propositions already exist in the belief system for expansionist states and the appropriate United States response – such as (united-states resist true goal expansionist-state) – but the Soviet Union was not classified as an expansionist state, then a new proposition – (soviet-union is-a true present expansionist-state) – would add the Soviet Union to the class of expansionist states. This would make all statements applicable to expansionist states applicable to the

Soviet Union, for which they may not have applied previously. Assume further that the statement (united-states resist true goal expansionist-state) has strategies associated with it, that is, ((united-states resist true goal expansionist-state) strategy true present (united-states embargo true goal expansionist-state)). Then, by inheritance, the addition of (soviet-union is-a true present expansionist-state) would result in (united-states embargo true goal soviet-union). Thus, this single proposition could drastically change problem representation created in response to situations involving the Soviet Union while producing only very small structural changes that in most cases would not be statistically significant.

WorldView does not provide sufficient information to discriminate between these possibilities. Without representing problem representation in this way, however, the possibilities would not have arisen. Furthermore, since the simulation results indicate that large-scale changes of discrete beliefs did not take place, then one of these four alternatives is likely. These results for Carter's problem representation suggest that large dramatic changes in foreign policy behavior can result from small subtle changes in a policy maker's beliefs. In addition, only small amounts of highly salient information may transform a policy maker's approach to international politics. The key for those seeking to influence policy makers is to identify the particular information that will effectively create desired changes, which appears to require extensive knowledge of the existing belief system and the goal hierarchies it contains.

Metrics

The discussion of cognitive restructuring highlights the need for problem-representation metrics to assist in the investigation of these possibilities. However, the creation of metrics depends on clear conceptualization of problem-representation structures. The careful representation of beliefs and problem representations in a manipulable structure using the WorldView system provides just such a clear conceptualization, and structural and comparative measures have been defined to analyze problem representations (Young 1996). Briefly, these measures assess the connectedness, dependency, size, and salience of individual problem representations and also assess the differences between them. This set of measures could be used to detect changes consistent with the mechanisms of change discussed earlier (change in probabilities, change in relative salience, change in existing assumptions, or addition of new beliefs). For example, one comparative measure, concept comparison, can provide lists of new concepts as they are used by Carter in his speeches and can also be extended to provide lists of new relationships as they appear in the speeches. Furthermore, routines can be designed to compare across the speeches and to detect translocation (the movement of a concept or subgraph from one superordinate concept to another), differentiation (splitting a concept into parts to preserve consistency), and transcendence (creating a concept superordinate to existing concepts that incorporates discrepant information but maintains consistency at a higher level), providing substantive information about changes in the belief system. When changes of these types are detected, the analyst can systematically run simulations with and without each addition or change to test the sensitivity of the simulation to these changes. This would provide excellent evidence for changes capable of producing behavioral change without large-scale belief changes. Although these measures may not provide answers to all the questions that could be profitably asked about problem representations, they do illustrate the usefulness of the modeling approach to the problem.

Groups

One of the difficulties in applying the problem-solving framework is that much of the work on groups views the group as an entity in and of itself and tends to classify groups on that basis. Consider, for example, much of the work on leader advisory groups (Johnson 1974), which focuses on the type of group (e.g., collegial versus competitive); analysis tends to proceed from the group down. WorldView, on the other hand, focuses on modeling individuals, with the recognition that if one individual can be modeled, then two can be modeled. Once two individuals have been modeled, modeling of their interaction is possible, that is, modeling group dynamics. The philosophy behind WorldView starts from the individual, and analysis proceeds up to the group. From this perspective, a plausible starting point for modeling a group is that of considering a group to be composed of individuals who pass, receive, process, and respond to messages from one another – just as WorldView responds to messages such as ''soviet-union invade true present afghanistan.''

In this formulation, a group is conceived of as a discussion space where group members pass messages to some or all other members of the group. (See Figure 9.11.) A group decision-making process can thus be described as an iterative cycle of passing, receiving, processing, and responding to messages from other group members. The group process terminates when a decision is reached and the group disbands. If all group members are identical (highly unlikely), then only a single cycle may be required as each group member affirms the first message passed. In real cases, group members are often required to engage in many cycles to combine their beliefs and repre-

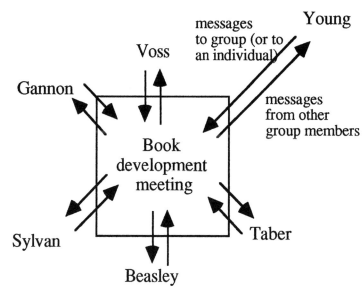

Figure 9.11. A group can be thought of as a discussion space where all group members may either pass arguments or receive messages from other group members.

sentations into a negotiated belief system (Walsh, Henderson, and Deighton 1988; see also Stasser and Titus 1985, 1987).

Group interaction is produced by group members initiating messages and attending to, processing, and responding to messages from other group members. However, not all messages will be treated equally by each of the group members. A number of factors are expected to influence whether an individual attends to a message, how that message is processed, and how people respond to the message (Markus and Zajonc 1985: 163): (1) the nature or content of the receiver's beliefs, (2) the nature or content of the input or stimulus information, (3) the fit between the receiver's beliefs and the message, (4) the state of the perceiver, (5) the context of the information-processing task, (6) and the reasoning style of the receiver. Within this formulation, the extension of the problem-solving framework to groups becomes a logically straightforward, although complicated, analysis of multiple problem-solving actors interacting in a variety of ways.

Goals and Data Bases

One of the assumptions of the WorldView model that comes from the problem-solving framework is that individuals are goal-driven – that is, they seek to obtain particular states of the world – and that some goals are more highly valued or more important to an individual than others. The representation used by WorldView incorporates this with the *goal* relationship modifier, which identifies goal statements and allows the analyst to extract goal hierarchies from the semantic network. The nature of this goal hierarchy and the interaction of various goal-driven reasoning models, such as Policy-choice, provides the ability to model problem solvers by modeling their beliefs and producing a trace of the decision process that illustrates which goals and information from the belief system (the data base) come into play for any particular decision. This trace can be compared with traces from actual problem solvers to determine if the process used is similar. In addition, the option exists to add to the belief system beliefs that may not have been expressed and to compare the new trace produced. In this manner, we can work toward an understanding of the processes underlying information use and goal trade-offs.

Prediction

The question of whether we should strive for predictive power in our explanations is in part philosophical but also arises from the goals of the theorists. Many of the psychologists who develop these problem-solving and decision-making theories are not directly interested in the questions that (at least some) researchers in the cognitively oriented research program in foreign policy are interested in: Why did this *particular person* act in this *particular way*, and how can we know how this person will act in the future in response to specified events? (Although this may be the ultimate goal of some psychologists, it is a long-term goal, and the typical large N experimental methodology does not lend itself to these questions.) The motivation for predictive power is to gain the ability to intervene in various political processes to produce particular outcomes, such as the prevention of war. This difference means that political scientists may find psychological theories underspecified *for their purposes*; therefore, political scientists must provide the necessary tools to fit these theories to our purposes and contexts rather than simply borrowing terminology and concepts to improve our storytelling. If political science cannot generate predictive theory, then any capacity for intervention in the world, for good or evil, is lost.

Conclusion

WorldView and, more generally, the modeling project embodied in this volume by WorldView and EVIN represent steps toward addressing the problems of problem solving identified by James Voss and satisfying Charles Kegley's call for maps of the "cognitive terrain" and a "dynamic process model" of actors in the international system. Both highlight the difficulty of building appropriate models of political decision making without knowing the beliefs of the decision makers involved or the processes of reasoning they used. WorldView addresses these difficulties by providing tools for (1) the identification of beliefs, (2) their representation in a formal structure, and (3) the operationalization of reasoning models. Research to generate and improve dynamic decision-making models will continue as better developed reasoning models and larger data bases are combined with the semantic network structure of the WorldView model, which can be more thoroughly tested. Once confidence is gained in the validity of the combined structural and process models, the research will shift to developing models of group interaction.

References

Abelson, R. P., and J. D. Carroll (1965). "Computer simulation of individual belief systems." *American Behavioral Scientist, 8*: 24–30.

Allison, Graham T. (1969). "Conceptual models and the Cuban missile crisis." *American Political Science Review*, Vol. LXIII, No. 3 (September).

Anderson, Craig A. (1983). "Abstract and concrete data in the perseverance of social theories: When weak data lead to unshakable beliefs." *Journal of Experimental Social Psychology, 19*: 93–108.

Axelrod, Robert (1976). *The Structure of Decision: The Cognitive Maps of Political Elites*. Princeton, NJ: Princeton University Press.

Bonham, G. Matthew, Daniel Heradstveit, Ove Narvesen, and Michael J. Shapiro (1978). "A cognitive model of decision making: Application to Norwegian oil policy." *Cooperation and Conflict, 13*: 93–108.

Bonham, G. Matthew, Michael J. Shapiro and Thomas L. Trumble (1979). "The October war." *International Studies Quarterly*, Vol. 23, No. 1 (March): 3–44.

Carbonell, Jaime (1978). "POLITICS: Automated ideological reasoning." *Cognitive Science 2*: 27–51.

Carey, Susan (1985). *Conceptual Change in Childhood*. Cambridge, MA: MIT Press.

Carter, Jimmy (1977). Speech at the United Nations, weekly compilation of presidential documents, administration of Jimmy Carter, pp. 1469–1477.

——— (1978a). Commencement speech at Wake Forest University, March 17, 1978, weekly compilation of presidential documents, administration of Jimmy Carter, pp. 529–535. Government Printing Office.

——— (1978b). Commencement speech at the U.S. Naval Academy, June 7, 1978, weekly compilation of presidential documents, administration of Jimmy Carter, pp. 1052–1057. Government Printing Office.

——— (1982). *Keeping Faith: Memoirs of a President*. New York: Bantam.

Chandrasekaran, B. (1986). "Generic tasks in knowledge-based reasoning: High-level building blocks for expert system design." *IEEE Expert* (Fall): 23–30.

Chandrasekaran, B., and William F. Punch, III (1988). "Hierarchical classification:

Its usefulness for diagnosis and sensor validation." *IEEE Journal on Selected Areas in Communications*, Vol. 6, No. 5 (June).

Clancey, William J. (1984). "Classification Problem Solving." Proceedings of the National Conference on Artificial Intelligence, Austin, Texas.

Cowan, David A. (1986). "Developing a process model of problem recognition." *Academy of Management Review*, Vol. 11, No. 4: 763–776.

Daehler, Marvin W. (1985). *Cognitive Development*. New York: Alfred A. Knopf.

Davis, Paul C. (1987). "A new analytic technique for the study of deterrence, escalation control, and war termination." In Stephen J. Cimbala (ed.), *Artificial Intelligence and National Security* (chap. 3). Lexington, MA: Lexington Books.

Duffy, Gavan, and Seth A. Tucker (1995). "Political science: Artificial intelligence applications." *Social Science Computer Review, 13*: 1–20.

Dutton, Jane E., and Susan E. Jackson (1987). "Categorizing strategic issues: Links to organizational action." *Academy of Management Review*, Vol. 12, No. 1: 76–90.

Estes, W. K. (1991). "Cognitive architectures from the standpoint of an experimental psychologist." *Annual Review of Psychology, 42*: 1–28.

Firebaugh, Morris W. (1988). *Artificial Intelligence: A Knowledge Based Approach*. Boston: Boyd & Fraser.

Gerner, Deborah J., Phillip A. Schrodt, Ronald A. Francisco, and Judith L. Weddle (1994). "Machine coding of event data using regional and international sources." *International Studies Quarterly, 38*: 91–119.

Halperin, Morton H. (1974). *Bureaucratic Politics and Foreign Policy*. Washington D.C.: The Brookings Institution.

Hastie, Reid (1988). "A computer simulation model of person memory." *Journal of Experimental Social Psychology, 24*: 423–447.

Heider, F. (1958). *The psychology of interpersonal relations*. New York: Wiley.

Hothersall, David (1985). *Psychology*. Columbus: Charles E. Merrill.

Hudson, Valerie (1992). "Situational predisposition model." In V. Hudson (ed.), *Artificial Intelligence and International Politics*. Boulder, CO: Westview Press.

Jackson, Peter (1990). *Introduction to Expert Systems* (2nd ed.). Wokingham: Addison-Wesley.

Jackson, Susan, E., and Dutton, Jane E. (1988). "Discerning threats and opportunities." *Administrative Science Quarterly, 33* (1988): 370–387.

Job, Brian L., and Douglas Johnson (1989). "UNCLESAM: The application of a rule-based model to US foreign policy." University of Vancouver mimeo.

Johnson, Richard T. (1974). *Managing the White House: An Intimate Study of the Presidency*. New York: Harper and Row.

Jones, E. E., D. E. Kanouse, H. H. Kelley, R. E. Nisbett, S. Valins, and B. Weiner, (1972). *Attribution: Perceiving the Causes of Behavior*. Morristown, NJ: General Learning Press.

Jordan, Hamilton (1982). *Crisis: The Last Year of the Carter Presidency*. New York: G. P. Putnam and Sons.

Kaplan, Craig A., and Herbert A. Simon (1990). "In search of insight." *Cognitive Psychology, 22*: 374–419.

Kegley, Charles, Jr. (1994). "How did the Cold War die? Principles for an autopsy." *Mershon International Studies Review*, Vol. 38, Supp. 1 (April).

Keil, Frank C. (1989). *Concepts, Kinds, and Cognitive Development*. Cambridge, MA: MIT Press.

Kotovsky, K., J. R. Hayes, and H. A. Simon (1985). "Why are some problems hard? Evidence from Tower of Hanoi." *Cognitive Psychology, 17*: 248–294.

Lamberti, Donna M., and Sandra L. Newsome (1989). "Presenting abstract versus concrete information expert systems: What is the impact on user performance?" *International Journal of Man-Machine Studies, 31*: 27–45.

Lehman, Fritz (ed.) (1992). *Semantic Networks in Artificial Intelligence.* New York: Pergamon Press.

Mallery, John C. (1991). "Semantic content analysis: A new methodology for the RELATUS Natural Language Environment." In Valerie Hudson (ed.), *Artificial Intelligence in International Politics.* Boulder, CO: Westview Press.

Maoz, Z., and A. Shayer (1987). "The cognitive structure of peace and war argumentation: Israeli prime ministers versus the Knesset." *Political Psychology,* Vol. 8, No. 4.

Markus, Hazel, and R. B. Zajonc (1985). "The cognitive perspective in social psychology." In G. Lindzey and E. Aronson (eds.), *The Handbook of Social Psychology* (3rd ed., Vol. 1). New York: Random House.

Mayer, Richard E. (1992). *Thinking, Problem Solving, Cognition.* New York: W. H. Freeman.

Mefford, Dwain (1992). "Steps toward artificial intelligence: Rule-based, case-based and explanation-based models of politics." In V. Hudson (ed.), *Artificial Intelligence and International Politics.* Boulder, CO: Westview Press.

Michotte, A. (1963). *The Perception of Causality.* New York: Basic Books.

Moreland, Richard L., and John M. Levine (1992). "Problem identification by groups." In S. Worchel, W. Wood, and J. A. Simpson (eds.), *Group Process and Productivity.* Newbury Park: Sage.

Newell, Allen, and Herbert A. Simon (1972). *Human Problem Solving.* Englewood Cliffs, NJ: Prentice-Hall.

(1976). "Computer science as empirical enquiry: Symbols and search." *Communications of the Association for Computing Machinery, 19* (March): 113–126.

Piaget, Jean (1982). *The essential Piaget* (H. E. Gruber and J. J. Voneche, eds.). London: Routledge & Kegan Paul.

Rosati, Jerel A. (1991). *The Carter Administration's Quest for Global Community.* Columbia: University of South Carolina Press.

Schrodt, Philip A. (1988). "Language, pattern and computational models of political behavior." Prepared for the Shambaugh Conference on Cognition and Politics, University of Iowa.

Sick, Gary (1986). *All Fall Down: America's Tragic Encounter with Iran.* New York: Penguin Books.

Simon, H. A. (1980). "Cognitive science: The newest science of the artificial." *Cognitive Science, 4*: 33–46.

(1985). "Human nature in politics: The dialogue of psychology with political science." *American Political Science Review,* Vol. 79.

(1990). "Invariants of human behavior." *Annual Review of Psychology, 41*: 1–19.

Stasser, Garold, and W. Titus (1985). "Pooling of unshared information in group decision making: Biased information sampling during discussion." *Journal of Personality and Social Psychology, 48*: 1476–1478.

(1987). "Effects of information load and percentage shared information on the dissemination of unshared information during group discussion." *Journal of Personality and Social Psychology, 53*: 81–93.

Sylvan, Donald A. (1987). "Political limits in the energy arena." In Stephen J. Cimbala (ed.), *Artificial Intelligence and National Security* (chap. 10). Lexington Books Massachusetts, 1987.

Sylvan Donald A., and Stuart J. Thorson (1992). "Ontologies, problem representation, and the Cuban missile crisis." *Journal of Conflict Resolution*, Vol. 36, No. 4 (December): 709–732.

Taber, Charles S. (1992). "POLI: An expert system model of U.S. foreign policy belief systems." *American Political Science Review*, No. 4 (December).

Taber, Charles S., and Richard J. Timpone (1996). "Beyond simplicity: Focused realism and computational modeling in international relations." *Mershon International Studies Review, 40*: 41–79.

Tamashiro, Howard (1989). "The Computational Modeling of Strategic Time." Syracuse University mimeo.

Tanaka, Akihiko (1984). "China, China Watching, and CHINAWATCHER." In D. Sylvan and S. Chan (eds.), *Foreign Policy Decision Making*. New York: Praeger.

Thorson, Stuart J., and Donald A. Sylvan (1982). "Counterfactuals and the Cuban missile crisis." *International Studies Quarterly*, Vol. 26, No. 4 (December).

Tversky, Amos, and Daniel Kahneman (1980). "Causal schemas in judgments under uncertainty." In Martin Fishbein (ed.), *Progress in Social Psychology* (chap. 2). Mahwah, NJ: Lawrence Erlbaum.

Walsh, James P., Caroline M. Henderson, and John Deighton (1988). "Negotiated belief structures and decision performance: An empirical investigation." *Organizational Behavior and Human Decision Processes, 42*: 194–216.

Young, Michael D. (1993). "Foreign policy reasoning: Modeling President Carter." Paper prepared for the 34th annual convention of the International Studies Association, Acapulco, Mexico, March 23–27.

(1994). "The foreign policy problem representation of President Carter." Unpublished dissertation, The Ohio State University.

(1996). "Cognitive maps meet semantic networks." *Journal of Conflict Resolution, 40*(3): 395–414.

CHAPTER 10

A Problem-Solving Perspective on Decision-Making Processes and Political Strategies in Committees: The Case of Controversial Supreme Court Justice Nomination Hearings

Katherine M. Gannon

In group decision settings, differences in how individuals represent problems may produce barriers to reaching consensus because the way an individual represents a problem may in large part determine the solutions or decision alternatives one considers (Newell and Simon 1972; see also Voss, Purkitt, and Breuning, all in this volume). Examples of this can be found in high-level government group decision-making units. A classic example is from the executive committee during the Cuban missile crisis.

> McNamara argued that the Soviet missiles did not fundamentally alter the strategic balance. The implication was thus that the US should either do nothing or restrict itself to diplomatic pressure on the Soviets.
>
> Bundy and Nitze argued that missiles in Cuba almost doubled Soviet Strategic power and reduced the warning time in the case of nuclear confrontation from twenty to two minutes. The implication was that the United States had to do its utmost to bring about a swift removal of the missiles. (Maoz 1990: 90)

Other examples on which this chapter focuses can be found in Senate Judiciary Committee decision making in controversial Supreme Court justice nomination hearings. These nominations are characterized by significant differences in individual problem representations at the hearing and lack of consensus in whether to support the nomination. Although this decision context differs in content from others discussed in this volume (i.e., it does not concern foreign policy), it does not differ significantly from these and other aspects of decision making that may be observed in more international domains. In this chapter, the process of the Senate Judiciary Committee's decision making in controversial Supreme Court justice nomination hearings is analyzed from a problem-solving perspective to illustrate how this perspective

249

provides a framework for understanding decision making and how its processes relate to decision outcome and political strategies employed.

Before beginning the specific analysis of decision making in controversial
Supreme Court justice nomination hearings, a brief review of various aspects
of problem solving in general is undertaken.

Problem Solving

When solving a problem, one first determines a *problem space* (Simon 1978).
Knowledge that is relevant to solving the problem, as well as goals of the
problem and imposed constraints, is included in the problem space. For example, the goal in solving a crossword puzzle is to fill in all the blanks with
words that correspond to the given clues. Constraints include choosing words
that fit into the pattern of letters already present in the puzzle and not consulting the answer key until one is finished with the entire puzzle. In problems
that are well structured, this space may be well defined. There is a clear
beginning and an end to the problem as well as clear algorithms that one
needs to follow in order to solve the problem. In ill-defined problem domains
such as political decision making, the constraints may not be readily apparent;
in fact, the problem solver sometimes needs to determine first what these
constraints are. This creates the possibility that the wrong constraints may be
imposed, which could prevent the problem from being solved (Reitman
1965).

Problem representation refers to the interpretation of the problem within
the problem space (Voss, Greene, Post, and Penner 1983). For example, if
one were faced with a hypothetical word problem in which one must determine the fastest way to get to a destination, one solver may interpret the goal
of the problem to be how to determine the rate of speed the vehicle must
travel given the time frame, whereas another may interpret the same problem
as having the goal of figuring out which route is best to take. Different
interpretations of the problem can lead to different constraints being imposed;
as a result, different solution alternatives are considered.

Boynton's cognitive model of the Senate Agricultural Committee is an
application of this perspective to Senate committee decision making (Boynton
1990). Boynton details how the problem space is determined and maintained
in this committee. *Boundary maintenance* includes the acceptance of five core
principles that the committee endorses – for example, the notion that "vol-
untary rather than mandatory programs are needed" and that "bringing supply into line with demand is accomplished by controlling supply rather than
improving demand" (Boynton 1990: 193). These ideas set the boundaries for
what is considered and is relevant to the decision making. Problem representation of particular decisions in the committee usually take the form of deter-

mining whether the agricultural cycle is in the "boom" or the "bust" phase of the agricultural economy. Each phase represents a different problem to be solved; therefore, different solutions are applicable.

Decision Making in the Senate Judiciary Committee

Senate Judiciary Committee decision making can also be considered from a problem-solving perspective. Several aspects of the Senate Judiciary Committee's decision task distinguish it, however, from other senatorial-committee decision making. The Senate Judiciary Committee is a decision-making body of about fourteen members organized along partisan lines in rough proportion to that of the full Senate. The Senate Judiciary Committee conducts the first hearings in the nomination process of Supreme Court justices. The committee transmits their decision to the full Senate for consideration in terms of numbers of those who oppose and those who support the nominee. In addition to the vote, a report of the majority and the minority views of the committee and individual views of some senators are transmitted to the Senate.

One aspect that distinguishes the Senate Judiciary Committee is that it does not explicitly identify problems that require solving. The decision-making event is initiated by the president after the resignation or death of a Supreme Court justice. Issues of problem identification thus do not exist as they might for a committee responding to a crisis.

A second distinctive aspect is that the committee does not generate options or decision solutions in the sense that other committees might. A particular nominee is selected by the president and presented to the committee for evaluation. The decision alternatives are predetermined; one can either support or oppose the nomination. Although this decision outcome is apparently clear cut and well structured, the problem solving is not. The decision process includes such ill-defined problems as how to determine the fitness of the nominee or how to best persuade another group member.

A third aspect that distinguishes Senate Judiciary Committee decision making from other committee decision making is that the decision criteria are supposed to be free from partisan considerations. Senators are expected to judge the Supreme Court justice nominee on such preset criteria as the nominee's ability to divorce political beliefs from his/her court rulings. The highly important nature of the task (a lifetime appointment) suppresses much of the overt political maneuvering of committee members that may be tolerated in other senatorial settings. This contention is supported by the fact that in most nomination hearings, there is unanimous or nearly unanimous agreement from Senate Judiciary Committee members of both political parties regarding whether to support the nominee. Problem representation does play a role in this decision context, albeit differently than in other senatorial committee decision making. Evidence of problem representation is perhaps most apparent in controversial Supreme Court justice nomination hearings, which are marked by lack of consensus. It is in such a situation that one may expect to find differences in problem space and representation. The next section discusses how such problem-solving components apply to controversial Senate Judiciary Committee hearings and how they provide a framework for analyzing the decision process.

Problem Space

The Problem Goal

The objective decision task of the Senate Judiciary Committee is to determine the fitness of the nominee to serve a lifetime appointment on the Supreme Court. However, not all senators on the committee have this goal. Many committee members have made their decision before the actual hearings begin for a variety of political reasons, such as willingness to oppose a lame-duck president or because of a shifting balance on the Supreme Court (Baum 1992; Watson and Stookey 1988).

Senators take on different roles during the hearings that are associated with different problem goals in the hearing. One role they can take is that of a *partisan* (Watson and Stookey 1988). This role is taken by senators who have made their decision before the hearing; they are distinguished from others by their "active efforts in the hearings to secure or defeat the nomination" (Watson and Stookey 1994). The problem goal associated with this role appears to be one of determining how best to secure or defeat the nomination.

Another role is that of the *advocate* (Watson and Stookey 1988). Senators in this role have also made their decision before the hearings begin, but unlike those in the partisan role, they do not openly display their partisan behavior; rather, they advertise and educate others about the nominee (Watson and Stookey 1994). The problem goal of this role appears to be to determine how to influence other senators' behavior in the nomination.

The *validater* is another role taken by senators who have made their decision before the hearings. They use the hearing to confirm their initial decision (Watson and Stookey 1994). The problem goal associated with this role is to determine whether there may be any unanticipated weaknesses of the nominee that would result in a change in decision.

Some senators remain undecided about the nomination until the hearings take place. The role they take in hearings is the *evaluator*. The evaluator uses the hearing evidence to come to a decision about the nominee (Watson and Stookey 1994). The problem goal of the evaluator during the nomination hearings is to evaluate the fitness of the nominee to be a Supreme Court justice. Senator Specter in the Robert Bork Supreme Court justice nomination hearings made statements consistent with this role: "I come to these hearings with an open mind, and I am prepared to listen to your views on these subjects and to make a decision based upon what I hear significantly in this room."

Senator Heflin in the Clarence Thomas Supreme Court Justice nomination hearings also made statements that are characteristic of a validater: "On the other hand, if your testimony persuades us that you will dispense justice fairly and impartially and that you will listen and be open-minded, then in my judgment, doubts will be alleviated."

The evaluator role in the Senate Judiciary Committee hearings bears some resemblance to the *cue taker* role identified by Stewart, Hermann, and Hermann (1989) in their modeling of the 1973 Soviet decision to support Egypt. The cue taker, like the evaluator, is a decision maker whose commitment to a preference is weak and is one who bases his or her position on situation-specific information. The cue taker has weak organizational affiliation, as did those taking evaluator roles in the Robert Bork and Clarence Thomas nominations (Cohodas 1987).

Constraints and Relevant Knowledge

Regardless of the role (and associated problem goals) that senators take in the hearings, they are constrained in the decision process by public accountability to preset decision criteria. Their decision is supposed to be based on the Supreme Court justice nominee's competence, judicial temperament, and integrity (Gannon 1995; cf. Watson and Stookey 1994). Senators explicitly mentioned these criteria in opening speeches of the Thomas and Bork Supreme Court justice nomination hearings and referred to them throughout their questioning of the nominee. The American Bar Association (ABA) also uses these criteria in their evaluations of potential nominees.

For senators whose problem goal is to evaluate the nominee, this constraint of being accountable to criteria in the public articulation of their decision outcome additionally influences their *decision process* (Gannon 1995). A later section of the chapter addresses how the constraints are used in the decision process of these Senators.

For senators who take the other roles in the hearing, however, the criteria may constrain only their discourse and not the decision process. These senators, who are already committed to a decision, must constrain their discourse to comments on the nominee's fitness while pursuing their political ends. Their potential problem-solving strategies are detailed in a later section of the chapter.

Problem Representation

The problem representations of uncommitted senators were evident in their opening statements in the Bork and Thomas Supreme Court justice nomination hearings. The senators clearly laid out the problem of having to decide on the fitness of the nominee by trying to decide which of two or more views of the nominee was accurate, as illustrated in the following extract from the testimony of Senator Heflin in the Clarence Thomas Supreme Court justice nomination hearing:

> To some you are the embodiment of the American Dream – you have overcome the bonds of poverty and racial segregation and deprivation and have risen to the top.
>
> To others you have succeeded but forgotten your past and turned your back on others now less fortunate than you. If the Senate is persuaded that you will pursue an ideological agenda, have a closed mind, and will be a judicial activist ignoring the will of the elected bodies, then these doubts will become impediments to your confirmation. On the other hand, if your testimony persuades us that you will dispense justice fairly and impartially and that you will listen and be open minded, then in my judgment these doubts will be alleviated.

Senator Deconcini similarly detailed two opposing views of Robert Bork in the Robert Bork Supreme Court Justice nomination hearing:

> Do I believe that faced with difficult decisions with wide-ranging implications– that you, Judge Bork, will listen carefully to the arguments on both sides and then apply the appropriate law in an objective and unbiased way? Or will you find an intellectually supportable and highly articulate way to decide the case as you see fit and how you feel it should come out?

Explicit evidence of the problem representation of precommitted senators is difficult to find in the hearing discourse. Given problem constraints that encompass the ideal of being nonpartisan in this context, it is unlikely that senators will let it be known that they are attempting to solve a political problem. Such political problems bring with them an additional constraint of being covert about the fact that one is viewing the problem as political. The addition of a constraint to the original problem statement is characteristic of such ill-structured problems (Voss, this volume).

Problem representation may indirectly be inferred by examining the discourse. For example, if the problem goal of a senator is to determine how to influence another senator, one can examine influence attempts in the discourse. The next section addresses these and other problem-solving strategies that can be inferred from the discourse.

Problem-Solving Strategies

Problem Solving of Uncommitted Senators

Uncommitted senators have the problem of evaluating the nominee's fitness to be on the Supreme Court and doing this within the bounds of preset decision criteria. A model applicable to understanding how senators solve this problem was developed by Gannon (1995). Transcript analysis of the Robert Bork and Clarence Thomas hearings and laboratory simulations provided support for this model, the Template-driven Construal (TDC) model. According to the TDC model, a senator's construal of the nominee is matched against a template (in this case, the ABA decision criteria) to determine whether the nominee is unqualified to serve as a Supreme Court justice. For example, a senator may construe the nominee as biased, dishonest, and untrustworthy. This construal may include simulations of the nominee's future actions in the Supreme Court and the resulting consequences of such actions. In this case, the traits biased and dishonest clearly do not match the template criteria of "integrity" and "judicial temperament," and the nominee would be viewed as unqualified.

The default of the nomination hearings is confirmation of the nominee (Baum 1992; Gannon 1995). If the senator is uncertain that the construal of the nominee matches the template (criteria indicating that he or she is qualified), then the presumption is that the nominee is qualified.

The TDC model includes one final step after the decision is made, that is, to make a judgment about the articulation of the decision. Specifically, an additional problem might be encountered by senators because the evidence used to make an evaluation of the nominee might not be publicly defensible. For example, in the Thomas hearings, the Senate Judiciary Committee members knew about the upcoming Anita Hill testimony before they wrote their decisions, yet there was no mention of the implications of this testimony in the final written decisions of the committee (Biskupic 1991). The articulation of the decision may become another problem complete with its own problem constraints. This is another example of an addition of constraint to the original problem statement, which is characteristic of ill-structured problems (Voss, this volume).

Problem-Solving Strategies of Precommitted Senators

An examination of hearing discourse of precommitted senators from a problem-solving perspective provided a pool of strategies they might use to influence best another senator or to secure or defeat a nomination.

Establish the Problem Interpretation: One strategy for senators trying to solve the problem of appearing to be nonpartisan at the same time as they are attempting to influence other senators to adopt their precommitted partisan position is to provide the problem interpretation for other senators. By providing an interpretation, one can create a problem space within which only certain information may be considered (Newell and Simon 1972). Putting bounds on the problem may increase the likelihood that an advocated solution is adopted.

Smith (1984) also notes the importance of interpretation for getting an advocated solution adopted in congressional decision making: "Presentations can influence the representations for two reasons. First, they structure how members search for information about consequences, and second, they can cause members to reconsider information they may have overlooked in prior searches" (Smith 1984: 47).

In the context of Senate Judiciary Committee hearings, one way to influence the decision process of uncommitted senators is to package or frame who the nominee is. Recall that the uncommitted senator's problem-solving strategy is to develop a construal of the nominee. The interpretation provided by precommitted senators may direct their search for information as well as determine what information is considered relevant to the problem solution.

The interpretative framework provided by the senators in the Judiciary Committee hearings may take the form of a cognitive representation of the nominee (Gannon 1995). The core organizing concept is a construal of the nominee. An example of alternative interpretation/frames of Judge Thomas given by a precommitted senator (Senator Metzenbaum) during the opening speeches of the Thomas hearings follows:

> But there is one thing upon which everyone including this senator agrees: Judge Thomas's life story is an uplifting tale of a youth determined to surmount the barriers of poverty segregation and discrimination . . . the question is not where does Judge Thomas come from? Rather the question for the committee is this: Where would Justice Thomas take the Supreme Court? I am deeply concerned about the answer to that question. The record suggests that Judge Thomas may be an eager and active participant in the Rhenquist court's assault on established judicial precedents which protects civil rights and individual liberties. Judge Thomas has harshly criticized important court decisions which have protected voting rights for blacks and promoted equal treatment for minorities and women. Indeed, he has suggested that many of these decisions be overturned.

Interpretation in this sense is akin to Gamson's (1989) use of the term *frame* in his work on media influence. "The media discourse can be conceived of as a set of packages that give meaning to an issue. A package has an internal structure. At its core is a central organizing idea, a frame for making sense of relevant events, suggesting what is at issue'' (Gamson 1989: 3).

Gamson also suggests that if ''packages are to remain viable, they have the task of constructing meaning over time by incorporating new events into their interpretative frames'' (Gamson 1989: 4). A construal of a nominee is flexible enough to provide meaning for new information about the nominee. For example, the ascription of personality traits such as ''dishonest'' or ''hardworking'' to a nominee allows one to assign meaning to newly encountered behaviors. Consider the Anita Hill testimony regarding alleged sexual harassment by Judge Thomas that became public after the close of the Senate Judiciary Committee nomination hearings. This initially unexpected and confusing information could readily be given meaning by being absorbed into more than one interpretive frame of Thomas. The opposing implications of the testimony could be assimilated by interpretation/frames of Thomas as either someone who was caring and committed to civil rights or someone who was a harsh critic of equal rights and was out of touch with his roots. The testimony may have been as controversial as it was precisely because the information could easily be interpreted into either frame without much modification of the already existing structure.

Attack Problem Constraints: Another strategy to achieve a solution to political problems of the hearings is to challenge the problem constraints themselves. In the context of Senate Judiciary Committee hearings, this may take the form of challenging the preset decision criteria.

Argument over the problem constraints in the Robert Bork hearing was one strategy senators used to tackle partisan issues while staying within the problem constraint of not appearing to be motivated politically. Explicit discussion ensued over the boundaries of judicial temperament, one of the decision criteria. Some senators argued that it was appropriate to abolish the constraint against consideration of Robert Bork's ideology because it was relevant to the decision criteria of judicial temperament. These senators argued that Bork's ideology was extreme enough to affect his judicial temperament. Others argued that ideology was clearly outside the problem space and should not be taken into account. Senator Heflin summarizes the conflict during the Bork nomination hearing:

> Some supporters of you, Judge Bork, argue that the Senate should not consider your philosophy and ideology but should decide only whether you have the appropriate intellect, temperament, and integrity. Some of your opponents on the other hand, argue that not only may the Senate consider philosophy and ideology, we must base our decision on the effect the nomination will have on future decisions.

Accuse Others of Violating Problem Constraints: A problem-solving strategy related to attacking the constraints directly is to accuse others of inappropriately violating the problem constraints. This is equivalent to accusing someone of attempting to solve a problem by cheating. This strategy allows the accuser to engage actively in partisan politics while virtuously remaining within the problem constraints themselves. It can also serve to erode the validity of the problem solution of another senator and possibly lessen its impact on the decision processes of uncommitted senators. Specifically in this context, the strategy is to comment on the use of partisanship or politics by other senators instead of the preset decision criteria when deciding whether to confirm the nominee. Senator Grassley in the Robert Bork Supreme Court justice nomination hearing used this tactic:

> The intense lobbying has transformed this nomination into the legislative equivalent of a pork barrel water project – all strong arm politics and no substance. The partisans who act as the generals in this war of mud slinging have had some success. In fact, some members of the Senate have outflanked each other for the honor of taking the most extreme position even before the first day of the hearings!

Conclusions

An application of the problem-solving perspective to Senate Judiciary Committee decision making resulted in asking how the individual members of the committee represented the problem and what strategies they could use in attempting to solve it. The framework directs research efforts at a cognitive level rather than at a systems level, in which one's focus may be on political variables accounting for a senator's decision. A focus on the cognitive level allows examination of questions such as the following: What is the decision process of the senators? Why are certain nominees perceived as controversial? What types of evidence or form of argument might create controversy or alleviate it? Why are certain strategies more effective than others in influencing the decision outcome? How do the interactions of the committee members affect the decision processes of uncommitted senators?

These questions are important ones to be addressed, particularly questions regarding how the uncommitted senators process hearing evidence. Senators who remain uncommitted play a pivotal role in controversial nominations because these nominations are characterized by a split of members' decisions down party lines even before nomination hearings have begun. Understanding their decision processes becomes a critical element in understanding the dynamics of the hearings and explaining the committee's final decision. Current models of Senate Judiciary Committee decision making, however, have not focused on the uncommitted senator's decision process (Baum 1992; Watson and Stookey 1988).

This chapter has attempted to demonstrate how the application of a problem-solving perspective can provide a framework for understanding and explaining decision making. Although the specific focus of this chapter has been on the Senate Judiciary Committee, at a more general level, the chapter has focused on decision processes and political strategies that may occur in a variety of other contexts entailing ill-structured problems. This perspective alerts one to the fact that in certain situations the possibility exists for individual decision makers to represent the problem entirely differently, pursue different problem goals, and as a result come to problem solutions very different from those of other decision makers even though all the decision makers possess relatively the same objective information. This perspective thus has implications not only for understanding an individual decision maker but for understanding group interactions. For example, an application of a problem-solving perspective to understanding group disagreement may lead one to discover that the source of the disagreement is either a difference in problem representations of group members or the consideration of different problem constraints. This information may be used to develop or select effective strategies to resolve the disagreement or, at the very least, make clearer what the disagreement entails.

References

Baum, L. (1992). *The Supreme Court*. Washington, D.C.: Congressional Quarterly Press.

Biskupic, J. (1991). "Thomas drama engulfs nation; Anguished senate faces vote." *Congressional Quarterly*, 2948–2957.

Boynton, G. R. (1990). "Ideas and action: A cognitive model of the Senate Agriculture Committee." *Political Behavior, 12*: 181–213.

Cohodas, N. (1987). "Deconcini, Heflin, Specter hold key to Judiciary committee vote on Bork." *Congressional Quarterly*, 1496–1497.

Gamson, W. A. (1989). "Media discourse and public opinion on nuclear power: A constructionist approach." *American Journal of Sociology, 95*: 1–37.

Gannon, K. M. (1995). "The Template-Driven Construal Model: An Application to Decision Making of the Senate Judiciary Committee in Supreme Court Justice Nomination Hearings." Unpublished doctoral dissertation, The Ohio State University, Columbus, Ohio.

Maoz, Z. (1990). "Framing the national interest: The manipulation of foreign policy decisions in group settings." *World Politics, 43*: 77–110.

Newell, A., and H. A. Simon (1972). *Human Problem Solving*. Englewood Cliffs, NJ: Prentice-Hall.

Reitman, W. R. (1965). *Cognition and Thought*. New York: Wiley.

Simon, H. (1978). "Information processing theory of human problem solving." In

W. K. Estes (ed.), *Handbook of Learning and Cognitive Processes: Human Information Processing* (Vol. 5). Hillsdale, NJ: Lawrence Erlbaum.

Smith, R. A. (1984). "Advocacy, interpretation and influence in the U.S. Congress." *American Political Science Review, 78*: 44–63.

Stewart, P. D., M. G. Hermann, and C. F. Hermann (1989). "Modeling the 1973 Soviet decision to support Egypt." *American Political Science Review, 83*: 36–59.

Voss, J. F., T. R. Greene, T. A. Post, and B. C. Penner (1983). "Problem solving in the social sciences." In G. H. Bower (ed.), *The Psychology of Learning and Motivation: Advances in Research Theory* (Vol. 17, pp. 165–213). New York: Academic Press.

Watson, G., and J. Stookey (1988). "Supreme Court confirmation hearings: A view from the Senate." *Judicature, 17*: 186–196.

(1994). *Shaping America: The Politics of Supreme Court Appointments*. New York: HarperCollins.

CHAPTER 11

When Gender Goes to Combat: The Impact of Representations in Collective Decision Making

Silvana Rubino-Hallman

Introduction

The traditional policy of excluding women from direct-combat positions in the U.S. armed forces has been a target of criticism by those who believe that this policy is nothing but a form of discrimination against women. These dissenting voices have been calling for the elimination of these last barriers and the opening to women of all positions within the military organization.

A brief – and certainly incomplete – narrative of policy-making evolution in this area should start in the early twentieth century, when women were used mainly as nurses in the armed forces. During World War II, owing to manpower needs to fight the Axis powers, it was decided that women would be employed more broadly in auxiliary roles. Later, women became actual members of the armed forces, but they were kept in separate corps. In 1948, the enactment of the Women's Armed Services Integration Act made the presence of women in the military permanent, even in peacetime, but it excluded them from direct-combat positions because such positions were seen as contrary to American culture and tradition. Women were significantly restricted in grade as well, because they could not go farther than the rank of colonel. When women were rotated out of a job, they reverted back to the highest permanent rank, lieutenant colonel or commander.

In 1967, Congress began loosening some of the restrictions on the positions that could be occupied by women. In 1972, women were allowed into Reserve Officers Training Corps (ROTC) units. In 1976, there was a further significant development when Congress required the Department of Defense to open the military academies to women. In 1978, the Navy statute was amended to broaden the availability of shipboard assignments to Navy women to include hospital, supply, and transport ships. In 1980, the Defense Officers Personnel Management Act (DOPMA) opened still more positions to women and indicated that women would be in competition with men for all jobs in the armed forces. In 1991, the Air Force statute was repealed by the House of Representatives, and restrictions on the assignment of women to air crew positions in the Navy were eliminated. The constraints on the assignment of women to ground combat and to combatant ships was left in place. As a result of discrepancies in the Senate version of this legislation, Congress included in the Defense Authorization Act of December 1991 the creation of a presidential commission to review all regulations concerning women in the military and to make recommendations on whether or not an amendment of such regulations was needed, particularly concerning the assignment of women to direct-combat positions. In March 1992, following congressional stipulations, President Bush appointed the Presidential Commission on the Assignment of Women in the Armed Forces (PCAWAF). At the time when the commission was appointed, the cockpits of fighters and bombers, as well as those of high-altitude reconnaissance aircraft, still remained closed to women in both services. Although women have been flying most of those planes – and have also served as instructors in combat squadrons – they were not allowed to train according to the "fighter syllabus" (fighter fundamentals and maneuvers); therefore, they were not qualified to fly combat missions.

On November 1992, the presidential commission concluded its duty by recommending to keep direct-combat positions closed to women, with the exception of positions aboard Navy combat ships. These recommendations astounded several audiences, including most of the commissioners themselves. The narrow difference registered in the vote on the recommendations reflects an intense and antagonistic debate. Indeed, whereas the commission's task was to make these recommendations as a collective body, the final report shows profound disagreements even within the majority.[1] The commission's final report was reviewed by President Bush and sent to Congress without changes in December 1992. In April 1993, President Clinton ordered the military to open combat positions to women in all services. The Air Force and the Navy implemented the presidential directive in combat aircraft, and the Navy also opened positions aboard combatant vessels. Navy submarines, amphibious combat positions in the Marine Corps, and ground combat positions both in the Marine Corps and Army remain closed to this date.

The characteristics of the debate that took place within this presidential commission provoke unexplored and innovative explanations on how decisions are made both individually and in a group environment when dealing with a particularly sensitive issue – the assignment of women to combat positions. By reviewing the commission's public transcript, it is clear that the issue became focused not on whether women *could* perform in direct-combat positions but whether they *should* do it. To ask the question whether women *should* be in combat involves a normative judgment and an embedded conflict of values; furthermore, it invites a confrontation of different positions, related not only to the military as an institution but also to the role of women in society. This involves not only structural and cultural factors but also the particular way in which actors involved in the assignment of women in the military "construct" their position and articulate their preferences through social practices.

The main focus of this chapter is on how the commissioners constructed their positions on whether or not women could or should be assigned to serve in combat aircraft. I also discuss how this group representation of women in combat aircraft influenced the commission's final decision to maintain the status quo in the assignment of women to combat aircraft, by recommending that those positions remain closed.

The Concept of Representations

In analyzing the case of this presidential commission, I argue that in order to understand how the commissioners constructed their positions and made their recommendations, one needs to analyze their *representations*[2] of the issue in debate: whether or not women should be assigned to direct-combat positions. I understand these representations to be preexistent constructions that are recalled in response to a certain event – in this case, the appointment of the presidential commission.

Representations are the product of an interaction of the following elements:

1. A set of beliefs (linked or not)
2. The presence or absence of some level of expertise on the issue in debate
3. A *recollection*[3] of past experiences
4. The use of common sense and heuristics
5. The preexistence of preferences and motives
6. The *reading* of contextual information

The way in which these elements interact is specific to the individual, and this interaction will always differ from another individual's representation of the same issue.

This study goes beyond reducing the role of cognition in group political decision making (the presidential commission in this case) to the consideration of cognitive components through which the individual *perceives* aspects of policy, the role of other actors, or any issue. First, it assumes that there is no "reality-out-there" to be "perceived" objectively – or, conversely, "misperceived" – and that individual representations of the issue of women in combat need to be analyzed and then taken as a given. Information processing becomes, then, "information selection" on the basis of consistency with the overall representation, having the sole objective of enriching its content.

Second, I consider that individuals not only are psychological beings but are also "socially and temporally situated beings connected with each other in a network of practices."[4] This supports the idea of "group representations," which I define as not a mere overlapping of individual representations but more of a synthesis of the collective reading of shared beliefs, reliable information, internal group dynamics, and decodification of the context in which the representation is being constructed. These group representations are constructed either in consent building or group polarization environments, and they have a strong impact on the group's outcome – in this case study, the recommendations to President Bush contained in the commission's final report. I would like to emphasize that (1) group representations may occur among members of the group with or without common preferences on the issue; (2) group representations are different than each of the individual representations of the members of the group; and (3) group representations are constructed during the decision-making process, and in this sense, procedural mechanisms are of key importance.

Third, these representational practices have an impact on the construction of reality, and this in turn has a feedback component that influences representations as well. As Shapiro puts it, "representations do not imitate reality but are the practices through which things take on meaning and value."[5]

The Representation of Women in Combat

The members of the Presidential Commission on the Assignment of Women in the Armed Forces brought to the debate previously acquired ideas and preferences concerning the role of women not only in the military but also in society, the family, in the workplace. Throughout the debate, commissioners interacted with their fellow members, listened to expert testimony from a variety of sources, and dealt with enormous amounts of information concerning women in the military.

During the public hearings conducted by the commission, experts, members of Congress, interest-group leaders, and others gave their testimony on the different aspects of this issue – from cultural and family considerations to physiological, physical, and psychological requirements imposed by combat conditions. Members of the armed forces – officers and enlisted, on active duty, reserve, or retired – provided their testimony as well. Commissioners also traveled to several military bases in the United States and overseas, searching for lessons to be learned and looking for more background on the issue. All the information gathered by the panels was meant to inform an impartial decision on the matter of the assignment of women in the military; more specifically, to decide on whether the still closed direct-combat positions should be opened.

Despite the availability of expert knowledge on the issue at stake, the commissioners always went back to the terrain of personal beliefs and emotions throughout the debate, as well as when making their final speeches. Information was used selectively, and there was not always a correlation between the commissioners' membership in interest groups and the commissioners' final vote. Previous deliberations on the issue of women in the military did not play a key role, and procedural regulations during the decision-making process influenced the framing of the issues. I argue that all of these factors, together with their personal and previously acquired approach to the issue at stake, shaped the commissioners' representations of women in combat.[6] Table 11.1 lists the pro and con positions and outlines some of their discursive components.[7] The differences between the two positions seem to reflect a conflict of values, a polarization of views on what the role of women in the military should be. But this apparent distinction needs to be analyzed further. Although the commissioners supported opposite positions on whether or not women should be assigned to direct-combat positions, in doing so they used the same arguments. The nuances in the arguments indicate that the positions were sometimes based on more empirical elements. Clearly, some combat specialties have specific physical requirements, and this influenced the position adopted by a particular commissioner. This discrepancy was conducive to the commissioners' favoring the opening of direct-combat positions in some areas but not in others, for example, ground combat.

Nevertheless, in other areas, the ability to identify elements that clearly support a certain position was more difficult, and commissioners found themselves trapped in circular discussions. This is the case with the assignment of women to aircraft in the Air Force and in the Navy. In the following section, I discuss the characteristics of the debate on the issue of opening combat positions to women pilots/aviators, in the Air Force and Navy, respectively. The content of the commissioners' representation of women pilots/aviators is examined, focusing on the possibilities of group representation.

The Characteristics of the Debate

Women have been flying for almost twenty years, and although they do not exceed 2 percent of the total number of Air Force pilots, their outstanding performance has been widely recognized. The same applies for women naval aviators. Unanimously, all wing commanders from both services who testified before the commission agreed that the inclusion of women in flying had resulted in improved crew performance. Despite this, the cockpits of fighter

Table 11.1. *Commissioners' representation of women in combat: discursive components*

Favoring the assignment of women in combat (Counterdiscourse)	Against the assignment of women in combat (Dominant discourse)
Equal opportunity	
Women should have equal access to all positions within the military.	Women should have equal access to all positions within the military except direct-combat positions.
Role of women in the military	
Since the increase in the participation of women in the all-volunteer force, women have demonstrated that they have the required skills to perform at the highest level. By not assigning women to direct-combat positions, the military institution is underutilizing them. Physical requirements need to be reevaluated taking into consideration the impact of technology.	Women have performed at the highest levels in the force. However, there is no manpower need that justifies their assignment to direct-combat positions. They do not possess the physical requirements to perform many of these missions. Moreover, combat unit cohesion and morale will be damaged by the incorporation of women.
Military readiness	
The inclusion of women will have a positive effect on military readiness. By depriving women of the opportunity to serve in combat, the military institution is reducing its pool of outstanding and best qualified personnel.	The inclusion of women in combat units is going to reduce the level of readiness of the force because of the impact upon unit cohesion and the extra burden that will be added to unit leadership.
Pregnancy and family issues	
Women who become pregnant should receive the same treatment as those who are injured.	Pregnancy is an obstacle very difficult to overcome because it reduces the possibilities for deployability and inflicts additional costs on training and requalification.
Interaction between men and women in a combat situation	
The relationship between men and women should not be threatening if regulations concerning sexual harassment and fraternization are strictly enforced. With strong leadership, there are no reasons why mixed combat units would be disruptive.	Sexual attraction, male protection of their female counterparts, double standards in training, fitness requirements, and job execution are all factors contributing to the disruption of unit cohesion and morale. Therefore, the inclusion of women in combat units has intrinsic negative effects on the readiness and ability of the military force to succeed.

planes are closed to women in both services. Although women fly most of those planes – and they serve as instructors in combat squadrons – they are not allowed to go over the fighter syllabus in their training; therefore, they cannot fly combat missions in those planes. Ultimately, the commission recommended keeping these positions closed.

The reasons for this unexpected recommendation were varied. First of all, the same legislation that established the presidential commission also repealed Air Force statutory regulations prohibiting the assignment of women to combat aircraft and eliminated similar limitations in Naval aviation. Second, women were already flying fighter aircraft, either as a part of their pilot training or as instructor pilots. The only thing that women were not allowed to do was to fly combat missions.[8] Third, some of the problems that were identified as unavoidable when considering the assignment of women to ground combat positions (e.g., women have less strength than men do, which has a direct impact on their performance within the unit) did not equally apply to combat aircraft. There are two main reasons for this: (1) The fact that women were already flying fighter aircraft implied that these women had the physical requirements needed for the job, and (2) the advances and applications of high technology are remarkable in aviation. Technological advances, such as the cockpit layout and the design of more G-resistant flight suits, have introduced numerous improvements that reduce the relevance of physical traits and concentrate more on other skills, such as ability to read and operate electronic instruments, decision reaction time, and so forth.

Fourth, by the end of the debate, although there was a general perception of the existence of a group of more conservative members within the commission, the expectation was that if these commissioners were to compromise with the presumed minority position – those favoring the opening of all combat positions to women – the issue on which they would compromise was going to be combat aircraft. These speculations proved wrong.

These reasons made the opening of direct-combat positions to women pilots a controversial issue. For those who supported the assignment of women in combat, women combat pilots were the best example of how women can perform as well as men can in a combat aircraft. For those who were against opening direct-combat positions to women, the pilot issue was the most difficult one to deal with, and one in which the bottom line of the debate is most difficult to grab.

In dealing with the fighter pilots/aviators issue, the commissioners listened to testimony from fighter elites in both services: Air Force F-15, F-16, F-111, and F-117 fighter pilots, one of them from the Air Force Fighter Weapons School (Nellis, AFB), and Navy fighter aviators from Top Gun at Miramar (F/A-18 and F-14 aviators). The fighter pilots comprised all-male panels because women do not fly combat missions in these planes. However, women who fly the same planes in noncombat missions also gave their testimony before the commission. What follows are excerpts from the discussion that took place. The questions of the commissioners – both those supporting and those rejecting the assignment of women to direct-combat positions – concentrated on two major issues that can be summarized as follows:

1. Can women do the job (fly the plane in a combat mission)? What are the physical requirements of the job? What is the required training, and what are the restrictions imposed by the equipment?
2. What would be the consequences of assigning women to fighter planes in terms of flying-schedule constraints (e.g., what would be the effects of menstrual cycles and pregnancy on their readiness status)? What would be the impact on unit cohesion? How would it affect life in a combat situation (e.g., issues like privacy, relationships between men/women in the same unit)?

Concerning the first set of questions, there was consensus on the notion that women are generally good at flying these planes, that most of the women excel as instructors, and that, overall, they perform as well as men do when flying the aircraft under normal conditions – as opposed to combat situations. In the words of Captain Dave Freaney, a U.S. Air Force (USAF) F-15 pilot:

> Well, just to start off, I'm about 100 percent opposed to this whole thing ... I could take anybody in this room right now, and you give me three months, and I can teach them how to fly the F-15 back and forth across this country. It's not such a difficult task. ... To the level and the capability to employ that jet as a weapon, I would seriously question the capabilities of women to do that.[9]

Because physical requirements and skills did not appear to be the problem, the discussion focused on the second set of questions. Many obstacles were identified concerning the effects of a female presence among fighter crews. The first was the pregnancy issue and its consequences in terms of pilot readiness. The time that women would be out of the cockpit during pregnancy would make them noncurrent in the aircraft, and training and requalification would be needed to put them up to their former level. This was seen as not only costly but also disruptive to unit operation, rotation possibilities, and level of cohesion. Second, women are perceived to lack the necessary traits of a fighter – such as aggressiveness, drive, competitiveness, willingness to live at the edge, and survival instincts and skills.

Third, the interaction between women and men was seen as problematic for many reasons, among them the lack of privacy, as well as the fear of accusations of sexual harassment (e.g., as the result of criticism of a woman pilot in a debriefing situation). Lieutenant John Claget (United States Navy

[USN], F/A-18 instructor pilot) expressed his concern on this matter as follows:

> I think I can bring up an example that I think goes on every day in a good fighter squadron or an attack squadron, and it is the example of what we kind of call the ready room debrief. A guy has made an obvious mistake out there in the combat or training environment, and it is a finger in his chest, it is, ''You never do that again, because potentially we're going to die because you did that, or I did that.'' And it is very personal, and what it teaches you in that squadron is that, yeah, for that second, you've got rage in you because somebody is accusing you of doing something wrong, and probably you did, and you know you did it wrong, but you'll never do it again. And I would contend that if you have a woman in that squadron, you don't have that option any more, because you are afraid that she is going to accuse you of using some sort of standard against her, and that is not – that is the farthest from the truth, but that goes on on a daily basis, and it goes on today.[10]

Fourth, and also in terms of unit cohesion, another element considered was the protective instinct that men have toward women, which together with others (sexual attraction, romantic relationships) could disrupt the unit's operation. Fifth, they considered issues such as the use of double standards to evaluate women, the potential for the introduction of quotas, and other potential privileges oriented toward the inclusion of more women in fighter cockpits.

Lieutenant Claget also voiced his concern on the consequences of double standards, not only as used today but also the effects of their use in the past. As an instructor pilot, he was not allowed to grade the women by using the same scale used to evaluate the men. He shared with the commission one of his experiences:

> There was one particular instance that always comes to my mind whenever we talk about females in the combat role, and it is always the one where I happened to be out with a female flight student. She didn't perform her mission what I considered up to standards. I chose at that time to try to give her an unsatisfactory for the flight and was told in private quarters that that wasn't what you did in this situation, that ''She not only will pass the flight, but it will be an average grading.'' And the reason at that time was – and I certainly cannot speak for the Training Command today, but as far back as 1988, or as near as 1988 – our attitude as instructors at that time was ''women will never fly combat aviation. You don't need to grade them on the same standards that the men are being graded on. They'll never get to tactical aviation. They're never going to fly the F-18s or the F-14s.'' The follow-on point to that is, yes, we do have women flying F-18s today, and that is a fact. They are certainly not flying the F-18s that any of us have

flown in the fleet or out in the combat missions. To compare the missions
that they are doing today to what we are doing is like comparing driving on
the [Los Angeles] Freeway to driving in the Indianapolis 500. It's just not
the same.[11]

Finally, the issue of prisoners of war (POWs) was raised, emphasizing the
negative effect that captivity might have on unit morale if the prisoner is a
woman. The idea of a woman POW's being raped in the presence of her
fellow unit members was considered appalling by the all-male panel.

But the enumeration of these and other reasons did not seem to justify the
exclusion of women from fighter cockpits, at least not in the minds of those
who supported the opening of these positions within the commission. Commissioner Draude, in an attempt to get to the bottom of the issue, asked the
following question: ''Setting aside the physical aspects, and the capabilities,
and the POW issue . . . , what is the intangible of what makes the fighter pilot
believe that the introduction of women is going to somehow adversely affect
the special uniqueness of being a fighter pilot?''[12] Almost all the pilots in
both the Air Force and Navy panels struggled with the question, and practically everyone repeated the list of factors that we discussed before (physical
capabilities, psychological needs, etc.), and none of their responses got to the
point that Commissioner Draude was trying to make. Lieutenant Tom Down-
ing (USN F/A-18, instructor pilot at Top Gun) articulated the following explanation:

> My feeling on women in combat units, and aviation in particular, since
> that's what I do for a living, is even if you give me someone – the strongest
> woman in the world, somebody that was – the Red Baron was her great-
> grandfather and [she] can fly a great airplane – the actual capability to move
> an airplane through the sky is one thing, but combat units – the ones that
> do well are the ones that come together in esprit de corps and cohesion, and
> that is what makes people winners. It's just like taking two football teams
> and looking at them. The physical capabilities are pretty much the same, but
> whoever is better as a team is what is going to be the winner. So my feeling
> is that if you put women into these combat units that are primarily all male
> right now, is that not only do combat aviators or naval aviators or infantry-
> men or artillery officers – we function differently when in fact we are
> amongst all men, when we are with external women, women who are exter-
> nal to the group, and also when there are women integrated into the group,
> and I think that goes across society. Men in general will act differently
> amongst men. They will act differently when women are involved. And I
> think the penalty that you pay when you put a woman into that particular
> unit is going to decrease the overall effectiveness of that unit to go out there
> and actively engage the enemy and kill people. And I think that is the
> bottom-line issue, because physically, yes, it is demanding. [But] you will
> be able to – there are women out there who can fly the jets. I'm sure of it.

There's probably women out there that can lift more weights, maybe pull more G than I can, but interaction amongst the combat unit, which we are – fighter aviation and attack aviation is to go out and actively kill the enemy. The cohesion involved there is what makes winners, and I think if women are put into that situation, that is going to decrease the overall effectiveness.[13]

Women Warriors?

What is it about combat that women cannot understand or prevents them to participate in it? As Karen Dunivin describes it, "Military culture is characterized by its combat, masculine-warrior paradigm. . . . The military's core activity, which defines its very existence and meaning, is *combat*."[14] Therefore, the uniqueness of being a fighter pilot is being a man fighter pilot, rather than merely a fighter pilot.

The debate on women in fighter aircraft needs to consider what it means to be part of this elite. In the Air Force, as in the Navy, if pilots in general are part of the elite, fighter pilots are the elite of the elite, the "knights of the air." The fighter pilot is the ultimate warrior, and he is also in control of the ultimate weapon, a sophisticated piece of machinery that each day becomes more effective in hitting an increasingly distanced target.

Women have been challenging the image of the "masculine warrior"[15] for more than two decades. During this time, they have performed extremely well, and today they have access to almost all the jobs in the military. But now, a group of these women want to tear down the last barrier to equal access in the armed forces. Nonetheless, the resistance to accepting women in direct-combat positions is still strong, even after President Clinton ordered the opening of combat specialties to women,[16] and this challenge to traditional military culture cannot be seen in isolation. The military institution is trying to resist these changes during an extremely difficult time characterized by uncertainty, budgetary reductions, the pressure of minority groups (women, gays, and lesbians), the instability of the international situation, and the lack of a powerful military threat.

Facing these threats to their survival, the institution as a whole and its members as individuals consistently attempt to preserve what is left of the traditional military culture, particularly by sustaining and promoting old traditions and rituals. Based on the foregoing textual analysis, attempts to keep women out of combat roles were not only an effort to guarantee the survival of the armed forces as institutions but also an effort for *male survival*. The military is one of the few contemporary social institutions valuing manhood, intolerance, strict discipline, subordinated relationships, symbolism, and rituals, all of which are no longer socially accepted or *en vogue*. For the mainstream military culture, the idea of *women warriors* is not only a deviation[17] but a threat to the last retreat for masculinity.[18]

Women Who Want to Be in Combat

Women pilots also came before the presidential commission to give testimony supporting the opening of direct-combat positions. Among them, the testimony of an Air Force U-2 pilot and two Navy aviators is of particular interest because these women were qualified to fly the same planes flown in combat missions by male fighter pilots in the Air Force and Top Gun and by male aviators in the Navy.

Most of the women pilots who testified before the commission were distinguished officers. For example, Captain Troy Devine (USAF, U-2 pilot) was the first woman to fly a U-2. Captain Devine discussed the issue of the special equipment requirements, and she stated that women could easily adapt to the few changes that needed to be introduced (i.e. the use of customized diapers instead of the urinary collection devices used by men) because of the long duration of their reconnaissance missions. She also addressed the issue of pregnancy, a major concern for the commissioners:

> Women do not fly if they become pregnant. I was asked not to become pregnant, and I have not become pregnant, and I don't plan on becoming pregnant. This seems to be an issue. I mean, those things don't happen spontaneously, and one of the stop-gap type procedures that we go through is every two weeks I administer a pregnancy test to myself and record the results to insure that I would not fly if I was pregnant and didn't know about it.[19]

This issue was also addressed by Lieutenant Brenda Scheufele (USN F/A-18 pilot), who stated:

> When you are attached to an operational squadron as a pilot, you are expected to remain in a flying status, and I don't think anyone is going to purposely get pregnant to not go on cruise. If they don't want to go on cruise, they wouldn't have joined the Navy. I mean, it's a responsibility as an officer. It's a – it just is ludicrous to me to say – for that issue to come up. There are opportunities, and there are – maybe not opportunities, but you are not going to be in the cockpit your entire career. You can't. If you want to continue in your career, you have to do shore billet tours. You have to go to Washington. You have to sometimes go to PG school. There are shore billets available that you can have a family if you wish. And, in my case, I'm not planning on children in the near future but if I did, it would be on a shore tour.[20]

They were also asked whether they saw the issue of physical requirements and necessary skills to fly the planes as an important one, and the answer was a definitive no. There was already a consensus among the commissioners and even among the male fighter pilots/aviators on the notion that women can fly the jets. Both Navy lieutenants were present in the audience when the all-male panel of fighter aviators was giving its testimony. They both answered the accusations made by the all-male panel in a defensive manner. Nevertheless, they made some very relevant points about why they want to be Navy fighter aviators.

When discussing the concerns over unit cohesion and morale, these women expressed their disappointment over the fact that the male colleagues doubted the women's willingness to risk their lives for someone they were flying with or for their country. They could not understand the basis for the men's concern. Indeed, Lieutenant Silvia Rivadeneira (USN COD pilot) stated that she could not believe that the men would take a "nugget" (a newly trained pilot [in this case male] without flight hours) over a woman who had been flying the aircraft and needed only to get her fighter training "just because she is a woman."

What was most surprising for both Lieutenant Rivadeneira and Lieutenant Sheufele is that they had been already in an all-male environment, and they did not experience any rejection or problem. Lieutenant Rivadeneira referred to her two-month deployments aboard a carrier as follows: "[I have been] in male environments at times when I was one, maybe one of two women on board as pilots, and it's possible, and I didn't have any problems. And the men treated me with the respect that I deserved because of my rank and because of my performance."[21]

Lieutenant Sheufele also commented on the issue of unit cohesion:

> I think it's the cohesion thing, and it's really funny that they [the men] should say, you know, "It's going to just destroy our cohesion," when I've worked with guys. I mean, obviously, every – most of the naval aviators are men, and I've worked with them, and the men that I have worked with come up to me and say: "Brenda, I would fly with you off the carrier on my wing any day, but I don't think I like the idea about women coming aboard the ship," because they don't equate me with, you know, the gender stereotype, mother, sister, daughter. I'm a professional pilot, I'm their squadron mate, and they can do the job with me and have no problem with it. We don't have a problem with unit cohesiveness in our squadron, and we have 40 percent of the women being female pilots, and we have a lot of enlisted women also in our squadron, and when we go on deck and we have to perform missions, that squadron just comes together and we do it and get the jets up, we go fly the missions, we do our job.[22]

In essence, these women do not have any problems in an all-male environment because they are not perceived as *women* by their male colleagues. Moreover, they do not see themselves mainly as women but, rather, as "professional pilots." Therefore, the issue for them is not whether they are equal to men but rather that they are professional pilots like the men. Even in a combat situation, things would not change:

> And, yeah, it's not in a combat situation, but I can't see how it would change. I really can't see that the relationships that I have with male pilots in my squadron would change if we were aboard the ship. I don't see it. It just – maybe it goes over my head, but I think I can fly with any man in any squadron, and, yeah, probably initially he would probably resent it or not know how to deal with me, but . . . I'd have no problems telling him exactly how I felt about a flight, and I don't think that they would have any problems telling me, because they haven't in the past.[23]

The Impact of the Representation of Women in Combat

As it appears evident after an analysis of the presidential commission's text, recommendations on the assignment of women to direct-combat positions cannot be formulated following the prescriptions of a rational actor model or the step-by-step procedure of information processing. Information is often incomplete, and when available, it is selectively used in consistence with the overall representation. The focus of attention shifts from the identification of the universe of options available to the argument in favor of a particular position within a more narrow array of alternatives.

An analysis of the commissioners' representations of women in combat positions in the Air Force and Navy shows that they had a strong impact not only on the way the commissioners read the context of this debate but also on the way in which they voted on the final recommendations to the president.[24] The commissioners' representation of the issue of women in combat had a similar composition between those who favored the maintenance of the exclusion and those who opposed it. What changed was the pattern of the representation, that is, the way in which its components interacted.[25]

Without considering the details of the structure of these representations, I would like to note that the result of this study shows that both those who were and those who were not favoring the assignment of women to direct-combat positions represented women in combat as *women*. Although this sounds more like a statement of an obvious fact rather than an essential element, in my opinion the fact that both sides of the debate constructed their position on the basis of the idea of *woman* had a direct impact in the outcome of the commission's decision-making process. Indeed, by highlighting the idea of *woman,* the commissioners' discourse focused more on the differences[26] than on the similarities between men and women. In simpler terms, if sex is biologically determined and gender is socially constructed, by focusing on *women* in combat, the outcome is segregation rather than integration.

When women pilots state their views on their integration into combat units, they do not do so as *women* but as *professional fighter pilots*. Furthermore, they told the commission that they are accepted within the all-male environment because they are professional pilots, because they know how to do their job. As they reported it, their male counterparts do not object to their presence in the wing, but they do not like the idea of having *women* in the squadron.

By focusing on *women in combat* rather than on *combatants* in general, the commissioners contributed to the creation of a *female warrior* opposed to a *male warrior*, the pillar upon which the essence of traditional military culture and warfare relies. The creation of the idea of the *female warrior* was the product of both the discourses of those favoring and those opposing the assignment of women to direct-combat positions. The commissioners' consideration of issues like pregnancy, child care, and single-mother deployment contribute to the portrayal of the *female warrior* as a symbol to embrace for those supporting the assignment of women in combat, and as a symbol to reject for those who did not.

This illustrates how the interaction of dominant discourse and counterdiscourse operates within the same textual space, no matter which one predominates. As a sine qua non, language is shared by both discursive practices, and through representations reality is constructed. Subscribing to Shapiro's notion of representational practices, I suggest that the commissioners' representations of women in combat in this group decision-making environment defined and constrained the *textual space* of the outcome of the process: the commission's recommendations. This, in turn, has implications for eventual policy implementation, because it delimits the discursive grounds upon which consequent policy is made. Finally, as already described, the women who want to be in combat represent themselves not as women but as *professional fighter pilots*, and this is in open contradiction of the textual space defined by the dominant and counterdiscourses. Future steps in this project are oriented toward examining the possibility of focusing on *gender similarities* rather than on gender differences. In doing so, it appears that efforts toward the integration of women should focus more on the *demasculinization of the warrior*[27] than on the creation of a subordinated *female warrior* confronting her masculine – and, by nature and number, dominant – counterpart.

Notes

1 The report includes the following sections: recommendations approved by the majority – in an 8 to 7 vote; alternative views supported by 5 of the 15 commissioners; 4 different dissents with the majority's recommendations and with the alternative views signed by different groups of 2 to 3 commissioners each, a minority statement on conscription, and individual statements by each of the 15 commissioners.

2 The development of the concept of representation is central to my dissertation

research. For a more detailed discussion, see Silvana Rubino, ''When Gender Goes to Combat: The Role of 'Representations' in the Assignment of Women in the Military.'' Ph.D. dissertation, unpublished, Washington, D.C.: The American University, 1995.

3 By using this term I mean that the individual's references to past experience are actually reconstructions, often presented in anecdotal form, which are necessarily altered with the passing of time, and also due to a striving for consistency with beliefs and preferences on the issue at stake.

4 See Michael Shapiro, ''Textualizing Global Politics,'' in James Der Derian and Michael Shapiro, eds., *International / Intertextual Relations: Postmodern Readings of World Politics* (Lexington, MA: Lexington Books, 1989, 18).

5 See Michael Shapiro, *The Politics of Representation* (Madison: The University of Wisconsin Press, 1988, xi).

6 To examine the content of the commissioners' representation of women in combat, I use textual analysis. The notion of representation that I propose embraces previous research on the effects of socialization and conditioning (see Berenice Carroll and Barbara W. Hall, ''Feminist Perspectives on Women and the Use of Force,'' in Ruth H. Howes and Michael R. Stevenson, eds., *Women and the Use of Force* [Boulder, CO: Lynne Rienner, 1993], 11–22), and the discourse on equal opportunity and on gender differences (see Christine L. Williams, *Gender Differences at Work: Women and Men in Nontraditional Occupations* [Berkeley, CA: University of California Press, 1989]). Also relevant is the literature on women in the military, especially the contributions arguing that the existence of limitations in the assignment of women within the armed forces is imposed by cultural values and is due to the fact that the military institution is male-dominated and war is considered ''men's business.'' It is beyond the objectives of this chapter to provide a detailed review of this literature.

7 This table partially summarizes – and simplifies – most of the central arguments referred to by the commissioners throughout the debate. These are not direct quotations but rather my own categorizations, which are the product of a textual analysis of the public transcripts.

8 Although women have been tested for their resistance when under high levels of G-force, these evaluations were done either in simulators or when flying the plane under normal conditions. Some of the fighter pilots and instructor pilots state that in a combat situation the issue is endurance under Gs rather than having the necessary strength initially to ''pull the Gs.'' Detailed explanations refer to the neck strength required to turn your head under 9 or more Gs, a necessary and common maneuver when engaging enemy aircraft. Captain Patrick Cooke (United States Marine Corps [USMC], F/A-18 instructor pilot) states, ''While doing that high G maneuver over your shoulder, still maintaining a tally-ho on the enemy, and potentially reversing the roles, you still have to have the physical capability under that high G situation to get the first weapon off on that opponent should there be a role reversal, and that's where the game of inches comes in. Not only do you have to be able to pull hard on the pole and make that maneuver, but you have to do it with visual acuity, while maintaining sight of your opponent and ensuring that your weapons system is on him before it's on you'' (Presidential

Commission on the Assignment of Women in the Armed Forces, Public Hearing Transcript [PCAWAF – PHT] of August 6, 1992).

9 PCAWAF – PHT of August 28, 1992.

10 Ibid. of August 6, 1992.

11 Ibid.

12 Ibid. of August 28, 1992.

13 Ibid. of August 6, 1992.

14 See Karen O. Dunivin, ''Military Culture: Changes and Continuities.'' Paper presented at the 101st Annual Convention of the American Psychological Association, Toronto, August 1993, 4.

15 Ibid., 4.

16 Overshadowed by the debate on gays in the military, the issue of women flying combat airplanes somehow drifted from the political agenda. Nevertheless, it has the chance to come back as soon as the first woman pilot completes her combat training and goes to a permanent assignment in a fighter wing.

17 Karen O. Dunivin, ''Military Culture . . . ,'' 7.

18 This is consistent with research on women's role in the military. In an insightful analysis of the role of women in the armed forces, Mady Segal emphasizes the fact that ''for women in the U.S. armed forces over the past twenty years, gender-based exclusions persist and military organizations are still resistant to full incorporation of women.'' The author identifies two factors that constrain the participation of women in the military: cultural values and structural patterns of gender roles. See Mady W. Segal (1993), ''Women in the Armed Forces,'' in Ruth H. Howes and Michael R. Stevenson, *Women and the Use of Military Force* (pp. 81–95), Boulder, CO: Lynne Rienner Publishers.

19 PCAWAF – PHT of September 12, 1992.

20 Ibid. of August 6, 1992.

21 Ibid.

22 Ibid.

23 Ibid.

24 The analysis also shows that these representations also had a strong impact on the procedural aspects of this group's decision-making process.

25 This is informed by the results of my dissertation research on the structure of representations, which I analyze by using a hybrid intelligence system (neural network and expert system combined) to replicate the interaction of the concept's components. See Silvana Rubino, ''When Gender Goes to Combat . . . ,'' Ph.D. dissertation.

26 This is also the case in the testimony of male fighter pilots.

27 This concept of demasculinized warrior calls for a focus on similarities between men and women rather than on differences. This may be a point of contention between my work and contemporary writings on women in the military. A lengthy discussion is beyond the purposes of this chapter, but without subscribing to the androcentric approach, I contend that the only way women can be accepted as equals in the combat environment is by challenging this male-defined environment, not just the male dominance. The problem with most theories of women's integration into the military is that they base their argument on the creation of a

female version of the traditionally male warrior. In doing that, they do not further integration; rather, they contribute to the segregation and marginalization of women within the institution, especially in combat specialties. Granted, viewed from the perspective of a male-dominated institution, if women are seen as the same as men, their "subordination" is ratified. I believe it will be more effective to challenge the male-defined character of the military by demasculinizing the warrior, focusing on a gender-neutral representation of warriors, which will give women a better chance at integration when assigned to direct combat positions.

CHAPTER 12

Representations of the Gulf Crisis as Derived from the U.S. Senate Debate

James F. Voss, Jennifer Wiley, Joel Kennet,
Tonya E. Schooler, and Laurie Ney Silfies

This chapter presents the results of an analysis of the contents of the U.S. Senate debate on the Gulf crisis. The analysis consists of using the argumentation of the debate to infer the representations of the Gulf crisis that were espoused by members of each side of the debate. Moreover, the analysis makes special use of the model of images described by R. Cottam (1977), R. Herrmann (1984, 1988), and M. Cottam (1994). Specifically, the analysis assumes that the image of Iraq held by the senators played a major role in establishing their respective representations of the crisis. Furthermore, we argue that the images provide a basis for interpreting the rhetorical features of the arguments of the senators.

There are a number of reasons for analyzing the contents of the Senate debate. First, at a relatively empirical level, it is simply of interest to extract the argumentation that was employed by each side, and it is of further interest to ascertain what can be inferred from such argumentation with respect to how the Gulf crisis was mentally represented by the senators of each side. Second, determining the images that were implied by the debate contents not only provides a basis for studying representations of the Gulf crisis; it also provides a basis for interpreting the arguments stated in the debate that were at least on the surface aimed at persuasion. Finally, analysis provides the opportunity to interpret U.S. policy with respect to Iraq in particular and the Middle East in general.

The chapter contains five sections. In the first, background information is presented that is relevant to the remainder of the chapter. In the second, the method we used to analyze the debate text is briefly described. The third section presents the analysis of the argumentation of the debate and what may be inferred regarding the problem representations and images of the senators. The final two sections present some tentative conclusions and speculations and discusses image representations.

279

Background Information

Brief Description of the Gulf Crisis

The Gulf crisis began in August 1990 when Iraq invaded Kuwait. In response, the United States sent troops to defend Saudi Arabia, and the Bush administration, in conjunction with the United Nations Security Council, organized an international embargo against Iraq. Subsequently, the Bush administration increased the military strength in Saudi Arabia, and an offensive posture was assumed. Iraq, however, did not withdraw from Kuwait, and a United Nations resolution was passed that gave Saddam Hussein until January 15 to pull out of Kuwait, with military intervention by an American-led coalition authorized on or after that date. The congressional debates were held on January 10, 11, and 12, 1991, prior to the United Nations deadline for Iraqi troop withdrawal from Kuwait. In the U.S. Senate, two resolutions were presented. The Dole–Warner resolution, advocating support of the policy of the Bush administration and the United Nations, authorized the use of military force to produce Iraqi withdrawal; the Mitchell–Nunn resolution advocated the continued use of sanctions to effect the same goal. The vote in favor of the Dole–Warner authorization of military force was 52–47, the vote being essentially known before the debate.

Problem Representation

Turning now to the theoretical basis of our analysis, the model of problem representation we employed in the present analysis was the general information-processing model of problem solving of Newell and Simon (1972), as the model has been applied to the solving of ill-structured problems (Voss, Greene, Post, and Penner 1983). Because the model is described in some depth in the second chapter of this volume, discussion of the model in this chapter is brief. In our analysis of the contents of the U.S. Senate debate, we were especially concerned about four components of the representation: the goal or goals that were stated or implied, the means advocated to accomplish those goals, the constraints that participants stated or implied, and the image of Iraq held by individuals as it related to the representation.

Image Theory

The study of the images that individuals have of another state has been primarily focused on the enemy image held by individuals in the United States and the Soviet Union during the Cold War (e.g., Bronfenbrenner 1961; Silverstein 1989). The present world situation, however, makes it imperative that images other than the enemy image be studied in order to develop a better understanding of how such images influence mental representations and possibly policy choices. The Cottam (1977) and Herrmann (1984, 1988) model is especially appropriate for this test because it provides a theoretical analysis of images other than that of an enemy, as demonstrated by Martha Cottam in her analysis of the dependent image of Latin America, as held by U.S. decision makers (Cottam 1994).

The Cottam-Herrmann model assumes that images are comprised of three dimensions that involve how the leaders of state A, for example, perceive state B. The dimensions include whether state B constitutes a threat or an opportunity with respect to state A, whether the capability of state B, broadly defined (military, economic, and other aspects), is perceived as superior, approximately equal, or inferior to the capability of one's own state, and whether the culture of the other state is perceived as superior, approximately equal, or inferior to that of one's own state. Our assumption is that these components play a major role in developing a problem representation in the context of a given situation.

In addition to the underlying dimensions, the model also delineates three indicators that help individuals to determine what image is being held by the leader of a given state. Assume that a leader of state A makes statements about state B. In order to determine what image the leader of state A holds of state B, the model states that the three indicators to be observed are what the leader says about state B's motivation, about state B's capability, and about state B's decision processes.

Table 12.1 presents the indicator statements that constitute the rhetoric used by a leader of state A when describing state B. In other words, when the leader of state A makes statements such as those indicated (in an abbreviated form) in the columns of Table 12.1, they are assumed to portray one of the six respective types of image indicated in the left column of Table 12.1. (See Herrmann 1988.)

The following aspects of the contents of Table 12.1 are noted. First, culture, which is also included in the Cottam-Herrmann model, is included in parentheses in the column heading because leaders of a given state may talk about the culture of another state, and the cultural statement may reflect one of the images given in Table 12.1. Second, statements of motivation map reasonably well onto the underlying threat or opportunity dimension, and capability maps well onto the underlying capability dimension. But the decision process indicator does not reflect culture in any direct way; instead, as noted in the table, the model assumes that statements about the way in which another state is governed reflect a particular image of that state. Third, the imperial image refers to the relation of a stronger state, A, to a weaker state, B. An important aspect of the imperial image, or what Martha Cottam (1994)

Table 12.1. Images of another state and indicators of each image as found in the Cottam-Herrmann model [after R. Cottam (1977) and Herrmann (1988)]

Indicators (and culture)

Image	Motivation	Capability	Culture	Decision process
Enemy	Aggressive, expansionistic, evil motives	Comparable, paper tiger (need to stand firm)	Comparable	Monolithic; citizens different from govt.; diabolical
Ally	Pursues mutually beneficial goals	Adequate but less than possible	Comparable	Well managed, complex; citizens support govt.
Degenerate	Leaders try to keep what they have	Country weaker than it was, power not used	Declining culture; inferior	Confused; unclear authority
Colonial	Do not believe in help of imperial power	Less capable; imperial power perceived as conspiracy	Comparable	Imperial country seeks control
Imperial (moderates)	Paternal leader; modernizer, nationalist, has people's interest	Inferior; as children who need help	Inferior	Cannot manage, need economic and military help
(Radicals)	Fanatic, extremist	Inferior, agitators, terrorists	Inferior	Well organized and clever
Complex	Combination of images with no extreme tendencies			

refers to generally as the "dependent" image, and one especially important for this chapter, is that a leader of state A perceives state B as having two groups vying for governance. One group, the "moderates," is usually controlled to some extent by state A, or at least the "moderates" are in agreement with state A's policies. A second group, the "radicals" or perhaps the "terrorists," are perceived as attempting to take over state B's government. State A then views state B's government as weak, often needing state A's economic, military, and political assistance. Of course, the group in B's government may be opposed by state A, as in the case of the Sandinista regime in Nicaragua, where the group opposing the United States became "freedom fighters." Fourth, the complex image refers to a situation in which a leader of state A does not hold one of the stereotypical images of state B but perceives B as having components that are complex. The leader of state A, for example, may not perceive state B as a strong threat or an opportunity.

Figure 12.1 is a diagram of the hypothesized interactive structure of a person's image and his or her problem representation. As noted, the underlying dimensions act to form the particular image, which in turn feeds into the problem representation. The problem-representational information, however, is assumed to influence what image is held because the situation or at least the individual's definition of the situation (Snyder, Bruck, and Sapin 1954; 1962) plays a role in defining and activating a particular image. Then, the image and problem-representational components jointly act to produce the rhetoric that is spoken by the individual in relation to a given state. The state's policy choices are presumably also influenced by the integrated image representation (cf. Herrmann and Fischerkeller 1994).

Nature of an Argument

An argument minimally consists of a claim and a supporting reason (Angell 1964). In our analysis a senator's position on a resolution was considered in relation to his basic claim, and the argumentation developed constituted his justification for supporting that claim. We examined the arguments of each senator and subsequently constructed two argument structures, each reflecting the cumulative position of the respective senators on each side of the debate. The analysis was conducted within the general framework of the Toulmin (1958) jurisprudence model of argument, although the amount of argumentation limited the model's application.

Method

The statements of each of the ninety-eight U.S. senators participating in the debate were taken from the 1991 *Congressional Record* of January 10, 11,

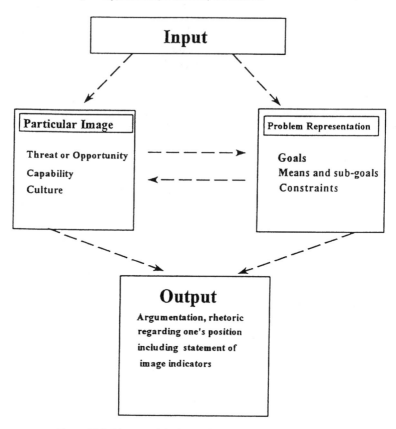

Figure 12.1. Diagram of the interaction of input, image, and problem representation components.

and 12. All quotations are from this record, and the numbers in parentheses denote the quotation's page number in this record. The two senators who did not contribute were Cranston, D-Calif., and Packwood, R-Oreg. Two individuals read the texts in their entirety. The arguments were extracted for each senator. A consensual argument structure was then determined for individuals on each side of the debate. The reliability of the judgments made by the individuals extracting arguments was 85.

Results

Argumentation Findings

Individuals voting in favor of the Dole-Warner resolution – that is, those supporting authorization of the use of military force – are termed *authorizers*,

Claim   Qualifier   Supporting Reasons

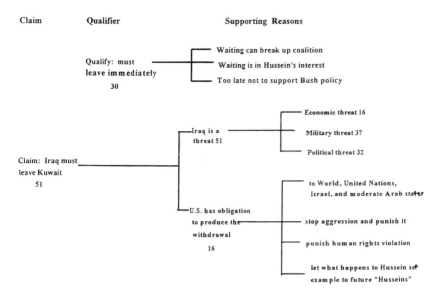

Figure 12.2. Representation-phase argument structure for the "authorizers." Numbers represent number of senators (of 51) making the particular point.

and those favoring the Mitchell-Nunn resolution are termed *sanctioners*. The two groups were split largely along party lines, with ten Democrats voting with Republicans in favor of the Dole-Warner resolution and two Republicans voting with the Democrats in opposition to the Dole-Warner resolution.

Authorizer Position: Figure 12.2 presents a summary of the arguments stated by the authorizers. The basic claim is that "Iraq must leave Kuwait," the claim being qualified by thirty senators with respect to timing – that is, "Iraq must leave Kuwait immediately." The reasons given for immediacy are provided at the top of Figure 12.2.

As shown, the claim is supported by two sets of reasons. The most extensive line of argument provided by the authorizers regarding why Iraq must leave Kuwait was that Iraq posed an economic, military, and political threat. Figure 12.2 presents the three categories and how many senators mentioned each type of threat. Figure 12.3 provides a more detailed description of the threat components. The economic threat, mentioned with relative infrequency, involved the possibility of Hussein's influencing and possibly controlling the world economy, as exemplified by Senator Danforth, R-Mo.: "Some people have asked whether this conflict is not 'just about' oil. To me, that is like asking whether it is not just about oxygen. Like it or not, our country, together with the rest of the world, is utterly dependent on oil. Our economy, our jobs, our ability to defend ourselves are dependent on our

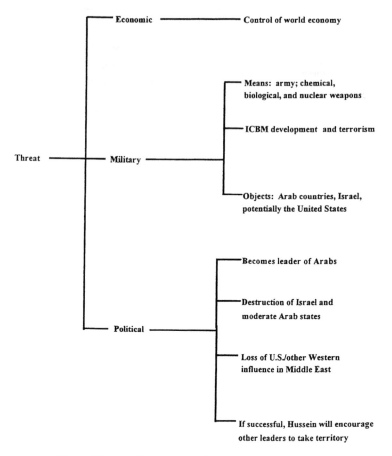

Figure 12.3. Authorizer argumentation of the economic, military, and political threat posed by Hussein.

access to oil. To control the world's supply of oil is in a real sense to control the world'' (122).

A large number of authorizers referred to Iraq as a military threat, which pertained to the possibility of Hussein invading other Arab countries, attacking Israel, and potentially being a threat to the United States. Senators asserted that Hussein was a threat via terrorism, that he had biological and chemical weapons, that Iraq had or would soon have a nuclear potential, and that Iraq was working on the development of an ICBM. Senator Bryan, D-Neb., stated: ''Hussein now today has under arms more men than Hitler when the German Army marched into the Rhineland . . . more tanks than when the Panzer Divisions crushed France . . . and most chilling of all, much closer to having a nuclear weapon than Adolf Hitler ever was'' (264). In addition, Senator Roth, D-Del., stated: "Hussein has demonstrated that with the Cold War fading, the real threat to freedom-loving nations is the proliferation of arms in the hands of despotic dictators. Intercontinental missiles, chemical, biological, and nuclear arms turn unstable Third World nations into first-rate military powers'' (137). Senator Cohen, R-Maine, stated: "Not one of us . . . is safe from the violence currently being inflicted in Kuwait. . . . Our security is only a Pan Am 103 away at any moment'' (333–334). The statement of possible direct military threat to the United States was perhaps best stated by Senator Cohen, R-Maine: "Whether he acquires them (nuclear weapons) in 6 months or 6 years, he eventually will have them; and he will have them and an intercontinental range for his ballistic missiles; and that means that the wheat fields of Kansas will fall under the same threat as the oil fields of Kuwait and Saudi Arabia'' (167).

It was also frequently mentioned that Iraq posed a political threat. Coats, R-Ind., stated: "Saddam Hussein's geopolitical designs on the Middle East are ambitious and ominous. His goals include becoming the leader of the Arab nation, the destruction of Israel, and the elimination of Western capabilities to influence events in the Middle East'' (362). Senator Hatch, R-Utah, also discussed the theme of Western influence: "We have a major political interest in preventing Hussein from radicalizing the Arab world. For decades, moderates and radicals have struggled for the heart of the Arab world. If we back down from this confrontation, Hussein would become the hero of the Arab man in the street. Revolutionary forces would topple moderate governments in the pivotal countries of Egypt, Jordan, and Saudi Arabia. Hussein's brand of anti-Americanism would soon dominate every Arab country from Morocco to Oman'' (142). Similarly, American prestige was seen to be on the line, as Senator Coats, R-Ind., stated: "In many ways we are the only remaining superpower, and our handling of this crisis will determine our international status. If we fail to achieve a satisfactory resolution to this crisis, U.S. global influence will be severely tarnished, and we will need to rethink our entire approach to foreign and defense policy . . . [O]ur involvement in a United Nations peacekeeping mission will never again carry the same weight. . . . We also risk undermining the United Nations just when this institution is becoming more relevant and effective in dealing with global instability'' (362–364). And success for Hussein would encourage other threats: "If Saddam Hussein in any way gains from his aggression . . . other aggressors will be encouraged to attack their neighbors, and place peace everywhere in the world in jeopardy'' (Domenici, R-N.Mex.: 325). Another set of arguments, presented at the bottom of Figure 12.2, involved the idea that the United States has a moral obligation and responsibility to stop Hussein, to punish Hussein's unprovoked aggression, and more generally, to punish his violation of human rights. This obligation is perceived as belonging to the world, to the United Nations, to Israel, and to the moderate Arab states. With respect to the argument that the United States must serve as the world leader to stop aggression, Senator Symms, R-Idaho, stated: "The reason it is the Americans who have to shoulder the biggest part of the responsibility is that we are the only people in the world who are capable: The history, the wealth, the military preparedness, to confront a Saddam Hussein" (378–379). Senator Rudman, R-N.H., argued, "Fundamental principles of international law cannot be permitted to be trampled with impunity . . . there is an ethical clarity to the situation which cannot but shake an often benumbed international conscience. . . . To cave in to such aggression . . . would mock every value we ascribe to an enlightened foreign policy" (325).

We pause here to note the nature of the threat stated by authorizers. The authorizers emphasized the military threat, also pointing to a related political threat. The economic threat was less emphasized, although it certainly was mentioned. The perception of threat is in agreement with the enemy image. With respect to indicator usage, some of the authorizer rhetoric referred to Hussein as highly aggressive and expansionistic, with respect to moderate Arab states, to Israel, and even the United States. What is especially interesting about this mode of threat is that the greatest emphasis is upon the threat to the nations being influenced by the United States, in Senator Hatch's terms. This fact points to the idea that if one views the Middle East as a whole, one sees a distinction of moderates and radicals, strongly suggesting that the view of the Middle East as a whole was imperial. Furthermore, there was some questionable lumping of "radicals" with Hussein; for example, Hussein was placed in the same category as Moslem fundamentalists of Egypt and Jordan. It seems that authorizers, out of conviction or in efforts to persuade, were attempting to portray Hussein and Iraq as America's enemies, using the rhetoric of the enemy image. On the other hand, when the authorizers' statements referring to the Middle East as a whole are considered, the image emerging is imperial. This is because Hussein was regarded as a threat to Israel, to moderate Arab states friendly to the United States, and generally to U.S. influence in the Middle East. There is, in other words, the distinction of "moderates" and "radicals" described in Table 12.1.

Turning now to the solutions proposed, we note again that the agreed upon goal was that Hussein should remove Iraqi troops from Kuwait. The issue at stake was how to accomplish this goal. The authorizers supported the possible use of military intervention, a position in support of the president's position, with such action regarded as important, at least in part because of the desire for immediate withdrawal.

Figure 12.4 presents a diagram of the solution proposed by the authorizers. The basic claim is that the Senate should authorize the use of force. This

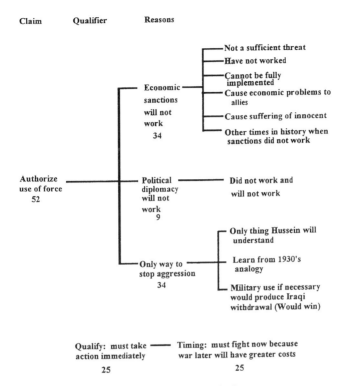

Claim   Qualifier   Reasons

Figure 12.4. Solution options considered by authorizers.

claim serves as the solution to the problem of means. One reason supporting this claim, as noted in Figure 12.4, is that the threat of the use of military force was regarded as the only way to prevent war, as Senator Simpson, R-Wyo., indicated: "Only by making him [Saddam Hussein] so absolutely certain that this has been a commitment of ours [taking whatever action is necessary to pull his taloned claw away from the slitted [*sic*] throat of Kuwait] and by giving it to him eyeball to eyeball in the tough, bully style that he seems to love, only then can we have any real hope of avoiding war" (392). In addition, the authorizers supported their position via reference to the 1930s, arguing that appeasement did not lead to peace then, because Hitler continued his aggression. Hussein should not be appeased, and even a delay in authorizing the use of force would constitute appeasement.

As also shown in Figure 12.4, the authorizers considered two other solutions, economic and political. Authorizers argued against the continued use of sanctions, saying they were not working. A variety of statements supported this view; for example, the CIA's head, Webster, stated that the Iran–Iraq war showed that Iraq could endure hardship and therefore would not yield to sanctions. It was also argued that sanctions could not be fully implemented, that they may cause suffering to the people of Iraq, and that they could pose economic problems to allied countries such as Turkey. It was also argued that other attempts at sanctions, as with Libya, have not worked. Relatively few authorizers discussed the diplomatic option, but those that did indicated that it had failed, that President Bush "had gone the extra mile," and that Iraq had indeed rejected diplomatic solutions proposed by Secretary of State Baker.

Once again, there also was a qualification of timing; in this case, military authorization was needed immediately because delay would increase the costs, would constitute appeasement, and would give Hussein a better chance to build up defenses. The counterargument, stated by authorizers to the argument that military force should not be used because of the potential cost in lives and money, was that although there might be costs now, the costs would be much greater if action was not taken immediately.

Pausing at this point, we find that the authorizer argumentation for endorsing possible military intervention appealed strongly to the idea that the threat of military action was the only thing Hussein would understand. But even more significant is the context of this argument. President Bush had already indicated that the military option was real and that he already had threatened in definite terms, via ultimatum, that it would be employed. Given this position, not supporting military action would be in direct conflict with the president's policy and would appear to be appeasing Hussein and showing a lack of will. In such a case, the pressure from the presidential office was quite substantial. Moreover, this position was in keeping with the capability perception of the enemy image; that is, one needs to be firm and stand up to the enemy so that he will back down.

As discussed in the next section, sanctioners generally took the position that although military action might be necessary, the United States should first continue to explore economic and diplomatic solutions before using military force. In a sense, this made the sanctioners' vote difficult because a vote against endorsing the president's policy could be interpreted either as being against any military intervention or being against only immediate military intervention. The authorizer argumentation was directed against both of these views, especially indicating that neither of these two avenues was feasible, that they would not work, and any delay in military action could be costly.

With respect to the representation employed, the authorizers showed a further tendency to portray Iraq in terms of the enemy image by noting that the United States should avoid harming the Iraqi citizens, thus employing the enemy-image rhetoric concerning decision processes; that is, Iraq had a government that suppressed its people, who disliked the government.

Sanctioner Position: The sanctioners agreed with the claim (Figure 12.1) that "Iraq must leave Kuwait." They also agreed that the United States had a sense of responsibility in stopping Hussein, as indicated by Senator Sanford's (D-N.C.) comment: "All of us share a common understanding, and have from the beginning, that we cannot let Saddam Hussein have any of the fruits of his aggression" (276). Similarly, Senator Wellstone, D-Minn., stated: "It is a bedrock principle of world order that no country has the right to go in and swallow up another country" (107). As previously mentioned, the sanctioners differed from authorizers in the means by which Hussein's withdrawal from Kuwait should be accomplished.

With respect to the three types of threats indicated in Figure 12.2, the sanctioners, while acknowledging Hussein's aggression, did not describe Hussein as a military threat to the United States. Senator Biden, D-Del., for example, in arguing that America had no vital interests in the region that merited going to war, stated: "Yes, we have interests in the Middle East. We wish to support the free flow of oil. We wish to promote stability, including the securing of Israel. But we have heard not one cogent argument that any vital American interest is at stake in a way that impels us to war" (337). Senator Biden also pointed out that President Bush had stated that the United States would not attack Iraq if the Iraqi troops were withdrawn from Kuwait, "notwithstanding the prospect of an Iraqi nuclear capability" (340). From the president's assertion, Biden was then able to argue that Iraq's military potential, and especially its nuclear potential, was not regarded as a substantial threat to U.S. security, because if it were, President Bush could not have made the foregoing statement. Also, with respect to capability, Senator Moynihan, D-N.Y., stated: "The Iraqis do not (even) have the technology to print their own paper money" (110).

Some sanctioners did, however, tend to see Iraq as an economic threat. Senator Inouye, D-Hawaii, stated:

> The threat posed by the Iraqi invasion extends far beyond the Middle East. Hussein's attempt to control a major portion of the region's oil supply continues to have a detrimental effect on the global economy. The price of basic commodities, food, fuel, and shelter has risen at an alarming rate, cutting deeply into the incomes of poor Americans and plunging the Nation into its worst recession in a decade. (365)

Figure 12.5 presents arguments used by sanctioners in support of the economic and diplomatic alternatives, and Figure 12.6 presents arguments stated in opposition to the use of military force. One claim is that the sanctions should be continued. As an example of this position, Senator Lautenberg, D-N.J., stated: "Historical analysis of the use of economic sanctions suggests that they can be effective over time in forcing the withdrawal of Iraqi troops

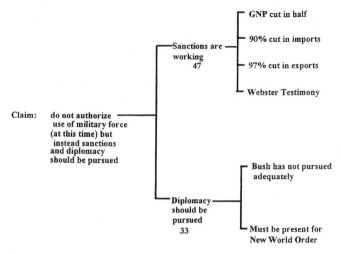

Figure 12.5. Solution options considered by sanctioners: Authorization of use of military force ($N = 47$).

from Kuwait. The prospects for the success of sanctions against Iraq are considerably higher than in previous international efforts because of the unprecedented coverage of sanctions which cover virtually all of Iraq's trade and finance, and the strong commitment to these sanctions by the global community. Sanctions have rarely been applied in such a comprehensive manner, even in wartime.... Iraq is unusually vulnerable to economic coercion like this because crude oil represents 90% of its total exports. It is easily monitored and easily interdicted'' (246).

A relatively large number of sanctioners indicated that in addition to economic sanctions, a diplomatic solution should be pursued.

> Prayerfully there are diplomatic operations taking place, but they are not coming from this country.... Our diplomacy consisted of sending the secretary of state to meet with the Foreign Minister; not to negotiate, but to deliver a message. I do not consider that negotiation, but that is the way this executive wanted to conduct his business.... He puts us in the position of giving up on diplomacy and having to vote for economic sanctions or for war. (Adams, D-Wash.: 138)

Figure 12.6 presents the sanctioner counterargument to the authorizers' claim that use of military force should be authorized. One set of reasons maintained that the action was unwarranted and inappropriate. Such a position was justified by statements indicating that, as stated before, no vital U.S. interests were at stake, that Hussein's increased control of oil was not as much of a critical threat as argued, that a defensive posture would prohibit

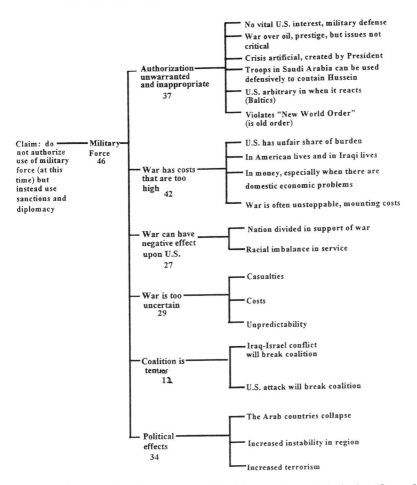

Figure 12.6. Solution options considered by sanctioners: Authorization of use of military force ($N = 47$).

further invasion by Iraq, that the crisis was artificially created by President Bush, and that the United States is arbitrary in its actions, not responding, for example, to Soviet aggression in Lithuania. It was also argued that the United States was not pursuing a "New World Order" but perpetuating the "Old Order" or developing a "New World Disorder." Senator Bradley, D-N.J., stated:

> What they have told us, however, . . . is that there is something far deeper than our national interest in the situation that compels us to take this impatient, belligerent, risky stance. It is the new world order, with America

offering a new paradigm for leadership. But if this first crisis in the post-cold-war is to be resolved simply by a blind rush to the use of force, what is so new about the new world order?. . . . [If] America truly hopes to lead the world in a new way . . . we will lead by the power of our example, not just by the firepower of our military. (136)

A second set of arguments stated that the costs of war in lives and money would be too high. "When a nation goes off to war and conducts it essentially itself, in terms of the cost in lives and dollars, it is even in a weaker position to deal with its fundamental economic problems here at home. We are way overdue in that respect. It is time to start investing in America and in our people" (Riegle, D-Mich.: 217).

A third set of arguments suggested that a possible war had already produced a divided United States and that with increasing casualties the division would be like that involving Vietnam. In addition, it was argued that war is uncertain and often unstoppable. It was suggested that a war would also be inappropriate for the political goals of the United States, as Senator de-Concini, D-Ariz., stated:

> We must ask ourselves before we commit to war, where will war lead us? What kind of regional order will result through the premature and massive use of force? I am not willing today to ask men and women to risk their lives for an action which in the end could further destabilize the region, increase the threat of terrorism and Moslem fundamentalist radicalism, and necessitate a prolonged military presence perhaps requiring even further military action. . . . The complex problems of the Gulf region do not lend themselves to simple solutions. We must find a course which will enable our Arab allies to find their own way to peace in the region. (283)

In addition, it was argued that a war could lead to the breakdown of the coalition and also to the possible overthrow of President Mubarak of Egypt and King Hussein of Jordan, thereby producing increased instability in the Middle East. Furthermore, it was argued that a substantial decrease in Iraqi strength might enable Syria or Iran to increase its stature and strength in the Middle East.

Sanctioners also presented counterarguments to particular arguments presented by the authorizers. For example, to the arguments that the 1930s should not be repeated, Senator Bradley, D-N.J., argued:

> If Hitler's earliest aggression – against the Rhineland – or Japan's earliest aggression – against Manchuria – or Mussolini's earliest aggression – against Ethiopia – had been met with strong deterrent measures, including precautionary international military preparations and strong economic reprisals, the Allies might never have had to face the awful choice of war or

appeasement. That's the lesson of the 1930's, and it is directly applicable to the Gulf. (136)

In terms of the images portrayed, it is clear that the sanctioners employed less enemy image rhetoric than did the authorizers. As Senator Biden's comment indicated, sanctioners tended to see the invasion of Iraq as a matter less vital to the United States than did the authorizers, and the image conveyed by the sanctioners' position was thus more complex than that maintained by the authorizers. At the same time, sanctioners did speak of the importance of U.S. influence in the Middle East and its goals of stability for Israel and for the Middle East in general. Indeed, it is interesting that the sanctioners argued that use of military force by the United States could produce an overthrow of the Egyptian and Jordanian governments, thus suggesting war was a threat to Middle East stability. The sanctioner position thus portrayed Iraq as less of an enemy, in terms of an enemy image, while viewing Iraq as a threat to the stability of the Middle East. This view may thus be regarded as both imperial and also more complex than the authorizer image.

Summary: The debate largely turned on the question of the use of sanctions and diplomacy to get Hussein to leave Kuwait versus the use of military force. Sanctioners indicated sanctions and diplomacy were working or had not been sufficiently pursued, whereas authorizers argued that both had been tried and they had not worked. Relatedly, the sanctioners argued that the potential costs and uncertainties of war suggested that military action should not be rushed into, and that sanctions should be given a chance; the authorizers argued that authorizing and thereby threatening use of military force was the only way to make Hussein withdraw the troops, and failing that, military action should be used. Furthermore, the authorizers had the cogent argument that failure to provide congressional authorization would essentially conflict with the president's position, and that a majority vote against authorization would make it look as if there was a split with the president and a lack of congressional and possibly popular support. We turn now to the discussion and speculation section.

Discussion and Speculation: Representational Issues

With respect to the issue of what caused the crisis, examination of the argumentation portrays a substantial difference between the two sides. The authorizer position held that the primary cause of the crisis was the Iraqi occupation of Kuwait. This action was attributed to one person, Hussein, who was said to be interested in power, in military strength, in becoming ''the'' Arab leader, in conquering other states, and in controlling the world's oil supply.

To accomplish these goals, it was argued, Hussein had created a powerful military machine designed to include poisonous gas, bacteriological warfare, nuclear weapons, and intercontinental missiles. The focus on Hussein as the primary cause of the crisis is underscored in another chapter, involving the use of metaphor in the Senate debate (Voss, Kennet, Wiley, and Engstler-Schooler 1992). The sanctioners used more metaphors than the authorizers in all of the categories of metaphor that were defined, except one – that of metaphors about Hussein himself. Hussein was not regarded as diabolical but as "crafty" and "guileful," as well as a "butcher," "glutton," "dog," "snake," "godfather," and other less-than-flattering terms (Voss et al. 1992). On the other hand, Senator Specter, R-Pa., stated: "I had an opportunity to visit with Saddam Hussein. I found him poorly informed. However, he was certainly no madman, he must have some other calculation . . . involving Israel in a war to destroy the coalition by forcing the Arabs to fight the Israelis" (115). Similarly, Senator Murkowski, R-Alaska, described Hussein as "cunning and he has a clear objective" (288); these characterizations are appropriate to the enemy image. In other words, Hussein generally was viewed by authorizers especially as a ruthless Hitler-type, motivated by power and expansionism. Indeed, the Dole-Warner resolution included the expression "threat to world peace" about Iraq, whereas the Mitchell-Nunn resolution did not. Given the perception of Hussein as the cause of the crisis, forcing withdrawal of Iraq from Kuwait was a necessity, and given what had transpired by January 10, a threat to U.S. prestige also became a critical factor. Additional goals were the destruction of Iraq's military potential and the removal of Hussein from his position, by death or by a coup d'état, although as previously noted, withdrawal from Kuwait would have been sufficient to avoid military attack.

The solution of authorizing military action was primarily justified by two reasons. First, it was the only action Hussein would understand, and if Hussein would not withdraw, then a military attack would certainly force withdrawal. Second, a quick victory was anticipated because, as opposed to the military constraints of Vietnam, a full force strike would be used. The certainty that military action would involve costs was met with the argument that delay would increase costs.

With respect to sanctioners, although they also had the goal of withdrawal of Iraqi troops from Kuwait, their causal analysis of the crisis was different from that of the authorizers in at least two ways. First, the sanctioners believed that the United States contributed substantially to the crisis, primarily via its "flawed policy" toward Iraq. This policy, as Senator Bradley noted, involved the support of Iraq in its war with Iran, including the furnishing of Iraq with weapons, the failure of the Bush administration to condemn Hussein's use of gas on Iraq's Kurdish population, and the American ambassador's statement to Hussein that Iraqi border issues were not an American concern. Second, sanctioners and authorizers had different perceptions with respect to the Iraqi position in the Middle East. Whereas authorizers regarded Hussein as a threat to moderate Arab states and to Israel, as well as a potential threat to the United States, sanctioners considered Hussein, while a threat primarily to moderate Arab states and Israel, to be only one player in a complex Middle East situation. Forcing Hussein's withdrawal by military action, they argued, could have undesirable repercussions, such as a gain in power by Syria and Iran, the overthrow of leaders of moderate states, and an increase in anti-American sentiment among Arabs. Yet the sanctioners were aware of the way in which the status of the crisis at the time of the debate constrained the possible actions. Indeed, Senator Nunn, D-Ga., argued that the "die was cast" (189) when President Bush placed 400,000 soldiers in the Middle East with no plans for rotation. The Bush offensive posture, in other words, acted to constrain subsequent American actions because the troops could not be kept in the Middle East indefinitely without rotation; attempting to resolve the conflict via military means was then, to Nunn, virtually inevitable.

Image Representations

The following interpretation is offered in the context of the Cottam-Herrmann model. With respect to authorizers, the decision to take military action required that Iraq be portrayed as an enemy; that is, arguments by authorizers consciously or unconsciously had to emphasize Iraq as a threat, or military action would have had questionable justification. Thus, Hussein was described, in the rhetoric of the enemy image, as ruthless, expansionistic, and aggressive. But not only was the rhetoric involving motivation that of the enemy image; so also was that involving capability. The authorizers in particular spoke of the strength of Iraq's army and the various weapons that Hussein had, thus emphasizing military capability. Iraq's economic capability was not spoken of much at all by the authorizers, but the potential for economic capability and control was mentioned in relation to Iraq's possibly gaining greater control of oil. Hussein was also regarded as a political threat, primarily to the moderate Middle East states, especially if he became the "Arab leader." Hence, authorizers characterized Hussein as a threat "to world peace," portraying Iraq as a possible nuclear threat to the United States, as an economic threat with respect to the control of oil, and as a political threat to U.S. influence in the Middle East.

The image portrayed by the sanctioners leads to the conclusion that the sanctioners perceived Iraq in a more complex way than did the authorizers. Some sanctioners held Iraq not to be a direct threat to the United States but possibly a threat to U.S. interests in the Middle East. They also spoke less of Iraq's expansionistic tendencies and regarded Iraq's military as less awesome than described by the authorizers. Both authorizers and sanctioners, however, viewed Iraq's decision process in a manner consistent with the enemy image, separating the government from the people, regarding Hussein quite negatively but not viewing the citizens of Iraq in a similar way.

An alternative image to that of Iraq as an enemy is that of Iraq as a "child," a child who in this case needed a lesson. Moreover, from the perspective of the model, this interpretation makes particular sense if the Gulf crisis is viewed in the context of the Middle East as a whole, including considerations of the Arab states, Iran, and Israel. Considered in this way, the Middle East is assumed to be an opportunity with respect to the interests of the United States, especially in relation to oil and in relation to achieving stability. Moreover, of particular importance is the fact that U.S. policy in the Middle East until shortly before the Gulf crisis had been oriented in relation to the Soviet Union (the competitive power), with states such as Syria, supported by the Soviet Union, also viewed as "radical." Thus, consistent with the "child" image, within the region there were two groups of states, those such as Saudi Arabia and Egypt, characterized by "enlightened" supporters of U.S. policy, and other states such as Iran, which were "radical."

With respect to motivation, Iraq's invasion of Kuwait constituted a move by a "radical," with Iraq then also constituting a threat to other "enlightened" Arab states and to Israel. With respect to capability, Iraq in fact was known to be quite poor economically compared to the United States and also relatively poor militarily, but relative to the other states of the Middle East (other than Israel), Iraq was regarded as a military power. Iraq was, in other words, an "agitator" that could provide a serious threat to the "enlightened." With respect to the decision-process indicator, viewing the Arab and Moslem Middle East states as a whole, the "enlightened" states were perceived as needing U.S. support in preserving their status, as shown, for example, by sending troops to Saudi Arabia as a defensive measure, while an "agitator" state, Iraq, needed to be "taught a lesson," the lesson being not to attack an "enlightened" state. Furthermore, such a "lesson," it was argued in the debate, could then be passed on to other would-be dictators who may think of attacking smaller, relatively unprotected countries. This idea was referred to as part of a "New World Order."

Turning to the issue of culture, the "child"–"imperial" interpretation made U.S. leaders view Iraq as culturally inferior to the United States. One would not expect such comments to be overt, but the direct or indirect statements that were made in the debate about culture were consistent with this interpretation. Senator Hatch was quoted earlier in reference to America's "moral commitment" to Israel and moderate Arab states, and his labeling of

Hussein as a "moral threat" to Israel, serves as an example. Senator Hollings, D-S.C., stated: "The culture of the United States is human rights and freedom and free elections. Arab culture is one of religion, a religion which teaches that you and I are the infidel – the No. 1 infidel." Hollings also stated: "We are not going to impose our culture and values through the barrel of a gun. We are not going to get free elections in the Mideast. . . . We have made it an American war and an American attack and an American invasion. It will be seen as a super power against a Third World country." Even regarding Kuwait, Hollings noted substantial cultural differences with the United States. "*Time* magazine said that the emir has four wives, four at one time. I do not know how many he has had when you add them all up. Twenty-one wives, one source said. *Newsweek* says 47 wives, dozens of children. I suppose the emir himself has lost count." Finally, Hollings also stated: "And let us optimistically say that within ten days, Saddam, if he is still alive, hollers 'Uncle.' What do we gain? Within 3 to 6 months, every Arab terrorist, every fundamentalist mullah, every Arab nationalist will say, 'The world power, the United States, came over here and invaded his Third World country for oil. The infidel came and killed tens of thousands of our brothers for oil.' And face it, they would be speaking the truth" (329).

In summary, the image-based interpretation that serves as an alternative to the "Iraq as enemy" image is that Iraq constituted an "agitator" of the Middle East that was regarded as a threat to moderate "enlightened" Arab states and ultimately to Israel. Hussein's motivation in this context was perceived as aspiring to become a Nasserlike Arab leader, a point made by both sides in the debate, and attempting to fill a power vacuum created by the Soviet loss of influence in the region. In addition, Iraq was regarded as militarily strong relative to other Middle East Arab states, but relative to the United States, Iraq's military and economic capability was quite weak. With the United States regarding the Arab and Moslem culture as inferior, that country was striving to protect its interests (opportunity) and influence in the Middle East, as indicated, for example, by the previously cited quotations of Senator Coats. Imperialism has a way of masking itself from the people who hold the view, and imperialism is usually found in a state believing it is doing what is morally correct and what is establishing order. To justify military action, it was therefore important that Hussein's threat, motivation, and capability be shown to be that of an enemy and not simply an "agitator" attacking the "enlightened."

A question that may be asked at this point is, What, if anything, by this analysis have we learned about post–Cold War images. M. Cottam (1994) has addressed the issue of U.S. policies toward Latin American countries in the post–Cold War period, especially considering U.S. policy toward Panama and toward Peru. She points out that U.S. policy toward Latin American countries had been one of viewing most countries in relation to a "depend-ent" image. In such an image, the dependent country usually relies on the dominating country for economic, political, and military strength. When a threat is perceived, then there may be elements of the enemy image that emerge. In the Middle East, the situation is not dissimilar. As hypothesized, the United States has interests, with the image generated being the imperial. Similarly, Martha Cottam, in Chapter 6, deals with the question of the U.S. image that helped shape policy decisions in Somalia.

Conclusions

We have endeavored to summarize the argumentation of the Gulf crisis de-bate and an interpretation thereof. Our analysis suggests that the argumenta-tion, while itself of interest, requires interpretation within some type of theo-retical framework or model in order to develop an understanding of the factors underlying the debate; it is not enough to simply show what claims were stated and how they were justified. In the current case, the argument at face value turned on the interpretation of sanction effectiveness and the will-ingness to initiate military action with its differentially perceived costs and benefits. But at a deeper level, the argumentation was a function or product of the nature of the underlying representations that senators held about the Gulf crisis, and most importantly, of the model that U.S. leaders held of the Middle Eastern Arab states: that they constituted an opportunity and that they had less capability and an inferior culture compared with the United States.

As noted by R. Cottam (1977), R. Herrmann (1984, 1988), and M. Cottam (1994), holding a particular extreme image essentially involves use of a ster-eotype, a stereotype that produces simplification of the given situation. This is an important idea because it seems that one aspect of post–Cold War images is a tendency to simplify via attributing fault to an individual rather than a situation, what in social psychology is termed the *fundamental attri-bution error* (Nisbett and Ross 1980). It is easier to think that the difficulties of a problem situation are a function of the actions or ideology of one person, as Hussein or Noriega, than to analyze in depth the overall situation and the complexity of the causal relations. (See Cottam and McCoy, Chapter 6 in this volume, regarding this point.)

One other point is that the present analysis, including argumentation, prob-lem representation, and images to interpret the Gulf debate, is not the only approach available. Boynton (1991), for example, in the context of a Senate committee decision, has shown that developing an acceptable narrative from available information may also be a fruitful means to analyze and interpret particular text. Such an analysis could conceivably be used in a debate con-text, although some qualification would likely be necessary. Similarly, Wallace, Suedfeld, and Thachuk (1993), using the cognitive or integrative complexity measure of text analysis demonstrated that integrative complexity was more simple in "hawks" than "doves" and that a lower amount of interpretation could also serve as a signal for possible action. Finally, we note that Renshon (1992), in his analysis of good judgment, has noted the importance of framing decisions, that is, decisions that frame an issue such that they influence future decisions. In the present account, the point is made that the image held by individuals of a given country influences the development of the problem representation and that the representation acts to constrain the policy choices as well as the rhetoric employed by the individual. This view, however, is not necessarily in conflict with Renshon's. For example, as pointed out by Nunn, Bush's decision to send a relatively large number of troops to the Middle East without a rotation plan constrained what could be done. To Renshon, the Bush decision would probably be a framing decision, whereas we would suggest that the decision was a function of Bush's mental representation of the problem.

A final note on this U.S. Senate debate on the Gulf War crisis is that the vote was essentially known beforehand. Individuals were not likely to change their minds, and the speeches made simply permitted each senator to "stand up and be counted," something relevant to the colleagues, the president, and especially to the senator's constituents. The debate apparently had virtually no effect on the vote, but it allowed individuals to express their positions on an extremely important issue, to make their constituencies aware of their positions, and to be able to look back at their positions afterward.

Author's Note: The research reported in this chapter was supported by a grant from the Mellon Foundation to the Learning Research and Development Center of the University of Pittsburgh. The opinions and conclusions expressed herein are not necessarily those of any of these organizations.

References

Angell, R. B. (1964). *Reasoning and Logic*. New York: Appleton-Century-Crofts.

Boynton, G. R. (1991). "The expertise of the Senate Foreign Relations Committee." In V. M. Hudson (ed.), *Artificial Intelligence and International Politics* (pp. 291–309). Boulder, CO: Westview Press.

Bronfenbrenner, U. (1961). "The mirror image in Soviet-American relations: A social psychologist's report." *Journal of Social Issues, 17*, 45–56.

Cottam, M. (1994). *Images and Intervention: U.S. Policies in Latin America*. Pittsburgh: University of Pittsburgh Press.

Cottam, R. W. (1977). *Foreign Policy Motivation: A General Theory and a Case Study*. Pittsburgh: University of Pittsburgh Press.

Herrmann, R. K. (1984). "Perceptions and foreign policy analysis." In D. A. Sylvan and S. Chan (eds.), *Foreign Policy Decision Making* (pp. 25–52). New York: Praeger.

——— (1988). "The empirical challenge of the cognitive revolution: A strategy for drawing inferences about perceptions." *International Studies Quarterly, 32,* 175–203.

Herrmann, R. K., and M. P. Fischerkeller (1994). "A cognitive strategic approach to international relations: Theory and practice in the Persian Gulf." (Unpublished manuscript.)

Newell, A., and H. Simon (1972). *Human Problem Solving.* Englewood Cliffs: NJ: Prentice-Hall.

Nisbett, R. E., and L. Ross (1980). *Human Inference: Strategies and Shortcomings of Social Judgment.* Englewood Cliffs, NJ: Prentice-Hall.

Renshon, S. A. (1992). "The psychology of good judgment: A preliminary model with some applications to the Gulf War." *International Society of Political Psychology,* 477–495.

Silverstein, B. (1989). "Enemy images: The psychology of U.S. attitudes and cognitions regarding the Soviet Union." *American Psychologist, 44,* 903–913.

Snyder, R. C., H. W. Bruck, and B. Sapin (1954). *Decision-making as an Approach to the Study of International Politics.* Princeton, NJ: Princeton University Press.

——— (1962). "Decision making as an approach to the study of international politics." In R. C. Snyder, H. W. Bruck, and B. Sapin (eds.), *Foreign Policy Decision Making* (pp. 14–185). New York: Free Press.

Toulmin, S. (1958). *The Uses of Argument.* Cambridge: Cambridge University Press.

Voss, J. F., T. R. Greene, T. A. Post, and B. C. Penner (1983). "Problem solving skill in the social sciences." In G. H. Bower (ed.), *The Psychology of Learning and Motivation: Advances in Research Theory* (Vol. 17, pp. 165–213). New York: Academic Press.

Voss, J. F., J., Kennet, J., Wiley, and T. Engstler-Schooler, (1992). "Experts at debate: The use of metaphor in the U.S. Senate Debate on the Gulf Crisis." *Metaphor and Symbolic Activity, 7,* 197–214.

Wallace, M. D., P., Suedfeld, and K. Thachuk (1993). "Political rhetoric of leaders under stress in the Gulf Crisis." *Journal of Conflict Resolution, 37,* 94–107.

CHAPTER 13

Configuring Issue Areas: Belgian and Dutch Representations of the Role of Foreign Assistance in Foreign Policy

Marijke Breuning

Belgian and Dutch decision makers represent the role that foreign assistance plays in the larger scope of their foreign policies in different ways. Specifically, there is some indication that Belgian decision makers represent foreign assistance as an aspect of their foreign economic relations, rather than as a separate issue area (Breuning 1992, 1994a). This representation of foreign assistance as subordinate to foreign economic policy in Belgium stands in contrast to the thorough separation of foreign assistance and foreign economic policy in the Netherlands. This difference in issue categorization provides a plausible explanation for the differences in the foreign assistance policy behavior between the two states.

But showing the existence of a contrast between the representations of the decision makers of these two states does not explain the origins of such differences in categorization. This chapter, therefore, is intended not only to outline the differences in issue categorization but also to explore plausible explanations for them and, finally, to outline the ingredients of a framework for the systematic empirical study of the manner in which groups of decision makers configure issue areas in foreign policy.

The roles foreign assistance plays in the respective foreign policies of Belgium and the Netherlands illustrate that the categorization of various issues may differ between groups of decision makers who represent different states. This supports the notion that the social context within which cognition takes place has significant effects on both cognitive content and processes (Resnick 1991; Levine, Resnick, and Higgins 1993). In other words, the social context within which a person is embedded affects not only what that person knows but also how that knowledge is structured and used. This is consistent with the notion that an individual's ontology constrains the manner in which problems can be represented and, consequently, the choices that are judged to be adequate responses (Sylvan and Thorson 1992; Voss, this volume). However, it differs in its additional claim that a person's ontology is shaped by the social environment within which that person is embedded. In other words, it assumes representations to be intersubjective (Levine et al. 1993). A group of people who share a social environment may be expected to share some similarities in the manner in which they represent phenomena in their environment: They share similarities in their "patterns of inference" (Cole 1991: 403). Representations may therefore be regarded as social phenomena, which have their roots in historically developed practices (Levine et al. 1993). This is not to deny individual differences but to emphasize the social context within which a person exists and to underscore that this social context constrains the range of possible problem representations.

Implicit in the preceding discussion is the conviction that decision makers' representations of issue categories help us understand the set of options such decision makers are predisposed to perceive, and thus provide insight into the policy choices they are likely to select. In other words, it assumes a connection between how problems are represented and how they are solved (e.g., Tversky and Kahneman 1981; Levy 1992; Sylvan and Thorson 1992; Sylvan and Haddad, this volume).

Foreign policy and its various subcategories represent problems that are solved at the national level. If structural similarities were to affect policy, Belgium and the Netherlands should exhibit similar foreign assistance policies. This is not the case. Unraveling what makes the social contexts of these two states different is expected to provide an explanation of the observed differences in the problem representations of the decision makers of these two states. This chapter hypothesizes that certain historical experiences extend their grasp across time and shape the social context within which decision makers are embedded.

Common themes and prescriptions in the parliamentary debates of Belgium and the Netherlands are analyzed to shed light on the current discourse on foreign assistance as a subset of foreign policy. Such analysis cannot, however, provide much insight into the historical antecedents that have shaped the issue categorizations and therefore the debate in these two states. Plausible explanations for the roots of current categorizations entail systematic comparison of what is common and what is distinct in the relevant historical experience of these two states. This chapter is an initial attempt at framing the questions that need to be asked to gain an understanding of the social context and its impact on how decision makers represent issues as belonging to similar or different categories.

Issue Areas and Problem Representations

The issue areas of foreign assistance and foreign economic relations have been used widely in the comparative study of foreign policy. Issue areas are generally employed to denote substantive issue categories of interest to researchers (Rosenau 1971). However, issue areas also entail specific problem representations. As such, issue categorization is dependent upon perception. The importance of decision makers' perceptions has been recognized (e.g., Jervis 1976; Vertzberger 1990), but this insight has most often been applied to specific cases. This study asks instead how decision makers of different states represent the dividing lines between various issue areas. More importantly, it asks how we can systematically obtain empirical evidence for decision makers' categorizations. The question is not merely a theoretical one: The separateness of foreign assistance from foreign economic relations, or the subordination to it, is an indication that different priorities guide the groups of decision makers who hold these different representations.

Issue areas are a device for categorizing policy problems into sets of problems that have like features. Problems that decision makers evaluate as having like characteristics are likely also to be candidates for like solutions. Therefore, the choice of whether groups of decision makers represent specific foreign policy problems that are confronted by their state as related or distinctly separate is expected to affect the kind of policy choices they consider and ultimately decide upon. Issue areas are distinct from issues in that the former are "persistent and general," whereas the latter "may be temporary and situational" (Rosenau 1971: 138). Issue areas, in other words, are devices to bring groups of like issues together in a manner that reflects the similarities between those issues.

Research in comparative foreign policy generally assumes representations of relatedness or distinctness of issue areas to be essentially constant across foreign policy–making settings. On the basis of that assumption, the concept of issue area proves itself very useful, because it facilitates comparisons of foreign policies, or subcategories thereof, of different states. It seems logical, for example, to compare the foreign assistance or national security policies of two states rather than the former type of policy for one state with the latter type of policy for another state.

> Indeed, the task of comparison may well be served if we hold issue area constant and depict the manner by which, within a given issue area, differences in political structure and political culture affect the general contours of the policy process. For most developed, pluralist states, the paradigm certainly seems plausible. (Zimmerman 1973: 1209)

The initial interest in issue area as a concept was to explain variations in foreign policy process and outcome not on the basis of a classification of decision-making structures of states but on the basis of the type of issue under investigation (Zimmerman 1973: 1212). Although these two approaches are not necessarily mutually exclusive, Evangelista (1989: 150) contends that researchers interested in the impact of domestic structures and processes on foreign policy outcomes have assumed that policy making in the issue area of military security is driven by international rather than domestic structures and processes. In other words, he argues that researchers have a priori assumed that the explanation for foreign policy decisions in different issue areas must be sought at different levels of analysis. He proceeds to make the case that domestic structures and processes must be considered equally valid explanations in the formulation of military security and foreign economic policy (Evangelista 1989). He does not throw out the issue area concept altogether but instead concludes that a general theory of foreign policy is unlikely to be a parsimonious one (Evangelista 1989: 171) and is more likely to resemble the rather elaborate scheme proposed in Rosenau's (1971) pre-theories essay.

For many researchers, the concept of issue area is used merely to denote the substantive issues they are interested in, such as military security policy, foreign economic policy, or foreign assistance policy. They use the concept of issue area intuitively and often without specific reference to it (Rosenau 1971: 136). Their interest is not so much to establish that variations in the foreign policy processes and outcomes of states can be explained on the basis of issue areas; instead, they are concerned with the processes and outcomes of policy making *given* a particular substantive issue area.

It has implicitly been assumed that if researchers carve up the whole of foreign policy into specific issues, then decision makers must do so as well; and moreover, decision makers representing different states must do so in the same manner (i.e., the division of the whole of foreign policy into various policy concerns has been assumed to be straightforward and self-explanatory). Potter (1980), however, has already alluded to the subjectivity of the definition of issue areas and the consequent importance of identifying decision makers' perceptions of issue areas.

If issue area is not a concept that can be assumed to contain a consistent meaning across foreign policy–making settings – because the decision makers of various settings may construct issue areas differently – the ability of the concept as generally employed to provide insight into the foreign policy making of various groups of decision makers must be called into question. Rather than assuming a particular categorization of issue areas, this chapter is an initial attempt at the construction of a framework designed to determine empirically decision makers' constructions of issue areas in foreign policy. The justification for such an effort derives from the hypothesized relation between such representations and the choices decision makers are predisposed to consider and arrive at as a result. In other words, issue categorization is treated as an independent variable (Brewer 1973, as cited by Potter 1980).

The idea that problem representation affects choice is not new. A series of experiments reported by Quattrone and Tversky (1988) and by Tversky and

Kahneman (1981) supports the notion that one's frame of reference affects the evaluation of problems. Sylvan and Thorson (1992) and Sylvan, Goel, and Chandrasekaran (1990) similarly argue that how problems are categorized has implications for the policy responses that are considered. Khong's (1992) case study of decision making during the Vietnam war illustrates this by showing that the set of possible policy responses was conditioned by the analogies that were considered. Specifically, the analogy of Dien Bien Phu was advanced but discredited. In other words, although there were individual differences in the analogies advanced, the perception that Munich belonged in the same category as Vietnam, and that Dien Bien Phu represented a different category of event, came to dominate decision making. Of course, analogical historical situations are not the same as issue areas, but both involve the principle of categorization of items as distinct or alike.

This example illustrates why an attempt at understanding how "representations are socially constructed and modified" (Sylvan and Thorson 1992) is important: Such categorizations have consequences for political decision making. Because what matters for decision making is the *prevailing* construction of issue categories, the focus is on representations that find common acceptance among groups of decision makers. A group of foreign policy decision makers representing a particular state is therefore assumed to be a set of people who share certain commonalities. This is not to discount the significant variations among people or parties within a state. It does, however, place emphasis on the socially shared aspects of problem representation (Resnick 1991).

Using the cases of Belgium and the Netherlands, I (1) show that the decision makers of these two states perceive the place of foreign assistance within the scope of their foreign policy differently, (2) explore plausible explanations for such differences, and (3) outline the ingredients of a framework to assess empirically groups of decision makers' constructions of issue areas in foreign policy.

First, the contention that Belgian and Dutch decision makers represent the role of foreign assistance in their foreign policy differently is supported with evidence from parliamentary debates of these two states. The nature, volume, and content of debate are examined for indications of distinctness and relatedness of foreign assistance and foreign policy. Questions that guide this investigation are: Are these issues debated separately or not? What is the relative volume of debate? What is said in these debates? Differences in these aspects of the parliamentary debate are expected to support a prevailing perception of distinctness of foreign assistance and foreign policy among the Dutch decision makers and a prevailing perception of relatedness among Belgian decision makers.

I argue in the next section that the comparison of Belgium and the Netherlands constitutes a variation of a most similar systems design (Lijphart 1971, 1975). An exploration, however, of what accounts for the differences in issue categorization and policy behavior necessarily focuses on those aspects that differentiate the decision makers of the two states.

An exploration of reasons why different representations have gained currency among groups of decision makers who represent otherwise similar systems must include an investigation of potentially different historical "lessons" passed down within each group (Vertzberger 1990; Carlsnaes 1993). Areas of difference in historical experience may include the existence of a *heroic history* and the extent and nature of colonial experience. The expectations can be expressed in terms of the following hypotheses:

1. If a state possesses a heroic history, it is more likely that decision makers perceive a proactive foreign policy as a realistic possibility. What I mean by heroic history is a memory of a time when the state was a powerful or significant actor in international affairs. Such a memory is likely to be kept alive through the teaching of national history to each new generation of citizens. A perception that proactive foreign policy is a possibility for the state means that decision makers perceive their state as able to influence other actors in the international system.

2. The past possession of colonies predisposes leaders to perceive foreign assistance as a separate issue area. The length and extent of the colonial experience must be taken into consideration in evaluating the impact of the past possession of colonies on the perception of the place of foreign assistance in the state's foreign policy.

3. The Belgian and Dutch cases are used in this chapter in an analytical, inductive (George 1979) manner in order to identify empirical indicators of decision-maker representations of distinctness or relatedness of various issues in foreign policy. The cases are used as "building blocks for theory development" (George 1979: 54). The ultimate objective is the creation of a generalized framework for understanding the connection between representations and foreign policy decisions, which can incorporate the various ways in which groups of decision makers construct the international environment within which they function. This study is limited in scope, however, and therefore has limited generalizability. It focuses on two small, industrialized Western European states and concerns the place of foreign assistance within the scope of foreign policy of these states. Without study of additional cases, the generalizability is limited to this type of state.

Similar Systems with Different Foreign Assistance Policies

The comparison of the Belgian and Dutch cases constitutes a variation of the most similar systems design (Przeworski and Teune 1970; Lijphart 1971, 1975). Belgium and the Netherlands were similar in terms of traditional measures of relative size, which according to structural theories of international relations would lead to the expectation that their foreign policies would be similar as well. This was not the case, however. Specifically, the two states pursued different foreign assistance policies.

In this section, I outline the structural similarities between the two systems in terms of both their international positions and their domestic political structure. In terms of their position in the international system, both can be classified as small states (East 1973). Both also have open economies that rely heavily on international trade (Katzenstein 1985). Both share similarities in the institutional framework regarding foreign policy making. The two states had comparable coalition governments throughout most of the 1980s.

The similarities in the institutional framework and coalitions governing the two states need some elaboration. The Administration for Development Cooperation is subordinate to the Ministry of Foreign Affairs in both Belgium and the Netherlands. The Belgian minister or state secretary for development cooperation heads the Belgian Administration for Development Cooperation (BADC), which is attached to the Ministry of Foreign Affairs, Foreign Trade, and Development Cooperation (Berlage 1984a; Franck 1987). The Dutch minister for development cooperation is officially a minister without portfolio. This individual oversees the Directorate General for International Cooperation (DGIC) housed within the Ministry of Foreign Affairs (Maas 1986; Everts and Walraven 1989).

In both cases, development cooperation is a separate, identifiable entity that is, however, attached to the Ministry of Foreign Affairs. Despite these institutional similarities, the roles played by the ministers within their respective governments differ. In Belgium, the office of minister for development cooperation is used to round out a coalition rather than being central to its formation (Vandommele 1982). This suggests that development cooperation is not seen as important subject matter among Belgian decision makers (Berlage 1984b). Van Elslande, a Christian Democrat (Christelijke Volkspartij, or CVP), argued during his tenure as minister of both foreign affairs and development cooperation (1974–1977) that this reflected attitudes prevalent in the society:

> As soon as both public and parliamentary opinion are won over to a particular objective, this objective will indeed be attained. If it is not attained this is often not only the fault of the government – which is only one of the mechanisms of the politically organized society – but because the necessity of a particular goal is insufficiently shared by many. (PH/AP, 8 June 1976: 3889)[1]

Officially, the authority of the minister for development cooperation is limited in the Netherlands as well. In practice, however, the extent to which he or she exercises influence depends on the political strength of the individual minister and the working relationship he or she establishes with cabinet colleagues. Over time the importance of the appointment has increased, due to the active role played within the cabinet by successive individuals who occupied the post of minister for development cooperation (Beerends 1981; Wels 1982; Voorhoeve 1985; Kruijssen 1986; Maas 1986). The institutional similarity is thus complemented by a notable difference in the type of politician that tends to occupy the office of minister of development cooperation. The institutional similarity, while important, tells only part of the story.

Belgium and the Netherlands were governed by comparable coalitions during most of the 1980s. One might expect coalitions dominated by similar parties to pursue similar policies. This would justify the expectation of similar foreign assistance policies from 1982–1983 until the 1987–1988 parliamentary year, when both states were governed by center-right coalitions. (See Table 13.1.) In addition, in both states the respective Christian Democrat parties furnished both the prime minister and the minister of foreign affairs. The similarity regarding which party held certain portfolios extended to the minister or state secretary for development cooperation, where for most years Liberals were in charge. The exceptions are the 1986–1987 and 1987–1988 parliamentary years, when the Dutch minister of development cooperation was a Christian Democrat, although the coalition remained center-right.

If the structural, institutional, and party-ideological similarities are important determinants of policy, then Belgium and the Netherlands should have exhibited strong similarities in their foreign assistance policies during most of the 1980s, but on the contrary, as Table 13.2 indicates, Belgium consistently spent a lower proportion of its gross national product (GNP) on foreign assistance than the Netherlands. Although the proportion of total assistance spent bilaterally was not significantly different for the two, the terms on which that bilateral aid was given did consistently differ: A higher proportion of Belgian bilateral aid was tied, meaning that the recipient had to use these funds for procurement in the donor state. This difference in tying status of Belgian and Dutch bilateral aid leads to the expectation that the distinction between foreign assistance and foreign economic relations is drawn less clearly in Belgium than in the Netherlands.

Foreign Assistance Debates Compared

The first indicator regarding the relatedness or distinctness of foreign assistance and foreign policy is the nature and volume of parliamentary debate. First, whether foreign assistance is addressed in parliament as a separate category furnishes an initial indication of whether it is represented as a distinct and separate policy category. If foreign assistance is never, or rarely, given its own place on the parliamentary calendar, the likelihood that it is represented as a distinct issue area is small. Second, the volume of debate is here taken as a rough measure of attention. Thus, the more words spoken about foreign assistance, the more significant a place it holds in the priority listing of issue areas in foreign policy. The converse might be argued: that issues get widely debated only when they are contentious, not when there is wide agreement on them. But a significant reconceptualization of the role of foreign assistance in a state's foreign policy is unlikely to take place during the annual debates on the various budgetary categories, but it is likely to occur during debates specifically scheduled to address government white papers and the like. The relative-attention measure used here involves relative attention paid to foreign assistance during the annual debates on the government's budget.

The period 1982–1988 includes six parliamentary years. In the parliaments of both Belgium and the Netherlands, there were annual discussions on a variety of subjects within the larger scope of debate on the budget, broken down into discussions on various policy or issue areas. The Belgian parliament devoted time to a separate discussion of development cooperation during two of these years (1983–1984, 1986–1987) and discussed development cooperation jointly with foreign affairs and foreign trade during two other years (1982–1983, 1984–1985), as reported in Table 13.3. During the 1985–1986 and 1987–1988 parliamentary years, there was no discussion of development cooperation at all. Therefore, whether and how much attention is paid to development cooperation vary from year to year. The Dutch parliament, on the other hand, debated development cooperation consistently as a separate subject. As a consequence, there was a debate on the budget for development cooperation for each year between 1982 and 1988.

In Belgium, the volume of debate fluctuated a great deal. The official parliamentary reports for 1983–1984 include a record of the debate on development cooperation that is 41 pages long, whereas the record of the comparable debate during the 1986–1987 year encompasses only 10 pages. The joint debates during the 1982–1983 and 1984–1985 parliamentary years presented a problem regarding the assessment of relative volume. It is difficult to establish exactly how much of the debate actually concerned foreign assistance versus other foreign affairs topics, especially because speakers often addressed Belgium's role within NATO in the same speech in which they addressed aid to the Third World. For instance, the 1982–1983 debate on foreign affairs, foreign trade, and development cooperation encompasses 52 pages in the official report, but only a portion of those pages addresses foreign assistance issues. (See Table 13.3.)

By contrast, the volume of debate on development cooperation in the Netherlands is fairly consistent. With the exception of the 1983–1984 parliamentary year, for which there are only 7 pages in the official parliamentary

Table 13.1. *Comparison of Belgian and Dutch coalitions of the 1980s*

Year	Belgium		Netherlands	
	Coalition		Coalition	
1980–81	Center-left: CVP/PSC, SP/PS	PM: Martens (CVP), Eyskens (CVP) MFA: Nothomb (PSC) MDC: Coens (CVP)	Center-right: CDA, VVD	PM: Van Agt (CDA) MFA: Van der Klaauw (VVD) MDC: de Koning (CDA)
1981–82	Center-right: CVP/PSC, PVV/PRL	PM: Martens (CVP) MFA: Tindemans (CVP) SSDC: Mayence-Goossens (PRL)	Center-left: CDA, PvdA, D'66	PM: Van Agt (CDA) MFA: Van der Stoel (PvdA) MDC: Van Dijk (CDA)
1982–83	Center-right: same	same	Center-right: CDA,VVD	PM: Lubbers (CDA) MFA: Van den Broek (CDA) MDC: Schoo (VVD)
1983–84	Center-right: same	same, except: SSDC: De Donnea (PRL)	Center-right: same	same
1984–85	Center-right: same	same	Center-right: same	same
1985–86	Center-right: same	PM: Martens (CVP) MFA: Tindemans (CVP) SSDC: Kempinaire (PVV)	Center-right: same	same
1986–87	Center-right: same	same	Center-right: CDA, VVD	PM: Lubbers (CDA) MFA: Van den Broek (CDA) MDC: Bukman (CDA)

198?/–88	Center-right: CVP	same	Center-right: same	same
1988–89	Center-left: CVP/PSC, PS/SP, VU	PM: Martens (CVP) MFA: Eyskens (CVP) MDC: Geens (VU)	Center-right: same	same
1989–90	Center-left: same	same	same	Center-left: PM: Lubbers (CDA) CDA, PvdA MFA: Van den Broek (CDA) MDC: Pronk (PvdA)

PM   = Prime Minister
MFA   = Minister of Foreign Affairs
MDC   = Minister of Development Cooperation
SSDC = State Secretary for Development Cooperation

Belgian coalition parties:

CVP = Christelijke Volkspartij   = Flemish Christian Democrats
PRL = Parti Reformateur Liberal   = Walloon Liberals
PS = Parti Socialiste   = Walloon Socialists

PSC = Parti Social Chretien   = Walloon Christian Democrats
PVV = Partij voor Vrijheid en Vooruitgang = Flemish Liberals
SP = Socialistische Partij   = Flemish Socialists
VU = Volks Unie   = Flemish Nationalists

Dutch coalition parties:

CDA = Christen Democratisch Appel   = Christian Democrats
D'66 = Democraten '66   = Democrats
PvdA = Partij van de Arbeid   = Labor
VVD = Volkspartij voor Vrijheid en Democratie   = Liberal

Table 13.2. *Belgian and Dutch foreign assistance expenditures*

Parl. debate year	Foreign asst. year	Belgium				Netherlands			
		$ million	% of GNP	% bilateral	% tied (of bilateral)	$ million	% of GNP	% bilateral	% tied (of bilateral)
1982–83	1983	479	0.59	62	74	1195	0.91	68	17
1983–84	1984	446	0.58	59	—	1268	1.02	69	—
1984–85	1985	440	0.55	63	67	1136	0.91	67	11
1985–86	1986	547	0.48	66	57	1740	1.01	68	12
1986–87	1987	687	0.48	62	—	2094	0.98	68	12
1987–88	1988	601	0.39	69	57	2231	0.98	70	15

Source: OECD, various years, *Development Co-Operation: Efforts and Policies of the Members of the Development Assistance Committee.* Paris: OECD.

Table 13.3. *Nature and volume of parliamentary debates*

	Belgium		Netherlands	
Year	Nature of debate[a]	Volume (in pages)	Nature of debate[a]	Volume (in pages)
1982–83	combined	52	separate	49
1983–84	separate	41	separate	7
1984–85	combined	16	separate	55
1985–86	no debate	0	separate	55
1986–87	separate	10	separate	47
1987–88	no debate	0	separate	40
	Total	119	Total	253
	Average	20	Average	42

[a] Nature of Debate:
combined   = development cooperation debated in conjunction with foreign trade and foreign affairs in general
separate   = development cooperation debated as a separate and distinct issue
no debate = no debate on the topic took place

report, there generally are around 50 pages of debate per parliamentary year. It should be noted that comparisons between the number of pages in the Belgian and Dutch official parliamentary reports provide only a sketch of differences in the volume of debate, because they are printed in different formats and use different fonts. In short, the comparison is only a crude approximation of differences in attention devoted to this subject matter.

The nature and volume of debate have given a first indication of differences between the role foreign assistance plays in foreign policy in Belgium and the Netherlands. These indicators, however, cannot provide information regarding how decision makers perceive the relatedness or distinctness of foreign assistance and foreign policy. An examination of the content of the debate on foreign assistance aids in an evaluation of Belgian and Dutch representations of the role of foreign assistance in foreign policy. This examination is based on a content analysis of parliamentary debates for the same parliamentary years as the measure on the nature and volume of debate. This analysis focuses on the thematic content of the speeches of the various speakers during parliamentary debates on foreign assistance. The following paragraphs outline the strategy employed for the content analysis.

The "speaking turn" was the unit of analysis. This was defined as a speech ranging from a sentence to several paragraphs, made by one speaker uninterrupted by other speakers. Each speaking turn was read in its entirety before making a coding decision, which consisted of determining whether one of six themes was present in the speaking turn. If none of these themes was referenced, then none was coded. Although a coding strategy focusing on themes is generally somewhat less reliable than a word count, the choice to use this type of coding scheme was made to enhance the validity of the research. Representations and conceptions are not likely to manifest themselves in single words.

The frequencies for the six themes are reported in Table 13.4. "Moral obligation" coded references to a perceived ethical or moral obligation to help one's fellow human beings. "Liberal order" coded the presence of references to the maintenance or extension of the liberal international economic order, including references to the need to protect or enhance free trade. "Mutual benefit" coded references to the fact that foreign assistance can be used to benefit the donor's trade and industry. "Privatization" coded expressed preferences for more extensive use of donor country trade and industry as vehicles for dispensing government aid funds, generally referencing the greater "efficiency" of such channels. "Social justice" coded references to concerns with an equitable distribution of wealth within the recipient society, including a concern for the most disadvantaged or poorest in society. This category included a concern with human rights as well. "Paternalism" coded references to the need to influence the regime of the recipient state in favor of democratization or other policies as preferred by the donor state. References coded into this category are sometimes couched in terms of a sense of responsibility toward the people in a developing society.

These themes occur with varying and not very high frequencies. Table 13.4 reports percentages for ease of comparison between years and between Belgium and the Netherlands. The most notable difference between the speakers in the two parliaments is a somewhat greater relative use of references to mutual benefit in Belgium and a somewhat greater relative emphasis on privatization in the Netherlands. References to social justice occur more frequently and more consistently in the Dutch parliament, as do references that indicate a paternalistic attitude toward the recipient state. The Belgians make no reference to a moral obligation, whereas the Dutch do mention it, albeit infrequently.

In addition to differences in the frequencies, the *manner* in which the decision makers of both states discuss these themes differs as well. It is here that the differences in Belgian and Dutch representations of the role of foreign assistance in their state's foreign policy become most evident. The Belgian decision makers often argue in parliament that there must be a return to the domestic economy to justify the foreign assistance program. For instance, Belgian State Secretary Mayence-Goossens, a Liberal (Parti Réformateur

Table 13.4. *Theme frequencies by year*

Theme	Belgium							Netherlands						
	1982–83	1983–84	1984–85	1985–86	1986–87	1987–88	Total	1982–83	1983–84	1984–85	1985–86	1986–87	1987–88	Total
Moral obligation	0% (0)	0% (0)	0% (0)	— (0)	0% (0)	— (0)	0% (0)	4% (1)	0% (0)	3% (1)	0% (0)	0% (0)	7% (2)	2% (4)
Liberal order	16% (3)	25% (3)	0% (0)	— (0)	0% (0)	— (0)	15% (6)	4% (4)	0% (0)	3% (1)	15% (5)	0% (0)	11% (3)	6% (10)
Mutual benefit	68% (13)	33% (4)	67% (2)	— (0)	20% (1)	— (0)	51% (20)	32% (9)	0% (0)	13% (4)	15% (5)	0% (0)	7% (2)	12% (20)
Privatization	0% (0)	8% (1)	0% (0)	— (0)	80% (4)	— (0)	13% (5)	25% (7)	17% (3)	38% (12)	15% (5)	47% (14)	15% (4)	27% (45)
Social justice	16% (3)	25% (3)	0% (0)	— (0)	0% (0)	— (0)	15% (6)	21% (6)	56% (10)	22% (7)	26% (9)	23% (7)	15% (4)	25% (43)
Paternalism	0% (0)	8% (1)	33% (1)	— (0)	0% (0)	— (0)	5% (2)	14% (4)	28% (5)	22% (7)	29% (10)	30% (9)	44% (12)	28% (47)
N	19	12	3	0	5	0	39	28	18	32	34	30	27	169

Libéral, or PRL), stated in a speech to the parliament that her policy was to an important degree driven by the need to "know how to aid the Third World while simultaneously stimulating the Belgian economy" (AP/PH, 26 October 1982: 181). Earlier in her tenure as state secretary for development cooperation, she had been more circumspect in her expression of the purposes of Belgium's foreign assistance program:

> I agree that our cooperation must be selective and must benefit especially the needs of those who suffer. . . . It must not be an extension of international trade, I emphasize this. But it is no less important . . . to come to a better integration of development cooperation and foreign trade. One must take care that our economy in crisis receives a just return, if possible. (PH/AP, 23 April 1982, 1426)

This sentiment was by no means limited to Mayence-Goossens alone. During the debate from which the last quotation was taken, Minister of Foreign Affairs Tindemans (CVP) called this approach to development cooperation "pragmatic and realistic as opposed to an ethical and humanitarian policy" (AP/PH, 23 April 1982: 1425). State Secretary Mayence-Goossens underscored this with the pronouncement that "our development cooperation cannot be solely charitable" (PH/AP, 23 April 1982: 1428). Kempinaire, another Liberal (Partij voor Vrijheid en Vooruitgang, or PVV), argued similarly that "one must not only think in terms of pure aid, but also in terms of opportunities for an economic return for our country. As you know, I have always been in favor of that" (PH/AP, 21 June 1989: 2795).

Although many of the statements made in parliament were of this general nature, the connection between foreign assistance and foreign economic relations was occasionally made specific. For example, Minister of Foreign Affairs Tindemans (CVP) explained to parliament that in Belgium's relations with Zaire there "are indisputably also economic interests. Our supply of raw materials should not unnecessarily and recklessly be endangered" (PH/AP, 27 October 1982: 210).

According to Franck (1987: 65), the relation between development cooperation and Belgium's dependence on international trade was coming more and more to the forefront. For instance, Christian Democrat Steverlynck (CVP) linked Belgium's extensive reliance on foreign trade with a necessity to play a role in building a more stable international order, claiming: "For our state international trade, and definitely export, are of vital importance for our employment and prosperity. Yet we also have a duty to cooperate for a new economic world order. Indeed, it is in our own interest" (PH/AP, 29 February 1984: 1899).

This focus on development cooperation as an instrument to enhance Belgium's long-term security was also articulated by the francophone Green party. Daras (Ecolo) argued:

> It is essential that we let go of the logic of short term interest in development cooperation. The true interest should aim at fighting extreme poverty, not only for moral reasons but also because in doing so, we will reduce tensions on a world scale and, as a result, we will enhance our own security. (AP/PH, 3 December 1984: 1995)

The observation that a stable international environment was in Belgium's long-term interest is another expression of the preoccupation with the economic welfare of Belgium that seems to characterize the foreign affairs of this state (Coolsaet 1987). Belgian parliamentary debate, despite the occasional reference to the humanitarian aspect of aid, tends to be straightforward about the need to receive a return for the Belgian economy on the foreign assistance program. In other words, Belgian decision makers tend to perceive foreign assistance as a tool in the service of their foreign economic policy, not as an end in itself. Put differently, Belgian decision makers represent foreign assistance as an aspect of foreign economic relations, not as distinct from it. The fact that Belgium has an open economy and depends heavily for its economic well-being on international trade may explain this concern with the international structure, although the same does not hold true for the Netherlands, which has an equally open economy.

Dutch decision makers are more circumspect in their discussions of the interrelation between foreign assistance and foreign economic policy. Generally, they stress that it is all right to benefit the domestic economy but that this is not what foreign assistance first and foremost should be about. After a few years of center-right coalition, Liberal member of parliament Weisglas (Volkspartij voor Vrijheid en Democratie, or VVD) reported that his party's representation in the chamber was "pleased that development cooperation policy in the past years has become more realistic and down-to-earth, but especially that in that process the needs of the third world have continuously been put first" (Handelingen, 24 October 1985: 828).

In other words, although the Liberals are generally proponents of pragmatic policies, their pragmatism does not go so far as to propose a foreign assistance policy that primarily serves Dutch foreign economic relations. The minister for development cooperation for this period, Schoo (VVD), perhaps came closest to an argument that might also have been made in the Belgian parliament when she said, "Development cooperation benefits not only developing countries. It is also in the interests of the rich states, both morally and materially. It keeps people in the Netherlands employed" (Handelingen, 17 February 1983: 2458).

Later during the same parliamentary discussion, however, she reiterated that the interests of the Third World were preeminent, declaring that her "policy is dedicated first and foremost to the developing countries" (Handelingen, 17 February 1983: 2459). Christian Democrat Aarts (Christen Democratisch Appel, or CDA) took the need to serve the interests of the Third World a little farther: "I have said that the minister for development cooperation must be the advocate of the interests of the Third World. . . . This minister is the only one of the sixteen who represents three-quarters of the world, albeit symbolically" (Handelingen, 18 December 1986: 2197).

He argued that although the other ministers represented the various interests of the Netherlands, the minister for development cooperation represented a constituency outside of the state, namely, the Third World. Most Dutch politicians would not go quite so far, but the viewpoint that development cooperation ought to serve the recipient states first and foremost is a frequent feature of Dutch parliamentary debate. Christian Democrat De Hoop Scheffer almost apologized for making the link between foreign assistance and its potential benefits to Dutch trade and industry: "We can and may talk about the relation between development cooperation and trade and industry, but we must understand that developmental relevance should always come first" (Handelingen, 29 November 1988: 1703).

De Hoop Scheffer implicitly acknowledged that Dutch trade and industry stood to benefit from the state's foreign assistance program, but his statement is typical of the manner in which the link between development cooperation and the Dutch private sector are often discussed in parliament. Development should be the primary purpose, but if Dutch trade and industry can benefit in the process, this is acceptable. The need to couch the rhetoric in this manner sets the Dutch decision makers apart from their Belgian counterparts. It is as if openly stating that aid must also benefit the domestic economy, as occurs in Belgium, is a taboo subject for Dutch decision makers.

Despite the similarity in the coalitions that governed Belgium and the Netherlands during the 1982–1988 period, there remain differences between the debates of the two parliaments. The comparison concerns a period of coalitions between Christian Democrat and Liberal parties for both states, and the differences in their rhetoric can not easily be attributed to differences in party affiliation. Although a more extensive analysis would be necessary for more conclusive results, at this point there are at least plausible indications that Belgian and Dutch decision makers perceive the role of foreign assistance in their foreign policies differently. What might account for the emergence of such differences in representation? The next two sections explore the representations of the international role and the experiences as colonizers of the two states to construct a preliminary answer to this question.

Representations of International Role

When decision makers of a state can refer to what I earlier termed a *heroic history*, they are more likely to perceive it possible for their state to play a significant role in international affairs. This would be especially true if the proud historical moment is defined as a time when the state was indeed a powerful and significant actor. The claim is that such a defining moment shapes national identity and extends its influence far into the future as each new generation of citizens is taught its nation's history.

With regard to foreign assistance, my expectation is that a heroic history will correlate with a perception of foreign assistance as a distinct issue area. Although an international norm has developed that prescribes for states to devote some portion of their GNP to foreign assistance, a distinct foreign assistance policy requires a vision regarding an alternative global future. Groups of decision makers who have little confidence that their state can have a significant impact on world politics are unlikely to formulate a distinct vision of the global future. Leaders of such states are more likely to represent foreign assistance as linked to the well-being of the state's economy.

Both Belgium and the Netherlands achieved independent statehood after seceding from larger entities, but the reasons for their success differ. The former was successful in seceding from the Netherlands in 1830 because of the interference of the great powers of the time (Witte, Craeybeckx, and Meynen 1990). The Netherlands, on the other hand, fought a war that spanned eighty years to be free of Spanish domination. This war coincided with the Dutch success as a commercial-maritime power, which accounts for the ultimate Dutch victory: The commercial success of the merchant marine enabled the Dutch provinces to purchase sufficient fighting power (Kennedy 1987). In short, the Dutch pride themselves on having secured their independence for themselves and in a history, however brief, as a world power. Even though both Belgium and the Netherlands are currently small states with a heavy dependence on international trade, they came into existence as independent states through very different events. These very different histories have left their legacies in different perceptions of the role that it is possible for the state to play in world politics.

A Christian Democrat member of the Belgian parliament, Van Wambeke (CVP) referred to Keohane's 1969 article "Lilliputians' Dilemmas" and used it as his basis for an assessment of Belgium's international role:

> We must conclude that our country is a small state, because neither in the world nor in the region are we able to impose our political will or protect our interests through power politics. . . . The foreign policy of a state like

ours must be primarily pragmatic, open to frank discussions and consultations and, with the permission of the large partners, be directed at a role of bridge-builder and mediator. Only in this manner can we, if modestly, have some influence on world politics. (PH/AP, 26 October 1982: 168)

Van Wambeke's assessment mirrored the judgment of Dewachter and Verminck (1987) – that Belgium was a "weak actor" in world politics. The former assessment was an attempt to sketch how Belgium could claim some level of influence in international affairs; Dewachter and Verminck's assessment was: "In international politics Belgium depends primarily on its economic strength and its technological skill and expertise" (1987: 24). In other words, foreign economic relations is the centerpiece of Belgian foreign policy, and a political role is not perceived as a strong possibility. In East's 1973 formulation, Belgian foreign policy priorities are typical of a small state.

Foreign policy decision makers in the Netherlands, on the other hand, saw foreign assistance as an issue area that "offered the Dutch an opportunity to build up a dynamic, constructive role" in a policy area not dominated by the larger powers (Voorhoeve 1985: 283). Pronk (Labor/ Partij van de Arbeid, or PvdA) in particular played a significant role in giving the Netherlands a distinct profile in foreign assistance during his tenure as minister for development cooperation from 1973–1977.[2] Pronk gave the Netherlands a distinct profile in a policy area that well suited the Dutch aspirations to status as a *gidsland* or "a guide to other nations that are locked up in their power and status quo interests" (Voorhoeve 1985: 283). Although this concept was formulated by decision makers of the left end of the political spectrum (De Gaay Fortman 1973), Voorhoeve notes that "the desire to set an example of international behavior can be found also among the center and right wing politicians in the country, even though it is translated differently in political action" (1985: 248).

Some rethinking about the pretentiousness of the concept of *gidsland* has taken place since the 1970s, but the concept does appear in parliamentary debates across the years and continues to play a role in the self-image of Dutch decision makers. During his first period as minister for development cooperation, Pronk himself reminded parliament that being a guide to others entailed certain limitations: "It is not the intention to be so far ahead in comparison to other states that we would have turned the corner and therefore could no longer function as a referent" (Handelingen, 13 November 1975: 1134). Nuis, a member of parliament for D66,[3] similarly argued that he did "not want to drag up the old pretension of *gidsland*, but we would be well suited for the more modest role of scout" (Handelingen, 2 December 1982: 717). Nuis's statement reflected an enduring desire to be out ahead and show others the way. Christian Democrat Gualthérie van Weezel echoed this:

The Dutch contribution is modest in comparison to the needs of the three southern continents. Nevertheless, the Netherlands is internationally ever lonelier at the top. . . . Securing presumed self-interest will turn out to be short-term-politics in this interdependent world. If only because of this the Netherlands will have to be the draft horse and give notice of this internationally. (Handelingen, 16 February 1983: 2378)

A few years later, fellow Christian Democrat Bukman, as minister for development cooperation, would negate this desire to play a defining role in this issue area: "Even though we occupy a prominent place, we do not always have to be the draft horse for all sorts of developments" (Handelingen, 25 November 1987: 1288). Nevertheless, the concept of *gidsland*, and perhaps the mere fact that such a concept emerges, illustrates the very different representations Dutch decision makers hold of their state's role in world politics compared to the representations of their Belgian counterparts.

Legacies of Colonialism

Belgium and the Netherlands both can be described as former colonial powers. This commonality in their histories might lead to the expectation that the decision makers of both states represent foreign assistance as a distinct issue area. Before coming to conclusions about the impact of the colonial experience on current relations with recipient states, whether or not they are former colonies of the donor state, the length and extent of the colonial experience must be considered.

Specifically, I expect that the farther the colonial history extends back into time and the more thoroughly the colony came to be seen as an extension of the European territory, rather than some alien land, the more likely it is that a vision for the future of the colony, and perhaps the Third World in general, emerged. Such a vision may be highly "Eurocentric" or even moralistic in tenor. Yet whatever the quality of the vision, it provides a justification for a more extensive aid program than could be justified without such a vision. In other words, not all colonial experiences are similar and therefore do not lead to similar representations of the role foreign assistance ought to play in the state's foreign policy.

The colonial experiences of Belgium and the Netherlands were quite different. Belgium acquired mandates over Rwanda and Burundi in the aftermath of World War I, just a little more than a decade after sovereignty over Zaire (then called Congo) had been transferred to the Belgian state in 1908. Before that, Zaire had been the personal possession of King Leopold II, who acquired the colony through a series of negotiations regarding Africa, which culminated in the adoption of the General Act of Berlin on February 26, 1885 (Pakenham 1991; see also Van Bellinghen 1990). The Belgian parliament initially refused to give the king or his colony any assistance, financial or otherwise (Van Bellinghen 1990), but became more involved as international opposition against the relentless exploitation of the colony grew. In essence, the parliament voted for the acquisition of Zaire by the Belgian state in order to prevent losing the colony altogether and governed it until its independence in 1960 (Witte et al. 1990). The colonial experience of the Belgian state was thus fairly short-lived.

The roots of Dutch colonialism extend to the 1600s, when the Netherlands was a commercial-maritime power, establishing trade connections in both the East and West Indies, as Southeast Asia and the Americas were then called (Wels 1982; Voorhoeve 1985; Kennedy 1987). Until the end of the eighteenth century, the emphasis was on trade rather than territorial acquisition (Wels 1982; Voorhoeve 1985). According to Voorhoeve, it was not until the nineteenth century that "the Dutch expanded their control over the Indonesian archipelago and became territorial colonial rulers" (1985: 252). Nevertheless, the Dutch had at that point a longstanding relationship with Indonesia, as well as with its other colonies, Suriname and the Netherlands Antilles. This conglomerate began to unravel in the aftermath of World War II, when the Dutch gave up control of Indonesia in 1949, after a bloody attempt to regain dominance. West New Guinea, or Irian Jaya, however, remained under Dutch rule until 1962, at which time it was incorporated into the Indonesian state (Lijphart 1966). This did not mean the end of the colonial era for the Netherlands. It was not until 1975 that Suriname became an independent state, and to this day the Netherlands Antilles remain an "overseas territory."

Although trade and other economic exploitation played a role both in the Belgian governance of Zaire and the Dutch governance of Indonesia, an important difference is that it was primarily the Dutch who exploited Indonesia, whereas King Leopold II's possession of Zaire was brokered on the condition that he permit free trade and economic exploitation by Europeans of other nationalities (Witte et al. 1990; Pakenham 1991). The Belgian king sought to facilitate a role for Belgian business in Zaire, but the nature of Belgian colonialism was inherently different from that of the Dutch: Rather than being staked through the establishment of trade relations, the claim preceded trade and was brokered in European palaces. In the end, King Leopold II acquired Zaire because this suited the European powers (Pakenham 1991).

Although some have argued that Zaire was important in that it "gave Belgium an international status which by itself it could not hope for" (Berlage 1984b: 2), business interests have always strongly influenced relations between the two states (Coolsaet 1987; Witte et al. 1990). Coolsaet went so far as to claim a very small role for foreign policy: In the relations between

Belgium and Zaire, "official diplomacy is limited to a few footnotes to decisions taken by the business community" (1987: 249; see also Doom 1990). The argument in Witte et al. that Belgium "governed the colony, in the interests of certain industrial and financial interests, in an autocratic-paternalistic manner, because of which it was not at all prepared for independence" (1990: 352) corroborates this for an earlier period.

Status also played a role in Dutch colonialism, fostering the belief that the Netherlands "counted for something in the world" (Wels 1982: 100). In light of this, it is not surprising that "whenever the possibility of giving up overseas territories came under discussion, international prestige was always brought into play alongside economic, legal and moral arguments" (Wels 1982: 101). The importance attached to the overseas territories also explains why Indonesia did not achieve its independence until the United States put pressure on the Netherlands by threatening to withhold Marshall Plan aid (Beerends 1981: 39; Smith 1981). Despite the economic factors that played a role in Dutch colonialism, over time there also developed a sense of what the British have called the *white man's burden*, a sense of paternalistic responsibility toward the colonies.

The differences between Belgian and Dutch patterns of colonialism lead to the expectation that the Dutch, through their long presence, longstanding trade relations, and more definite control over their colonies acquired more of a sense of responsibility for the population residing there. They came to represent their colonies as overseas territories that were a source of economic riches, but for which they also felt a paternalistic responsibility. The Belgian state acquired Zaire only reluctantly and late, forced to salvage the free-for-all conditions that had resulted from the conditions under which King Leopold II had assumed jurisdiction over it. Trade may have followed King Leopold's acquisition of Zaire, but the initial impetus for gaining control over it was adventure and politics. In its initial refusal to become involved in King Leopold's African possession, the Belgian government did not deny its citizens the opportunity to benefit materially from investments or other economic involvements in Zaire. It did, however, refuse to accept any responsibility for its administration and therewith hindered any development of a representation of Zaire as an extension of Belgium rather than some alien place fit only for fortune hunters.

Issue Areas as Decision Makers Define Them

The categorization of foreign assistance and foreign economic policy as distinct issue areas reflects the representations of Dutch decision makers much better than those of Belgian decision makers. Whereas Belgian decision makers are quite frank about the need for their state's foreign assistance to serve

economic interests, Dutch decision makers prefer to draw a sharp line between the two issue areas. The Belgian decision makers tend to represent
foreign assistance as a tool in the service of their foreign economic policy.
The Dutch decision makers represent it as an issue area that should remain
distinct from the state's immediate economic interests, although economic
benefit is regarded as an acceptable second-order consequence.

This difference in the representation of the role of foreign assistance in
foreign policy is poorly explained with reference to structural factors. Table
13.5 (top third) shows that Belgium and the Netherlands share similarities in
terms of their position in the international system, the structures of their
foreign policy–making institutions, and the coalitions governing the two
states for the period under study. On the other hand, the historical factors
examined in this chapter draw a clear distinction between the experiences of
the two states, as the bottom third of Table 13.5 illustrates. The experiences
of initial state formation and of colonialism are quite different for Belgium
and the Netherlands. The Belgian secession owed its success to the intervention of the great powers of Europe. It owed its status as a colonial power to
the adventurism of its king, and the state initially refused to take administrative responsibility for the colony. The Dutch, on the other hand, boast of a
heroic history, owed their colonial possessions to the explorations of their
seventeenth-century merchant marines, and regarded these possessions as
overseas extensions of the homeland.

These differences in national historical experiences provide a plausible
explanation for the differences in the Belgian and Dutch representations of
the role of foreign assistance in foreign policy, as shown by a comparison of
the center and bottom thirds of Table 13.5. The differences in the national
historical experiences of Belgium and the Netherlands predispose the decision
makers of the latter to perceive foreign assistance as a distinct issue area.
Moreover, it gives them a vision for the future of North-South relations that
not only justifies a generous aid program but the aspiration to ''light the
way'' for other donor states as well.

This study indicates that an explanation of foreign policy behavior that
takes into account how decision makers *themselves* represent the similarities
and differences between categories of issues may allow us to explain foreign
policy differences between states that appear to be similar on the basis of
structural comparisons. In other words, it makes sense to approach the issue-
area concept cognitively.

Author's Note: This research was supported by a grant from the National Science Foundation
(DIR-9113599) to the Mershon Center Research Training Group on the Role of Cognition in
Collective Decision Making at the Ohio State University and by a research grant from the
Fulbright College of Arts and Sciences of the University of Arkansas.

Table 13.5. *System, history, and issue representation*

		Belgium	Netherlands
Similar systems	Similar position in international structure?	Yes	Yes
	Similar domestic structure regarding foreign assistance policy?	Yes	Yes
	Similar coalitions during period 1982–1988?	Yes	Yes
Foreign assistance debate	Foreign assistance always debated separately?	No	Yes
	Lot of debate on foreign assistance?	No	Yes
	Foreign assistance separated from foreign economic relations?	No	Yes
Historical experience	Heroic history?	No	Yes
	Long colonial history?	No	Yes
	Paternalistic sense of responsibility?	No	Yes

Notes

1 PH/AP refers to Parlementaire Handelingen/Annales Parlementaires. If PH is listed first, the quotation was originally in Dutch. If the order is reversed (i.e., AP is listed first), then the quotation was originally in French.
2 Jan Pronk returned as minister for development cooperation in a center-left cabinet in 1989.
3 Irwin (1989) described D66 as a liberal party, noting that since the early 1980s its members referred to themselves as ''progressive-liberals.'' Voorhoeve (1985), on the other hand, placed the party at the left end of the spectrum.

References

Beerends, Hans (1981). *30 Jaar Nederlandse Ontwikkelingshulp 1950–1980 [Thirty Years of Dutch Development Cooperation 1950–1980]*. Utrecht, the Netherlands: Landelijke Vereniging Wereldwinkels.
Belgium, Parliament, Chamber of Representatives (various years). *Annales Parlementaires/ Parlementaire Handelingen [Official Parliamentary Reports]*.

Berlage, Lodewijk (1984a). "Trends in the performance of European aid donors and the distribution to the LICs." In Olav Stokke (ed.), *European Development Assistance* (Vol. 2). Tilburg, Netherlands: EADI.

——— (1984b). "The Organizational Structure of Belgian Development Cooperation: Evolution and Problems." Unpublished manuscript.

Breuning, Marijke (1992). "National Role Conceptions and Foreign Assistance Policy Behavior: Toward a Cognitive Model." Ph.D. dissertation, The Ohio State University.

——— (1994). "Belgium's foreign assistance: Decision maker rhetoric and policy behavior." *Res Publica, 36*, 1: 1–21.

Carlsnaes, Walter (1993). "On analysing the dynamics of foreign policy change: A critique and reconceptualization." *Cooperation and Conflict, 28*, 1: 5–30.

Cole, Michael (1991). "Conclusion." In Lauren B. Resnick, John M. Levine, and Stephanie D. Teasley (eds.), *Perspectives on Socially Shared Cognition*. Washington, D.C.: American Psychological Association.

Coolsaet, Rik (1987). *Buitenlandse Zaken [(Belgian) Foreign Affairs]*. Leuven, Belgium: Kritak.

De Gaay Fortman, Bas (1973). "De Vredespolitiek van de Radicalen [The Peace Policy of the Radicals]." *Internationale Spectator, 27*.

Dewachter, Wilfried, and Mieke Verminck (1987). "De Machtsbases van Belgi in de Internationale Politiek [The Powerbases of Belgium in International Politics]." *Res Publica, 29*: 21–27.

Doom, Ruddy (1990). *Derde Wereld Handboek, vol. 1 [Third World Handbook, Vol. 1]*. Brussels, Belgium: NCOS/NOVIB/METS.

East, Maurice A. (1973). "Size and foreign policy behavior: A test of two models." *World Politics, 25*, 4: 556–557.

Evangelista, Matthew (1989). "Issue-area and foreign policy revisited." *International Organization, 43*, 1: 147–171.

Everts, Philip, and Guido Walraven (1989). *The Politics of Persuasion: Implementation of Foreign Policy by the Netherlands*. Brookfield, VT: Avebury.

Franck, Christian (1987). "La Prise de Décision belge en Politique extérieure [Belgian Foreign Policy Decision Making]." *Res Publica, 29: 61–84*.

George, Alexander L. (1979). "Case studies and theory development: The method of structured, focused comparison." In Paul Gordon Lauren (ed.), *Diplomacy: New Approaches in History, Theory, and Policy*. New York: Free Press.

Irwin, Galen (1989). "Parties having achieved representation in parliament since 1946." In Hans Daalder and Galen Irwin, *Politics in the Netherlands: How Much Change?* London: Frank Cass.

Jervis, Robert (1976). *Perception and Misperception in International Politics*. Princeton, NJ: Princeton University Press.

Katzenstein, Peter J. (1985). *Small States in World Markets: Industrial Policy in Europe*. Ithaca, NY: Cornell University Press.

Kennedy, Paul (1987). *The Rise and Fall of the Great Powers*. New York: Random House.

Keohane, Robert O. (1969). "Lilliputians' dilemmas: Small states in international politics." *International Organization, 23*: 291–310.

Khong, Yuen Foong (1992). *Analogies at War: Korea, Munich, Dien Bien Phu, and the Vietnam Decisions of 1965*. Princeton: Princeton University Press.

Kruijssen, H. A. J. (1986). "Ontwikkelingssamenwerking als Rijksoverheidsdienst [Development Cooperation as a Governmental Department]." In A. Melkert (ed.), *De Volgende Minister [The Next Minister]*. The Hague, Netherlands: NOVIB.

Levine, John M., Lauren B. Resnick, and E. Tory Higgins (1993). "Social foundations of cognition." *Annual Review of Psychology, 44*: 585–612.

Levy, Jack S. (1992). "An introduction to prospect theory." *Political Psychology, 13*, 2: 171–186.

Lijphart, Arend (1966). *The Trauma of Decolonization*. New Haven: Yale University Press.

——— (1971). "Comparative politics and the comparative method." *American Political Science Review, 65*, 3: 682–693.

——— (1975). "The comparable-cases strategy in comparative research." *Comparative Political Studies, 8*, 2: 158–177.

Maas, P. F. (1986). "Kabinetsformaties en Ontwikkelingssamenwerking 1965–1982 [Coalition Formations and Development Cooperation 1965–1982]." In A. Melkert (ed.), *De Volgende Minister [The Next Minister]*. The Hague, Netherlands: NOVIB.

Netherlands, Parliament, Second Chamber (various years). *Parlementaire Handelingen [Official Parliamentary Reports]*. The Hague, Netherlands: Staatsuitgeverij.

Pakenham, Thomas (1991). *The Scramble for Africa*. New York: Random House, Inc.

Potter, William C. (1980). "Issue area and foreign policy analysis." *International Organization, 34*: 405–427.

Przeworski, Adam, and Henry Teune (1970). *The Logic of Comparative Social Inquiry*. New York: Wiley.

Quattrone, George A., and Amos Tversky (1988). "Contrasting rational and psychological analyses of political choice." *American Political Science Review, 82*: 719–736.

Resnick, Lauren B. (1991). "Shared cognition: Thinking as social practice." In Lauren B. Resnick, John M. Levine, and Stephanie D. Teasley (eds.), *Perspectives on Socially Shared Cognition*. Washington, D.C.: American Psychological Association.

Rosenau, James N. (1971). *The Scientific Study of Foreign Policy*. New York: Free Press.

Smith, Steven M. (1981). *Foreign Policy Adaptation*. New York: Nichols.

Sylvan, D. A., A. Goel, and B. Chandrasekaran (1990). "Analyzing political decision making from an information processing perspective: JESSE." *American Journal of Political Science, 34*: 74–123.

Sylvan, Donald A., and Stuart J. Thorson (1992). "Ontologies, problem representation, and the Cuban missile crisis." *Journal of Conflict Resolution, 36*, 4: 709–732.

Tversky, Amos, and Daniel Kahneman (1981). "The framing of decisions and the psychology of choice." *Science, 211*: 453–458.

Van Bellinghen, Jean-Paul (1990). "Belgium and Africa." In Marina Boudart, Michel Boudart, and Rene Bryssinck (eds.), *Modern Belgium*. Palo Alto, CA: Society for the Promotion of Science and Scholarship.

Vandommele, Mark (1982). "Twintig Jaar Belgisch Ontwikkelingsbeleid [Twenty years of Belgian development cooperation]." *Internationale Spectator, 36*, 9: 499–506.

Vertzberger, Yaacov Y. I. (1990). *The World in Their Minds: Information Processing,*

Cognition, and Perception in Foreign Policy Decision Making. Stanford, CA: Stanford University Press.

Voorhoeve, Joris J. C. (1985). *Peace, Profits and Principles: A Study of Dutch Foreign Policy*. Leiden, Netherlands: Martinus Nijhoff.

Wels, C. B. (1982). *Aloofness and Neutrality: Studies on Dutch Foreign Relations and Policymaking Institutions*. Utrecht, Netherlands: HES Publishers.

Witte, Els, Jan Craeybeckx, and Alain Meynen (1990). *Politieke Geschiedenis van België van 1830 tot Heden [Political History of Belgium from 1830 to Present]*, *5th ed*. Antwerpen, Belgium: Standaard.

Zimmerman, William (1973). "Issue area and foreign-policy process: A research note in search of a general theory." *American Political Science Review, 67*: 1204–1212.

PART IV
CONCLUSION

Reflecting on the Study of Problem Representation: How Are We Studying It, and What Are We Learning?

Donald A. Sylvan

How decision makers understand and represent problems they face is crucial to the decisions they make. That has been the primary theme of this volume. But how have the contributors to this book helped us learn more about the manner in which problem representation occurs and how it has affected foreign policy decisions? That question and the question of the consequences of the manner in which problem representation is studied are the two themes of this final chapter.

Information Processing

One important way to conceptualize problem representation is commonly termed *information processing*. In Chapter 2 of this volume, Voss carefully explicates an information-processing perspective. Such a perspective posits that foreign policy decision makers have goals that can be articulated and that guide decisions they make. An information-processing perspective also assumes that a domain can be described as having properties, such as "ill structured" or "well structured," that can be spoken of as though they are independent of the decision maker operating in the area of foreign policy. In addition, Voss points out that an information-processing approach assumes that decision makers are serial processors and have a working memory system with a finite capacity.

To varying degrees, most of the chapters in this volume share these assumptions of an information-processing approach. What are the implications of those assumptions for the analysis of decision making, including any conclusions we might draw concerning the role of problem representation? Perhaps the most important implication flows from the information-processing assumption that actors studied have goals that motivate them. Of the empirical chapters (Part III), this assumption clearly plays a role in Young's Chapter 9, Gannon's Chapter 10, Voss et al.'s Chapter 12, and Breuning's Chapter

13. In Young's study of Carter, for instance, the notion of a goal hierarchy is central to his analysis. Were one to adopt the contrasting assumption that Carter administration actions were largely determined by bureaucratic inertia, the substantive conclusions of Young's work would be called into question. The very notion of the Soviet invasion of Afghanistan as a potential Carter goal impediment defines the manner in which "problem representation" is employed, and it predisposes the analyst to find order (no matter how prone to change) in Carter's pronouncements. Similarly, the concept of "worldview" is predicated on the existence of an identifiable representation of problems that guides the processing of information in foreign policy decisions.

As mentioned, Gannon, Voss et al., and Breuning also emphasize the role of information processing on decision making. As a result, each of these chapters can be characterized as focusing on representations that are *instrumental* to the goals of political actors. Discourse-analytic works, such as Rubino-Hallman's, do not adopt this instrumental view, instead characterizing representations with such terms as *dominant discourse* and *counterdiscourse*. Although Rubino-Hallman is the only contributor to employ discourse analysis in this volume, the approach – especially when empirically grounded, as in the case of Rubino-Hallman – has the potential to add to the approaches discussed in this closing chapter and Chapter 1, and to enrich our understanding of problem representation. Even though a discursive-practices approach differs philosophically with some of the assumptions of the information-processing approach adopted throughout much of this volume, I do *not* see the two as fundamentally antagonistic approaches to understanding problem representation. Rather, I argue that each illuminates critical portions of the way in which problems are represented, and that it is important to learn from both approaches. A discursive-practices approach focuses on the manner in which groups of decision makers use language to communicate and thereby define the nature of the issues with which they are dealing. Using a discursive-practices framework, objects and events become inseparable from the processes of apprehension within which they are formed. This emphasis on language as a key to problem representation is quite compatible with virtually all of the chapters of this volume. As the reader has seen, only the work of Rubino-Hallman sees discursive practices as its primary vehicle for observing problem representation. A number of chapters in this volume, however, reflect the reasoning behind both the aforementioned discursive-practices philosophy and the information-processing understanding and terminology communicated by Voss. For example, the emphasis of discursive practices on a social level of analysis is quite consistent with such information-processing–oriented works as Beasley's chapter, where the author deals with the issue of groups and problem representations. Voss et al., like many who undertake discourse analysis, employ texts as the primary focus of analysis. Voss et al.

adopt the view that "argumentation, while itself of interest, requires interpretation within some type of theoretical framework or model in order to develop an understanding of the factors underlying the debate." Rubino-Hallman's work is premised on a view that objects and events are inseparable from the processes of apprehension within which they are formed. The two chapters may point to similar evidence in making their arguments, but for Voss et al., that evidence is to be interpreted by a theoretical framework offered by the analyst. For the type of approach adopted by Rubino-Hallman, a separate, abstracted theoretical framework is not the goal: A statement of the discursive practices themselves – in her case, practices dealing with women pilots – is sought. There are clearly contrasting fundamental propositions in these works. While the reader may want to choose between them, I prefer to see what aspects of decision making each can illuminate.

"Findings"

Keeping in mind the caution that "measures" of problem representation, and not "the representations themselves," are being investigated in this volume, we now turn our attention to the issue of the "findings" of the chapters in this volume in the areas of foreign policy and of political psychology. Cottam and McCoy's examination of U.S. foreign policy toward the Third World in general and Somalia in particular finds that the United States still holds a largely dependent image of Third World countries, even after the Cold War. The image has begun to disintegrate slightly in the case of Somalia, but there has not been a fundamental change in problem representation.

Two of Beasley's conclusions stem from his focus on aggregation principles and on the Munich crisis. He concludes that in discussions among the British foreign policy elite, "models of the world were not promoted as much as were building blocks from which models could be constructed." Also, Beasley finds that "the Single Representation Embellishment aggregation principle was approximated more frequently at the beginning of new decision episodes, and that these meetings were characterized by higher focus on categorical relations between concepts and fewer stated preferences." Although Beasley's conclusion obviously needs to be corroborated in other studies, his focus on problem-representation aggregation principles in groups opens up an important area for expanded research.

Michael Young does not dispute the notion that a change in President Jimmy Carter's beliefs and behavior took place after the Soviet invasion of Afghanistan. However, after observing very few specific changes of belief in Carter's speeches, Young advances the study of beliefs as well as our understanding of Carter's presidency by offering four mechanisms that could produce behavioral change without producing detectable belief changes. They are (1) a change in an assumption already existing in the belief system, (2) changes in relative salience of beliefs, (3) change in probabilities attached to beliefs, and (4) the addition of a few new propositions to the belief system. Although Young is not able to offer conclusive evidence of one of these four mechanisms prevailing over others, it is clear that without studying problem representations as he does, it is unlikely that he would have been able to gain these insights into the relationships between Carter's beliefs and behavior.

One of the more detailed empirical examinations in this volume is Helen Purkitt's "Problem Representation and Political Expertise: Evidence from 'Think Aloud' Protocols of South African Elite." Recall that she examines in some detail the "structure and content of the problem representations developed by diverse members of the political elite" in South Africa. Purkitt is quite reflective about the utility of the concept of "problem representation." Her work contrasts with many of the other approaches advocated and employed in this volume in that it prompts key political leaders to create their own problem representations by supplying them with a task statement asking how they would develop a policy. This was not a completely open-ended exercise, in that respondents were explicitly asked to consider these factors: "the future of the Nationalist Party, the need to maintain political order and economic growth, proposed reforms of police and security forces, the current and future demands of key economic and political forces in society, regional security issues, and current and future actions by key actors in the international community." An interesting comparison study might be to provide no such cues and see to what degree the task statement influenced the "think aloud" responses.

Purkitt's categorization scheme for coding the responses is based in the information-processing tradition. Expertise, age, and political background are each explored as possible correlates of the information-processing patterns that emerge. Purkitt deals on a level of process (e.g., "describe," "predict," "recommendation") as well as content (e.g., "society," "security-military," "governmental"). A key conclusion of Purkitt's is that "expertise in solving complex but ill-structured political problems is closely coupled with verbal articulateness and a person's social status rather than to problem-solving successes or cognitive abilities." Some might argue that an empirical distinction between verbal articulateness and cognitive ability is a difficult one to maintain, but Purkitt is quite clear in her distinction. Conceptualizing problem representation in terms of verbal expressions is a productive path for Purkitt. Although she urges future researchers to study further the "determinants of problem representation," she has clearly shown us how verbally self-articulated problem representations can give us insight into an important set of international political issues.

In dealing with the issue of problem re-representation, Billings and Hermann have conceptualized the issues involved in the re-representation process. They do not undertake an empirical analysis, but they review literature and note a paucity of empirical evidence on this subject in general. By employing such concepts as "problem location," they are clearly adopting information-processing assumptions. They are also assuming a prior, identifiable representation and location for a problem that is a candidate for re-representation.

Voss and his collaborators study U.S. Senate debates of the Gulf crisis and find that those debates can best be understood as a disagreement between two alternative "image-based interpretations" of Iraq: as an enemy versus an agitator threatening moderate Arab states and Israel.

Breuning offers some noteworthy observations based on her analysis of the ways in which Belgian and Dutch decision makers represent the role that foreign assistance plays in foreign policy. Perhaps more than any other author in this volume, Breuning employs multiple sources of evidence in her chapter. Parliamentary debates on foreign assistance, governmental expenditures, and characterizations of national histories are all studied for evidence bearing on the issues of how foreign assistance is being represented and why. Breuning's work is a good example of work that complements both an information-processing perspective and one that emphasizes discourse analysis. In fact, parliamentary discourse is studied in order to draw conclusions relevant to the aspects of problem representation employed by students of both discourse analysis and information processing.

Sylvan and Haddad find that the Story Model of problem representation – prominently explicated by Pennington and Hastie in their study of jury decisions – seems to hold in the realm of foreign policy content tasks as well. Given the contrasting nature of a close-ended jury verdict and a foreign policy choice, this was not at all a foregone conclusion. Sylvan and Haddad also find that explanation-based reasoning predominates along with the Story Model of problem representation when subjects are given foreign policy–related scenarios.

Although Gannon's chapter is the only contribution that does not deal with foreign policy, she does illustrate how a focus on problem representation can illuminate a political process more than would be possible with a focus on only more narrowly political variables. She makes a convincing case that one would have less of an understanding of the U.S. Senate confirmation process for Supreme Court nominees if one were to look only at politics and not at problem representations of senators.

Rubino-Hallman finds that the representation of women in combat positions in the Air Force/Navy was a crucial factor in both the way members of the presidential commission read the context of the debate and the way they voted on the final recommendations to the president. Creation of the idea of the "female warrior" was the crucial representation influencing the process and outcome of the committee's work.

Bases of Evidence

How does the type of evidence accumulated affect both the type of conclusions reached and the picture of foreign policy decision making presented? Authors in this volume have employed "think aloud" protocols (Purkitt), experiments (Sylvan and Haddad), textual analysis (Beasley, Young, Gannon, Rubino-Hallman, and Voss), and multiple sources including summaries of analyst accounts (Cottam and McCoy) and government expenditure data (Breuning).

One illuminating comparison is that between two examples of textual analysis: Silvana Rubino-Hallman's and Katherine Gannon's. Rubino-Hallman's methodology differs from Gannon's in that Gannon emphasizes information processing while Rubino-Hallman employs a discursive-practices approach. Despite the different emphases between the two approaches, there are overlaps between the two chapters, perhaps attributable to the similar textual evidence each brings to bear on their puzzles. If the reader agrees with this argument, then the logical conclusion is that it is not only the basic philosophical assumptions but the type of evidence considered[1] that determines the type of conclusions reached, and the picture of foreign policy decision making presented.

Employing "think aloud" protocols means that Helen Purkitt's concept of problem representation and her picture of foreign policy differ from those of other authors in this volume. Purkitt has clearly assumed that individuals (in this case, South African political leaders) can and will accurately report their values, reasoning, and the substance of their political understandings. Contrasting sets of political assumptions would lead a researcher to mistrust the self-reporting of any set of political elites, given their political biases and agendas. In addition to mistrust, a contrasting psychologically based argument would hold that even if the subjects wanted to be "honest," they might not be capable of self-reporting on their problem representations. Therefore, for Purkitt, problem representations are both understood and articulated by subjects. Foreign policy, then, takes place in a problem space defined by these prompted self-reports. A common textual forum is not necessary to define foreign policy given the assumptions underlying Purkitt's base of evidence, in contrast to many of the views inherent in the textual evidence presented in other chapters in this volume.

In a parallel vein to the arguments advanced regarding Purkitt's use of "think aloud" protocols, Sylvan and Haddad's use of a particular set of experimental subjects and Breuning's reliance on economic data mean that each has employed a somewhat divergent concept of problem representation, and that each has presented a different picture of foreign policy. Sylvan and Haddad rely primarily on undergraduate students in their experimental study. Their focus, then, is about people understanding, reasoning, and representing problems in the realm of foreign policy. In previous work that they cite (e.g., Sylvan, Ostrom, and Gannon 1994; Sylvan, Haddad, and Ostrom 1994), they have studied subjects with contrasting expertise, nationality, and age. They have also examined both individuals and groups and have seen how the same subjects reason in domains other than foreign policy. Those studies have found that there is little difference between the performances of the aforementioned subject pools, even in contrasting task domains. As a result, Sylvan and Haddad assume that representations of foreign policy problems by undergraduate students can provide some insight into the way elites reason when dealing with foreign policy issues. The manner of arriving at a problem representation is their focus, rather than the particular substantive representation of a foreign policy problem. Therefore, verbal references and connections, as well as a few nonverbal aspects of the group decision making found on the videotapes, are the focus of the evidence they collect. Given their substantive conclusion of the Story Model's being the predominant mode of problem representation, they offer a picture of foreign policy decision making in which the adoption by a group of a narrative structure or framework is the crucial element in understanding a foreign policy decision-making process.

Breuning's use of Belgian and Dutch foreign assistance expenditures as part of the evidence that she accumulates in drawing conclusions about foreign assistance problem representations sets her apart from most of the authors in this volume. She implies that in order to corroborate evidence from texts (parliamentary debates in this case) and to set problem representations in historical context, one should look at data that can be seen as an overt manifestation of the policy (foreign assistance policy) being represented in the particular study. Foreign policy, then, involves a clear linkage between words and deeds, according to Breuning. Cognitively based factors such as problem representation are crucial policy determinants, she implicitly argues, and the linkages can be shown by studying economic data in her case. Recall that a key conclusion reached by Breuning through this approach is that Belgian and Dutch political elites have historically different reasons behind their foreign assistance policies, and that those reasons and their attached problem representations still exist in current times. More specifically, Dutch decision makers see foreign assistance as a distinct issue area, and they have a vision for the future of North-South relations that justifies their foreign assistance activity. In the Belgian situation, by contrast, foreign assistance is seen as a vehicle to serve Belgian economic interests.

Young, Gannon, Voss et al., Beasley, and Breuning all analyze publicly available texts. If they were to assert on the basis of such analysis that they had captured the problem representations of the individuals whose speeches they were examining, one might question the degree to which public figures express their "true" thinking in such fora. These contributors are generally careful to note, however, that they are trying to capture either the public persona and problem representation of the individuals involved or the problem representation of a group, the documents of which they are analyzing. But their choices to examine such public documents and to adopt an information-processing point of view still open them to the charge that they may have captured reasoning for public consumption rather than a logic or problem representation "in use." Their choices of bases of evidence lead us to conclude, though, that in their views, foreign policy is a public enterprise, and therefore, one can meaningfully refer to publicly expressed problem representations.

Cottam and McCoy's decision to use journalistic and scholarly accounts of foreign policy elites' views gives us some insight into their conceptualizations of problem representation and foreign policy. Most of the statements referenced by Cottam and McCoy are from policy makers,[2] and in those cases, the foregoing comments about the textually oriented chapters apply. But Cottam and McCoy also cite such analysts as John Bolton and Meg Greenfield to support their arguments. By doing so, they imply that the characterizations by these authors of the manner in which U.S. policy makers represent the problem of U.S. policy in Somalia is one with which Cottam and McCoy agree. In fact, one could read into this analysis the assumption that the images held by and the problem representations operating for these officials are discernible in a relatively uncontroversial manner by more than one analyst. In other words, the basic idea is that the representation is clear, and the task of the analyst is to uncover it through careful observation of the utterances of policy-making elites. Foreign policy, then, results from the interaction of the images and problem representations of officials involved in decisions.

Impact of This Volume

Most of the chapters in this book have already laid out their own implications. In some other cases, the implications follow clearly from the "findings" mentioned earlier in this chapter. They range from what might be termed *metapolicy*[3] implications to substantive politics conclusions. In the former category, one would offer the following advice based on Sylvan and Haddad's Chapter 8: Those who seek to have impact on a particular policy process should first study the predominant story of the decision-making group. In the latter category, Young's conclusion that the seeds of what many see as

Carter's "abrupt" change of policy toward the Soviet Union were present well before the Soviet invasion of Afghanistan.

In addition to the individual contributions of each of the chapters of this volume, the book itself should be seen as making some important statements. First and foremost, *systematically studying problem representation can provide insights into foreign policy decision making that would not necessarily be forthcoming without such systematic study.* This statement is agreed upon by all of the authors in this book.

Another potentially significant observation coming from this closing chapter and the entire book deals with the relation between philosophical assumptions and bases of evidence employed in the study of foreign policy decision making. *The philosophical assumptions and the bases of evidence employed in foreign policy decision-making research will each independently influence the possible types of conclusions that can be reached, and the relative efficacy attributed to competing categories of factors affecting foreign policy.*

This book has addressed a variety of conceptual issues, employed a variety of methodologies, and used a number of different types of data. Both the impact and the determinants of problem representation have been examined. It is to be hoped that the reader has now seen that if one attempts to study foreign policy decision making by focusing only on option selection, one will not have a comprehensive understanding of the process of decision making in foreign policy.

Notes

1 Philosophical assumptions and type of evidence considered are clearly related in that certain philosophical frameworks (e.g., discourse analysis) clearly lead the analyst to consider particular types of evidence (e.g., texts). However, as has been pointed out, there is not a one-to-one relationship between these assumptions and evidence. Texts, for instance, have been employed in this volume by authors whose assumptions differ substantially.
2 Unlike most of the authors in this volume, however, Cottam and McCoy selectively choose key quotations from leaders rather than sample or analyze an entire data base of speeches from one leader or a few leaders.
3 *Metapolicy* is used here in a manner consistent with Dror (1971): policy on how to make policy.

References

Dror Y. (1971). *Design for the Policy Sciences.* New York: Elsevier.
Sylvan, D. A., D. M. Haddad, and T. M. Ostrom (1994). "Reasoning and Problem Representation in Foreign Policy: Groups, Individuals, and Stories." Paper pre-

sented at the 35th Annual Meeting of the International Studies Association, Washington, D.C. (March).

Sylvan, D. A., T. M. Ostrom, and K. Gannon (1994). "Case-based, model-based, and explanation-based styles of reasoning in foreign policy." *International Studies Quarterly, 38,* 1: 61–90.

Index